2007

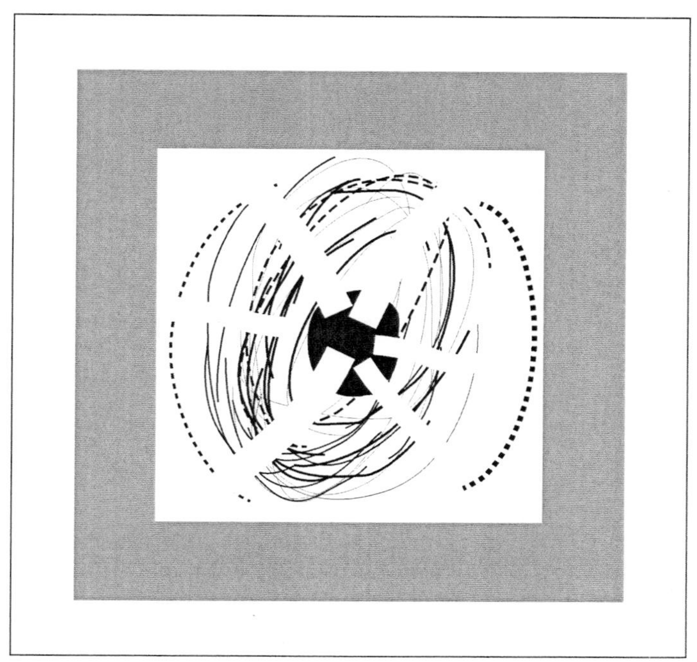

Latin America and the Caribbean in the World Economy

2008 TRENDS

UNITED NATIONS

Alicia Bárcena
Executive Secretary

Laura López
Secretary of the Commission

Osvaldo Rosales
Director of the Division of International Trade and Integration
and document coordinator

Diane Frishman
Officer in Charge
Documents and Publications Division

www.cepal.org/de

Latin America and the Caribbean in the World Economy is an annual report prepared by the Division of International Trade and Integration of ECLAC. The Statistics and Economic Projections Division, the Economic Development Division, the Division of Production, Productivity and Management and the Commission's country office in Washington, D.C. assisted with the preparation of this year's edition. The production of the report as a whole was overseen by Osvaldo Rosales, Director of the Division of International Trade and Integration. Mikio Kuwayama, Chief of the International Trade Unit, was responsible for its technical coordination.

In addition to Osvaldo Rosales and Mikio Kuwayama, the following individuals were involved in preparing and drafting the chapters included in this year's edition: Mariano Alvarez, Claudia de Camino, Jaime Contador, José Elías Durán, Myriam Echeverría, Alfonso Finot, German King, Raúl Holz, Ekaterina Krivonos, Marcelo La Fleur, José Carlos Mattos, Graciela Moguillansky, Nanno Mulder, Andrea Pellandra, Gastón Rigollet, Indira Romero, Sebastián Sáez, Juliana Salles and Gingyi Zhang.

The statistical appendix was prepared by Jaime Contador in collaboration with Andrés Yáñez. It is appended to this document as a CD-ROM and is also available online at: http://www.eclac.org/Comercio/ paninsal/Anexo2007_2008/ingles/.

Notes
The following symbols have been used in this Study:
Three dots (…) indicate that data are not available or are not separately reported.
A minus sign (-) indicates a deficit or decrease, unless otherwise indicated.
A full stop (.) is used to indicate decimals.
The word "dollars" refers to United States dollars, unless otherwise specified.

United Nations publication
ISBN: 978-92-1-121676-9
ISSN printed version: 1680–8657 ISSN online version: 1681–0295 ISSN CD-ROM: 1811-6205
LC/G.2383-P
Sales No: E.08.II.G.36

Printed in Santiago, Chile

Contents

Tables

Figures

Boxes

Abstract

This year's edition of *Latin America and the Caribbean in the World Economy* is divided into seven chapters.

Chapter I contains an analysis of recent trends in the main industrialized and emerging economies and reviews the possible impact of the financial crisis that began in the United States on the world economy and on the economic and trade performance of Latin America and the Caribbean. The effect of the crisis on the prices of commodities (especially food and oil) and the implications for growth, inflation and the region's external sector are also examined. Lastly, the chapter looks at the region's trade figures for 2007 and projections for 2008.

Chapter II describes recent developments in the Doha Round, including documents disseminated in July 2008 on negotiations relating to agriculture and non-agricultural market access. It also provides a summary of the main advances and obstacles emerging from those negotiations, with emphasis on the repercussions for Latin America and the Caribbean.

Chapter III discusses some new trade-related topics: (i) new security requirements for freight transport; (ii) the development and legal status of private quality standards; (iii) the state of play in discussions on trade and labour rules; and (iv) the debate on the links between climate change, trade and the multilateral trading system. It is argued that these and other issues will be on the international agenda for the next few years and that the region must begin to form unified positions on such topics.

Chapter IV examines recent progress in regional integration and the main initiatives under way in the region's integration schemes (the Southern Common Market (MERCOSUR), the Andean Community, the Central American Common Market (CACM) and the Caribbean Community (CARICOM)). The chapter also analyses: (i) Mexico's active policy aimed at strengthening its trade and infrastructure links with Central America; (ii) the Latin American Pacific Basin Initiative; (iii) the South American Community of Nations (UNASUR); and (iv) the hosting by Brazil in December 2008 of a Summit of Heads of State and Government of Latin America and the Caribbean on the subject of regional integration schemes. The chapter concludes with an analysis of the links between investment and services as an instrument of de facto integration.

Chapter V reports on the status of negotiations for the adoption of an association agreement between the European Union and each of the above-mentioned subregional integration schemes. In each case, there is a description of the negotiation process, controversial issues and the main challenges. It is noted that, since there is a similar framework for all these negotiations (covering Caribbean and Central American countries, the Andean Community, MERCOSUR, Mexico and Chile), they may generate important synergies for the subsequent convergence of trade and investment rules among the region's integration schemes.

Chapter VI presents an in-depth analysis of trade and investment relations between the Latin American and Caribbean region and the Asia-Pacific region, as well as within the latter. It is established that: (i) biregional trade remains inter-industrial in nature, despite the emergence of some new export commodities and high-technology manufactures; (ii) so far, efforts to forge closer links between the Latin America and Caribbean and the Asia-Pacific regions have been undertaken by individual countries on a somewhat sporadic basis; and (iii) there needs to be a more coordinated strategy among countries, so as to strengthen the nexus between trade and investment and to reinforce production and trade linkages through various types of public-private alliances (including free trade agreements).

The subject of chapter VII is the foresight analyses carried out by some countries of the Organisation for Economic Co-operation and Development (OECD) with a view to strengthening innovation, competitiveness and export diversification. Despite the importance of such exercises for building consensus around strategic development guidelines, they are not frequently used in Latin America and the Caribbean. Advances achieved in other parts of the world could therefore encourage the countries of the region to use such exercises as an effective tool for promoting competitiveness, innovation and export development.

Executive summary

Global economic trends and Latin American and Caribbean trade flows

In 2003-2007, world economic activity was at its most vibrant in 40 years, with high growth rates, low inflation, low interest rates, fluid financing and buoyant international trade. The major emerging countries (Brazil, the Russian Federation, India and China —the so-called "BRIC" group) accounted for almost half of world economic growth. This favourable international context, combined with improvements in the region's macroeconomic policies, enabled the Latin American and Caribbean region to achieve its best economic performance in 40 years. An important factor in this positive regional performance was high world demand for energy, food and other commodities, which boosted the region's exports.

The year 2008 will be a landmark in the economic history of globalization.[1] This year has broken the upward phase of the cycle with powerful interrelated shocks, which have their origins in the five years running up to 2008: (i) the subprime mortgage crisis, which started in the

Figure 1

CONTRIBUTION OF SELECTED REGIONS TO WORLD GROWTH

(Percentages of annual world growth)

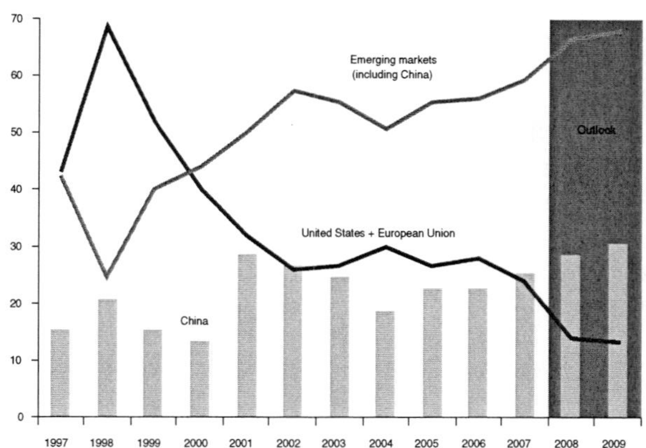

Source: Economic Commission for Latin America and the Caribbean (ECLAC), on the basis of International Monetary Fund (IMF), World Economic Outlook (WEO) database.

Note: Gross domestic product (GDP) based on purchasing power parity (PPP).

1 The world financial debacle triggered by the subprime crisis in the United States, following decades in which emphasis had been placed on deregulation, has, once again, set off the debate on the deficiencies of the regulatory framework for international finance (just as occurred after the "Asian crisis"). Having led the bail-out of European banks by deciding that his government would assume an active role as a shareholder, the Prime Minister of the United Kingdom, Gordon Brown, stated that it seemed that the time had come to rethink the world's financial system in the global era.

United States in 2007 and threatens to throw that country and the world economy into recession; (ii) the weakening dollar during the first half of the year and steady demand from emerging economies, which have caused oil and food prices to soar and increased speculative movements and volatility in those markets, thereby putting inflation back on the agenda of global concerns; and (iii) the domino effect of the subprime mortgage crisis, which has triggered a series of bankruptcies and shake-ups in the financial industry in the United States and Europe. In late September, these repercussions toppled the United States investment banking sector, which had led the way in engineering the recent financial innovations of the global economy, and the threat of an international financial crisis loomed. Fears of recession have since led to a fall in raw material prices, especially those of oil, copper and other commodities of interest to the region.

In short, the subprime mortgage crisis is the aftermath of a real estate bubble in the United States which, when it burst, sent ripples through financial institutions that had large quantities of assets backed by such mortgages. The losses incurred by these operations raised these institutions' levels of indebtedness and reduced their capital, thereby limiting their capacity to meet the credit needs of the economy. Faced with this situation, they proceeded to sell off assets, intensifying the fall in the price of such assets and consequently exacerbating their own debt and capital problems. This downward spiral triggered a loss of confidence among the banks themselves, which sparked a credit crunch and set the stage for the failure of financial giants that had imprudently saddled themselves with excessively risky operations and short-term financing. At this point, it became absolutely indispensable for the State to step in to restore confidence and normalize financial flows.

The crisis has reverberated through financial markets in the United States and Europe, creating solvency and liquidity problems and causing turmoil in credit markets worldwide. Authorities in industrialized economies have responded —with varying degrees of timeliness and coverage— by providing liquidity and recapitalizing financial institutions in need of assistance. Notwithstanding the enormous efforts that have been made, volatility remains high, fuelled, on the one hand, by uncertainty about the duration and intensity of the financial crisis, and, on the other, by questions as to how the measures will be implemented and how the costs will be divided up among the different stakeholders.

Regardless of exactly how the crisis is eventually resolved, it is already having a serious impact on the real economy in the industrialized countries, and lower growth and job-creation figures are being forecast for the rest of 2008 and for 2009 in those economies. This situation, whose duration and intensity are still impossible to predict, has started to filter through to the Latin American economies and will have deeper repercussions in 2009. In particular, a fall in external demand and in unilateral current transfers is to be expected, which would reduce inflows to the region. This drastic change in external conditions will have an adverse effect on growth and employment in the region and, thus, on the number of people living in poverty in Latin America and the Caribbean.

According to information available as of early October 2008, the European banking system has also suffered. This has further undermined confidence in the financial and stock markets and, in some cases, has generated panic situations to which some of the major emerging economies are exposed to as well. Despite massive injections of liquidity in the United States and Europe, interbank interest rates remain at a record high, and there is a serious danger of defaults along the payment chain in the United States. If this unfortunate situation were to arise, the economies of the United States and the European Union would face a much more dramatic slowdown and perhaps even a recession in late 2008 and for much of 2009. This would drive down growth projections sharply for 2009 and 2010 for the world economy, including developing economies.

Current events are therefore interlinked, and they are increasing the level of uncertainty and volatility in financial systems, sapping confidence and shrinking credit in the major economies. The effects on production, investment, employment and trade will be felt more keenly in 2009. The present financial crisis is the most serious event of its kind to take place in the United States since the Great Depression, and although the world is now better prepared to cope with its effects, it will nonetheless leave a deep mark on the global economy, as is only to be expected when such a severe crisis occurs in what is not only the most dynamic sector of the world's largest economy but also the one that has the most far-reaching ramifications for other economic activities in the United States and the wider world economy. With the bailout of Bear Stearns by JP Morgan Chase, the acquisition of Merrill Lynch by Bank of America, the bankruptcy of Lehman Brothers and the change of status of Goldman Sachs and Morgan Stanley to regulated bank holding companies, in the space of just six months the five leading investment banks in the United States have disappeared. These events, in addition to the bailout of Fannie Mae and Freddie Mac (the country's main mortgage lenders) by the United States Treasury and the rescue of the nation's biggest insurance company, American International Group Inc. (AIG), and Washington Mutual (a major commercial bank), demonstrate that this is a systemic crisis with serious ramifications not only for world finance but also for the real economy.

Given the off-balance-sheet operations conducted by these investment banks, it is still difficult to predict the depth and duration of the crisis. The bursting of the real estate bubble therefore needs to come full circle, so that the prices of all "toxic" assets can return to sustainable levels. Only then will the scale of the losses be known, and the financial sector can begin to put its accounts in order and recapitalize. These processes will take time, and this is why the rescue package proposed by the United States authorities to restore confidence in the system amounts to some US$ 700 billion. As of mid-October 2008, implementation of the financial "megaplan" was a matter of urgency, as was an announcement of the plan's operational details so that "toxic" assets could be isolated and liquidity could be provided to distressed financial institutions in order to restore confidence among banks and normalize financial flows. In early October, the main financial challenge in the United States was to ensure continuity in the chain of payments in order to enable well-managed financial agencies and enterprises to avoid bankruptcy and thus avert severe impacts on employment and production activity.

The massive rescue package finally approved by the United States Congress did not succeed in restoring confidence in the world's financial and stock markets. Whether this was due to design failings or problems of implementation, the inadequacy of this response became evident when the United Kingdom announced its own rescue package. The overall matrix of that package was endorsed a few days later by the other European governments, which coordinated their operations to lower interest rates and throw a lifeline to the European financial system. The impact of the coordinated European action, following a few weeks of vacillation, was dramatic, reviving financial and stock markets and reducing interbank rates. The markets rewarded the idea of a coordinated global effort to deal with a global, systemic problem.

In essence, the rescue package proposed by Prime Minister Brown was broader, deeper and swifter than that of the United States Treasury and Federal Reserve. Its main components were: (i) an injection of liquidity into the financial system; (ii) an equity injection consisting of the recapitalization of weakened financial institutions in exchange for a government stake; (iii) guarantees for interbank debt; (iv) insurance for bank deposits; and (v) public purchase of subprime assets.

Table 1 shows the breakdown of the total amount of liquidity —some US$ 3.1 trillion— which central banks and other government agencies have recently injected into the banking system. By mid-October, the US$ 700 billion rescue package announced by the United States and the European countries' firm resolution to take decisive, coordinated action on the basis of the matrix proposed by the Government of the United Kingdom, had generated commitments totalling US$ 2 trillion. The markets responded positively and many stock markets recovered ground lost since the start of the crisis.

Table 1

LIQUIDITY INJECTIONS AND RESCUE PACKAGES ANNOUNCED UP TO 20 OCTOBER 2008

(Trillions of dollars)

Countries	Liquidity used [a] (as at 20 October)	Rescue packages (as at 14 October)	Rescue packages (as at 20 October)
United States	1.38	0.7 [b]	4.3 [e]
European Union	1.62	2.41 [c]	2.42 [f]
15 euro zone countries	1.16	1.54 [c]	1.56 [f]
United Kingdom	0.46	0.87 [c]	0.87 [c]
Japan	0.11	...	...
Other	0.05 [d]	...	...
Total	3.17	3.11	6.72

Source: Economic Commission for Latin America and the Caribbean (ECLAC), on the basis of International Monetary Fund (IMF), *Global Financial Stability Report*, October 2008; and international financial press reports (*New York Times, ABC, The Guardian, Estrategia, BBC News*, among others).

[a] Refers to the liquidity supplied by the United States Federal Reserve, the European Central Bank and other central banks through repurchase agreements (repos) and short-term (less than 90-day) loans. The amounts spent by governments to purchase equity in banks are also included.

[b] First United States rescue package.

[c] Includes guarantee commitments for inter-bank loans, bank deposit insurance and public purchase of subprime assets by the Governments of France, Germany, Ireland, the Netherlands and Spain.

[d] Includes injections of liquidity in Australia and Sweden.

[e] Includes the announcement by the United States Federal Deposit Insurance Corporation that it would insure the deposits of subordinate banks up to US$ 1.5 trillion, non-interest-bearing deposits up to US$ 500 billion and commercial paper up to US$ 1.6 trillion. The three commitments add up to US$ 3.6 trillion.

[f] Includes the intervention by the Government of the Netherlands in the bailout of ING.

In adopting their rescue model, the United States authorities had rejected the idea of having the State acquire equity in the banking system, probably for ideological reasons, and had instead placed emphasis on government purchase of "toxic" assets through mortgage securitization. This, however, did not manage to restore confidence in financial markets. Given the success of the European rescue programme and the coordinated interest-rate measure, the United States followed suit, reinforcing the improvement in financial expectations worldwide. The United States authorities announced that US$ 250 billion of the rescue package approved by Congress would be used to purchase equity in large and small banks. In the days that followed, the Federal Deposit Insurance Corporation announced that it would guarantee deposits in subordinate banks, non-interest-bearing current accounts and commercial paper amounting to approximately US$ 3.6 trillion. These guarantees, plus the US$ 700 billion bailout package, bring the total United States rescue programme to US$ 4.3 trillion (see table 1).

It is not yet possible to ascertain whether these measures will be sufficient to resolve the crisis. They are certainly a step in the right direction, however, and the more alarming problems that were looming at the beginning of October, that is, widespread panic on financial markets and the threat of a break in the payment chain, seem to have abated.

It is precisely the positive characteristics of the cycle (high growth, low interest rates and low inflation) that increased risk-seeking and made financial innovation, securitization and off-balance-sheet operations seem more attractive. Overconfidence in the market and deregulation were responsible for the rest, creating a climate that encouraged fraud and set off the worst financial crisis since the 1930s. Just as the external debt crisis in Latin America and the Caribbean led to more sensible economies policies (following the lost decade and some painful adjustments), the current financial crisis in the United States could result in a rethinking of financial regulation in terms of risk management and levels of capitalization and leverage, as well as stronger economic policy incentives for saving (to deter excessive public and private borrowing in that country's economy).

The repercussions of the financial crisis will be even more keenly felt in 2009, as they manifest themselves in economic activity and employment levels. The world economy will therefore grow less in 2009 than in 2008. Depending on the results of the financial rescue package in the United States and the effectiveness of the support measures introduced in Europe, the situation could even give rise to a significant recession, unless the crisis is prevented from spreading to real economic activity via a serious credit crunch. For the time being, the slowdown is concentrated in the main advanced economies, although Asian and other emerging economies will also be affected, albeit to a lesser degree. The United States economy has been grappling with strong recessionary pressures since late 2007, but buoyant net exports, which have been boosted by the weak dollar, have averted a worse slump in the economy as a whole. Japan and the European Union are being severely hurt by the crisis in the United States, and their performance, in terms of both domestic and external demand, has taken a considerable turn for the worse as they seem to be headed towards a virtual recession in late 2008.

Up to mid-2008, emerging economies were maintaining high levels of growth despite the slowdown in advanced economies, which suggested that there was some degree of decoupling between the two groups. In the second quarter of 2008, new signs pointed to a more nuanced outlook, as the trading partners of developed countries began to be affected by the sharp drop in demand in the latter. Furthermore, the financial crisis has aggravated the liquidity squeeze in international markets, which has pushed up interest rates. This will have a further negative impact on growth in developing economies. So long as the financial crisis does not continue to worsen, most emerging countries will be better prepared than previously to weather external shocks, thanks to their substantial international reserves, orderly fiscal accounts and low external debt. Nevertheless, the scale of the crisis is so great that the entire global economy, including the emerging economies, will feel its impact.

The financial crisis and the slowdown in world growth have halted the upward trend in food and oil prices. These prices rose until mid-July 2008, in a context of growing demand for such commodities from China, India and other Asian countries, combined with tight and inelastic supply. In real terms, the price of oil was higher than it had been during the 1979 energy crisis, while metal prices have tripled or quadrupled since 2003. Food prices have also shot up since 2006. In the second half of 2008, commodity prices started to fall as a result of the financial panic, the threat of a global recession and the sharp slowdown in industrialized economies. Between July and mid-October, wheat and maize prices fell by 70%, oil prices by 55% and aluminium, copper, nickel and platinum prices by nearly 50%. Long-term trends still place these prices at relatively high levels and they will probably remain high as long as China and the other emerging economies remain buoyant. The financial shock has watered down the speculative component in price volatility, but structural supply and demand factors continue to push up the prices for these products, especially energy, minerals and metals. Everything points to these prices remaining relatively high but ceasing to exert inflationary pressure.

The improvement in the trade balances of Mexico, South America and the region as a whole between 2004 and 2006 was due mainly to high and rising commodity prices. In 2007, these trade balance worsened slightly, owing to the strong increase in import volumes and prices. In contrast, the rise in commodity prices had the opposite effect on Central America and the Caribbean, as they are net importers of oil and food.

The projected fall in commodity prices in the final quarter of 2008 and in 2009 is bad news for developing countries that export raw materials, such as those of Latin America and the Caribbean. As already mentioned, however, those prices will probably remain above 2006 and 2007 levels, which should bring some relief in terms of inflation and will be of benefit to the net oil-importing countries of Central America and the Caribbean (with the exception of Trinidad and Tobago). The years 2008 and 2009 are expected to see a decline in export volumes, while imports will continue to rise. As a result of the worsening terms of trade and a drop in trade volumes, the trade and current account balances will deteriorate in all subregions except Central America and the Caribbean. In 2009, the external sector will therefore no longer be a growth factor for the region.

Given this complex world scenario, the Latin American and Caribbean region has to deal with both immediate and long-term challenges. In the short run, the region's governments must find a way to cope with international financial and economic turmoil at a time when they have less access to external financing, they must pay higher interest rates, local stock exchanges have been hit hard by world trends, capital is being shifted to safer destinations and into less risky assets, exports are lower, migrant remittances from industrialized countries in recession are declining and foreign direct investment is down. As a result, credit lines for exports and investment plans will be tighter, thereby limiting growth.

If the crisis were to deepen beyond the situation observed in early October (when this summary went to press), then the avoidance of contagion from the financial crisis in industrialized economies would clearly become the highest priority. In that case, the region's governments would have to ensure liquidity in the financial system (particularly credit lines in United States dollars) and reinforce prudent supervision of the soundness of the banks and financial institutions with the most (direct and indirect) links to international financing and risky operations. If such a negative scenario were to become more likely, with recession in the United States and the European Union and a severe liquidity squeeze, then a less stringent monetary policy would be justified.

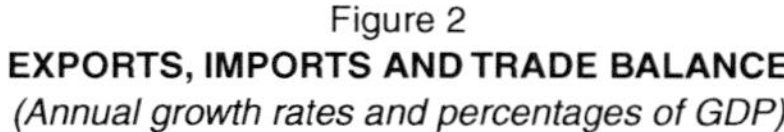

Figure 2
EXPORTS, IMPORTS AND TRADE BALANCE
(Annual growth rates and percentages of GDP)

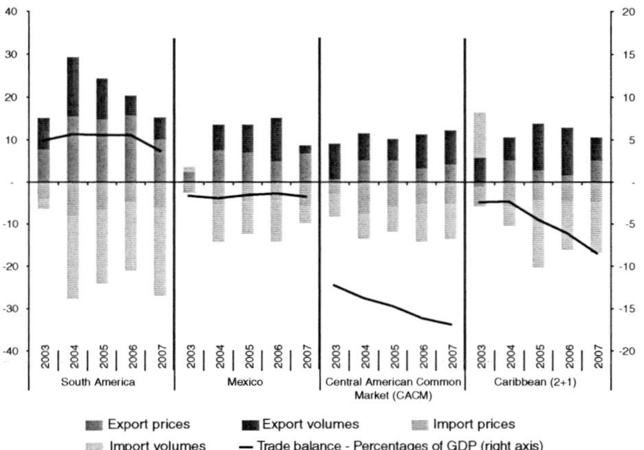

Source: Economic Commission for Latin America and the Caribbean (ECLAC), on the basis of official figures.

Note: The increase in prices refers to the annual variation in the unit values of imports and exports. Growth in volume refers to the annual variation in the quantities exported. The trade balance is the weighted net result of growth rates. Caribbean "2 + 1" refers to Panama, Haiti and the Dominican Republic.

The higher cost of capital and the restriction of global financial and investment flows will continue for the rest of 2008 and 2009 and will be coupled with stronger inflationary pressures, and this situation, for the time being, calls for somewhat more monetary policies. Given these conditions, such pressures have to be eased through the use of appropriate monetary and fiscal policies, along with other social and production measures to support low-income groups. In any event, the world economic slowdown can be expected to reduce demand for commodities, especially food and energy, thereby gradually easing the disturbing inflationary pressures observed since the beginning of 2008. Curbing inflation should continue to be the aim as long as this remains the most pressing challenge. Achieving this objective may entail adapting policies to the scale of the inflationary pressure generated by external factors. As stated previously, all indications are that the international situation will cease to be a source of inflationary pressure in the rest of 2008 and in 2009.

In order to deal with the foreseeable external shocks, governments should strengthen their countercyclical macroeconomic policies, maintain sound fiscal accounts and monitor external account trends in order to prevent the emergence of unsustainable disequilibria. Depending on how the financial crisis evolves, fast-acting expansionary policies will probably have to be devised, as a matter of urgency, in order to support liquidity in the financial system. This will call for financing and appropriate policy arrangements to avoid the creation of new disequilibria. In the medium term, the governments of countries that maintain favourable terms of trade should improve the management and use of additional income from above-trend commodity prices by promoting activities that boost medium-term competitiveness, human resource development and export diversification.

Although 2009 will be a tighter year for all the economies in Latin America and the Caribbean, the extent of the constraints will vary in each case, depending on each economy's specific circumstances. The opportunities or constraints influencing each economy's performance in 2009 will be determined by a number of variables, including: (i) the solvency of its financial system; (ii) whether it is a net debtor or net creditor vis-à-vis the rest of the world; (iii) the sustainability of its fiscal accounts and the level of its public debt; (iv) the level of inflation and inflationary expectations; (v) the balance-of-payments current account balance; (vi) the relative importance of remittances and FDI as stable sources of current account financing; (vii) the degree of export diversification in terms of destination markets; and (viii) whether the country is a net exporter or net importer of food and energy. Beyond any national differences, the global situation is one that recommends fiscal caution, exchange-rate flexibility and prudent supervision of the financial system's performance in order to ensure its liquidity and to make sure that the terms, currencies and types of risk involved in financial operations match up.

The current global financial crisis and the threat of recession in 2009 pose an enormous challenge in terms of the soundness of the economic reforms that the region's countries have been making considerable efforts to implement in recent decades. Thanks essentially to these reforms, and notwithstanding the need to determine whether these reforms have effectively contributed to growth, equity and competitiveness, there is no doubt that the region is now better prepared to face this adverse situation. Although this crisis may well have a considerable impact, there is no doubt that, without such reforms, that impact would have been much greater. Now is the time to keep the reforms that are enabling countries to weather the financial storm with relatively limited damage firmly on track, with emphasis on: fiscal responsibility and control of inflation; trade openness and market diversification; and debt reduction and the build-up of international reserves. These are the assets that have prevented Latin America and the Caribbean from falling into a recession such as the one towards which the United States and the European Union appear to be heading. These same assets will also stimulate a rapid recovery once global financial flows return to normal.

To sum up, it is difficult to see how the world economy could remain the same after 2008. Changes need to be made in terms of financial regulation, energy efficiency, the search for renewable energy sources and the provision of international funds to reduce hunger and increase the food supply in the poorest countries. In the first half of 2008, the combined effect of the energy crisis and soaring food prices not only triggered inflation in a number of countries within the region and elsewhere, but also posed serious threats to democratic governance in some developing nations. These concerns were expressed at many international summits, which highlighted the urgency of tackling the issues of governance associated with the globalization process.

Indeed, once efforts to resolve the financial crisis are on the right track, the governance of globalization, with emphasis on redefining the modalities for regulation and prudential supervision of the financial system, should be the main item on the international agenda. In this regard, and against the backdrop of the current financial crisis, the main European leaders —Prime Minister Brown of the United Kingdom, Chancellor Merkel of Germany and President Sarkozy of France— are calling for an international summit to address the urgent reforms needed in the international financial system, including rules on greater transparency, the definition of global standards for cross-border regulation and supervision, and the establishment of crisis early warning systems. In a similar vein, proposals are being made to update institutions such as the International Monetary Fund, the World Bank and even the World Trade Organization in order to bring them into line with the new state of the global economy in the twenty-first century. The United Nations has expressed its full willingness to make its Headquarters in New York available for such a summit to facilitate this increasingly urgent process. Decades of economic reform are now threatened by volatility and a lack of governance in financial markets, as well as by shocks in energy and food prices that have been exacerbated by speculative operations. An international recession in 2009 would seriously jeopardize the achievement of the Millennium Development Goals. This seems to be the right time for Latin American and Caribbean countries to adopt a unified position on these issues, to speak with one voice in various international forums and to formulate proposals that will help to shape the global agenda. The Summit of Heads of State and Government of Latin America and the Caribbean on Integration and Development, due to be hosted by Brazil on 16 and 17 December 2008 in Salvador, Bahía, will be an excellent opportunity to do so.

The Doha Round: failure or temporary setback?

In 2008, the climate at the Doha Round deteriorated from reasonable optimism to a state of pervasive uncertainty, following the failure of the "mini-ministerial meeting" convened by the Director-General of the World Trade Organization (WTO), Pascal Lamy, in the final week of July. This round of negotiations is especially important because it is the first to take place in 15 years, i.e., since the end of the Uruguay Round of the General Agreement on Tariffs and Trade (GATT) in December 1993. For developing countries, the Doha Round represents the possibility of reinstating the development dimension on the international trade agenda; hence the term "Doha Development Agenda".

The Doha Development Agenda originated out of a recognition that, although advances made in the new multilateral system were significant, they had not benefited all members in an equitable way. One of the problems was that developing countries needed support tools to deal with the complexity of World Trade Organization (WTO) agreements, which is why there was interest in identifying problems of application in each agreement and assessing special and differential treatment for the developing countries concerned. The second aim of the Doha Round was negotiation in the traditional areas of market access for agricultural and non-agricultural products and trade in services, which would capture part of the liberalization process that members have been implementing since the close of the Uruguay Round. A third aim was to continue the process of reforming agricultural trade by creating effective access opportunities, reducing the subsidies that distorted trade the most and agreeing to eliminate export subsidies applied by developed countries. Lastly, the Doha Round provides for improvements in the trade rules on antidumping duties, fishing subsidies and the link between trade rules and environmental agreements with a view to improving consistency between the former and the goals of sustainable development.

The purpose of the "mini-ministerial meeting" was to consolidate the informal progress made on various negotiation topics during 2007 and 2008 and to provide a new political impetus to the most sensitive issues in relation to trade in agricultural and non-agricultural products. With regard to market access for agricultural products, for instance, the proposal was for a minimum average tariff reduction of 54% for developed countries and 36% for developing countries. Countries could designate a percentage of tariff lines as "sensitive products", and developing countries could, in addition, designate "special products" and apply safeguards. Sensitive and special products were to be subject to smaller reductions, and certain special products would have been completely exempt.

In terms of total domestic support (production subsidies),[2] the proposal on the table would oblige the European Union to reduce total subsidies by between 75% and 85%. For the European Union (15 members), the estimated reduction would be from the existing level of € 110.3 billion to € 27.6 billion. The United States and Japan would have to reduce their subsidies by between 66% and 73%. For the United States, this would mean a reduction from the current consolidated figure of US$ 48.2 billion to between US$ 16.4 billion and US$ 13 billion. In the case of the most trade-distorting (amber box) subsidies, the proposals would translate into a reduction of 70% for the European Union, i.e., a drop from the current ceiling of € 67.16 billion to a new maximum of € 20.1 billion. For the United States, the reduction would be 60%, from the current ceiling of US$ 19.1 billion to around US$ 7.6 billion. Although the objection raised to these proposals is that the United States would retain some margin for raising subsidies above current levels, these would nonetheless be lower than those applied in four of the last seven years.[3] Following the collapse of the negotiations in July 2008, if the current situation (no agreement) is compared with the commitments undertaken in the Uruguay Round (the status quo), the European Union could now triple the most trade-distorting subsidies it applies without breaching its international commitments. Similarly, the United States could double its subsidies.

In terms of non-agricultural market access, it was suggested that bound tariff reductions should be introduced using a formula that distinguished between developed and developing countries. For developing countries, there would be three different rates, based on the degree of flexibility chosen. The larger the reductions (and the lower the rate), the greater degree of flexibility there would be (and vice versa). There would also be additional flexibility that could be used to exempt certain products or apply smaller reductions to them. There were also provisions for special modalities for the 32 least developed countries (which would be exempt from tariff reductions) and special arrangements for 31 small and vulnerable economies and for 12 developing countries with a low percentage of bound tariff lines.

The failure of the "mini-ministerial meeting" in July 2008, which was marked by disagreements between China, India and the United States as well as less visible conflicts of interest among developing countries, is creating uncertainty about the capacity of the protagonists of the negotiations (beneficiaries of the process of globalization) to make the multilateral trading system more governable. This latest failure could be seen as a justification for regional policies and bilateral negotiations undertaken in a context where the positive complementarity between multilateralism and regionalism appears weaker than in the past. Multilateral trade rules are lagging behind regional ones, endangering the relevance of the multilateral system for its members and weakening its ability to tackle the challenges of an expanding membership. Once again, questions are being raised about the ability of WTO to handle the international agenda of the future, and unless negotiations are reopened very soon, the Doha Round and its pro-development agenda will be delayed until late 2009 or 2010 at the earliest.

In Latin America and the Caribbean, there are many viewpoints on developments in the Doha Round. There is consensus that industrialized nations have the scope to be more generous in their proposals regarding agricultural trade in terms of both access and reductions in distortions. No such consensus exists, however, about how the region can shape its proposals concerning non-agricultural and services market access in order to contribute to a good agreement in the Doha Round. There are also differences of opinion on the urgency of concluding the Round. Some countries would prefer no agreement to an unsatisfactory one. For others, what is on the table constitutes significant progress, particularly in view of the protectionist tendencies that may be triggered by the current financial crisis in industrialized economies.

---

2 This includes the most trade-distorting subsidies (amber box), subsidies decoupled from production (blue box) and *de minimis* (or minimum) subsidies.

3 *The Economist*, 2 to 8 August, 2008.

Figure 3

TRADE-DISTORTING AGRICULTURAL SUBSIDIES, 1995-2007

(Billions of dollars and billions of euros)

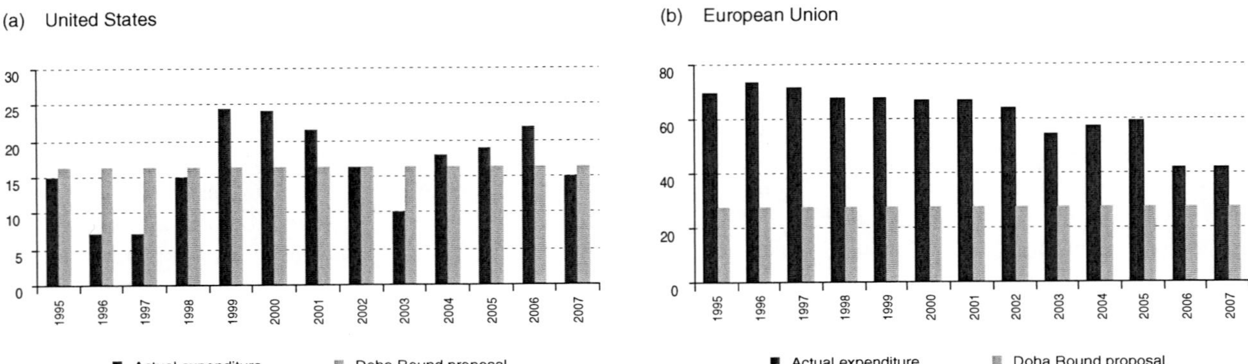

Source: Sébastien Jean, Tim Josling and David Laborde, "Implications for the European Union of the May 2008 Draft Agricultural Modalities", International Centre for Trade and Sustainable Development (ICTSD), June 2008; David Blandford, David Laborde and Will Martin, "Implications for the United States of the May 2008 Draft Agricultural Modalities", International Centre for Trade and Sustainable Development (ICTSD), June 2008; Kimberly Ann Elliott, "Last Gasp for Doha? [online] http://blogs.cgdev.org/globaldevelopment/2008/07/last_gasp_for_doha.php; and World Trade Organization (WTO), "Unofficial guide to the 10 July 2008 'revised draft modalities'", 2008.

Note: The figures compare actual expenditure in 1995-2007 with the proposed new limits on expenditure. Includes the most trade-distorting subsidies (those directly linked to prices and production), which are officially called Aggregate Measurement of Support (AMS) and are also known as "amber box" subsidies. Also includes blue box subsidies, which are not linked to prices or production, and the *de minimis* category, which includes amber box support but in smaller quantities or the minimum allowed in relative terms (currently 5% of production for developed countries and 10% for developing countries). The three programmes together are equivalent to the concept of Overall Distorting Domestic Support (ODDS), as shown in the figures. The reforms proposed in the Doha Round include limiting blue box subsidies to 2.5% of the value of production for the period 1995-2000 and reducing *de minimis* subsidies to 2.5% of the value of production. The Doha Round proposal also seeks to amend the Agriculture Agreement to include disciplines in these categories and to define a new concept of trade-distorting subsidies. Both figures use the most conservative estimates of the possible results of the Doha Round according to current proposals. For the United States, results range from US$ 13 billion to US$ 16.4 billion. For the European Union, estimates vary between € 16.5 billion and € 27.6 billion.

It is in light of the above that the quality of the agreement and the urgency of concluding it must be assessed. Assuming a tight schedule and adopting an optimistic outlook, if the Doha Round is postponed, it could still be completed in 2010 and approved by national parliaments in 2011, but even then its first benefits would not be felt until 2012. In this scenario, however, the Doha Development Agenda could easily be sidetracked by the impact of either the financial crisis in the United States and the European Union or new global problems such as energy or food crises or climate change. It is said that negotiations never fail, but are only postponed. However, it is also true that their political relevance is not eternal.

Although the July 2008 agreement was far from fully satisfactory to developing countries, it was nonetheless a step in the right direction: improved access to the agricultural markets of developed countries, elimination of subsidies for agricultural exports by 2013 and a reduction in bound levels of domestic support for agriculture. These bound commitments were almost double the effective levels, but this was because of the high prices of agricultural products in July 2008, which means that the support was less necessary. The idea is to bind domestic support at a ceiling rate so that, when prices fall, a glut in supply can be avoided. The level at which such support would be bound would be lower than that applied by the United States in four of the last seven years, and this restriction would be permanent. This remains pending while a detailed study is made of the costs, benefits and opportunities of the Doha Round. In this process, the Latin American and Caribbean region could strengthen its internal consensus so that it would be in a position to play a more prominent role in the Doha Round without losing sight of the synergic and facilitating effect these negotiations could have on other trade talks (such as those with the European Union) if the Doha Round were to be concluded soon.

Globalization and new trends in international trade

In recent decades, the international economy has undergone sweeping changes, mainly in the form of advancing globalization, dramatic technological change and the emergence of strong new competitors such as China, India and the Asia-Pacific region in general. The implications of these three developments are varied and complex. For instance, there have been drastic changes in the world map of trade flows and competitive advantages, with new winners and losers emerging in terms of economic areas, countries, production sectors and enterprises. The most striking element is the stronger competitive presence of China, India and the Asia-Pacific region, as well as of emerging economies in general. Even though they have coincided with a strong upswing in the business cycle (2003-2007), this complex reconfiguration of the world economy has not banished the dangers of traditional protectionism.

At the same time, the uncertainty associated with the new world economic order is hampering progress in multilateral negotiations (see chapter II). If the world economy slows in 2009 and 2010 as suggested by the available evidence, not only will the Doha Round become more problematic but, against the backdrop of an economic slowdown and a credit crunch in industrialized economies, the competitive challenges posed by emerging economies may trigger pressure for new forms of protectionism.

In analysing these new trends in international trade, care must be taken to distinguish those that stem from technological change and new ways of organizing business activities from those that are based on efforts to preserve market share by establishing rules that, although not formally binding, do in practice influence the competitiveness of products and companies. In production, for instance, advances in information and communications technologies (ICT), telecommunications and transport are increasingly shifting the dividing line between tradable and non-tradable goods and between manufactures and services. This facilitates the management of global value chains based on a twenty-first century template for the organization of production. Although this template of industrial organization may not represent more than 15% or 20% of existing business enterprises, these are the leading companies that are setting international business standards and that are managing to have some of them incorporated into international trade rules. Innovations such as bar codes, online connections with suppliers and distributors, and new forms of online information sharing have facilitated flexible mechanisms for matching demand, thanks to processes such as outsourcing, offshoring and insourcing. This value chain incorporates logistics into the production function so that, in addition to production per se, the chain also encompasses research and development, design, distribution, marketing, financing, after-sales service and product recycling or disposal. These processes can now be regarded as structural trends in international trade, and innovation and competitiveness policies therefore need to adapt to that fact.

Growing awareness of environmental issues and the importance of climate change and the increasing political influence of consumer groups (particularly in Europe) are also establishing new parameters in international trade. Energy conservation and environmental protection are becoming higher profile issues in corporate discussions concerning innovation and competitiveness. Furthermore, industrialized countries are introducing an increasing number of safety and traceability requirements for the production and international trade of foodstuffs.

The issues of security and trade have become extremely important to the international community since the attacks of 11 September 2001. This has resulted in the establishment of new requirements for freight transport, some of which have emerged from cooperation among countries via the World Customs Organization (WCO), while others have been created unilaterally. This will lead to a significant increase in trade costs as requirements for the inspection of all containers and certification of security methods throughout the export chain are introduced. Although meeting these requirements could bring benefits such as greater delivery speed and predictability, considerable investments would also be required, and there are doubts about how smaller countries and small and medium-sized exporters would be able to finance their implementation.

The top private corporations have recently been playing a regulatory role in terms of product quality and the establishment of private-sector trade standards, which, although voluntary, can nonetheless influence countries' competitiveness. These private standards include Good Agricultural Practices (GAP), safety certificates, the criteria of the International Standards Organization (ISO) and quality certification. Chapter III goes on to discuss the current public-policy debate in the United States and the European Union regarding the links between trade and employment and between trade and climate change. The issue of climate change will definitely be prominent on the international agenda. The link between trade and measures to mitigate or remedy climate trends will become increasingly important, and the discussion therefore turns to the proposals made by Europe and the United States concerning trade measures designed to limit greenhouse gas emissions and border taxes aimed at levelling internal and external competitiveness. The analysis is not exhaustive, but instead focuses on those aspects that may have the most impact on the external trade of Latin America and the Caribbean. Attention is also devoted to the link between trade-related measures and WTO trade rules, with emphasis on the most relevant provisions and some potential conflicts.

All of these events may generate additional pressure in terms of the competitiveness of the region's countries and may lead to the emergence of barriers that are not regulated by international trade disciplines. These trends do not necessarily translate into precise multilateral rules that define the playing field for the international economy of the twenty-first century. Here again, the multilateral trading system is failing to keep up with the rapid pace of technological change and the evolving structure of business stakeholders that are often more relevant to and hold more sway over trade issues than the governments of industrialized countries. This interaction, which could be described as encompassing technological and business developments, on the one hand, and, on the other, new issues and institutions, is highly complex as it combines requirements arising from technological advances (such as quality certification) with business models that use technological change to attempt to limit competition and protect private business (as is the case with certain certification requirements linked to specific laboratories and enterprises).

There is a fine line between technological progress, the creation of new agencies and institutions, and protectionism, and it is one that can easily be crossed, particularly if developing countries do not focus on creating the technical capacity to distinguish between changes that they will have to adapt to and those that are merely new forms of private business that may limit competition or encourage protectionism.

Integration and trade initiatives

In 2007, intraregional trade once again posted double-digit growth, although the rate of expansion (around 19%) was slower than in previous years. During 2008, intraregional exports continued to climb, thereby offsetting poor sales to the United States. All groups show an increase when compared with the first quarter of 2007 (see figure 4).

Figure 4
INTRAREGIONAL AND INTRA-SUBREGIONAL EXPORTS, 1990, 1998, 2007 AND JANUARY-MARCH 2008 [a]
(Percentage of total exports)

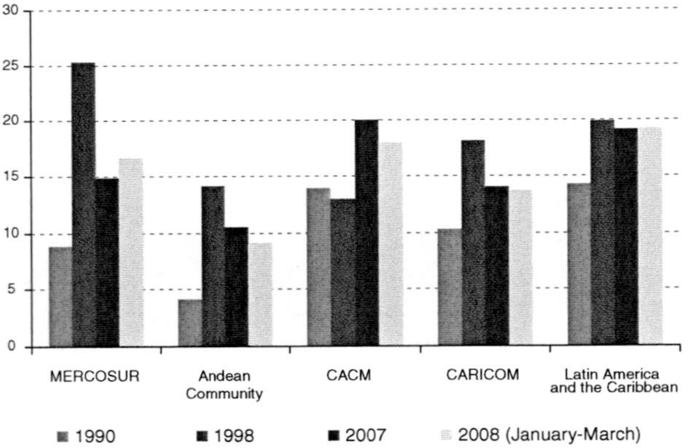

Source: Economic Commission for Latin America and the Caribbean (ECLAC), on the basis of official information.
[a] Total exports used to calculate the ratio include exports from the maquila sector and free-trade zones.

With considerable uncertainty prevailing in the international economy, especially with regard to exports to the United States by members of integration schemes, strenuous efforts were being made in 2007 and the first half of 2008 to move forward with community commitments on trade facilitation. One example is the adoption of a unified customs document and the harmonization of customs regimes within the Andean Community. Similarly, the Central American Common Market (CACM) approved and updated a series of technical regulations on standardization measures, metrology and authorization processes, as well as sanitary and phytosanitary measures and procedures. Similar advances have been made in the context of MERCOSUR.

Efforts are also being made to promote trade strategies aimed at increasing regional interdependencies. Examples include the re-launch of the South American Community of Nations (UNASUR) and the Meso-American Integration and Development Project (Meso-America Project), formerly the Puebla-Panama Plan (PPP), as well as efforts by countries that make up the Latin American Pacific Basin Initiative to generate synergies in trade relations with countries of the Asia-Pacific region (especially China, India and members of the Association of Southeast Asian Nations (ASEAN)). Lastly, countries of the Caribbean (in 2007) and of Central America and the Andean Community (in 2008) have been involved in trade negotiations with the European Union.

In recent years, the international expansion of certain companies has resulted in an increase in foreign investment, especially from Brazil, Chile and Mexico. Trans-Latins have become an increasingly significant phenomenon and currently account for around 8% of inflows of FDI to Latin America and the Caribbean, especially in the sectors of natural resources and natural-resource-based manufactures, food and beverages, commerce and services (with this last sector representing approximately half of the total). However, for Central America and the Dominican Republic, trans-Latins represent 20% of total FDI, or almost 40% if United States investment is removed from the equation. It is interesting to note that, in the case of services, FDI is the principal means for suppliers to offer services abroad. América Móvil (Telmex) and the retailer Cencosud of Chile are two examples.

Although this growing internationalization is one of the most noteworthy features of economic events in the region, unfortunately it has not been linked with integration decisions. Any effort to deepen integration should seek to strengthen links with the regional actors in the internationalization process; this would reinforce both the expansion of the companies involved and the relevance and effectiveness of the integration process. Generally speaking, this process has not resulted from specific public policies or measures arising from integration commitments. Initiatives could be undertaken within the framework of trade agreements and trade facilitation measures to strengthen this vital de facto integration process. In addition to increasing the credibility of dispute settlement mechanisms, steps could be taken to promote the convergence of regulatory frameworks in the services sector and perhaps to update trade agreements in order to deepen their coverage of trade in services. Trade facilitation measures include investment in logistics and infrastructure and the harmonization of regulations, as well as mobility of technical and professional workers and the gradual harmonization of tax and financial procedures.

In many countries, the current integration process is coupled with more ambitious, broader and deeper approaches to liberalization than in the past. This is reflected in aspects of trade that either featured only partially in previous integration models (as with investment) or not at all (as in the case of services). One of the most radical changes in approaches to integration is that several Latin American and Caribbean countries have sought to conclude trade agreements with their main trading partners (especially the United States, the European Union and, more recently, the Asia-Pacific region).

It is well known that the past decade has seen rapid changes in technology and in the world economy, as well as the emergence of new competitors and markets (China and India, along with the rest of the Asia-Pacific region). This has dramatically altered the world map of trade flows, comparative advantages and investment location decisions, and it will no doubt continue to do so. It is in this global context of new opportunities and challenges that the progress made in terms of integration falls short of the mark, particularly in South America. Indeed, integration schemes do not figure in major business decisions, and integration is not high up on the countries' political agendas; when it does appear, it amounts to little more than statements of intention. Against that backdrop, it should come as no surprise that the range of possible avenues for integration into the world economy are increasing. By the same token, sharp structural and policy differences are to be found across the countries of the region. Structural differences exist in terms of size, production structures, export capacities, comparative advantages, structure of main destination markets and degree of complementarity with or substitution of the main agricultural products of industrialized economies that heavily subsidize exports or support domestic producers. Policy differences have to do with the role that each country aspires to play in the regional and world economy, the strength of its economy and institutions and, hence, its bargaining power and alliance structure —all of which is reflected in trade policy and trade negotiations.

The different visions that have emerged therefore need to be acknowledge and reconciled in order to preserve the objective of integration. Integration has to be built up from these diverse realities with a view to making an expanded regional market more attractive. The time is ripe to update the notion of "open regionalism" by reinforcing the complementarity between integration into the world economy and subregional or regional integration schemes. This would not only broaden access to the main markets for labour- and natural-resource-intensive products, but would also encourage the development of technology- and knowledge-intensive activities, including the incorporation of value added in natural-resource-based products.

Integration schemes involve elements of development and policy coordination that are not present in free trade agreements concluded with partners outside the region. Therein lies the superiority of integration, but the serious political and technical efforts that this process requires have thus far not materialized. Of course, integration is about more than just trade, and more attention must indeed be paid to the social dimension (especially in a continent blighted by social inequality). However, this must not be done at the cost of delaying or compromising the economic and trade aspects of integration, but should rather reinforce the complementary nature of its commercial and social dimensions. With this in mind, efforts should be redoubled to build subregional value chains that enable members to export to third markets, and measures should be introduced to encourage the inclusion of less developed countries in those chains. This would represent an appropriate form of "open regionalism" that combines growth, the quest for third markets and social cohesion and in which structural support for reducing inequality among member countries promotes the development of competitive export supply in the less developed nations.

Viewed from this perspective, the summit meeting of heads of State and government on regional integration which will be hosted by Brazil in December 2008 offers an ideal opportunity to discuss these issues and agree upon an agenda for renewing and deepening regional integration.

Association agreements between the European Union and Latin America and the Caribbean: from preferences to reciprocity

Forging stronger economic and commercial ties with the European Union is an item of key importance on the regional agenda. This chapter focuses on the fact that Europe's importance as a trading partner of Latin America and the Caribbean has declined as the region's trade with the United States has expanded and as the Asia-Pacific region has become an increasingly significant export market and source of imports for the region.

These negotiations are important for the Latin American and Caribbean region, especially in view, on the one hand, of the recent failure of the Doha Round and, on the other, of the need to deepen its own regional integration. A possible association agreement between the European Union and each regional integration scheme (MERCOSUR, the Andean Community, the Central American Common Market (CACM) and the Caribbean

Community (CARICOM)) could act as a catalyst for the convergence of the various trade agreements that exist among Latin American and Caribbean countries. The European Union promotes agreements that cover the three pillars of trade, cooperation and political dialogue. The aim of all the ongoing negotiations is the creation of a free trade area supplemented by a series of trade clauses and cooperation initiatives. The accompanying political dialogue tends to focus on aspects relating to democracy, human rights and efforts to combat corruption and drugs.

In late 2007, the Caribbean countries successfully completed negotiations for an association agreement with the European Union, while the Central American and the members of the Andean Community each embarked upon negotiations for similar agreements. The negotiation process with MERCOSUR, which began eight years ago, is at a standstill. In mid-2008, the European Commission announced its intention to negotiate a strategic partnership with Mexico that could take economic relations to a new level. This is in addition to the strategic partnership agreement that the European Union signed with Brazil at the first European Union-Brazil Summit, held in Lisbon in July 2007.

If and when all these negotiation processes are brought to a successful conclusion, 13 economies of Latin America will have association agreements with the European Union (the number could rise to 18 if MERCOSUR reaches an agreement which includes the Bolivarian Republic of Venezuela). The agreements between the European Union and Mexico (2000) and Chile (2002) are in full swing. While Chile has managed to increase and diversify its exports as a result, the trade benefits for Mexico are less obvious (given its large and widening trade deficit with the European Union). The opportunity for reconfiguring its relations with the European Union through a strategic partnership could provide Mexico with a promising avenue for diversifying trade and attracting investment.

Caribbean exports to the European Union are concentrated in services and a few agricultural products (sugar and bananas). Until now, trade relations have been based on the preferences granted by the European Union to the African, Caribbean and Pacific (ACP) countries. The economic association agreement that was concluded in December 2007 (although not yet officially approved by the Caribbean countries) is a comprehensive accord that provides for the gradual removal of tariffs and the liberalization of services. The commitments of the Caribbean Forum of African, Caribbean and Pacific States (CARIFORUM) in the areas of services and investment go much further than the offers made by developing countries under the General Agreement on Trade in Services (GATS). However, the European Union has offered limited concessions in terms of what is contained in GATS. The total benefits for CARIFORUM countries will become clearer once the crucial provisions (such as the one concerning temporary work permits for professionals in European Union countries) have been implemented. Putting an agreement of such depth and scope into operation will not be easy in countries with limited institutional capacity. Furthermore, participating countries will have to face the fiscal impact of tariff reduction. The main challenge, however, will be to diversify from sugar and bananas to other production and service sectors.

Central America, for its part, receives the lion's share of the assistance which the European Union provides to the region. This aid is mainly focused on rural development, disaster prevention and reconstruction, social cohesion and regional integration, as well as on various programmes aimed at strengthening democracy and human rights. Agricultural products constitute the subregion's main exports to the European Union, and it is in this area that the negotiations will be most difficult (especially with regard to bananas). The challenge for Central America is to convert and expand the current Generalized System of Preferences, plus unilateral preferences, into more permanent market access for strategic goods. The parties have agreed that negotiations should be completed by mid-2009, and the trade talks are on schedule. These negotiations will nonetheless be difficult in areas that are important to Central America, such as exports of banana and other tropical fruit.

In the Andean Community, the effort to combat illegal drugs is one of the main topics of the dialogue on politics and cooperation. The Andean Community exports mainly agricultural and mining products to the European market. The European Union has suspended negotiations, citing the lack of a common position within the Andean Community as the main reason. There are significant differences between the negotiating positions of Peru and Colombia, on the one hand, and Bolivia and Ecuador, on the other. Bolivia has stated that it will exclude itself from certain sections of any free trade agreement. The position of the European Union is that negotiations should be carried out at the level of groupings and that agreements should be as comprehensive as possible. It would appear that, in order for these negotiations to move forward, a greater degree of flexibility needs to be introduced so that countries in differing situations can choose different coverage options. In terms of merchandise trade, the long-standing dispute about bananas also poses a major challenge in these negotiations.

Although it has been eight years since negotiations between MERCOSUR and the European Union were formally opened, there is no sign of an agreement being reached in the next few years. Talks have been hampered by disagreements on the European Union's agricultural subsidies and access to MERCOSUR markets for manufactures and services. There is every indication that the deadlock could be broken once an overall agreement is reached on agricultural subsidies in the Doha Round.

There are several quite complex issues under discussion. For Central America, the sticking point is market access for the subregion's textiles and agricultural products, as well as the European demand for ratification of the Statutes of Rome of the International Criminal Court. The Andean Community needs to arrive at a common negotiating position, at least on the main issues being considered. If this is not achieved, bilateral negotiations (as requested by Colombia and Peru) cannot be ruled out as a way of overcoming the current standstill. Another requirement is the solution of the long-running controversy with the European Union over banana exports, a crucial issue for Central America (and Colombia and Ecuador). In this respect, the agreement on bananas that the European Union had accepted in Geneva in order to unblock negotiations in Doha in late June 2008 paved the way for more rapid progress in negotiations with Central America and the Andean Community. In contrast, the way in which the European Union is tying that agreement to a final agreement in Doha is an obstacle to those same negotiations. For MERCOSUR, agricultural market access and the Singapore issues are the main stumbling blocks.

The association with the European Union could act as a catalyst for regional integration. Indeed, the European Union prefers to negotiate with subregional or regional groups and offers cooperation to strengthen integration schemes. No less importantly, the fact that a large number of Latin American and Caribbean countries will probably have a similar and wide-ranging trade agreement with the European Union offers a real opportunity for the convergence of intraregional trade agreements, thereby facilitating the standardization of regional rules and disciplines in various chapters of those agreements. There will be intense negotiations between the European Union and Central America throughout 2008 and 2009, and an agreement does appear to be in sight. Negotiations with the countries of the Andean Community will be more difficult unless a more flexible approach is adopted. Progress with MERCOSUR will depend on the outcome of the Doha Round. Agricultural market access is the top priority in the negotiations being pursued with these three subregional integration schemes.

The Latin American and Caribbean and Asia-Pacific regions in search of closer trade and investment relations

In the last seven years, the Asia-Pacific region has increased its share of the world economy. In terms of output measured in constant prices and purchasing power parity (PPP), the economy of the region as a whole represented 20.5% and 28.0% of world GDP, respectively, in 2007, compared with 6.4% and 8.3% for Latin America and the Caribbean. The Asia-Pacific region accounted for just over 36% of the 4.9% growth in the world economy during 2007.

The Asia-Pacific region plays a major and growing role in world trade, representing 28% of world merchandise exports and 23% of commercial service exports (compared with 5.7% and 3.3%, respectively, for Latin America and the Caribbean). The merchandise exports of ASEAN amounted to US$ 863 billion, exceeding the total for all of Latin America and the Caribbean. In terms of services, China, India and Singapore have become major exporters, especially of "other services" (i.e., services other than the traditional sectors of transport and travel).

In 1980-2006, the stock of FDI received by Asian countries amounted to US$ 1.2 billion (10% of worldwide stocks). Latin America and the Caribbean, on the other hand, received just under 8% of world FDI. Thus, among developing regions, Asia has outpaced Latin America and the Caribbean in this respect.

The Asia-Pacific region plays an increasingly important part in maintaining global economic equilibria. In terms of the world current account, the combined US$ 727 billion surplus of China, Japan, the newly industrialized Asian economies and ASEAN practically covered the US$ 740 billion deficit of the United States. What is more, emerging Asian economies and Japan have almost 60% of the world's international reserves. It is estimated that the Asia-Pacific region holds 53% of United States Treasury bonds. As a result, any indication of what Asia-Pacific (and China in particular) may do with its huge reserves has immediate repercussions on global financial markets.

For some countries of Latin America and the Caribbean, the Asia-Pacific region represents a massive market: nearly 36% of Chile's exports go to that region; the figure for Dominica is 31%; for Cuba, 29%; Peru, 24%; Costa Rica, 24%; Brazil, 18%; Bahamas, 17%; Argentina, 16%; Uruguay, 12%; and Bolivia, 12%. Most of these exports are from South America, while Central America and Mexico account for a smaller proportion. For many Latin American and Caribbean countries, the Asia-Pacific region remains a relatively untapped market.

The Asia-Pacific region is a much more important trading partner in imports than in exports, which means that the Latin American and Caribbean region has a growing trade deficit with it. Of total Latin American and Caribbean imports, a larger proportion originates from the Asia-Pacific region than from the European Union, with China displacing Japan as the main destination and origin. For some countries, such as Argentina, Brazil, Costa Rica and Uruguay, ASEAN has become a major trading partner. However, for China, Japan, the Republic of Korea and ASEAN, the Latin American and Caribbean region accounts for no more than 4% of imports and exports.

As pointed out in recent editions of *Latin America and the Caribbean in the World Economy*, the region's exports to the Asia-Pacific region are largely in the form of inter-industry trade, contrasting with the intra-industry focus in Asia, which is embarking on a considerable de facto vertical and horizontal integration process. In recent years, however, the inter-industrial trade structure has been taking on certain aspects of intra-industry trade associated not only with new commodities but also some high-technology manufactures. The Grubel-Lloyd index shows that Mexico is increasing its level of trade with the Asia-Pacific region, while Brazil and Costa Rica are beginning to engage in trade of a more intra-industrial nature with the region. Nonetheless, the low level of vertical and horizontal intra-industry trade continues to act as a major limitation on biregional trade and mutual investment.

Figure 5

LATIN AMERICA AND THE CARIBBEAN: SHARE OF THE ASIA-PACIFIC REGION IN TOTAL EXPORTS, BY COUNTRY, 2007

(Percentages)

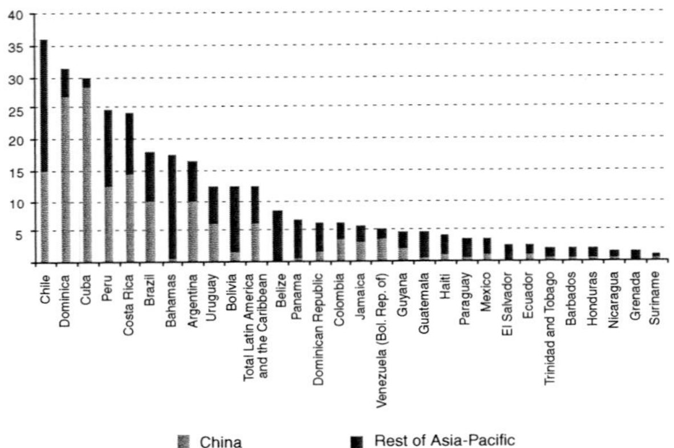

Source: Economic Commission for Latin America and the Caribbean (ECLAC), estimates based on official national figures.

To promote biregional trade, a two-pronged strategy is called for that would be directed towards: (i) making the most of the present surge in demand from Asia for commodities by incorporating knowledge, technology and value added; and (ii) becoming better integrated into Asian production and marketing networks for intra-industry trade and investment.

Intra-Asian trade and FDI are both concentrated in manufactures. An analysis by destination and origin of the trade and FDI of China, Japan, the Republic of Korea and ASEAN shows that their own region is becoming increasingly important. It is vital for the Latin American and Caribbean countries to become part of the regional process of productive integration that is under way in Asia.

This is confirmed by the high values of the Grubel-Lloyd index for Asian countries. The Latin American and Caribbean region has not been a preferred destination for FDI from China, Japan and the Republic of Korea. Much of what investment there is goes to tax havens such as the British Virgin Islands and the Cayman Islands. The Latin American and Caribbean region receives little investment in manufacturing, with most of the inflows being concentrated in various service sectors. Even in natural resource sectors (except mining), the Latin American and Caribbean region has not been a favoured destination for Asian investment.

De facto integration in Asia has been further intensified by intra-industrial and intra-firm trade. This can be observed in the fragmentation (slicing up) of value chains, especially in machinery sectors. This creates an increasingly close trade-investment nexus in which China serves as an export platform for neighbouring countries.

The proliferation of trade agreements in Asia-Pacific indicates that the region has entered a second stage of economic integration in which it is seeking a greater synergy between the de facto and de jure dimensions of this process. A network of trade agreements is being created around ASEAN which includes ASEAN+3 (ASEAN plus China, the Republic of Korea and Japan) and ASEAN+6 (ASEAN+3 plus Australia, India and New Zealand). This de jure integration process may place Latin America and the Caribbean at a disadvantage.

Approaches to the Asia-Pacific region have thus far been undertaken by individual countries on a somewhat sporadic basis by means of bilateral free trade agreements (FTAs). A more coordinated strategy is needed among countries or country groupings for the establishment of closer ties with this region. Such a strategy should focus on reinforcing the nexus between trade and investment and on strengthening production and technological linkages through various types of public-private alliances (including FTAs when such an option is deemed feasible and recommendable). It is important to link this strategic partnership with regional integration, to seek greater externalities and to move forward with enhanced legal certainty and macroeconomic stability, as well as forging more unified markets by streamlining and/or harmonizing trade rules (dispute settlement mechanisms, sanitary and phytosanitary measures, technical barriers to trade, accumulation of origin). Such advances in the regional integration agenda can be expected to increase the region's negotiating capacity vis-à-vis Asia-Pacific and broaden the scale and variety of business ties between Latin American and Caribbean firms and their Asia-Pacific counterparts.

Prospective analysis: a tool for strengthening international integration

Foresight studies have become an important consensus-building tool, particularly as regards the core components of strategies for strengthening countries' positions within the international economy and promoting export development. This kind of exercise is not common today in Latin America and the Caribbean, and progress made in this area by other countries and continents may thus serve as a stimulus for studies of this sort in the region.

Numerous analytical approaches to the preparation of prospective studies can be found in the literature. The scope of such studies has been growing in complexity over the last few decades, however, and the focus has shifted to decision-making in the present. The participation of multiple stakeholders (scientists, business people, other professionals, public authorities) helps create conditions conducive to planning and to well thought-out, systematic and participatory approaches to the creation of long-term development strategies geared towards improving a country's position in the international economy.

In a number of OECD countries, this type of long-term perspective is embodied in export development strategies having four strategic pillars around which programmes and polices are structured: attraction of foreign investment; export promotion and diversification; linkage and internationalization of SMEs; and innovation. These foresight exercises have helped to build consensus in priority-setting and in decision-making around these strategic pillars.

Although at first prospective studies focused on technology, they have since been expanding in scope to include other fields, such as sectoral strategies, and even broader development issues, such as sustainable growth. Prospective analysis is evolving through the convergence of trends in public policy analysis, strategic planning and future studies. This process therefore brings together the main agents of change in order to develop a strategic outlook based on advance intelligence.

Between the late 1940s, when future studies were first undertaken, and the present day, when prospective exercises have become a public policy instrument, the methodology used for this purpose has expanded enormously. Prospective studies are now conducted in many different ways depending, for the most part, on the characteristics of each country and each exercise, but the available methodologies are the same.

One key element in the latest studies has been the high degree of participation by stakeholders. Experience indicates that a policy's effectiveness depends on the involvement of the widest possible range of stakeholders, and that this is just as important as the expertise of those in charge of its implementation. The form that stakeholder participation takes depends on the type of exercise involved and the type of methodology used. An analysis of experiences in this regard points up the existence of distinct phases, each of which elicits differing degrees of interest and participation. If the exercise is at a diagnostic or exploratory stage, the level of participation may be lower owing to the specificity of the issues that are being addressed. During the decision-making stage, the range of stakeholders involved will tend to be wider. In contrast, at the implementation and coordination stage, the number of participating stakeholders will decrease considerably.

Although there are numerous research institutes and centres in the world that undertake future analysis exercises, governments are the ones that have taken the initiative in the use of prospective analyses as a decision-making and strategy-definition tool.

Foresight analysis is also being conducted in Latin America and the Caribbean, but, except in a few countries, governments have not systematically applied this practice at the national, subnational or sectoral level. In most cases, these exercises have been carried out only sporadically, and the capacity to adapt them in a creative way to the conditions found in the countries of the region has yet to be developed sufficiently.

Prospective studies help to build consensus and to determine strategic courses of action for overcoming obstacles to competitiveness. Energy policy provides one example. Such analyses are not widespread in Latin America and the Caribbean, but some interesting cases can be found in Brazil and the Bolivarian Republic of Venezuela. The study carried out by the Latin American Energy Organization (OLADE) is also a point of reference in this respect.

The United Nations Industrial Development Organization (UNIDO) has been promoting a sectoral form of prospective analysis in the region. In 2005, an analysis of the future of the South American fishing industry was carried out which covered Chile, Colombia, Ecuador and Peru. The corresponding chapter describes foresight analyses at the sectoral level that may help to detect potentials in new sectors as well as to define the future of an industry in crisis and to identify possible options.

The types of prospective exercises outlined in this chapter can be used to help strengthen public-private partnerships. Experience shows that such studies, by identifying the priorities and strategic guidelines that need to be taken into account in the present, are useful in building consensus as to how to construct a desirable future that is achievable in the long run.

Some foresight studies have been undertaken in Latin America and the Caribbean, but they have not influenced policy. Changes in administrations also reduce the continuity of recommended actions. A consensus as to how obstacles to competitiveness or future challenges should be addressed greatly reinforces support for the policies that are adopted and increases their sustainability and ability to withstand changes in government administrations. This is of fundamental importance for the implementation of State policies underpinned by long-term strategies. Prospective studies are a useful tool for countries striving to meet this challenge.

Chapter I

Trends in the global economy and developments in Latin American and Caribbean trade

Introduction

After expanding rapidly for five years, the global economy has slowed down substantially in 2008. Between 2003 and 2007, world output increased at an impressive rate of more than 5% in terms of purchasing power parity (PPP) (4% in terms of the weighted nominal exchange rate), and the volume of world trade in goods expanded at an even higher rate of 7% per year. Economic growth was concentrated in emerging markets where high financial returns and strong export performances encouraged high levels of foreign and domestic investment. This five-year period, which ended in 2007, was also exceptional for Latin America and the Caribbean in several respects.[1]

The global slowdown in 2008 is mainly due to the major financial crisis that originated in the United States and has spread to Europe and Japan. The financial crisis is pushing these three major advanced economies into recession. In the third quarter of 2008, the United States posted negative growth owing to a sharp drop in consumption. This raised concern, although until the second quarter of 2008 the United States continued to post positive growth thanks to dynamic net exports. Net exports have grown at high rates in part thanks to a weakening dollar,

[1] First, 2007 was the fifth consecutive year of per capita GDP growth of over 3%. A similar period of growth in the region occurred some 40 years ago. Second, the region has reduced its external vulnerability, as illustrated by primary fiscal and current account surpluses, the decline in external debt and the increase in reserves. Third, foreign direct investment in the region reached an all-time high in 2007. Fourth, exports have been very dynamic, in part, because of soaring commodity prices. Last but not least, social indicators reveal marked improvements during this five-year period, in poverty-reduction, education, health care and labour markets (ECLAC, 2008a; Machinea and Kacef, 2008).

which has counterbalanced the meagre growth of the domestic economy.[2] Other factors currently hampering global growth include the unwinding of housing market bubbles in several large economies, soaring commodity prices (despite a slight drop at the end of 2008) and the liquidity problems in the global financial markets.

However, the deceleration of world economic growth has so far been mild due to the vigorous performance of large emerging markets, the so-called "BRICs" (Brazil, the Russian Federation, India and China). Nowadays, the BRICs and emerging economies in general account for the bulk of global GDP growth and a significant proportion of international trade. In 2007, the BRICs accounted for 42% of the world population and 22% of world GDP (in PPP terms). These four countries were responsible for almost half of the increase in global GDP between 2000 and 2007. Between 1990 and 2007, their share in world exports rose from 5% to 14%, while their participation in foreign direct investment (FDI) inflows almost quadrupled. The BRICs (mainly China) also accumulated large foreign exchange reserves thanks to their enormous trade surpluses, as shown by their increasing share in global reserves (see table I.1). China, together with the world's major oil producers (Kuwait, Saudi Arabia and the United Arab Emirates), has placed a significant portion of these reserves in sovereign wealth funds, which, according to International Monetary Fund (IMF) estimates, total over US$ 3 trillion and are expected to reach US$ 12 trillion by 2012 (Hudson Teslik, 2008; IMF, 2007).

Another aspect of the rapid economic development of China, India and Asia is their increasing demand for energy and food, which has been a mixed blessing for the world economy. On the one hand, fast-growing demand explains most of the upsurge in global prices for these commodities. In turn, this has led to sharp increases in not only headline but also core inflation around the globe, in particular in emerging market economies. As a result, central banks in many countries acted to raise interest rates to stem inflation and inflationary expectations. On the other hand, commodity exporters have benefited considerably from rising Asian demand and high prices. Strong commercial ties with Asia have driven up exports in Latin America and the Caribbean and boosted GDP growth in the region.[3]

Table I.1

CHINA, BRAZIL, INDIA, THE RUSSIAN FEDERATION AND DEVELOPING ASIA-PACIFIC ECONOMIES: SHARE IN WORLD AGGREGATES, 1990, 2000 AND 2007, AND CONTRIBUTION TO VARIATIONS IN THOSE AGGREGATES, 1990-2000 AND 2000-2007

(Percentages)

	China					Brazil, India and the Russian Federation					Other developing Asia-Pacific economies				
	Share			Contribution to variation in 1990-2000	Contribution to variation in 2000-2007				Contribution to variation in 1990-2000	Contribution to variation in 2000-2007	Share			Contribution to variation in 1990-2000	Contribution to variation in 2000-2007
	1990	2000	2007			1990	2000	2007			1990	2000	2007		
(a) Population	22	21	20	16	11	22	22	22	23	23	14	15	15	19	20
(b) GDP (PPP)	4	7	11	20	23	10	9	11	3	15	4	4	5	13	9
(c) Exports	2	4	9	6	13	3	3	5	4	6	3	4	4	13	9
(d) Inward FDI	2	3	6			1	3	5			4	0	2		
(e) International reserves	3	8	19	14	27	1	5	10	9	14	11	5	5		4
Petroleum products															
(f) Consumption	3	7	12	26	35	12	10	11	-10	8	6	11	13	35	13
Imports															
(g) Agricultural materials	2	4	8	11	16	1	3	4	11	7	12	12	10	10	8
(h) Mining	2	7	23	36	32	3	4	6	10	8	9	12	10	28	9
(i) Raw energy	0	3	5	6	7	4	4	5	5	5	11	15	15	20	15
(j) Petroleum products	0	3	6	7	8	4	4	5	5	5	12	16	16	22	16

Source: World Bank, World Development Indicators [online database]; British Petroleum and United Nations Commodity Trade Database (COMTRADE) for import data.

Note: Columns 1-3 show the participation of each country or group of countries (China; Brazil, India and the Russian Federation; and other developing Asia-Pacific economies) in world aggregates in 1990, 2000 and 2007. Columns 4 and 5 give the contribution of each one to the variation in world aggregates.
Details of world aggregates: (a) Total population; (b) World GDP in constant 2005 international dollars (GDP in PPP terms); (c) Global exports of goods and services in current dollars; (d) Net inflows of FDI in current dollars; (e) Gross international reserves is monetary gold, special drawing rights (SDRs), the reserve position of members in IMF and foreign exchange holdings in the hands of monetary authorities.

2 The United States economy grew by -0.2% and 0.9%, with net exports contributing 0.9 and 0.8 percentage points to this growth, respectively, in the last quarter of 2007 and first quarter of 2008. In the second quarter of 2008, net exports contributed 2.9 percentage points to overall GDP growth of 2.8%. The latest data available indicate that in the third quarter, net exports contributed 1.1 percentage points to overall GDP growth of -0.3% (BEA, 2008).

3 GDP growth has also been boosted by stable macroeconomic environments and prudent fiscal, monetary, and debt policies.

It seems increasingly unlikely that the emerging markets are sufficiently decoupled from the advanced economies to remain unaffected by the sharp slowdown in those economies. For some time, emerging economies did succeed in maintaining economic growth at near potential levels despite the slowdown in industrialized countries, in part, because the rapidly-growing Asian region had intensified trade with other developing regions around the world. Therefore, despite modest growth in Europe, Japan and the United States, global growth retained most of its momentum. However, since mid-2008, it has become increasingly clear that the emerging markets are being affected by the financial crisis in the United States economy through many channels and that the "myth of decoupling has been exploded" (ADB, 2008). The first channel is international trade as the drop in import demand in the United States and other advanced countries is increasingly affecting export growth in the emerging economies. The second channel is the financial market since investors are losing confidence because of the financial crisis and, consequently, capital flows to emerging markets are drying up, interest rates have risen, and stock markets in these countries have come down. Nevertheless, Latin America and the Caribbean and most other emerging regions are better prepared to withstand this shock thanks to their abundant external reserves, primary fiscal surpluses and relatively low levels of external debt. As a result, although global growth is predicted to slow down in 2008 and 2009, the major emerging economies, in particular China, are expected to continue expanding at robust rates, albeit more slowly.

As of mid-2008, the world is facing two major short-term challenges: containing the risks associated with the financial crisis and coping with higher energy and food prices and other inflationary pressures. This chapter examines recent trends and their likely impact on trade in Latin America and the Caribbean. It also discusses possible policy responses in the face of deteriorating global growth prospects, high commodity prices and rising inflation.

A. Main developments in the financial markets

1. The United States financial crisis and its economic impact

The financial crisis stemming from the collapse in the real-estate market in the United States is the main event affecting global growth in 2008. In 2007, difficulties in credit markets started to impact the real sector of the United States economy as growth slowed. The crisis has its origins in a combination of low interest rates (in particular for mortgages), innovative debt instruments and the expectation of continuously rising housing prices (see box I.1). Other factors that played a role are the lack of regulation that allowed the development of huge shadow markets with risky investments, the lack of restraint on the part of lenders and borrowers and misguided federal policies that failed to minimize the obvious risks to credit markets. The depth of the United States crisis and the degree of its transmission to industrialized and emerging economies will define global economic conditions over the next two years.

From mid-2007 to the second half of 2008, the financial crisis steadily worsened. Around mid-2007, major financial institutions around the world started to announce poor financial results, with bad debts affecting their results and balance sheets. The British bank Northern Rock was nationalized after a run on its deposits. In January 2008, Bank of America bailed out a troubled mortgage lender (Countrywide Financial). In March, Deutsche Bank reported massive losses, and investment bank Bear Stearns was bought out by JP Morgan Chase, with the help of the Federal Reserve. In July, major problems arose in mortgage lending markets as lenders in Spain, the United Kingdom and the United States began to fold or be bailed out by larger rivals. The United States mortgage lender IndyMac collapsed and was taken over by the Government.

Box I.1

ORIGINS OF THE FINANCIAL CRISIS IN THE UNITED STATES

The United States subprime crisis has its origins in an explosive mix of cheap credit, innovative debt instruments and the expectation of continuously rising home prices. Low interest rates following the 2001 recession made home-buying a more attractive financial option. Banks and mortgage brokers also relied less on loan repayments as a source of income and the incentive for careful due diligence on mortgage applications was removed. Mortgages with features such as low initial interest rates and no down payment were offered to borrowers with little repayment capacity. By selling mortgage contracts to Wall Street, lenders were then able to earn fees while passing the risk on to the financial market.

Financial-sector demand for mortgage-backed securities was insatiable. New mortgage-backed debt instruments (such as the infamous collateralized debt obligations or CDOs) allowed investors to participate in the booming housing sector and leverage it. These new assets consolidated mortgage types, such as subprime mortgages, into vehicles that relied on preferential payment schemes to differentiate buyers' risk exposure. Investors could pay a premium for the right of preferential repayment, hoping that delinquency rates in the underlying mortgages would not affect them. Thus, sellers were able to create a pseudo-diversified financial instrument that leveraged some of the worst risks in the mortgage sector (Mollenkamp and Ng, 2007). Buyers of these securities had little information on the quality of the underlying mortgages. Ratings companies also failed to fully understand the risks, justifying high ratings with the guarantee of mortgage insurance companies ("monolines") that were also exposed to mortgage-backed instruments.

The cycle became self-fulfilling, with greater demand for mortgage contracts leading to lower credit standards and lower interest rates, sustaining the demand for homes and causing a boom in real-estate prices. Regulators were unable, or unwilling, to keep pace with these developments (Ip, 2007). This unsustainable model began to unravel as rising interest rates and excessive inventory burst the bubble of perpetually increasing home prices. From July 2006 to July 2008, prices declined by 20% and buyers who had hoped to either refinance or sell their homes at higher prices found an illiquid market and unaffordable monthly payments. This led to a spike in default rates —initially among less-qualified borrowers (thus the origin of the term "subprime crisis") but eventually encompassing even prime-rated securities— and a leveraged impact on the financial instruments backed by these mortgages. The obscure nature of the underlying risk of derivative contracts made their market worth suspect, leaving many highly exposed institutions with assets of unknown value and close to violating prudential requirements.

Source: Economic Commission for Latin America and the Caribbean (ECLAC).

In September and October 2008, the financial crisis intensified rapidly. Early in September, the financial problems of mortgage lenders Fannie Mae and Freddie Mac forced the Government to bail both of them out to avoid a collapse of the United States financial system. Shortly afterwards, investment bank Lehman Brothers filed for bankruptcy protection. Stock prices fell, which obliged credit agencies to lower their debt assessment of several financial institutions. Counterparties were forced to reduce their debt exposure to these organizations and reacted by calling in their loans. Bank of America agreed to take over Merrill Lynch. When American International Group Inc (AIG) proved unable to raise new capital, the Federal Reserve stepped in to rescue the company and took control of 80% of its assets. Similarly struggling with liquidity shortages, Goldman Sachs and Morgan Stanley, the two remaining major independent investment banks in the United States, chose to become bank holding companies. This move enabled both firms to secure easier access to credit, at the price of stricter Government supervision and regulation, in order to survive the current crisis. This ended the era of American investment banking, which had lasted 75 years and been characterized by massive risk-taking and its extraordinary potential for generating profits. By the end of September, the largest commercial bank failure ever witnessed in the United States occurred when Washington Mutual collapsed, and major banks in Europe began to run into difficulties as well.

The present crisis is the most costly economic event since the Great Depression in the United States (Reinhart and Rogoff, 2008). Its origins fit into a familiar pattern of rapid increases in equity and housing prices (one of the leading crisis indicators in countries experiencing large capital inflows), as well as changes in real GDP growth, public debt, and current account deficits. Although there is some novelty in both the causes of the United States crisis and the policy response it has produced, it is reasonable to expect that the economic impact will be significant and will bring about a reduction of real per capita growth of two percentage points in the United States, the effects of which will be felt for at least two years.[4]

The actions of regulators to contain the crisis have been unprecedented. First, the Federal Reserve increased credit availability to banks and financial institutions through new lines of credit and reduced interest rates, but this move was unable to solve the underlying problems of the financial system. Institutions were holding assets whose markets had suddenly disappeared and were in dire need of capital to sustain their balance sheets.[5]

---

4 If the impact is more severe and matches the experience of the five most catastrophic cases (Finland, Japan, Norway, Spain and Sweden), the decline in growth could be greater than 5% and could last over three years.

5 An institution's use of the Federal Reserve Bank Discount Window is often seen as a sign of financial weakness and is therefore stigmatized. The Federal Reserve, recognizing this, arranged for more anonymous access to funds through new instruments.

In recognition of this, the Federal Reserve began to accept lower-quality assets as collateral, swapping a significant portion of its safe Treasury holdings for new debt instruments —some of which were guaranteed by mortgage-backed securities.[6] The Federal Reserve then had to step in to guarantee the mortgage-related losses being incurred by financial institutions, and the United States Government committed at least US$ 25 billion to bail out Freddie Mac and Fannie Mae.[7] The Government also nationalized one of the country's largest mortgage lenders, IndyMac, among others. The Federal Reserve meanwhile increased its existing currency swaps with other major central banks worldwide in an effort to infuse liquidity into the global financial system.

At the end of September, when the crisis was spiralling out of control, the United States Treasury and the Federal Reserve put forward a US$ 700 billion bailout plan to purchase large amounts of troubled mortgage securities and other "toxic" assets from financial institutions. The total mortgage debt is estimated at US$ 12 trillion, with approximately 9% of loans either seriously delinquent or in foreclosure. Other aspects of the bailout plan include the Government's acceptance of equity stakes in companies, restrictions on executive compensation packages ("golden parachutes") for certain companies that sell assets to the Department of the Treasury, rules on future compensation in case the Government is unable to recover its payments, help for homeowners with delayed payments and the study of a possible regulatory overhaul of the United States financial sector. For example, there are strong demands to regulate the so-far unregulated US$ 62 trillion market for credit-default swaps amid concerns that they may drive down stocks.[8] Also, regulators probably will tighten controls on hedge funds, private equity firms and investment banks by imposing stricter rules on capital requirements and limits on leverage. Since the announcement of this plan, the Treasury has opted to change the focus of the bailout plan and concentrate first on using US$ 250 billion to recapitalize the country's largest banks by purchasing preferred and common stock. The plan follows the proposal by Britain's Prime Minister, Gordon Brown, which announced a three-point plan to recapitalize banks in the United Kingdom, inject liquidity into financial markets, and provide government guarantees to the interbank lending market. This plan has since become the template for rescue packages in many other countries, including the United States, France, Germany and Austria.

It is highly uncertain whether the bailout package approved by the United States Congress will be sufficient to keep the financial system afloat and to save the United States economy from sinking into a deeper recession. In particular, there is enormous uncertainty about how the subprime mortgage crisis is affecting other credit segments, including prime mortgages, commercial real estate, unsecured consumer credit (credit cards, student loans and auto loans), industrial and commercial loans, corporate bonds and credit-default swaps. It is also unclear how thousands of small and medium-sized United States banks will be affected by the current crisis. Furthermore, the credit crunch caused by the undercapitalization of the financial sector may push the housing market into a deeper crisis and cause more financial institutions to file for bankruptcy.

The impact on the private sector is expected to be considerable. According to IMF, banks and insurance companies had lost between US$ 640 billion and US$ 735 billion by the end of September 2008, while losses for the entire global financial system may amount to US$ 1.3 trillion (IMF 2008e). An important part of these losses is directly related to residential loans (subprime and prime) and creates a significant solvency risk in many banks, which have been forced to raise capital and access various types of financing in order to remain within prudential regulations.

The crisis is also affecting investment and consumer spending. Economic growth slowed sharply in 2007 and contracted at an annualized rate of 0.2% in the fourth quarter of that year. Slow growth continued during the first half of 2008. As shown in figure I.1, the slowdown has so far been led by a reduction in private consumption and private investment caused mainly by a fall in residential investment, which has averaged a negative 1% annualized contribution every quarter since mid-2006, contrasting with a positive 0.3% average since the end of the 2001 recession. In the third quarter, consumption shrank 3.1% compared with the previous quarter, which translated into a 2.3% drop in GDP growth. In 2007, four fifths of the deceleration was concentrated in four sectors: finance and insurance, construction, real estate and rental, and mining (BEA, 2008). In mid-2007,

---

6 Prior to the onset of the credit crisis in August 2007, 87% of the Federal Reserve's assets were Treasury securities. By mid-October, Treasury securities accounted for 27% of these assets, having been replaced by repurchase agreements, term auction facility instruments, and other loans. Impaired collateral held against these new instruments are reported as "other assets pledged" and was zero in August 2007 (Federal Reserve Statistical Release, H.4.1 [online] http://www.federalreserve.gov/releases/h41/20081008/, 16 October 2008).

7 The bailout of Fannie Mae and Freddie Mac marks an important regulatory shift as the authorities reversed their position of not guaranteeing the companies' debts. The stakes are also much higher than in the case of Bear Stearns as the companies have debts of US$ 1.5 trillion and own or guarantee US$ 5 trillion in mortgages. They also have contracts worth US$ 2 trillion more to hedge the risks behind those mortgages.

8 Speculators may use credit-default swaps to bet a company's financial condition will worsen. The contracts pay holders face value for the underlying securities or the cash equivalent should a company fail to repay its debt. The swaps' value increases as perception of the company's stability deteriorates. Speculators who buy swaps without owning the underlying debt may flood the market and drive down stocks (Bloomberg, 2008).

consumption in the United States started to weaken as a result of falling household wealth, stagnant real wages and tighter credit conditions. Efforts by policymakers to increase credit availability have not had much impact on consumer lending, as banks have used the additional funds to bolster balance sheets. A recent survey by the Federal Reserve on lending practices and demand showed that the number of banks reporting tighter credit standards was the highest since the survey began in 1991, indicating significant risk aversion. At the same time, demand for consumer loans has dropped to historic lows, and banks have increased spreads over their cost of funds (Fed, 2008).

The economic crisis is curbing recent inflationary effects. Higher import prices have not yet been fully passed on to the domestic economy, and other macroeconomic indicators (such as payroll reports, consumer and business confidence, industrial production and durable goods orders) have also pointed to a bleaker outlook. In the meantime, the United States economy continues to benefit from strong export growth due to a weak dollar and the fact that other regions remain dynamic. Real exports were over 10% higher in the first half of 2008 than in the same period in 2007, but import demand has weakened: real imports fell by 1.7% during the same period. In this context, the issue of decoupling is highly important as demand for United States exports also depends on the rest of the world's economic performance.

Figure I.1
UNITED STATES: GROSS DOMESTIC PRODUCT BY EXPENDITURE COMPONENTS
(Year-on-year growth rates each quarter)

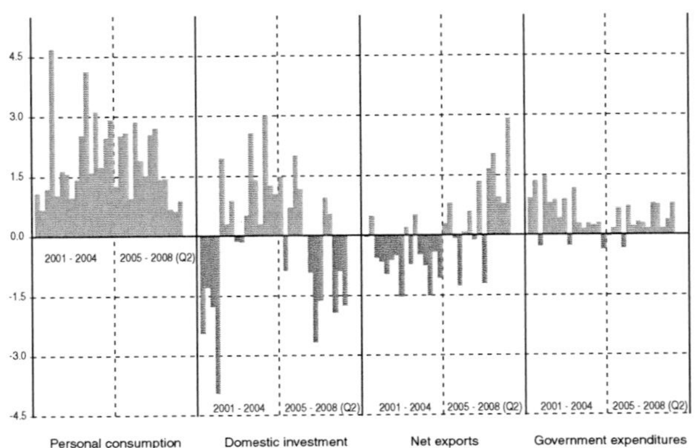

Source: Economic Commission for Latin America and the Caribbean (ECLAC), on the basis of United States Bureau of Economic Analysis.

2. The impact of weakening import demand in the United States on global trade

A prolonged slowdown in the United States will not only threaten the economies of Latin America and Caribbean economies directly through lower import demand and a decline in remittances, but also indirectly through its impact on Asian economies and trade. On the one hand, the declining share of the United States as an export destination for Latin America and the Caribbean, combined with improvements in the region's terms of trade and robust growth in Asia, helps to offset the direct impact of the economic slowdown. On the other hand, the effects of slower growth in the United States will be felt in Asia as lower demand for Asian exports will reverberate through the region's large processing sector, eventually affecting Asian demand for Latin American and Caribbean exports. Given the increasing importance of trade for Latin America and the Caribbean —both relative to GDP and as a source of growth— the impact of the United States crisis on commercial activity warrants careful consideration.

Shifting global trade patterns should mitigate the direct impact of slowing United States demand for imports from Latin America and the Caribbean. The share of the United States in world imports declined from over 21% in 2000 to just over 14% in 2007. For exports from Latin America and the Caribbean, the share directed to the United States fell from 60% to just 42% between 2000 and 2007. Mexican exports to the United States declined from nearly 90% of the total in 2000 to 76% in 2007 (see table I.2).

Table I.2
EXPORTS TO THE UNITED STATES AS A SHARE OF TOTAL EXPORTS, 1980-2007
(Percentages)

	1980	1990	2000	2005	2007
Canada	61	75	87	82	79
European Union (27 countries)	5	7	9	8	7
Japan	24	32	30	23	20
South America	21	30	29	26	21
Caribbean	56	36	54	54	45
Central America	38	41	36	54	39
Mexico	65	69	89	86	76
ASEAN	16	19	19	14	12
Singapore	12	21	17	10	9
China	5	8	21	21	20
Republic of Korea	27	29	22	15	12

Source: United Nations Commodity Trade Data Base (COMTRADE) and International Monetary Fund (IMF), Direction of Trade Statistics.

= Denotes a decrease from the previous period.

The United States slowdown may also have an indirect impact on Latin American and Caribbean exports, as weakened import demand in the United States reduces export and income growth in other regions in the world, which may in turn depress their demand for Latin American and Caribbean products. The economic slowdown in the United States has already had an impact on that country's imports from Asia and the European Union, although the depreciation of the yen against the dollar since 2005 has helped to sustain United States imports from Japan (see figure I.2). The average growth in the volume of United States imports from China for the period from January to August dropped from 14% in 2007 to 1.5% in 2008, and there is some evidence of slower Chinese demand for key Latin American and Caribbean products (see figure I.2). For the ASEAN region, the decline was from 3.5% to -1.9%. The growth of exports from the European Union to the United States has been slowing since December 2007 and has averaged 1.4%, well below the figure of over 7% recorded in the previous six months.

Figure I.2

GROWTH OF UNITED STATES REAL IMPORTS FROM SELECTED COUNTRIES AND REGIONS, 2007 AND 2008 (JANUARY TO JULY)

(Year-on-year growth rates by month)

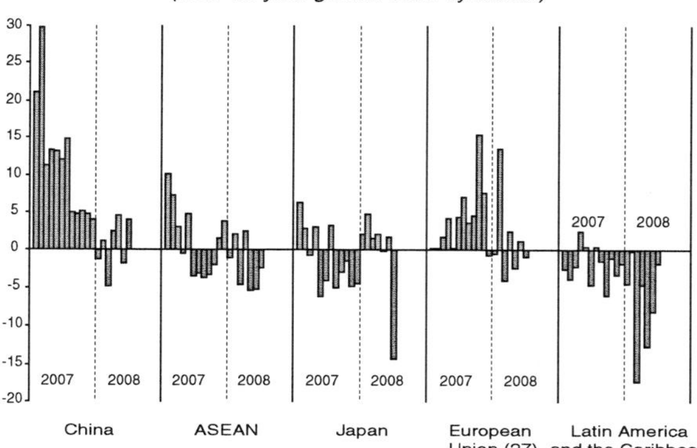

Source: Economic Commission for Latin America and the Caribbean (ECLAC), calculations based on United States International Trade Commission, Bureau of Labor Statistics.

As exports from Asia to the United States slow, Asian intraregional linkages via China's processing trade are of particular importance to Latin America and the Caribbean (given the increasing weight of Asia in Latin American and Caribbean trade). Of the region's total exports, the proportion which went to the Asia-Pacific region (including China) doubled between 2000 and 2007, from 6% to 12% (see table I.5 for country-specific shares). This increases the exposure of Latin America and the Caribbean to a decline in United States demand for Chinese exports. Falling Chinese demand for inputs from Asia would slow regional growth and eventually Asian import demand.[9]

The European Union, Japan, and the other industrialized economies will see a significant drop in their growth rates during 2008 and 2009 to levels below their medium-term averages. In the second quarter of 2008, GDP in the European Union contracted by an annualized rate of 0.2% relative to the previous quarter, and Japan saw its economy contract by 0.6% in the same period. The *World Economic Situation and Prospects* projects decrease in real GDP growth rates as of mid-2008 for the advanced countries from 2.5% in 2007 to 0.6% in 2008 and 0.9% in 2009 (United Nations, 2008). The euro area will experience a drop from 2.6% to 1.1% with significant downside risks. Housing prices in the European Union have mirrored developments in the United States, although the scale of financial leveraging of the housing sector in the United States has resulted in the impact being much greater there.[10]

Other regions, including Asia and Latin America and the Caribbean, will also see lower growth rates than in recent years, but will remain at or near their medium-term performance. Within Asia, the difference between the growth of industrialized and emerging economies is also highly evident: Japan, which represents 42% of the region's GDP, is expected to experience economic growth of just 0.2% in 2008. Economic growth in China, which represents 31% of Asia's GDP, will slow from 11.9% in 2007 to 9.7% in 2008 (IMF, 2008e). Within Latin America and the Caribbean, individual countries' prospects will depend a great deal on their commercial ties. Countries with greater dependence on the United States and the European Union, such as the Bolivarian Republic of Venezuela, Mexico and a number of Central American and Caribbean countries, will face lower demand for their exports, which tend to consist of energy and manufactured products. Those countries that have more connections within the region and with other emerging markets, such as Argentina, Bolivia, Paraguay and Uruguay, will benefit from their net exports of high-priced commodities and from robust intraregional economic activity.

All in all, the Latin American and Caribbean region is relatively well placed to withstand a slowdown in the United States and the resulting direct and indirect effects on its exports. Economic activity in Asia, led by China, will decelerate but remain relatively dynamic, which will help offset some of the decline in export demand. In addition, improvements in the terms of trade of many countries in the region will help sustain balance-of-payment positions. The region also enjoys strong fiscal and debt positions that may discourage drastic shifts in financial flows.

[9] See section C for more details on the importance of China's performance to Latin America and the Caribbean.

[10] According to figures from the *2008 World Economic Outlook* (IMF, 2008a), issues of residential-mortgage-backed securities (RMBS) in the United States averaged nearly US$ 100 billion per month during 2006 and early 2007 (with a peak of US$ 145 billion in June 2006). In Europe, 12-month average issues of similar instruments never surpassed US$ 30 billion.

3. Exchange rates

Since early 2002, the dollar has generally depreciated at a rate of between 2% and 9% per year, as measured by the broadest trade-weighted index. The evolution of the dollar against most of its main trading partners since its high in early 2002 has helped the United States to improve its trade balance by lowering the relative cost of its exports. Between November 2004 and May 2008, the yuan appreciated by 13% in real terms relative to the dollar, affected by the decision of Chinese regulators to increase the rate of appreciation and relative inflation rates between the United States and China. In June 2007, the yen reversed its depreciating trend that had begun in 2005; by May 2008 it had gained 12% against the dollar. The euro has also continued to rise against the dollar, gaining 23% since late 2005. In mid-2008, the dollar regained most of the nominal value it had lost during the year, following disappointing economic news in Europe and reports that the United States Government would provide support to Fannie Mae and Freddie Mac. The large movements in foreign exchange markets mark a period of increased volatility as traders react to economic news and search for safe havens.

Figure I.3

REAL EXCHANGE RATES INDICES AND REAL DEPRECIATION RATES

(a) Real exchange rates against the United States dollar (2005=100)

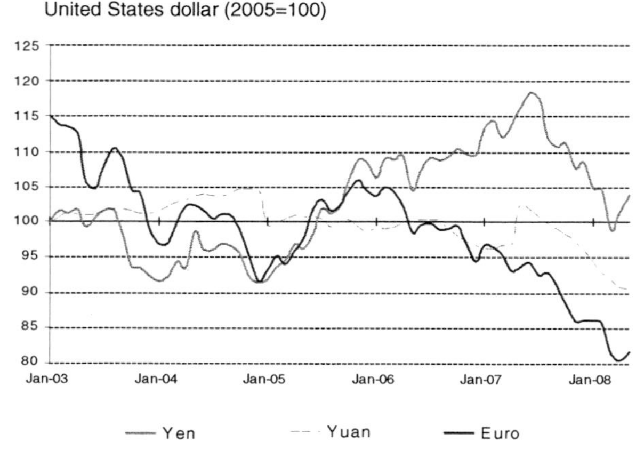

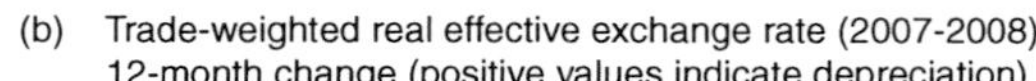

(b) Trade-weighted real effective exchange rate (2007-2008) 12-month change (positive values indicate depreciation)

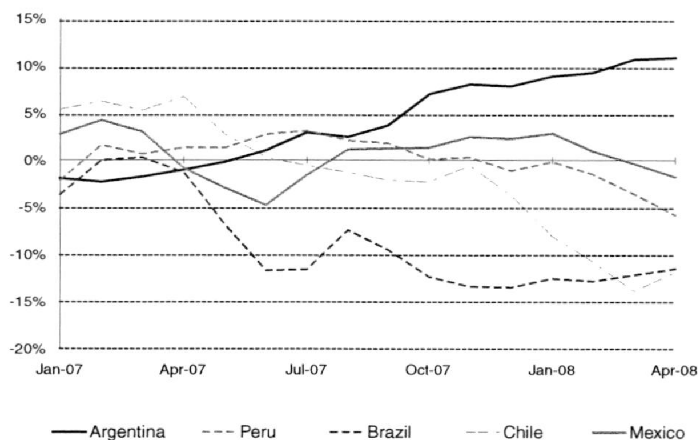

(c) Brazil: year-on-year change in real exchange rate against selected countries (positive values indicate depreciation of Brazil's currency)

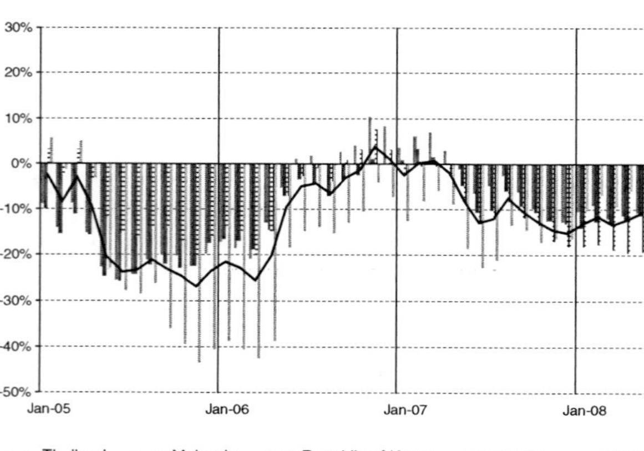

(d) Chile: year-on-year change in real exchange rate against selected countries (positive values indicate depreciation of Chile's currency)

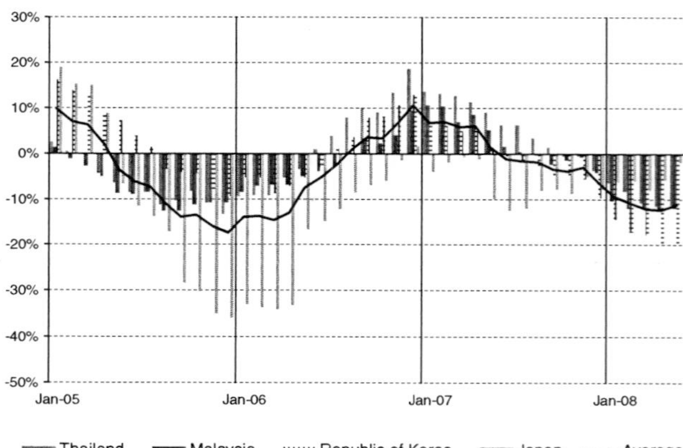

Source: Economic Commission for Latin America and the Caribbean (ECLAC), on the basis of International Monetary Fund (IMF), International Financial Statistics.

Relative to the United States dollar, Latin American and Caribbean currencies have on average appreciated by less than those of Asian countries since the dollar began to fall in 2002, leading to improved competitiveness in the United States market over that period.[11] A comparison of the relative exchange-rate movements of China's main sources of imports in Asia and Latin America and the Caribbean in the last two years paints a different picture. Since 2005, Brazil and Chile have seen their currencies appreciate at a faster pace than those of their Asian competitors. The Republic of Korea has gained the most as the won has lost 25% of its nominal value against the yuan. As such, Asian exports to China are becoming more competitive than those from Latin America and the Caribbean.

B. Recent trends in commodity markets

1. Recent price developments

For much of 2008, the world experienced an across-the-board commodity price boom, which was both broad-based, encompassing all the major commodity groups —energy, metals, foodstuffs and agricultural commodities— and persistent, lasting longer and producing larger price hikes than earlier booms such as that of the early 1970s.[12]

The price rises were particularly pronounced in the case of oil and other energy products. The price of crude petroleum increased from approximately US$ 25 per barrel in 2002 to over US$ 100 for most of 2008, reaching an unprecedented high of US$ 140 in June 2008. This surpassed the peak of the 1979 energy crisis in both nominal and real terms. Coal prices have also jumped relative to the 2002 level, and the price of natural gas increased more gradually during the same period (see figure I.4).

Figure I.4
COMMODITY PRICE INDICES
(2000=100, deflated[a])

(a) Energy

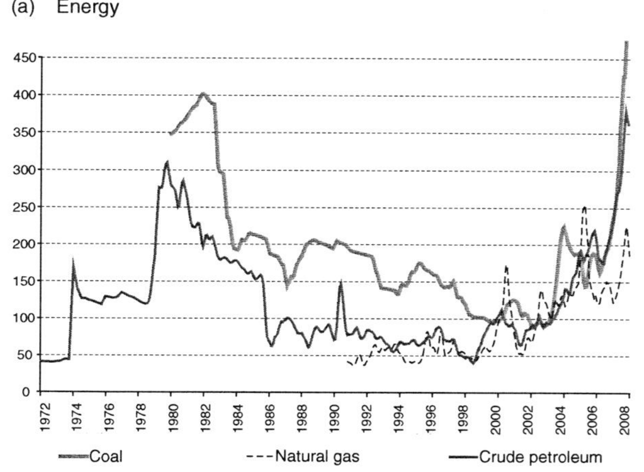

(b) Minerals, ores and metals

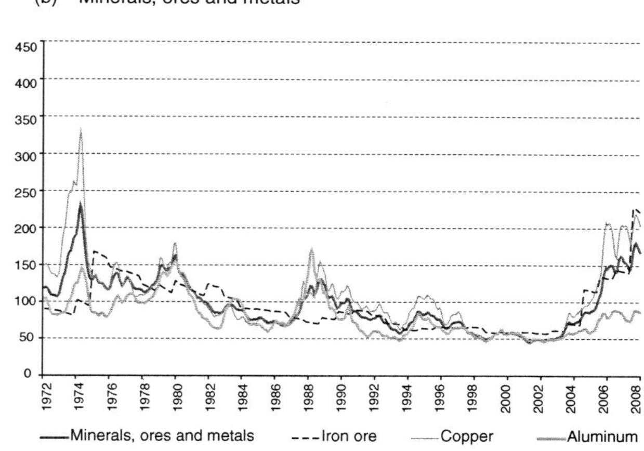

[11] Available data for 18 countries in Latin America and the Caribbean show an average appreciation against the United States dollar of 12.5% from February 2002 to April 2008. Data on 13 Asian countries show an average appreciation of 16.3% during that time. Hong Kong Special Administrative Region of China, Mexico, Nicaragua, Panama and Taiwan Province of China have experienced depreciations. Since 2007 and mid-2008, the average rates of appreciation have been 6.8% and 5.9%, respectively.

[12] See IMF (2008a), box 5.2, for a comparative analysis.

Figure I.4 (concluded)

(c) Agricultural products

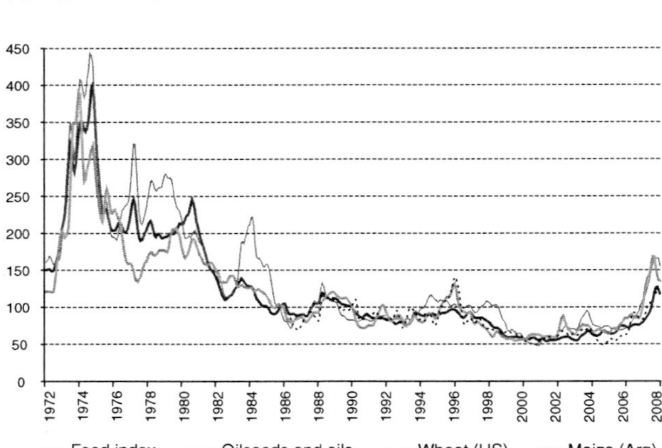

Source: Economic Commission for Latin America and the Caribbean (ECLAC), on the basis of United Nations Conference on Trade and Development (UNCTAD), Commodity Price Statistics [online database].

[a] Deflated by United States Consumer Price Index (excluding food).

The boom has also been seen in metals and ores, although current prices are still below those of the early 1970s. Between mid-2003 and mid-2008 the nominal price of aluminium doubled, the price of zinc tripled, and iron ore and copper prices increased four and five times, respectively. Even when adjusted for overall inflation, iron and copper prices have performed strongly, growing 270% and 330% over the course of the past five years, respectively. The current deflated price of iron ore is at a historic high since 1960, and the price of copper is at its highest since 1974.

As for agricultural commodities and foodstuffs, there has been a sharp and simultaneous upswing in all prices since early 2006 (see figure I.4c). The prices of grains and oilseeds more than doubled between January 2006 and June 2008, although the prices came down slightly afterwards. The increase has been particularly steep in the case of wheat, with the price surpassing US$ 450 per ton in March 2008,[13] a 150% increase over the course of two years. Wheat prices declined slightly through May and June and fell again in September, but the average for the first three quarters of 2008 remains almost three times higher than the 2000-2005 average. Although the recent price hike is dramatic relative to the levels of five years ago, from a historical perspective, the recent increase in food prices could be said to represent a recovery from the exceptionally low levels of 1985-2005. For most grains and oilseeds, the current prices are still far below those of the 1970s and early 1980s, allowing for overall inflation.

2. Commodity markets: real versus financial determinants

(a) Real factors affecting commodity prices

A number of common factors have brought about hikes in the prices of all commodities. In the last few years, the growth of demand has outpaced that of supply. Robust economic growth and rapid industrialization in China, India and other developing economies, in a context of inelastic supply in the short term, explain part of the price boom (see figure I.5).[14] Developing countries overall accounted for 82% and 99% of the increase in demand for rice and wheat between 2000 and 2007, while consumption in the industrialized countries, in particular the United States,

13 For United States hard red winter wheat (grade 2).

14 In both 2006 and 2007, while growth in Japan, the United States and the European Union economies was well below 3%, most low- and middle-per capita income economies performed strongly, averaging 7% to 8% growth per year, with prospects for continued expansion, albeit at a slightly slower rate (United Nations, 2008).

declined. Together, China and India account today for half of the world's consumption of rice and one third of wheat and soybean oil consumption.

Demand from China has an even stronger impact on metal and oil consumption than on food markets, accounting for more than 100% of the increase in world demand for refined copper between 2000 and 2007 and three quarters of the increase in global consumption of refined aluminium and slab zinc. China's share in worldwide consumption of steel products, refined aluminium, and refined copper increased from 2000 onwards, and its demand for oil and petroleum products grew almost six times faster than world demand in the same period, contributing 35% to the increase in global demand for these products.

Figure I.5
CONTRIBUTION OF CHINA AND INDIA TO THE VARIATION IN GLOBAL CONSUMPTION OF SELECTED AGRICULTURAL COMMODITIES, PETROLEUM AND METALS, FROM 2000 TO 2007
(Percentages)

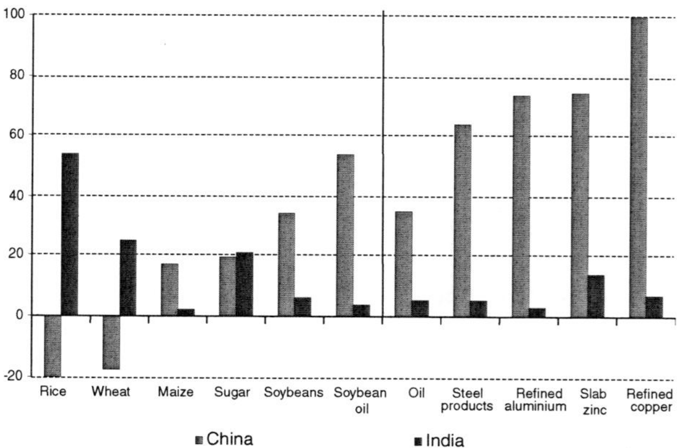

Source: Agricultural commodities: United States Foreign Agricultural Service, official estimates of the United States Department of Agriculture (USDA); oil and metals: British Petroleum, International Iron and Steel Institute and World Bureau of Metal Statistics.

(i) Agricultural commodities

The interplay of numerous mutually reinforcing factors is perhaps most complex in agricultural markets. On the supply side, the last three years were characterized by negative yield shocks primarily caused by weather-related production shortfalls: cereal yields fell by about one fifth in Canada and drought-stricken Australia between 2005 and 2007 (OECD/FAO, 2008). Another factor is the soaring cost of agricultural inputs, particularly fertilizers, which doubled in price between October 2006 and October 2007.[15] Higher transport costs have also impacted the cost of agricultural commodities. Ocean freight rates for grain shipments from United States ports in the Gulf of Mexico to Europe have almost tripled.[16]

The supply response to the price boom has been slow in materializing, constrained not only by lags associated with planting and investment decisions, but also by government-imposed distortions that impede the transmission of price signals to domestic markets. These include price controls, consumption subsidies and export restrictions. Measures introduced in many countries to retain domestic supply and protect domestic consumers reduced supply on world markets and put further pressure on world prices. These include export restrictions, such as those on rice recently announced by India and Viet Nam, and increases in export taxes in Argentina and elsewhere.[17]

On the demand side, a sharp increase in the use of food grains for biofuel production (ethanol and biodiesel) was a major engine of demand growth between 2005 and 2007. In that period, global biofuel consumption of wheat and coarse grains doubled, accounting for over half of the increase in total grain use. Policies adopted by the United States and, to a lesser extent, the European Union have stimulated the use of food grains for biofuels and led countries to switch to growing crops for biofuel production. The International Food Policy Research Institute (IFPRI, 2008) and World Bank (2008) find that increased biofuel production is largely to blame for higher agricultural prices.

In short, there has been a persistent gap between the growth rates of supply and demand. The markets are tight, and neither supply nor demand has been able to respond to price signals in the short run. In addition, the shocks to supply and demand took place in the context of record low stocks, which otherwise would have acted as a buffer and softened the impact of these shocks on prices.

(ii) Energy products and metals

According to estimates by the International Energy Agency (IEA, 2008), the current level of oil prices is high due to the combined effect of strong demand growth and limited supply expansion in recent years. While there has been some weakening of demand in the countries of the Organisation for Economic Co-operation and Development (OECD), global consumption has continued to expand, driven mainly by rising demand in non-OECD Asia and the Middle East. At the same time, oil production by the member States of the Organization

[15] For example, ammonium sulphate and triple super phosphate (TSP) (see FAO, *Food Outlook*, various issues).

[16] From US$ 28 to US$ 75 per ton (FAO, 2008b).

[17] An increase in the export tax on soybeans was rejected by the Argentine Senate on 16 July 2008.

of Petroleum Exporting Countries (OPEC) has been stalled at approximately 35 million barrels per day since 2005, mainly because of the rising cost of oil exploration and development. Production has been hampered by a sharp increase in marginal costs since 2003, as well as limited access to low-cost oil reserves. There are also geopolitical concerns. Most oil is produced in politically fragile or even war-ridden zones such as Nigeria, where a number of oilfields have been closed down recently after attacks by militant groups.

On the demand side, developing and emerging countries use relatively more energy to produce their output.[18] The economies of China, India, the Russian Federation and other major players are concentrated in sectors with high energy requirements: mining, smelting, cement, iron and steel, meat and dairy products. These countries' energy demand will therefore remain high in the near future.

There is evidence that this strong demand is the main factor behind high mineral and metal prices, driven in particular by Chinese imports of copper and iron as described above. Per capita use of refined copper in China is about 3 kg, double the Latin American average and well above other developing and transition economies, except the Russian Federation (ICSG, 2007).

Raw metals are characterized by highly inelastic supply, at least in the short term, since production is capital-intensive. It often takes 6-10 years to bring a new mine into production, requiring heavy investments in construction and machinery. At the same time, demand is also inelastic, since substitution among different metals is very limited, constraining a demand response to high prices. As the result of inelastic supply and demand, both periods of surplus supply and shortages are frequent, and the market experiences cycles with strong price swings.

(b) The roles of exchange rates, interest rates and speculation

Several analysts argue that prices increased not only because of rising demand and inelastic supply, as outlined above, but also owing to the real effective depreciation of the dollar, low interest rates and speculation. First, the depreciation of the real effective exchange rate of the dollar has indeed put upward pressure on commodity prices quoted in that currency (Bastourre, Carrera and Ibarlucia, 2007; FAO, 2008c; UNCTAD, 2008). Following the real depreciation of the dollar from 2002 to April 2008 (except in 2005), and in the context of rising demand and low reserves, commodity producers have raised their prices to compensate for the loss of purchasing power. Second, expansionary monetary policies in numerous countries (such as China, India and the United States) with low nominal interest rates and negative real ones have stimulated economic growth and contributed to the growing demand and rising prices for commodities around the world.[19] Moreover, low interest rates in the United States have weakened that country's currency, with the aforementioned effect on dollar-quoted commodity prices.

Third, other analysts point to the increasing role of speculation in driving up commodity prices (Kregel, 2008; Masters, 2008; UNCTAD, 2008) although there is as yet no solid evidence to support this. Partly in response to the real depreciation of the United States dollar, the financial crisis and downward movements in equity and mortgage markets, many investors have turned to commodity-based index funds because their prices seem to be negatively correlated to other types of investment, such as equities and bonds. From 2002 to 2008, investments in commodity-based index funds increased from less than US$ 15 billion to more than US$ 260 billion (Commodity Futures Trading Commission). Nonetheless, there is no conclusive proof of the role of speculation in determining commodity prices.[20]

---

[18] The indicator of energy intensity (GDP per kg of oil equivalent) is 2.6 for the Russian Federation and 3.1 for China (2005), among the lowest in developing countries. The average energy intensity for high-income countries is 6.0 and the world average is 5.0 (World Bank, World Development Indicators, online database).

[19] Based on an analysis over the past 30 years, Merrill Lynch (2008) finds that a reduction of one percentage point in real interest rates results in a 17.5% increase in spot commodity prices.

[20] Krugman (2008), Merrill Lynch (2008) and *The Economist* (2008) suggest speculation cannot be held responsible for the price spikes because not all commodity prices have increased (for example, nickel, sugar and lean hogs) in recent years; statistical tests suggest that the increase in index-linked commodity investments has not contributed to the increase in spot prices of commodities as diverse as maize, gold and oil; non-index-linked commodities have also seen dramatic price gains (including coal, rice, iron ore and steel); and there are few signs of inventory building (for example, in crude aluminium, oil, or wheat).

3. Short-term commodity price prospects

There is much uncertainty regarding the future course of commodity prices. One scenario is that the commodity price boom continues, in which case, more weather-related yield shocks occur, the use of cereals for biofuels expands, and oil production levels remain constant although geopolitical tensions trigger periodic supply disruptions. Another scenario is that prices begin to decline relative to 2008 levels. Under this scenario, growth in developing countries slows, there is a strong supply response in agriculture and, to some extent, in metals, oil extraction increases in OPEC and non-OPEC countries, and global demand for oil is curbed by recession fears, changed consumer behaviour and the introduction of alternative fuel technologies in OECD countries. A more realistic scenario lies somewhere between the two and is consistent with the price projections made by most agencies, as listed in table I.3. The consensus among international and government organizations (IMF, World Bank, OECD, Food and Agriculture Organization of the United Nations (FAO), International Energy Agency (IEA), United States Department of Agriculture) is that global demand for commodities will continue to be strong, driven by developing countries. This means that consumption of raw agricultural and metallic materials, as well as fuels, is unlikely to slow in the medium term.

There are, however, factors that could positively affect supply capacity and loosen the market tightness observed during 2007 and 2008. In agricultural markets, supply response is picking up, in particular for grains, as planted areas are expanding and investment in agriculture is increasing both in the industrialized world and in developing economies. Thus, after peaking in early July, the price of soybeans had fallen 14% by mid-September. Wheat prices reached an all-time high of US$ 12 per bushel in mid-March, but dropped by over 70% to US$ 7 by mid-September, reverting to the level attained a year ago. Maize prices went down by 25% from a record of US$ 7 per bushel in early July to approximately US$ 5.3 in mid-September.[21] On the other hand, it seems that agricultural yields will continue to be affected by adverse climate conditions, and this will contribute to supply instability. A recent example is the flooding in the Midwestern United States in June 2008.[22] In addition, the use of cereals for biofuel production will continue to increase, albeit at a slower pace than in the last two years.

Table I.3

SHORT TERM PRICE PROJECTIONS, CHANGE FROM PREVIOUS YEAR

(Percentages)

Percentage change	Economist Intelligence Unit		International Monetary Fund		International Energy Agency	
	2008	2009	2008	2009	2008	2009
Food						
Maize	58.7	14.7	28.6	4.8		
Wheat	43.9	-2.0	41.1	-2.8		
Rice	107.5	-3.5	50.4	4		
Soybeans	63.6	6.8	30.8	-3.6		
Soybean oil	66.9	6.1	25	-5		
Sugar	30.3	11.7	2.4	1.2		
Grains	47.3	-1.3				
Oilseeds	62.6	2.9				
Metals						
Copper	9.1	-11.9	-1.8	-14.3		
Aluminium	12.8	-7.5	2.3	-7.4		
Iron ore			65.3	-14.3		
Zinc	-36.7	-10.7	-38.5	-10		
Crude petroleum						
Crude West Texas Intermediate (WTI)	69.1	-8.3			60.1	9.2

Source: The Economist Intelligence Unit, "World commodity forecast: food, feedstuffs and beverages", July 2008; International Monetary Fund (IMF), *World Economic Outlook*, Washington, D.C., April 2008; Energy Information Administration (EIA), *Short-Term Energy Outlook 2008*, Washington, D.C., United States Department of Energy.

Most analysts expect agricultural commodity prices to peak in 2008 and flatten or decrease slightly in the following years, although on average they will remain higher than during the decade prior to the boom. Table I.3 shows that, following strong growth in 2008, a decline in wheat prices in 2009 is widely expected. Overall, the consensus is that agricultural prices will remain higher than in 2005, but not as high as in 2007.

Oil price projections made earlier this year placed an emphasis on the continued growth of global oil consumption, driven primarily by demand in developing countries and China in particular. However, in the second half of 2008, slower than expected growth in world petroleum

[21] Data from Bloomberg.

[22] The Midwest was hit by the worst flooding in 15 years, Iowa being one of the states most seriously affected. Of around 10 million hectares of crop area in Iowa, 16% was under water, including 810,000 hectares of soybeans and 530,000 hectares of maize. The United States exports half of all maize traded worldwide and, in 2005, it accounted for 40% of exports of soybeans in quantity terms (FAO Statistical Databases-FAOSTAT). Wheat yields will not be affected by the flood, as most of the wheat is grown in the Great Plains states (Kansas, Montana, North and South Dakota, Texas and others).

demand became evident. Sluggish consumption in the OECD countries driven by a slowdown in the global economy[23] and prospects for increased supplies from producers outside OPEC have put downward pressure on crude prices. So far, concerns regarding an economic downturn have overshadowed supply concerns: neither the disruption of Caspian export flows in August, nor the continued tensions between Russia and Georgia nor Hurricane Gustav raised oil prices (EIA, 2008c). As a result, the West Texas Intermediate (WTI) crude oil price dropped by one third from the peak of over US$ 140 per barrel in mid-July to slightly over US$ 90 per barrel in mid-September and fell to less than US$ 80 in mid-October. Highly sensitive to the exchange rate of the United States dollar and to developments in the financial markets, spot prices for oil have continued to trend downwards.

The short- and medium-term prospects for oil prices are closely linked to expectations regarding the global economy. Weak economic activity and a steady supply of oil from OPEC countries would keep prices down. On the other hand, it is plausible that the current sluggishness of demand is temporary, and that global consumption will pick up towards the end of 2008 and drive up oil prices. Be that as it may, OPEC member countries are continuing to take steps to maintain oil prices within a range of US$ 70-US$ 90 per barrel, since they consider that the minimum price for the final quarter of the year should be US$ 70 per barrel.

Although Chinese demand for metals grew strongly in 2007 (consumption increased by 43%, 35% and 13% for aluminium, copper and steel, respectively),[24] Chinese imports of iron ore, copper and zinc slowed in the first half of 2008, a trend that is expected to continue through 2008 and 2009. Slower growth in China and the end of Olympics-related investment are affecting demand. A global economic slowdown is expected to put a brake on global demand as well, especially in the construction, machinery and automotive industries, and this will ease price pressures. As a result, the rise in metal prices is expected to slow during the second half of 2008 and reverse in 2009. The prediction is therefore that some metal prices will decrease by 10% or more in 2009, with the overall index for base metals declining by 7.6% (EIU, 2008b). Some of these price drops have already begun to appear: copper prices, for example, fell 24% between the beginning of July, when they peaked, and mid-September. On the other hand, there are also signs that the supply of some metals will pick up: Chilean copper production, for example, is set to expand as various investment projects are under way in the mining sector.[25]

C. Trade in Latin America and the Caribbean: recent performance and impact of global economic conditions

1. General trends

In 2007, several changes took place in the dynamics of Latin American and Caribbean trade with respect to the boom period of 2004 to 2006. Goods export growth fell back sharply, mostly because of reduced import demand from the United States, while import growth retained the momentum it had built up in the previous three years thanks to thriving domestic economies. The slowdown in export expansion was mainly due to smaller rises in volume: from 8% in 2004-2006, the annual growth rate was down to only 3% in 2007 (figure I.6). This slowdown in the growth of export volumes took place

23 Consumer behavior is also changing in these countries: There is an observed switch away from SUV and light trucks in the United States. Moreover, the big car makers are slowing production of these vehicles, replacing them with more energy efficient and environmentally friendly cars.

24 Data from International Iron and Steel Institute and World Bureau of Metal Statistics.

25 Projected investments in the mining sector grew threefold between 2007 and 2008 from US$ 804 millions to US$ 2,431 millions (*El Mercurio*, 17 July 2008). Also, the state copper company, Codelco, has announced plans of US$ 5 billion expansion of the Andina mine, targeting an increase in extraction from 220 thousand tons in 2007 to 800 thousand tons annually in the coming years (see Portal Minero [online] http://www.portalminero.com/noti/noticias_ver_ch.php?codigo=4129&fecha=07).

in all the subregions, but was most evident in the Andean nations, Brazil and Mexico. Export price rises also dipped in most countries in 2007, with Chile being the most notable case. Other subregions experienced only minor increases in export prices. In contrast, export prices in Argentina, Paraguay and Uruguay rose faster in 2007. All in all, three quarters of export growth in 2007 was due to increasing prices and only one quarter to higher volumes.

Figure I.6

GOODS EXPORTS AND MERCHANDISE TRADE AND CURRENT ACCOUNT BALANCES, 2004-2006 AND 2007

(a) Goods exports: volume and prices

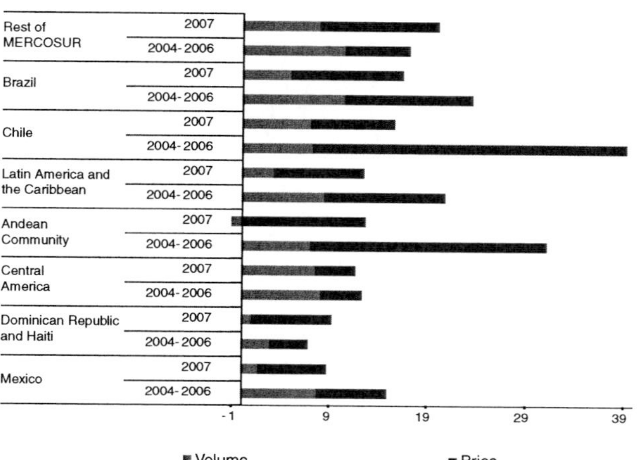

(b) Merchandise trade and current account balances as a percentage of GDP

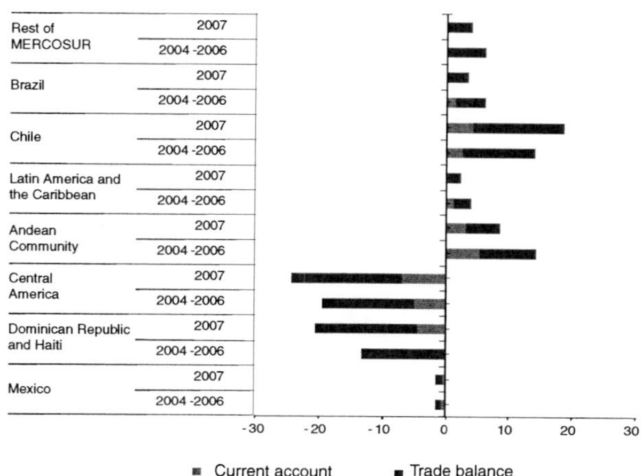

Source: Economic Commission for Latin America and the Caribbean (ECLAC).

In 2007 import growth remained strong in relation to the previous three years, in keeping with buoyant domestic consumption and investment in the region, with volume rising more slowly but somewhat faster price rises. Growth in import volumes was very uneven across the region, with some countries (Brazil and the Central American countries) showing higher rates in 2007 than in 2004-2006, and others lower ones (rest of MERCOSUR, Dominican Republic, Haiti and Mexico). In both periods, import prices rose at about the same rate in all the countries.

The trade balance and current account weakened in 2007, although the region as a whole remained in positive territory for the sixth year in a row. With respect to GDP, trade balances declined in all subregions and countries except Chile. Overall, the largest merchandise trade deficits were recorded in Central America, the Dominican Republic and Haiti, where they reached more than 15% of GDP. Current account balances showed deteriorations similar to the merchandise trade accounts in all countries and subregions, again with the exception of Chile. The services trade balance also worsened in 2007 in relation to previous years, mainly owing to falling tourism revenue and a larger deficit on the transport account as a result of rising costs. Migrant workers' remittances also increased by less than in previous years.

The improvements seen in the region's trade balance from 2004 to 2006 were related more to terms-of-trade gains than trading volumes, whereas the deterioration in 2007 was explained in large part by trading volumes. This is illustrated in figure I.7, which shows a breakdown of the variations in the trade balance as a proportion of GDP.[26] The dash illustrates the total variation, with a positive number indicating that the trade balance improved in that year and a negative one showing that it deteriorated. The South American countries have experienced an average improvement of 32% in their terms of trade since 2003. In contrast, the Central American and Caribbean countries have seen their terms of trade decline by an average of 7%, as the region imports most of its energy requirements and exports a large proportion of labour-intensive manufactured products that compete against China for the United States market.

[26] For a formal breakdown of the trade balance, see Beynet and others (2006) and Gianella and Chanteloup (2006).

Figure I.7
CONTRIBUTION TO CHANGES IN THE TRADE BALANCE, 2004-2006 AND 2007
(GDP percentage points, annual averages)

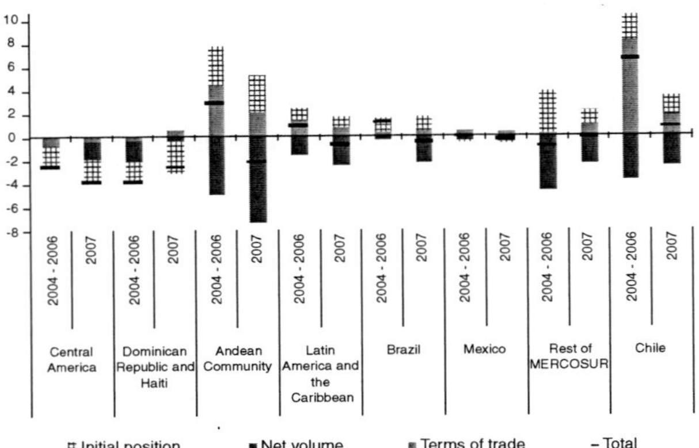

Source: Economic Commission for Latin America and the Caribbean (ECLAC), estimates on the basis of national accounts.

Note: Each dash represents the percentage point variation in the trade balance as a share of GDP. The variation has three components: (a) *Initial position effect*, showing how the trade balance would have changed if exports had grown at the same rate as imports in the current year, given the position of the trade balance in the previous year, (b) *Net volume effect*, illustrating the net contribution of real export and real import growth, and (c) terms of trade.

Between 2003 and 2006, terms-of-trade improvements accelerated as many countries' export baskets benefited from global increases in commodity prices.[27] The change in relative prices was most significant in 2006, when they added 1.3% to the region's GDP in contrast with an average yearly gain of 0.8% between 2003 and 2005. This trend was particularly marked in Chile and the Andean Community, which gained the equivalent of 12.6% and 5.1% of their respective GDP from terms of trade improvements. The figures for Central America, which had seen average annual losses of 0.6% of GDP in 2003-2005, worsened to a 0.7% loss in 2006. Price increases tapered off in 2007, as did the gains and losses in all countries except Colombia, the Dominican Republic, Mexico and Paraguay, which experienced greater gains that year (see table I.4).

Table I.4
NET GAINS OR LOSSES FROM VARIATIONS IN TERMS OF TRADE, 1995-2002, 2003-2005, 2006 AND 2007
(Percentages of GDP, annual averages)

	1995-2002	2003-2005	2006	2007
South America	0.1	0.9	2.2	0.8
MERCOSUR	0.0	0.1	0.6	0.4
Andean Community	0.6	3.4	5.1	2.1
Chile	0.3	4.1	12.6	2.1
Central America and Mexico	0.3	0.4	0.1	0.2
Central American Common Market	-0.2	-0.6	-0.7	-0.3
Costa Rica	0.1	-1.1	-1.1	-0.4
Mexico	0.4	0.5	0.2	0.3
Latin America and the Caribbean	0.1	0.8	1.3	0.6

Source: Economic Commission for Latin America and the Caribbean (ECLAC), on the basis of official data.

2. The slowdown in the United States: direct and indirect impacts on the region's exports

Import demand from several regions has slowed. Average growth in the volume of Latin American and Caribbean exports to the United States fell from a positive 7.5% in 2006 to a 2.1% contraction in 2007. The fall was even sharper in the first quarter of 2008, when the region's export volume declined by 8.2% relative to the first quarter of 2007 (see figure I.8).

Demand from the European Union is more stable for the region as a whole, though this is largely explained by the weight of South America in the region's basket of exports. Mexico, Central America and the Caribbean have seen large fluctuations in the volume of their exports to Europe, while South America has seen steady growth in the last three years, averaging 5.7% per year since the second quarter of 2005.

27 Net gains from variations in the terms of trade are calculated on the basis of the change in the terms of trade between year 1 and year 0, multiplied by exports in year 1 at 2000 prices. This number is then divided by the GDP of year 1 at 2000 prices. An increase in this indicator shows that a country can buy more imports today than it could last year thanks to an improvement in the terms of trade.

Figure I.8
VOLUME OF LATIN AMERICAN AND CARIBBEAN EXPORTS TO THE UNITED STATES AND THE EUROPEAN UNION, 2005-2008
(Quarterly growth over previous year)

(a) United States

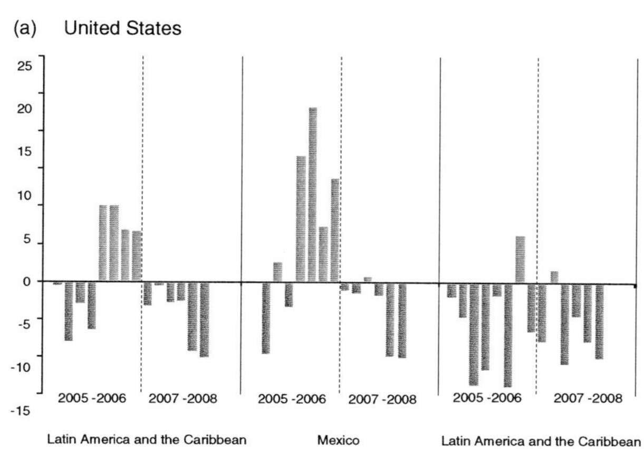

(b) European Union

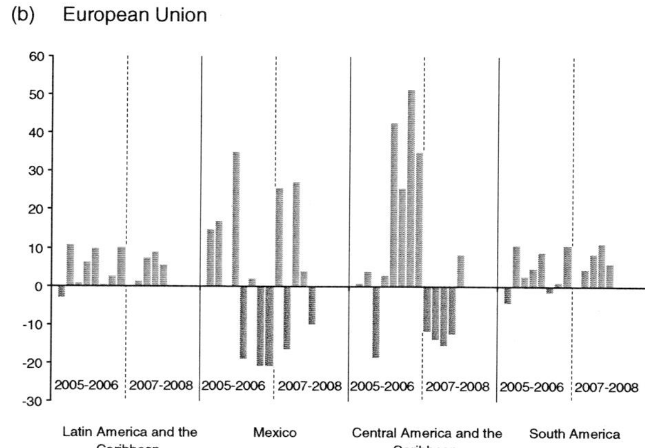

Source: Economic Commission for Latin America and the Caribbean (ECLAC), on the basis of the United States International Trade Commission and the Statistical Office of the European Communities (EUROSTAT).

Import demand from developing economies has remained buoyant, growing in volume terms by an average of 11% each year since 2000 (IMF, 2008a). IMF forecasts point to annual growth rates of 12% and 11% in 2008 and 2009, respectively, nearly double the rate of growth in global import volumes. Exports to these countries are expected to continue growing at a strong pace, though recent data for China's imports of key Latin American and Caribbean exports, while not yet showing widespread effects from global economic events, do point to some weaknesses (see figure I.9).

Figure I.9
CHINA: GROWTH IN IMPORT VOLUMES OF SELECTED COMMODITIES
(January-June 2004-2008, year-on-year growth)

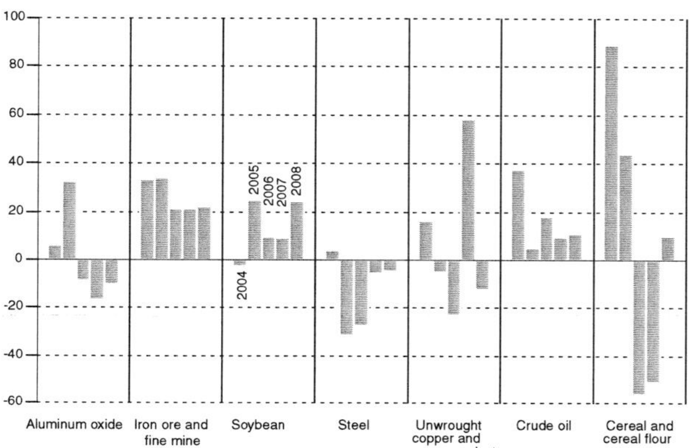

Source: Economic Commission for Latin America and the Caribbean (ECLAC), on the basis of Ministry of Commerce of China.

Should United States demand for products from China remain weak, the slowdown in China's exports would create problems for many countries in Asia. Approximately 20% of China's total exports are sold to the United States, which is showing signs of lower demand (see figure I.2). Overall, Chinese export growth slowed slightly in the second quarter of 2008, although the country's total import growth continues to accelerate owing to strong domestic demand. As of 2006, over 50% of China's exports come under the heading of processing trade, which drives the country's large processing-trade imports (41% of total imports). As United States imports from China slow, Asian economies will see falls in export revenues and economic growth, and this will eventually impact on Asian imports from Latin America and the Caribbean. Growth in the volume of Brazil's exports to China and to Asia-Pacific countries has slowed in the last year, showing a clear downward trend.[28] The importance of the processing trade must be weighed against the decline of the United States as a destination for exports from the region. With the exception of Ecuador, Honduras and four Caribbean countries, revenues from exports to Asia-Pacific have increased relative to those going to other regions for all the Latin American and Caribbean economies (see table I.5). This shift increases the importance of the dynamic Asian continent for Latin American and Caribbean trade.

28 The lack of high-frequency trade volume data broken down by trading partner prevents a fuller analysis of recent trends in Latin American and Caribbean exports to Asia.

Table I.5

EXPORT SHARES BY MAIN DESTINATION, 2000 AND 2007

(Percentages of total exports)

Country/region		Latin America and the Caribbean		China		Asia-Pacific		United States		European Union (27 countries)	
		2000	2007	2000	2007	2000	2007	2000	2007	2000	2007
South America	Argentina	48	39	3	10	8	16	12	8	18	19
	Bolivia	47	61	0	1	1	12	24	9	17	6
	Brazil	25	25	2	10	12	18	24	15	28	24
	Chile	22	16	5	15	29	36	18	13	25	24
	Colombia	29	36	0	3	3	6	51	31	14	18
	Ecuador	32	32	1	1	12	3	40	43	16	16
	Paraguay	75	72	0	1	4	4	3	3	11	21
	Peru	22	18	7	12	20	24	28	19	21	18
	Uruguay	55	37	4	6	10	12	8	10	16	22
	Venezuela (Bol. Rep. of)	20	15	0	4	1	5	55	52	5	9
Central America	Costa Rica	19	25	0	14	3	24	38	25	21	24
	El Salvador	28	39	0	0	1	3	24	48	11	6
	Guatemala	36	41	0	1	3	4	59	42	10	6
	Honduras	6	21	0	0	4	2	77	69	10	10
	Nicaragua	23	22	0	0	1	2	41	63	20	7
	Panama	20	19	0	0	3	6	50	21	19	50
	Mexico	3	6	0	1	1	3	89	78	3	6
Caribbean	Bahamas			-	1	4	17	29	21	52	44
	Barbados			0	0	2	2	5	12	20	17
	Belize			-	-	3	8	52	28	38	35
	Cuba	8	11	5	28	8	29	0	0	39	21
	Dominican Republic	4	5	0	2	1	6	87	67	6	17
	Dominica			-	27	7	31	7	2	31	18
	Grenada			-	0	0	1	51	21	31	14
	Guyana			1	2	4	5	25	17	30	33
	Haiti			0	1	0	4	87	75	5	5
	Jamaica			1	3	3	5	38	35	32	31
	Saint Kitts and Nevis			0	0	1	0	68	61	23	20
	Saint Lucia			0	0	1	0	18	26	55	48
	Saint Vincent and the Grenadines			-	-	2	0	3	1	46	69
	Suriname			0	0	5	1	25	9	29	21
	Trinidad and Tobago			0	0	1	2	47	59	14	9
Latin America and the Caribbean		16	18	1	6	6	12	60	42	12	15

Source: United Nations Commodity Trade Data Base (COMTRADE) and International Monetary Fund (IMF), Direction of Trade Statistics.

Indicates >10% increase.

Indicates >10% decrease.

However, despite the declining importance of the United States market for the region as a whole, trade relationships within the Americas remain strong. The United States is still the single largest destination for the region's exports and absorbs at least 20% of the exports of 19 countries in the region. In addition, 54% of exports from Latin America and the Caribbean are primary products and natural resource-based manufactures, which in turn represent over 82% of the region's exports to Asia-Pacific countries. As such, trade between Asia and Latin America and the Caribbean is more vulnerable to variations in commodity prices. Trade with the United States and Europe and within the region is more balanced, with a greater share of high-, medium-, and low-technology manufactures (see chapter VI for more details).[29]

[29] Calculations by ECLAC based on COMTRADE data.

3. Impact of the commodity price boom on Latin American and Caribbean exports

Latin America and the Caribbean is a major producer and exporter of commodities on a global scale. In 2006, the region produced 44% of the world's soybeans and 13% of global maize output. Its share in the production of zinc, aluminium and copper is also sizeable, at 28%, 22% and 19%, respectively, of the world total. The region is a net exporter of fuels, metals and agricultural products. Thus, although net commodity importers in the region (mostly in the Caribbean and Central America) are adversely affected by rising prices, the region as a whole gains from higher commodity prices in terms of export earnings and external balances. In total, agricultural commodities and fishery products, metals and oil represented 40.5% of exports in 2006.[30] The commodity price boom therefore has major implications for the region's external position and growth. In terms of their contribution to GDP, commodity exports are most significant for the Bolivarian Republic of Venezuela, Bolivia, Ecuador, Guyana and Trinidad and Tobago (see figure I.10).

Figure I.10
EXPORTS OF PRIMARY PRODUCTS AND NATURAL-RESOURCE-BASED MANUFACTURES [a] BY COUNTRY, 2006
(Percentages of total exports and GDP)

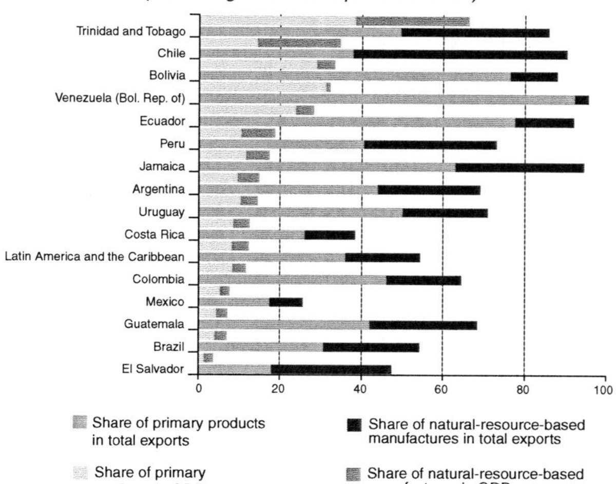

Source: Economic Commission for Latin America and the Caribbean (ECLAC), calculations on the basis of United Nations Commodity Trade Data Base (COMTRADE).
[a] Primary products are defined as unprocessed outputs of the agricultural, mining and energy sectors, such as cereals, oilseeds, metal ores, crude petroleum, coal and gas. Natural-resource-based manufactures include refined petroleum and petroleum products, processed agricultural and forestry products, such as flour and sugar, as well as basic metals and minerals such as copper, aluminum and zinc.

The rise in commodity prices has had several consequences for exports from Latin America and the Caribbean. Monthly export earnings have grown rapidly in nominal terms since 2003, as shown in figure I.11. Annual exports from the region were 17.3% higher in June 2007-May 2008 than in the previous 12-month period. However, this development is due mostly to increases in prices rather than in volume. In real terms, annual exports grew by only 1.2% in the same period.[31]

Figure I.11
MONTHLY EXPORT VALUES FOR LATIN AMERICA AND THE CARIBBEAN, 2000-2008 [a]
(Billions of dollars)

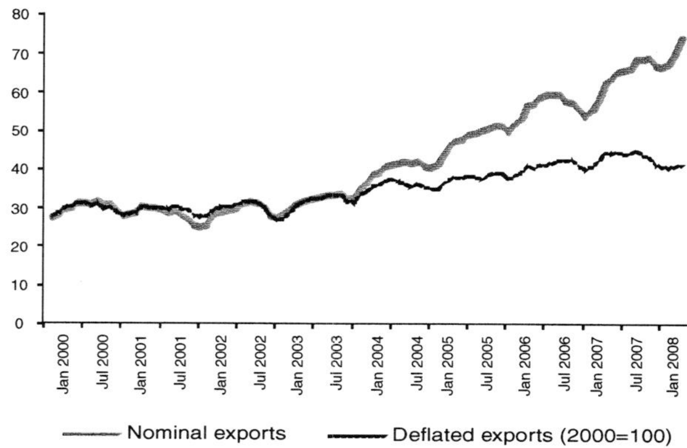

Source: Economic Commission for Latin America and the Caribbean (ECLAC), on the basis of official information from the relevant countries.
[a] Excluding Antigua and Barbuda, Dominica, Grenada, Saint Kitts and Nevis, Saint Lucia and Saint Vincent and the Grenadines, for which the monthly data are incomplete.

A potential negative consequence of the commodity price boom would be greater reliance on commodities for exports and a slowdown in exports of manufactures, which have a higher value added content. From the mid-1980s until 2000, the share of primary products in Latin American and Caribbean exports declined rapidly, reflecting a shift towards manufactures, greater export diversification, higher value added and greater technology content in exports. Between 1990 and 2000 the share of primary goods in total export values declined from 49% to 28%. However, their nominal share increased from 28% in 2000 to 36% in 2006. This reversal is entirely due to the rising prices of commodities, in particular petroleum. From 2000

---

30 The main agricultural commodities and fishery products (such as bananas, beef, coffee, maize, soybeans, soybean oil, sugar, wheat, and fish and shellfish) made up 7.6% of the region's total exports. Key metals and ores (iron and steel, zinc, aluminium and copper) represented 12.8%, and oil and petroleum products 20%.

31 Nominal exports were deflated by the United States price index for imports from Latin America (2000=100) from the Bureau of Labor Statistics.

to 2006, the share of oil and petroleum products increased from 16% to 20% of all Latin American and Caribbean exports in value terms, while that of copper (including copper ore) expanded from 2.8% to 6.8%, and that of iron and steel (including iron ore) from 3.2% to 4.3%.

Rising commodity prices offer high returns on exports of primary products and natural-resource-based manufactures, which may undermine the progress made by the region in the previous 20 years in diversifying its export basket. The region's commodity export boom in recent years is also closely linked to its growing commercial ties with China and other Asian economies, whose imports from Latin America and the Caribbean are highly commodity-intensive. This fact could also contribute to a potential move away from export diversification.

However, there is no indication that commodities exports have increased as a share of total exports in real terms. The share of commodities in total exports expanded only marginally in real terms between 2000 and 2003, from 27% to 28%, but then declined to 25% in 2006. Despite rapid price increases in the last few years, in quantity terms primary exports grew at an average annual rate of 4.1% between 2000 and 2006, compared with 5.6% for other exports. In 2006 primary export volumes actually declined, while other exports kept growing at almost 10% (see figure I.12). Export volumes of agricultural commodities, especially maize, coffee and sugar, have increased since 2005, but metals exports from Latin America increased only slightly in 2006 and then declined in 2007 (refined copper by 3.3%, aluminium by 4.1% and zinc by 12.8%).[32]

Another concern regarding greater reliance on commodity exports is that export earnings could become more volatile.[33] So far, however, this does not seem to be the case. Clearly, the impact of commodity prices on economies in the region depends on the relative weight of commodities in each country's total exports. A few countries account for the bulk of exports of each commodity from Latin America and the Caribbean. Most grain exports are from Argentina and Brazil, the latter also being the largest exporter of coffee and sugar. Colombia exports almost all of the region's coal and Bolivia accounts for half of the region's natural gas exports. The Bolivarian Republic of Venezuela dominates petroleum exports. Chile accounts for three quarters of the region's total copper exports. Brazil is the main exporter of iron and steel, as well as aluminium. Peru exports half of the region's zinc. In this context, Argentina and Brazil are the main beneficiaries of the boom in agricultural prices, while the Bolivarian Republic of Venezuela, Bolivia, Chile, Mexico and Peru gain the most from metal and energy price increases. Analysis of the correlation between the commodity price index and export values by country supports this hypothesis.[34]

Figure I.12
ANNUAL GROWTH OF PRIMARY AND OTHER EXPORTS FROM LATIN AMERICA AND THE CARIBBEAN, BY VOLUME
(Percentages)

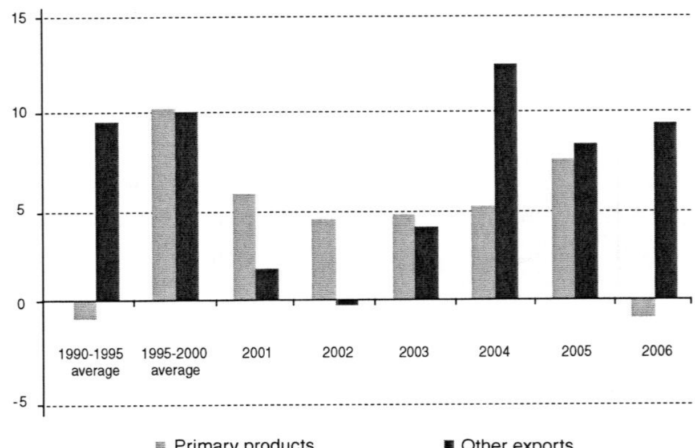

Source: Economic Commission for Latin America and the Caribbean (ECLAC), on the basis of national statistics and the United Nations Commodity Trade Database (COMTRADE).

The effect of commodity price increases on the trade balance also depends on each country's trade patterns. Net commodities exporters improve their external balances as commodity prices increase, while net importers will see deterioration. Accounting only for first-order effects, IMF finds that commodity price increases between 2005 and 2007 improved trade balances relative to GDP by 9% in Chile, 7% in Peru, and 6% in the Bolivarian Republic of Venezuela (IMF, 2008c). Argentina, Brazil and Colombia also benefited (with Argentina gaining most and Brazil least of the three). By contrast, the trade balances of the Central American countries were affected negatively.

[32] Data from WBMS (2008).

[33] The coefficient of variation relating to the values of monthly exports from the region remained unchanged between 2000 and 2007. The coefficient of variation relating to monthly export flows from Latin America and the Caribbean in the past two years (from March 2006 to March 2008), which is when most of the price increases took place, is still slightly lower than in the two previous years. During that period, there was increased volatility in Argentina and to a lesser degree in Central America and Jamaica.

[34] In 14 out of 33 Latin American and Caribbean countries, the correlation between export values and commodity prices was over 0.9, and in 21 countries it was above 0.8 (based on monthly data from January 2002 to March 2008). Exports from the major commodity exporters, such as Argentina, Bolivarian Republic of Venezuela, Bolivia, Chile, Colombia, Ecuador, Mexico and Peru, were very closely correlated with the commodity price index. Only the Caribbean countries (except Trinidad and Tobago) and Panama showed correlation lower than 0.6, which is consistent with the lower share of commodities in their exports.

Commodity prices also affect exports through transportation costs, which depend to a large extent on fuel prices. Higher transport costs have mixed effects on the competitiveness of Latin American and Caribbean exports. Local products become more attractive compared to imports, favouring import substitution. Also, because of shorter distances, Latin American and Caribbean exports may become more attractive for the United States market compared to Asian exports. Conversely, high transport costs make the region's products less attractive in more distant markets.

4. Inflationary implications of the commodity price boom

Apart from the effect on foreign trade, commodity prices affect Latin America and the Caribbean through the costs to consumers and producers of using these commodities as inputs. Rising commodity prices have raised the import bill for net importers of food and energy and the poverty impacts are potentially devastating.

Table I.6 shows that overall inflation in Latin America and the Caribbean has increased.[35] Moreover, low-income households spend a large proportion of their budgets on food and are affected the most by commodity price increases. The commodity price boom therefore has important implications for poverty and inequality in the region (see box I.2). Thus, it is a major priority for the region to implement policies to attenuate the negative effects of the food and energy crisis. Inflation in Argentina, Bolivia and Nicaragua is also accelerating. The exact contribution of commodity prices to inflation is debatable, as other factors, such as monetary policy, may have a greater impact.

Table I.6

INFLATION RATES IN SELECTED COUNTRIES AND REGIONS

(Percentages)

Country/Region	Change in consumer price index from the previous year (end of period)									
	2006				2007				2008	
	Q1	Q2	Q3	Q4	Q1	Q2	Q3	Q4	Q1	Q2
United States	3.5	**4.3**	2.1	**2.6**	**2.8**	2.6	**2.8**	**4.1**	4.0	**4.9**
European Union	2.2	**2.4**	1.8	**1.9**	**1.9**	1.9	**2.1**	**3.1**	**3.6**	**4.0**
Asia										
ASEAN	6.4	5.8	4.8	3.5	3.1	**3.4**	4.0	**5.6**	**8.8**	
China	0.8	**1.5**	1.5	**2.8**	**3.3**	**4.4**	**6.2**	**6.5**	**8.3**	7.1
Japan	-0.2	**0.5**	**0.6**	0.3	-0.1	-0.2	**-0.2**	**0.7**	**1.2**	**2.0**
Latin America and the Caribbean	6.8	6.5	6.0	**6.1**	**6.2**	**6.4**	**7.2**	**8.6**	**10.3**	12.1
Argentina	11.1	11.0	10.4	9.8	9.1	8.8	8.6	8.5	**8.8**	**9.3**
Brazil	5.3	4.0	3.7	3.1	3.0	**3.7**	**4.1**	4.5	4.7	6.1
Chile	4.0	3.9	2.8	2.6	2.6	**3.2**	**5.8**	**7.8**	**8.5**	**9.5**
Mexico	3.4	3.2	**4.1**	4.1	**4.2**	4.0	3.8	3.8	**4.2**	**5.3**
Venezuela (Bol. Rep. of)	12.1	11.8	**15.4**	**17.0**	**18.5**	**19.4**	15.3	**22.4**	**29.1**	**30.8**
World	3.4	**4.0**	3.3	**3.5**	**3.5**	**3.5**	**4.0**	**4.9**	**5.7**	...

Source: Association of Southeast Asian Nations (ASEAN) Finance and Macroeconomic Surveillance Unit Database; International Monetary Fund (IMF), International Financial Statistics Database; official government statistics; and European Central Bank.

Note: Bold font denotes an increase from the previous year.

[35] In the second half of 2008, inflationary pressures have started to ease as commodity prices have begun to stabilize or even decline.

Box I.2

POVERTY IMPLICATIONS OF THE FOOD CRISIS IN LATIN AMERICA AND THE CARIBBEAN

The steep increase in food prices over the last two years has severe implications for poverty and indigence in Latin America and the Caribbean through its effect on consumption. Most worrisome is the growing expenditure on maize, wheat, rice and oilseeds. According to ECLAC calculations, the growing cost of food in Latin America and the Caribbean may increase the number of poor and indigent by over 10 million. Based on indigence projections for 2007, ECLAC estimates that a 15% rise in food prices, which was the average variation in the food price index in 2007, will increase indigence by almost three points from 12.7% to 15.6%. This means that rising food prices will push another 15.7 million people into indigence. A similar number will also fall below the poverty line. However, if household incomes were to go up by 5%, close to the average inflation rate in the region, the number becoming indigent as a result of price increases would be nearly 10 million, and a similar number would swell the ranks of the poor. While the data reveal the clearly negative effects of the rising cost of food on people's welfare, they do not take into account the poverty impacts of rising fuel prices, which are pushing up the price of transportation and public utilities.

POVERTY AND INDIGENCE PROJECTIONS WITH REGARD TO FOOD PRICE INCREASES

(Percentages and millions of people)

	2007 projection		Assuming a 15% food price increase			
			Without a rise in income		With a 5% rise in income	
	%	Millions of people	%	Millions of people	%	Millions of people
Indigence	12.7	68.5	15.6	84.2	14.7	79.1
Poverty	35.1	189.5	37.9	204.5	37.0	199

Source: Economic Commission for Latin America and the Caribbean (ECLAC).

D. Outlook for the global economy and for Latin America and the Caribbean

1. Prospects for the global economy

The outlook of the world economy for the remainder of 2008 and 2009 looks increasingly grim. Economic growth projections have been revised downward for 2008 (United Nations, 2008; IMF, 2008b), while for 2009 most projections indicate an even weaker performance. The depth and duration of the financial crisis are very uncertain, even considering the bailout package approved by the United States government.

Economic growth in the United States, the European Union and Japan will decelerate further in the fourth quarter of 2008 and in 2009. United States consumption is expected to contract in the context of more job losses, stagnant or falling wages and income from equity and other assets and tight credit, while investment may be cut further because of the credit crunch and weak overall growth prospects. United States export growth is also likely to weaken against a background of near or outright recession in the other G-7 economies, slowing growth in emerging markets, and a stabilizing dollar. The recession in Europe and Japan may also deepen, amid weak business and consumer sentiment, terms of trade losses, poor partner-country growth, the impact of their strong currencies on net exports and the credit crunch. Financial institutions in these countries may also be more seriously hurt through their investments connected with the United States' and some European countries' housing markets.

Growth rates in China, India and other emerging economies will also decline from current levels but will remain robust, while those countries have to deal with increasing inflation. In China, to some extent, economic growth remains dynamic because swelling domestic demand is partly offsetting the slowing of net export growth. The Chinese authorities also stimulate growth through low nominal and negative real interest rates (although there have been some increases recently), controlled exchange rates and energy subsidies. Moreover, most emerging economies are well prepared to face the current international turbulence, with strong foreign-exchange reserves and low external debt. All in all, the robust performance of the key emerging markets will help sustain global growth despite the slowdown of the United States economy and deceleration of growth in other OECD markets.

The weakening of global demand, together with some easing of supply constraints, will continue to moderate commodity prices, although they are expected to remain high and volatile, partly because emerging markets will continue to expand and thus push up demand. Although interest rates and the real exchange rate of the United States dollar also affect prices, the most important drivers are real supply and demand. Oil prices are likely to remain high and volatile for some time. Agricultural commodity prices will peak in 2008 and probably flatten or decrease slightly in the coming years. Finally, the upward trend in metal prices will probably slow in the second part of 2008.

The main effect of rising food and energy prices is an increase in headline inflation worldwide, although more so in the emerging economies. Many analysts and central banks view the accelerating rate of inflation as a prime concern. Elevated food and fuel prices are starting to have "second-round effects", meaning that price increases spread through the economy, for example in the form of wage demands. The most worrying sign is that people in various (mostly developing) countries expect higher inflation in the medium term. For several reasons, this acceleration of price increases may backfire on economic growth and contribute to poverty.[36] However, in advanced countries, inflationary pressures are easing in the context of the slowdown in economic growth.

A number of policy actions are required to avoid a worsening of global growth prospects (IMF, 2008b; OECD/FAO, 2008; United Nations, 2008). To prevent the financial crisis from spreading worldwide and to avoid recession in the United States, some form of government rescue plan will be necessary. To avert similar problems in the future, banking and other financial regulation needs to be strengthened, in particular in the areas of trading derivatives, mortgage-backed securities and the extensive use of leveraged investments by banks. In the euro area, concerns over inflation have eased somewhat as the economy had slowed more than expected by mid-2008, a downturn which is expected to last several quarters.

In China and other emerging economies, the main concern is to hold down inflation and avoid overheating the economy. Possible measures include interest rate hikes, control of fiscal spending and more flexible exchange rate policies; for several emerging economies this will mean faster appreciation of their currencies against the United States dollar. In energy-exporting countries, energy consumption subsidies should be lowered and cooperation with other (advanced) countries should be expanded in order to spur oil exploration. Last but not least, protectionist measures must be avoided in the current complex economic context, as discussed in more detail below.

2. Projections for Latin American and Caribbean international trade

The financial crisis in the United States and the bleak outlook for the global economy will without doubt impact on Latin American and Caribbean international trade. In particular, growth in export volumes will slow, while imports are expected to keep their momentum in 2008. As most commodity prices (in particular oil and agricultural commodities) grew in 2008 relative to 2007, the region's terms of trade have also improved, since it is a net commodity exporter. The net result will probably be a bigger trade surplus for 2008. A lot of uncertainty remains with regard to the evolution of commodity prices in the remainder of 2008. A simulation of three different scenarios for the oil price for the second half of 2008 shows major effects on trade balances in the region (see box I.3). The expansion of the region's exports is expected to slow because import growth has slipped, mostly in the United States and, to a lesser extent, in the European Union and Japan. Each country's export growth will depend on those markets' shares in its export basket and the degree to which it succeeds in redirecting its foreign sales to more dynamic markets, in particular China and other Asian countries, which is easier for standardized products such as commodities than for manufactures.[37] Consequently, the Caribbean, Central America and Mexico will be worse affected than South America. This is illustrated by ECLAC projections, which show that the real export growth of Costa Rica, Dominican Republic, Guatemala, Mexico, Nicaragua and Panama will decrease substantially in 2008 compared to 2007.

36 Most of all, it creates uncertainty about the future purchasing power of money, and this reduces not only current production, but also saving and investment as people shorten their time horizons. Moreover, high inflation reduces a country's international competitiveness unless offset by a depreciation of its currency.

37 Standardized products are easier to redirect to other markets than manufactures, as the latter are often produced according to technical standards which are specific to each destination market.

Box I.3

OIL PRICE ASSUMPTIONS FOR SECOND HALF OF 2008 AND IMPACT ON TRADE BALANCE [a]

Despite the recent drop in the oil price from its peak of US$ 140 per barrel in July to slightly over US$ 70 in mid-October, most analysts agree that prices are likely to stabilize towards the end of 2008. As discussed in section B.3, the sluggish global demand observed in the past few months is anticipated to pick up, driven by persistent demand in the non-OECD countries. However, depending on the severity of the global economic slowdown triggered by the banking and financial sector meltdown in the United States, the demand for oil consumption could decline substantially, especially if spending on government infrastructure projects is affected. In these uncertain circumstances, it seems practical to assume a wide range of possible price fluctuations. As such, oil prices could continue dropping below the October levels or they could revert to the peak recorded in July.

Therefore, three different scenarios for the oil price in the second half of 2008 are simulated to estimate the effect on the region's trade balance: (i) a "neutral" scenario of US$ 120; (ii) a "low-price" scenario of US$ 80; and (iii) a "high-price" scenario of US$ 150. All other variables —other commodity prices and trade volumes— are held constant. Compared to 2006, trade balances would worsen for both net importers and Brazil in 2008 under all three scenarios. However, for net oil exporters, the trade balance would improve under the US$ 120 and US$ 150 scenarios. Under these two scenarios, the improvement of the trade balance of oil exporters would be bigger than the decline of the trade balance of oil importers, and therefore the region as a whole would gain. As Brazil's net oil imports are close to zero, its trade balance is only slightly affected by changes in oil prices.

OIL PRICE SCENARIOS AND TRADE BALANCE, 2008

(In billions of dollars)

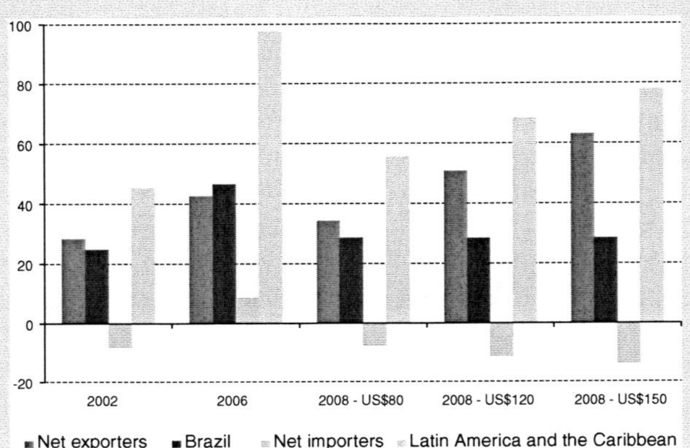

Source: Economic Commission for Latin America and the Caribbean (ECLAC).

Note: Net oil exporters are Argentina, Colombia, Ecuador, Mexico and Bolivarian Republic of Venezuela. Net oil importers are Bolivia, Chile, Costa Rica, Dominican Republic, El Salvador, Guatemala, Haiti, Honduras, Nicaragua, Panama, Paraguay, Peru and Uruguay.

[a] The three scenarios for the oil price in the second half of 2008 (80, 120 and 150 dollars) were defined in September 2008 and did not anticipate the sharp drop in the price per barrel in the ensuing months.

Commodity exporters in South America may experience divergent trends in 2008 (see table I.7). Some, such as Argentina, Brazil and Chile, show a decline in export growth, each for different reasons. In Argentina, growth in export volumes may be dampened in 2008 by export restrictions and domestic tensions. In Chile, export growth in 2008 will be lower than in 2007 despite substantial new investment in mining-sector expansion: one reason is that this investment will take time to mature as a result of a strike by copper workers under contract in April and May, and another is that non-traditional export growth seems to be hampered by an appreciated exchange rate. Brazilian exports are also expected to lose some momentum, in part owing to falling demand from the United States and exchange rate appreciation. On the other hand, Colombia, Peru and Uruguay have seen their export volumes expand in 2008. In Peru, this is thanks to new mining capacity coming on-stream in 2008. In Uruguay, favourable production trends and continued strong demand for agricultural products (such as cereals, beef, dairy products and wool) are keeping export growth dynamic. Moreover, strong demand from MERCOSUR (growing about 20% in volume terms in 2008) may offset a fall in demand from the United States.

In 2008, import growth is expected to remain robust in commodity-exporting countries, but will decelerate in the rest of the region. In the former group, import demand remains strong in the context of persistently high commodity prices and appreciated exchange rates. In the latter group, including most Central American countries and the Dominican Republic, economic growth will probably slacken and growth in demand for imports will likely fall, partly because of the effect of the United States slowdown.

Table I.7
REAL GROWTH RATES OF EXPORTS AND IMPORTS OF GOODS AND SERVICES, 2006-2008

	Exports			Imports		
	2006	2007	2008	2006	2007	2008
Argentina	7.3	8.9	5.1	15.4	20.7	19.3
Bolivia	11.3	3.1	7.4	5.2	4.4	12.0
Brazil	4.6	6.6	2.8	18.1	20.7	19.6
Chile	5.5	7.8	3.7	10.5	14.3	16.0
Colombia	9.4	7.5	11.6	17.3	16.4	18.0
Costa Rica	9.6	9.1	0.0	7.9	4.6	4.5
Ecuador	8.6	2.6	6.0	9.2	7.0	12.0
El Salvador	8.1	3.9	3.5	8.4	8.1	5.0
Guatemala	4.8	10.5	3.5	6.5	7.8	4.5
Haiti	3.1	-2.3	-6.0	4.6	-0.3	2.0
Honduras	-0.4	3.6	3.0	3.8	8.0	4.0
Mexico	10.8	6.2	1.0	12.8	7.0	6.5
Nicaragua	12.5	9.6	4.5	5.5	14.2	5.0
Panama	11.1	14.0	5.5	7.7	12.5	6.5
Paraguay	14.6	9.6	9.6	16.5	10.8	10.8
Peru	0.8	6.2	9.8	13.1	21.3	23.9
Dominican Republic	0.7	2.4	1.0	8.2	11.7	4.0
Uruguay	8.0	9.7	11.0	17.6	10.3	18.0
Venezuela (Bol. Rep. of)	-4.5	-5.6	-3.2	31.1	33.6	8.2
Latin America and the Caribbean	7.1	6.2	2.8	14.3	13.2	11.8

Source: 2006 and 2007 from national sources, 2008 projections by the Economic Commission for Latin America and the Caribbean (ECLAC).

3. Dealing with an uncertain global outlook

Faced with uncertainty over global economic prospects and the direction of commodity prices, Latin America and the Caribbean needs to address both immediate and longer-term challenges. Overall, the information up to the end of October suggests that the economic slowdown and financial crisis in the United States will have a relatively modest impact on the Latin America and the Caribbean region in 2008, except for its exports. Compared to previous shocks in the United States economy and the world at large, Latin America and the Caribbean is much less vulnerable than in the past, with a current account surplus, sounder public finances, a lower level and better profiles of public and external debt, and larger international financial reserves (Machinea and Kacef, 2008).

Apart from trade and commodity prices, global trends will affect the region in at least two other ways. First, the economic slowdown in the United States will cause migrant workers residing there to reduce the amount of their remittances, an important source of finance for several countries in the region, particularly Mexico and Central America and some Caribbean countries. Second, the turmoil in financial markets across the globe is causing investors to shift their portfolios to lower-risk assets in a "flight to quality", and this is increasing risk premiums for Latin America and the Caribbean. Higher risk premiums make financing more expensive, although in the short term this should not pose a problem given that most countries in the region have small external borrowing requirements and abundant foreign reserves. As a result, the region's economic growth is forecast to decline from 5.7% in 2007 to 4.6% in 2008 (ECLAC, 2008b) and probably around 3.6% in 2009.

In this context, it is essential to maintain macroeconomic stability by reinforcing the countercyclical components of fiscal policy and closely monitoring trends in the external accounts, since the region's economies face increasing risk premiums which are worsening external financing conditions. Governments should maintain their hard-won sound fiscal balances, which could be jeopardized by large subsidies on fuel consumption against a background of persistently high oil prices. Keeping inflation in check while maintaining sound fiscal balances and sustainable external accounts will facilitate economic growth, reduce poverty and promote competitiveness. High inflation affects the lowest income groups disproportionately. Moreover, keeping inflation low may help Mexico and Central America to recover some of their lost competitiveness in the United States market relative to China and other Asian economies, as the latter experience double-digit inflation rates (Viet Nam has an annualized rate of 30%), which will soon translate into higher nominal wages and unit labour costs.

The main challenge with regard to commodity prices is to allow the export sector take full advantage of the boom while protecting the most vulnerable groups from the adverse effects of those prices on consumption and containing overall inflationary expectations. Policy actions should take into account the fact that the prices of oil and other commodities will not revert to pre-2006 levels even if they decline slightly relative to 2008.

Latin America and the Caribbean is a net exporter of commodities, so the region stands to gain overall from the price boom. Some countries, in particular those of Southern Cone, have clearly benefited from the higher food prices. However, while most countries are net exporters of raw agricultural products, many are net importers of food and oil. The countries most dependent on food imports typically have the highest poverty rates. At the same time, on average, the poor spend a larger proportion of their budget on food and are therefore the worst affected by commodity price increases.

Many countries in the region have already taken steps to deal with the price increases in order to buffer the negative impact on consumption and poverty. The most widely used or proposed measures by the governments in the region include:

- Quantitative export restrictions, as in the case of rice in Brazil and cereals and beef in Argentina and Bolivia;
- Price controls and price agreements in certain food markets, as in Argentina, Bolivia, Honduras, Mexico and Paraguay;
- Reduction or elimination of import tariffs and non-tariff barriers; and
- Bilateral agreements on food and grain imports, for example the arrangement concluded recently between Bolivia and Argentina (ECLAC, 2008b).

According to the Food and Agriculture Organization of the United Nations (FAO, 2008d), 14 countries of the region have adopted measures to compensate consumers for the loss of purchasing power, through food distribution programmes, income transfers or tax cuts. Twelve countries have taken steps to support domestic food production, including input subsidies and public-private production agreements. Lastly, 11 countries have introduced trade measures and 9 have taken steps to control domestic prices directly. Protective trade measures, such as increasing export taxes, could, however, have an adverse effect on prices. While this measure curtails exports and boosts domestic supplies, it could also help to push up world prices as global supply shrinks, provided that the country has considerable market power for a certain good, as in the case of Argentine wheat exports.

To deal effectively with rising food prices in order to avoid inflationary pressures and impoverishment of the population, it is necessary to combine an immediate response (emergency food assistance and conditional income transfers) to protect the most vulnerable groups with longer-term measures to boost domestic productive capacity. A number of governments in the region have successfully negotiated agreements with producers to increase supplies, contain price rises or both in exchange for public support in the form of input subsidies, breaks in taxes and utilities payments, technical assistance and assistance with processing, packing, marketing and distribution. Subsidization and tariff protection of biofuel production also needs to be rethought, to take into account their impact on food security.

These measures should be complemented with efforts to minimize trade distortions. It is important to maintain open economies and avoid protectionist measures. It is unadvisable to impose quantitative export restrictions and export taxes because, by constraining supply, they place additional upward pressure on world prices and exacerbate global price volatility. Countries should facilitate imports by lowering or eliminating tariffs and reduce transaction costs, including those related to import financing. At the same time, governments need to undertake additional tax-reform measures to recoup at least part of the revenue lost through tariff reduction.

Removal of trade barriers should be accompanied by measures to facilitate trade. Red tape should be reduced in order to lower import and export costs, in particular by relaxing regulations that affect entrepreneurship and the development of SMEs. Further reforms are needed to improve the efficiency of customs, logistics, ports and transport.

With regard to energy, policy recommendations generally focus on improving energy security, boosting energy efficiency and diversifying sources of energy, in particular by increasing the use of renewables. The use of generalized energy subsidies as a means of coping with high oil and gas prices should as limited as possible. Insulating domestic prices from world price fluctuations impedes supply response, prevents consumers from switching from fossil fuels to alternative energy sources and discourages energy conservation. Moreover, these subsidies tend to be regressive as they favour higher-income groups. Instead, such price distortions should be corrected and the countries should focus on removing barriers to greater use of renewable energy, encouraging investment and development of new technologies to speed the change and adopting appropriate urban infrastructure and land-use policies to curb the demand for fossil fuels for transportation (ECLAC, 2008c).

Another challenge for the longer term is to avoid a slowdown in the growth of non-commodity exports —which generally have a higher value added content— in a context of persistently high commodity prices and appreciated exchange rates. This can be done in several ways. First, maintain a competitive real exchange rate, to favour the development of new (non-commodity) exports. Various policies can contribute to this if the price hike is only temporary (Mulder, 2006). Second, the government can use its resources to provide special incentives for the development of new goods or services. These measures can be financed (in part) with a special tax on the rents associated with rising commodity prices. However, it is important that this tax should not discourage private investment in these sectors. Also, decisions on where and how to invest are far from trivial, and should be coordinated with the private sector. Policy decisions are best guided by priorities set according to a development strategy defined by the public and private sectors jointly. Policies seem to be most effective when their implementation and impact are systematically assessed in the light of their established goals (see chapter VI and ECLAC, 2008a).

Bibliography

ADB (Asian Development Bank) (2008), *Asian Development Outlook 2008: Update*, Manila.

ASEAN (Association of Southeast Asian Nations) (2008), Macroeconomic Indicators [online] http://www.aseansec.org/18135.htm.

Bastourre, D., J. Carrera and J. Ibarlucia (2007), "Commodity prices in Argentina. What does move the wind?", Buenos Aires, Banco Central de la República Argentina.

BEA (United States Bureau of Economic Analysis) (2008), "Downturn in Finance and Insurance Restrains Real GDP Growth in 2007" [online] http://www.bea.gov/newsreleases/industry/gdpindustry/gdpindnewsrelease.htm, 29 April.

___ (2007), "Table 1.1.2. Contributions to percent change in real gross domestic product [online] http://www.bea.gov/national/index.htm.

Beynet, P. and others (2006), "Pourquoi le solde commercial américain a-t-il continué de se dégrader depuis 2002 malgré la dépréciation du dollar?", *Économie et statistique*, N° 397.

Bloomberg (2008), "Credit Swaps Must Be Regulated Now, SEC's Cox Says", 23 September.

China, People's Republic of (2008), official site of the Ministry of Commerce [online] http://english.mofcom.gov.cn/index.shtml.

ECB (European Central Bank) (2008), European Central Bank Statistical Data Warehouse [online] http://sdw.ecb.europa.eu/.

ECLAC (Economic Commission for Latin America and the Caribbean) (2008a), *Structural Change and Productivity Growth - Twenty Years Later. Old problems, new opportunities* (LC/G.2367(SES.32/3)), Santiago, Chile.

___ (2008b), *Economic Survey of Latin America and the Caribbean, 2007-2008* (LC/G.2386-P/I), Santiago, Chile.

___ (2008c), International Price Volatility and Economic Policy Challenges in Latin America and the Caribbean (LC/L.2958), Santiago, Chile.

EIA (Energy Information Administration) (2008a), *Annual Energy Outlook 2008*, United States Department of Energy.

___ (2008b), *International Energy Outlook 2008*, United States Department of Energy.

___ (2008c), *Short-Term Energy Outlook 2008*, United States Department of Energy.

EIU (The Economist Intelligence Unit) (2008a), "World commodity forecast: food, feedstuffs and beverages", July.

___ (2008b), "World commodity forecast: industrial raw materials", July.

EUROSTAT (Statistical Office of the European Communities), Statistical database [online] http://epp.eurostat.ec.europa.eu.

FAO (Food and Agricultural Organization of the United Nations) (2008a), *Crop Prospects and Food Situation*, various issues.

___ (2008b), *Food Outlook*, various issues

___ (2008c), Soaring food prices: Facts, perspectives, impacts and actions required (HLC/08/INF/1), document presented at the High-level Conference on World Food Security, Rome, 3-5 June.

___ (2008d), "Situación alimentaría en América Latina y Caribe", FAO Regional Office for Latin America and the Caribbean, May-June.

Fed (United States Federal Reserve) (2008), "The April 2008 Senior Loan Officer opinion survey on bank lending practices" [online] http://www.federalreserve.gov/boarddocs/SnloanSurvey/200805/.

Gianella, C. and C. Chanteloup (2006), "Assessing Russia's non-fuel trade elasticities: Does the Russian economy react "normally" to exchange rate movements?", *Economics Department Working Papers*, No. 510, Paris, Organisation for Economic Co-operation and Development (OECD).

Goldman Sachs Global Economics Group (2007), *BRICs and Beyond.*

Hudson Teslik, L. (2008), "Sovereign wealth funds", *Backgrounder*, Council on Foreign Relations, 18 January.

IDB (Inter-American Development Bank) (2008), *The Changing Pattern of Remittances, 2008. Survey or Remittances from the United States to Latin America*, Washington, D.C., April.

ICSG (International Copper Study Group) (2007), *The World Copper Fact Book 2007* [online] http://www.icsg.org/.

IEA (International Energy Agency) (2008), *Mid-Term Oil Market Report*, June.

IFPRI (International Food Policy Research Institute) (2008), "Biofuels and grain prices: impacts and policy responses", Mark W. Rosegrant, Director, Environment and Production Technology Division, Testimony for the U.S. Senate Committee on Homeland Security and Governmental Affairs, 7 May.

IMF (International Monetary Fund) (2008a), *World Economic Outlook*, April.

___ (2008b), *World Economic Outlook Update: Global slowdown and rising inflation*, June.

___ (2008c), *Regional Economic Outlook: Western Hemisphere*, April.

___ (2008d), *Global Financial Stability Report*, April.

___ (2008e), *World Economic Outlook*, October.

___ (2007), *World Economic Outlook*, September.

___ (n/d), Direction of Trade Statistics [online database] http://www.imfstatistics.org/dot/.

___ (n/d), International Financial Statistics [online database] http://www.imfstatistics.org/imf/.

Ip, G. (2007), "Did Greenspan add to subprime woes?", *The Wall Street Journal* [online] http://online.wsj.com/article/SB118134111823129555.html, 9 June.

Kregel, J. (2008), Background document presented at the Regional Consultation Preparatory to the Follow-up International Conference on Financing for Development to Review the Implementation of the Monterrey Consensus, Panel 3, Economic Commission for Latin America and the Caribbean (ECLAC), Santo Domingo, 12 June, unpublished.

Krugman, P. (2008), "Fuels on the hill", *The New York Times*, 27 June.

Machinea, José Luis and Osvaldo Kacef (2008), Latin America and the Caribbean in the New International Economic Environment (LC/L.2908), Santiago, Chile, Economic Comission for Latin America and the Caribbean (ECLAC), June.

Masters, M. (2008), Testimony before the Committee on Homeland Security and Governmental Affairs, United States Senate [online] http://hsgac.senate.gov/public/_files/052008Masters.pdf, 20 May.

Merrill Lynch (2008), cited in "Loose money driving commodity prices, not speculation, Merrill insists", FP Posted [online] "http://network.nationalpost.com/np/blogs/fpposted/archive/2008/06/17/loose-money-driving-commodity-prices-not-speculation-merrill-insists.aspx.

Mollenkamp, C. and S. Ng (2007), "Wall Street Wizardry Amplified Credit Crisis; A CDO Called Norma Left 'Hairball of Risk'; Tailored by Merrill Lynch", *Wall Street Journal* (Eastern Edition), p. A.1.

Mulder, N. (2006), "Aprovechar el auge exportador de productos básicos evitando la enfermedad holandesa", *Comercio internacional series*, No. 80 (LC/L.2627-P), Santiago, Chile, Economic Commission for Latin America and the Caribbean (ECLAC).

ODEPA (Agrarian Research and Policy Office of Chile) (2008), "Las alzas en los precios de los alimentos", Santiago de Chile.

OECD/FAO (Organisation for Economic Co-operation and Developmet/Food and Agriculture Organization of the United Nations) (2008), *Agricultural Outlook 2008-2017*.

Reinhart, C. and Rogoff, K. (2008), "Is the 2007 U.S. subprime financial crisis so different? An international historical comparison", *NBER Working Paper*, No. 13761.

Rodríguez, A. (2008), "Análisis exploratorio de la evolución de los mercados mundiales de materias primas agrícolas y de los precios de los alimentos", Santiago, Chile,

Economic Commission for Latin America and the Caribbean (ECLAC), unpublished.

Sachs, J. (2008), "Stagflation is back. Here's how to beat it, CNN-money" [online] http://money.cnn.com/2008/05/27/news/economy/sachs_stagflation.fortune/index.htm.

Southwood, Jim (2008), "CRU's new process for managing copper price risk", document presented at the seventh CRU World Copper Conference, Santiago, Chile, April.

Stürmer, Martin (2008), "The international raw materials boom. A challenge for multilaterial trade policy", *International Politics and Society*, No. 2/2008.

The Economist (2008), "The oil price: don't blame the speculators", 3 July.

UNCTAD (United Nations Conference on Trade and Development) (2008), "Addressing the global food crisis: key trade, investment and commodity policies in ensuring sustainable food security and alleviating poverty", document prepared for the High-Level Conference on World Food Security: the Challenges of Climate Change and Bioenergy, Rome, 3-5 June.

United Nations (2008), *World Economic Situation and Prospects 2008, Update as of mid-2008*, New York.

___(n/d), Commodity Trade Database (COMTRADE) [online] http://comtrade.un.org/.

United States Department of Agriculture, "Exchange Rate Database" [online database] http://www.ers.usda.gov/Data/ExchangeRates/.

USBLS (United States Bureau of Labor Statistics), "Import/Export Price Indexes" [online] http://www.bls.gov/mxp/#data.

USGAO (United States General Accounting Office) (1996), "Financial Audit: Resolution Trust Corporation's 1995 and 1994 Financial Statements" [online] http://www.gao.gov/archive/1996/ai96123.pdf.

USGS (United States Geological Survey) (2008), "2006 Minerals Yearbook: Copper" [online] http://minerals.usgs.gov/minerals/pubs/commodity/copper/myb1-2006-coppe.pdf, May.

USITC (United States International Trade Commission), "Dataweb" [online database] http://dataweb.usitc.gov/.

WBMS (World Bureau of Metal Statistics) (2008), *World Metal Statistics*, March.

World Bank (2008), "Rising food prices: policy options and World Bank response", a background note.

___(2007), *Global Development Finance*, Washington, D.C.

Chapter II

Latin America and the Caribbean and the Doha Round of trade negotiations

Introduction

Points of view about the evolution of the Doha Round vary in Latin America and the Caribbean. It is generally agreed that the industrialized countries' agricultural offers could be more generous in terms of market access and the reduction of trade distortions. Opinions differ, however, about what the region should contribute in order to achieve a good multilateral agreement, particularly in the area of non-agricultural market access (NAMA) and services. Some maintain that, given how uneven the playing field is in globalization, developing countries should not have to give up anything in return for the long-overdue offer to open up the agricultural markets that the industrialized countries have now placed on the table. Such a position may reflect an accurate appreciation of the asymmetries of global trade and finance but is a politically unrealistic approach to adopt. Regardless of what may or may not seem fair, the industrialized countries are, for obvious reasons, hardly likely to approve a package within the Doha Round that only dismantles the protectionism their farmers enjoy without opening up any new trade opportunities in the manufacturing and services sectors. The region is thus facing a real negotiation, which means understanding the give-and-take that these processes entail and that the most important goal is to achieve a favourable outcome for developing countries. The question now is whether the world is anywhere near to obtaining that result and whether the political climate is ripe for it to happen. The momentum of the talks will not last for ever. Moreover, if they fail, it may prove tricky to resume them quickly, and the process could be stalled for a considerable period of time.

The sense of urgency about the need to conclude the Round has already waned. Some countries would rather not reach an agreement at all than accept a "bad" one. Others feel that the offers on the table do not represent real progress, especially now that the current financial crisis could heighten protectionist tendencies in the industrialized economies.

The agreement reached in July 2008 did not fully satisfy the developing countries, but it was headed in the right direction: access for agricultural goods to the developed countries' markets was improved; subsidies for agricultural exports were eliminated by the end of 2013; and the levels of domestic support for agriculture were lowered. The levels offered were almost twice as high as the ones being effectively applied now, but only because the high prices of agricultural products since July 2008 has rendered domestic support less necessary. The important point is to establish a maximum level for domestic support for when food prices come down again so as to avoid the oversupply of markets. The levels contemplated in the agreement were lower than those that the United States has applied in four of the last seven years. The restriction would, moreover, be permanent. The time has thus come to carefully weigh the costs, benefits and opportunities posed by the Doha Round of talks. Latin America and the Caribbean could consolidate consensus within the region with a view to playing a more prominent role in the Round, without losing sight of the synergy between those talks and other trade negotiations (such as those with the European Union), which could proceed more smoothly if the Doha Round were to be concluded soon.

The experience of the Doha Development Round has shown that, in the age of globalization, the interests of developing countries tend to vary according to how strongly they are integrated with the international economy. This means that, except in the agricultural talks, the interests of the developing countries have been highly divergent. Even in agriculture, the main points of coincidence have been about the need to eliminate export subsidies and reduce domestic support measures, while huge discrepancies have arisen regarding tariff cuts (market access) and special safeguards for developing countries. The divergent interests of the Caribbean countries, on the one side, and the Central American and Andean countries, on the other, in the banana controversy with the European Union reveals how these differences can play out in the region.

This makes it difficult to assess the outcome of a negotiation process from the viewpoint of development as there is no common denominator that can benefit everyone. All trade negotiations involve costs and benefits. The Doha Development Round should try to minimize those costs and distribute them over time and among the members of the World Trade Organization (WTO) in such a way that does not hamper economic growth and poverty reduction in developing countries. The Round should also harness the initiatives that could lead to the development of new and more dynamic export activities in the short term as a means of improving the distribution of costs and benefits within each economy. In the case of the least developed countries, which in Latin America and the Caribbean only refers to Haiti, many of the initiatives agreed to so far are working along these lines. In the case of the other developing countries, however, it is less clear how these matters could be coherently addressed.

After a period of reflection, agreed to by the countries participating in the Doha Development Round negotiations, talks resumed in February 2007. In July and August 2007, the Chairs of the Negotiating Group on Agriculture and the Negotiating Group on NAMA presented documents that reflected the possible negotiation modalities for these subjects (ECLAC, 2007).[1] Throughout the second semester of 2007, the Chairs of the other negotiating groups also presented documents on their areas.[2] On 19 May 2008, new documents reflecting the status of the talks in the agriculture and NAMA were distributed. On 26 and 28 May that same year, the Chairs of the Negotiating Group on Services and the Negotiating Group on Rules submitted reports on the status of their negotiations. A mini-ministerial meeting was held from 21 to 29 July 2008, but ended in failure.

The document presented by the Chair of the Negotiating Group on Agriculture on 10 July 2008 moves the negotiations forward in two important ways: on the one hand, the number of issues awaiting policy decisions (bracketed text) is reduced; and on the other, the scope of the talks in areas in which no agreement has been reached is narrowed, and progress made so far is consolidated by confirming the proposals previously discussed (regarding export competition, for example). Some of this has been achieved, however, by establishing flexibility for WTO members to make smaller cuts than those agreed to in general, and this could reduce the gains made in the negotiations (ECLAC, 2007) (see table II.1).

---

1 In WTO negotiations, the modalities establish the general parameters (such as formulae or approaches for tariff reductions) of the definitive commitments.

2 Further information on the objectives of the Doha Round, the negotiating groups and the documents available so far can be obtained from the WTO website [online] at: http://www.wto.org/english/tratop_e/dda_e/dda_e.htm.

Table II.1
AGRICULTURAL NEGOTIATIONS - PROGRESS

	Falconer proposal (May 2008)			
	Developed Countries		Developing Countries	
Market access	Tier 0-20% >20-≤ 50% >50-≤ 75% >75% Average cut:	Cut 50% 57% 64% 66-73% ≥ 54%	Tier 0-≤ 30% >30-≤ 80% >80-≤130% >130% Average cut:	Cut 33.3% 38% 42.7% 44-48.7% < 36%
Other access issues	Special reductions for 45 small and vulnerable economies. The least developed countries (32) do not have to make reductions. Some exceptions for very recently-acceded members. Sensitive products: 4%, 6% or 8% of tariff lines for developed countries and 5.3% or 8% of tariff lines for developing countries. Tariff cuts of 1/3, ½ and 2/3 under the general formula for developed countries and developing countries. Tariff quotas for developed countries must represent new access opportunities equivalent to 4%-6% of domestic consumption in the case of a 2/3 reduction and less in the case of other reductions. For developing countries, the tariff quota expansion must be 2/3 of the volume for developed countries. Several deviations from this rule were proposed. Special Products: developing countries can designate a maximum of 20% and a minimum of 8% of tariff lines as special products. In this case, 40% (8% of lines) may be exempted from cuts. In all other cases, there must be an average cut of 15% and a minimum cut of 12%. Special Safeguard Mechanism: the possibility of protection for all developing country products is included, and possible application mechanisms are proposed. Tariff ceilings: these are not mentioned, but additional access commitments are established for cases in which over 4% of a developed country's products are subject to tariffs of over 100%.			
Export competition	Export subsidies to be eliminated by the end of 2013 and reduced in value by 50% by 2010. Additional disciplines are established for export credit, trading companies and food aid.			
Total domestic support (US$ billions)	Tier ≤ 10 10 ≤ total domestic support ≤ 60 ≥ 60		Cut 50-60% 66-73% 75-85%	
	Initial cuts of 33.3%, five-year implementation period and base established for reductions.			
Amber Box (US$ billions)	Tier <15 15 ≤ Amber Box ≤ 40 > 40		Cut 45% 60% 70%	
	Initial cuts of 25%, five-year implementation period and base established for reductions			
	Maximum limits for products equivalent to those for 1995-2000 are established. De minimis is reduced by 50%-60% for developed countries from the current level of 5% of the value of production and by 2/3 for developing countries from the current limit of 10% of production value.			
Blue Box	The current Blue Box causes some trade distortion. These measures consist of direct payments to farmers based on the number of heads of livestock they have or the area of land they cultivate, but under production-limiting schemes. The Agreement on Agriculture would be modified to include a new type of Blue Box based on payments that are not production-linked but based on the fixed amount of previous production. A maximum limit of 2.5% of the average value of agricultural production in the base period is set, with caps for individual products.			
Green Box	The provisions of the Agreement on Agriculture would be modified to allow developing countries to implement more development programmes and to apply stricter criteria for developed countries.			

Source: Word Trade Organization (WTO), Revised draft modalities for agriculture (TN/AG/W/4/Rev.2), 19 May 2008; and "Unofficial guide to the revised draft modalities – Agriculture, 19 May 2008" [online] http://www.wto.org/english/tratop_e/agric_e/chair_texts08_e.htm.

Under these proposals in the area of agriculture, overall trade-distorting domestic support in the United States would drop from the current level of US$ 48 billion to between US$ 13 billion and US$ 16 billion (see table II.2). In the case of the European Union, such support would be lowered from 110 billion euros to 28 billion euros. The cuts in Japan could be greater given that 40% of the value of Japanese agricultural products is currently subsidized.[3] The final outcome of the proposed market access commitments summarized in table II.1 will depend on the use and workings of the flexibilities that are established. These are difficult to assess on the basis of the information currently available. The lowering of tariffs for sensitive products and the increase of quotas within the future tariff-quota scheme are two of the most notable provisions under consideration. Again, the lack of information makes it impossible to gauge the extent of the new level of access that these will create. In the case of the United States, the flexibilities will most likely be used for raw and refined sugar, industrial cheeses, butter and powdered milk. In the European Union, beef, pork, poultry, rice and sugar might be included in this category.[4]

[3] See WTO, "Revised draft modalities for agriculture" [online] http://www.wto.org/english/tratop_e/markacc_e/nama_10july08_e.htm.

[4] *Inside US Trade* (2008a).

Table II.2
SIMULATIONS OF PROPOSED DOMESTIC SUBSIDY CUTS

	Overall trade-distorting domestic support (OTDS)		Amber box (distorting programmes + measures)	
	Uruguay round	Doha proposal	Uruguay round	Doha proposal
Euro zone	€ 110.3 billion	€ 27.6 billion	€ 67.2 billion	20.1 billion
United States	US$ 48.2 billion	US$ 13 billion – US$ 16 billion	US$ 19 billion	US$ 7.6 billion

In the case of the European Union, the proposed modalities could mean the effective restriction of trade-distorting disbursements as of 2013 or 2014. In the case of the United States, the amount of domestic support would be reduced, but the country could still increase OTDS by US$ 4 billion and its Amber Box measures by US$ 1 billion. Limits might also be set for dairy products, sugar, cotton, corn, rice and other items. In both the European Union and the United States, there would be less room for Blue Box measures.

Source: World Trade Organization (WTO); Sébastien Jean, Tim Josling and David Laborde, The Consequences for the European Union of the WTO Revised Draft Modalities for Agriculture, International Food Policy Research Institute (IFPRI), 2008; and David Blandford, David Laborde and Will Martin, Implications of the February 2008 WTO DRAFT Agriculture Modalities for the United States, International Food Policy Research Institute (IFPRI), 2008.

Although it was an impasse regarding the special safeguard mechanism (SSM) for the agricultural products of developing countries that brought the negotiations to a standstill in July 2008, agreements were reached on several aspects of the SSM. One of these was the provision whereby developing countries could use the mechanism to raise tariffs temporarily to deal with import surges and prices falls. The least developed countries (as defined by the United Nations) and the small and vulnerable economies were to receive the most generous treatment in this regard.

The problem arose within the group of seven countries (Australia, Brazil, China, the United States, India, Japan and the European Union) that was negotiating the general terms of a proposal to be submitted to the other members of the WTO on the possibility of raising tariffs above the levels agreed to in the Uruguay Round (or at the time of accession in the case of countries that subsequently joined the WTO). The controversy arose between some members of the G-33 (net agricultural-goods importers) and certain exporting countries. On the one hand, some countries maintained that the SSM should be freer and easier to use, with smaller triggers and larger tariff increases. On the other, certain members felt that the use of the SSM should be more restricted: there should be no tariff increases above pre-Doha Round levels, the mechanism should not be activated by normal fluctuations in prices or normal trade expansion, and it should be limited to the period of liberalization. In other words, the mechanism should not be a permanent one.[5] One proposal that was discussed contemplated allowing tariffs to rise above pre-Doha levels but subject to constraints imposed by additional criteria, such as larger increases in imports for the mechanism to be triggered, limits on how high the tariff could rise above pre-Doha rates and limits on the percentage of products that could benefit from this flexibility. The impasse was about the size of these constraints. It should be borne in mind that this would be the third safeguard mechanism in the WTO. The first consists of the general safeguards that are applicable to all products and triggered by import surges. The second is set forth in the current Agreement on Agriculture and covers agricultural products tariffied in the Uruguay Round. The third is the mechanism under discussion in the Doha Round, which is to be used exclusively by developing countries.[6]

The document presented by the Chair of the Negotiating Group on NAMA in July 2007 provoked a strong reaction among some developing countries that felt there was a lack of balance between the agricultural proposals and the high level of ambition presented in the NAMA document. There were at least three problems: (i) the level of precision and the thematic scope of the document left little room for negotiation; (ii) the proposed flexibilities did not moderate the substantial opening of the set of sectors subject to the so-called "Swiss-formula" tariff cuts; and (iii) the cuts involved in the proposed formula were tantamount to a tariff reduction (see table II.3).[7]

---

5 See the explanation provided in WTO [online] http://www.wto.org/english/tratop_e/agric_e/guide_agric_ safeg_e.htm. This is the position of the countries of Latin America and South-East Asia, as well as other members of the Cairns Group and the United States.

6 See the explanation provided in WTO [online] http://www.wto.org/english/tratop_e/agric_e/guide_agric safeg_e.htm.

7 See ECLAC (2008).

Box II.1

THE UNITED STATES FARM BILL

The Director-General of the WTO stated that the passing of the 2008 version of the United States Farm Bill, which will guide agricultural policy up to 2012, "is not sending a great signal that the U.S. are serious about reducing their subsidies". WTO members voiced similar concerns in the wake of the ninth Trade Policy Review of the United States, which took place on 9 June 2008.

The United States Farm Bill is subject to renewal every five years. It is a complex legal instrument due to the large number of issues it addresses and the interests it affects. It covers support programmes for commodities, especially wheat, rice, cotton, sugar, dairy goods, oilseed products and peanuts. These consist of direct payments, counter-cyclical payments and commodity marketing loans. It also establishes provisions for government purchases of agricultural goods, quota administration and trade barriers. Other titles of the bill refer to: land conservation; agricultural trade and food aid; nutrition; credit; rural development; research; energy; and miscellaneous programmes covering assistance, insurance, natural disasters, labelling and other issues.

The largest objections to the new bill were that it did not dismantle the most trade-distorting support programmes, and this represented a lost opportunity to introduce changes that could have paved the way for an agreement in the Doha Development Round.

In budgetary terms, the new bill will add between US$ 5 billion and US$ 6 billion to the total budget allocated to the agricultural sector, which will reach US$ 286 billion. White House press releases indicated that the budget increases topped US$ 20 billion for the various programmes covered by the bill. The United States Congress reports, however, that the increase was only US$ 10 billion. The difference arises from the exclusion of certain programmes in the figure released by Congress, such as the fund for aiding farmers in times of natural disaster, which has been allocated US$ 4 billion, and other provisions that boost payments to the agricultural sector by approximately US$ 4.5 billion.

Commodity support programmes will be allocated from about US$ 32 billion to US$ 35 billion (not all of these programmes are necessarily trade-distorting by WTO definitions). This is slightly less than the current level of support of US$ 36.5 billion. In some programmes, the eligibility requirements for farmers have been modified, tightened in some cases and relaxed in others, with the net impact remaining unclear. Products that previously did not benefit from certain programmes have also been incorporated.

Source: Economic Commission for Latin America and the Caribbean (ECLAC), on the basis of information from "CRS Report for Congress", No. RS 22131, 1 April 2008 [online] http://www.whitehouse.gov/news/releases/2008/05/20080509.html; and "CRS Report for Congress", No. RL 33934, 10 April 2008 [online] ww.boston.com/news/world/europe/articles/2008/05/29/wtos_lamy_says_us_farm_bill_poor_trade_signal/.

Table II.3

IMPACT OF THE SWISS FORMULA ON BOUND AND APPLIED TARIFFS

Country	Coefficient [a]	Average tariff (percentages)			
		Base bound tariff	New bound tariff	Base applied tariff	New applied tariff
Argentina	19	30.6	11.6	10.4	7.4
	26	30.6	13.8	10.4	8.4
Brazil	19	29.8	11.4	11.0	8.5
	26	29.8	13.6	11.0	9.7
Chile	19	25.0	10.8	6.0	6.0
	26	25.0	12.7	6.0	6.0
Colombia	19	35.4	12.4	11.3	9.1
	26	35.4	15.0	11.3	10.2
Costa Rica	19	43.4	12.7	4.7	4.6
	26	43.4	15.7	4.7	4.7
Mexico	19	34.9	12.2	12.2	9.1
	26	34.9	14.8	12.2	10.2
Peru	19	30.0	11.6	9.2	8.1
	26	30.0	13.9	9.2	8.1
Venezuela	19	33.7	12.1	11.6	9.2
(Bol. Rep. of)	26	33.7	14.6	11.6	10.4

Source: Economic Commission for Latin America and the Caribbean (ECLAC), on the basis of simulations conducted by the WTO Secretariat [online] http://www.eclac.org/comercio/noticias/documentosdetrabajo/8/32098/BAL-COM2007-I.pdf.

[a] Countries in the region that would have to apply the Swiss formula agreed to in the document. The simulation is made using the coefficients of 19 and 26, respectively. The exercise supposes that the countries do not use the flexibilities permitted under the formula, which consist of: (i) applying less than formula cuts to up to 10% of the tariff lines provided that the cuts are no less than half the formula cuts and that these tariff lines do not exceed 10% of the total value of a member's imports; or (ii) keeping, as an exception, tariff lines unbound, or not applying formula cuts for up to 5% of non-agricultural tariff lines provided they do not exceed 5% of the total value of a member's non-agricultural imports. The countries not included could make use of other flexibilities contemplated in the document presented by the Chair. Eighteen countries of Latin America and the Caribbean are considered small and vulnerable economies.

Consequently, the new proposal presented on 19 May 2008 focussed on defining new flexibilities for the developing countries that would have to apply the Swiss tariff reduction formula in full. These included the possibility of applying three coefficients. The lower the coefficient used (i.e. the greater the tariff cut), the greater the flexibility, and vice versa. The application of this formula would substantially reduce the gap between bound and applied tariffs, which would make trade far more predictable.

An important number of additional flexibilities are included in the proposal, especially regarding tariff lines that could be excepted from tariff reductions or subject only to smaller cuts. Special modalities are contemplated for the other developing country members (of which there are approximately 75) that would not apply the Swiss formula in full. The 32 least developed countries would be exempt from making tariff reductions, and special provisions would apply to the 31 small and vulnerable economies (18 of which are in Latin America and the Caribbean) that represent less than 1% of world trade and for the 12 developing countries that have a low percentage of bound tariffs. Their contribution to market access would be made through the significant increase in bound tariffs. Moreover, the treatment of certain specific cases was under negotiation. Finally, special modalities were contemplated for the 16 recently acceded members.[8]

[8] See WTO, "Revised draft modalities for agriculture" [online] http://www.wto.org/english/tratop_e/agric_e/agchairtxt_may08_e.doc.

Under the proposals, the maximum tariffs applied by the developed countries were to reach between 7% and 9%, and the average tariff for non-agricultural goods were to be below 3%. Average tariffs in the developing countries that had to apply the formula would range between 11% and 15% (and higher in some cases) depending on the flexibilities and coefficients used.

Opposition to the NAMA proposals has been headed by the NAMA-11 group, which includes Argentina, the Bolivarian Republic of Venezuela and Brazil. Argentina in particular has criticized the proposals vehemently and highlighted the imbalance between the outcomes of the agricultural and the non-agricultural goods negotiations (Inside US Trade, 2008a and Bridges Daily Update, 2008).

There are other areas in which the Doha Development Round has yet to produce concrete results. These include the negotiations on services and the negotiations on antidumping measures. Little headway has been made in the services negotiations despite plurilateral talks being held, and the differences regarding the proposed level of ambition remain marked. The developed countries are seeking at least a commitment from developing countries to bind current levels of market access and national treatment, a proposal that developing countries are likely to resist (Inside US Trade, 2007a). The developed countries have also proposed the liberalization of environmental goods and services, which has stirred up opposition among some developing countries, especially Brazil, which insists on ethanol being treated as an environmental good while developed countries consider it an agricultural product.

The Negotiating Group on Services held an informal meeting during the mini-ministerial held in July at which countries presented the commitments they would be willing to assume in the services sector. Although the results were not translated into concrete proposals, both the developed and the developing countries viewed the stated intentions positively (Bridges Daily Update, 2008).

As far as antidumping measures are concerned, the text proposal presented by the Chair of the Negotiating Group on Rules in November 2007 provoked strong reactions because it was held to reflect the suggestions made by the United States on the subject, especially with regard to zeroing.[9] In the document presented on 28 May 2008, prior to the mini-ministerial in July, the Chair basically compiled the proposals that have been made by WTO members on the topic and the comments of members to the text proposal. Similar situations arose regarding subsidies in general and fisheries subsidies in particular.[10]

The mini-ministerial held 21-29 July 2008 did not manage to capitalize on the informal progress made in various areas of the negotiations or to generate new political momentum to resolve the more sensitive issues involved in agricultural and non-agricultural trade talks. The meeting in fact failed to meet its objectives even though only 35 of the 153 WTO members (counting the European Union as one) were present. This outcome is particularly poignant given that in 18 of the 20 subjects addressed, significant progress had been made, and the negotiations failed owing to differences among the trading partners in two main areas: the commitments to participate in the sectoral talks and the special agricultural safeguards for developing countries. This is troubling because, by concentrating on solving the problem of market access for goods, other topics (such as services, rules on antidumping rights and fishing subsidies, the environment, and the link between intellectual property, the Convention on Biological Diversity and development) were never addressed in any depth. In other words, the talks did not fail in all areas. The lack of agreement surrounds one subset of highly relevant subjects. There were even concrete signs of willingness to advance with the services negotiations once the problems in the agricultural talks and NAMA had been resolved. It was hoped that an agreement would be reached on modalities, in other words on the terms of reference for the next stage of the negotiations. The goal was to lay the foundations to move ahead with the agenda of the negotiations, not to conclude them.

The conclusion of the mini-ministerial sent out three worrying messages to the multilateral trade system. The first is that the capacity of those handling the negotiations (and even of those who benefit from the globalization process) to make the system governable is now in doubt. The second is that it may not be possible for the WTO and its members to further a gradual and inclusive multilateral trade opening process that can accommodate the policies being adopted at the regional level. These policies are increasing the fragmentation of the multilateral trade system by discriminating in favor of their participants at a time when the complementary nature of multilateralism and regionalism seems to be weaker than it was in the past. The third negative message is that the Doha process and its development programme will be on hold for as long as other difficulties (such as the worsening of the international economic situation, the food and energy crisis and the problem of climate change) corner the attention of the international community. The situation is further complicated by the widely differing opinions of the WTO held by important political figures on both sides of the Atlantic.

---

9 See Inside U.S. Trade (2007a). Zeroing in simple terms consists of excluding negative numbers in the dumping margin, which means that the margin increases. Antidumping duties therefore also increase.

10 See Negotiating Group on Rules, Working document from the Chairman (TN/RL/W/232), 28 May 2008.

The confirmed end of the North-South dichotomy could be seen to be another source of concern. After the mini-ministerial, some participants were even speaking of the emergence of a new world order. Opposition to the special agricultural safeguards had come not only from the United States, but from developing countries that export agricultural goods, such as Paraguay and Uruguay. The differences in the interests at stake, in the current international context, were also apparent in the Caribbean countries' opposition to the agreement reached between the European Union and the banana-exporting countries of Latin America. Opinion among developing countries regarding the NAMA negotiations also varied considerably, and the hopes of some African countries for a definitive decision on distortions in the cotton trade were consequently thwarted.

Given the organization's inability to resolve traditional trade issues, doubts have once more been raised about the capacity of the WTO to tackle the issues that the international community will need to address in the future, such as the relations between trade and the measures taken to lessen the impact of climate change. Multilateral trade rules have not kept up with regional ones, and this is threatening to render the multilateral system irrelevant and to make it increasingly difficult for the WTO to handle the challenges posed by the deepening integration of its members. The option of negotiating substantive aspects of trade-related issues in other forums is already under discussion. The Group of Eight, for example, declared the negotiation of different mechanisms for enforcing intellectual property rights to be a priority this year, and the non-binding SECURE initiative (Standards to be Employed by Customs for Uniform Rights Enforcement) is currently being negotiated within the WCO with a view to preventing the violation of intellectual property rights.[11]

In September 2008, consultations were held and contact was made among WTO members with a view to breaking the impasse in which the talks had ended in July. Members have stated their interest in not losing the ground gained so far in the negotiations, especially during the first semester of 2008, which attests to the importance of the progress made. The talks still have a long way to go, however, even once the modalities have been agreed to. The legal scrub of the final text will have to be performed, and then there will be additional negotiations. Moreover, there are some areas, such as rules and services, in which concrete progress has yet to be made. Finally, the results of the Doha Round will have to be approved by the legislative branches of the WTO member countries within an increasingly uncertain international context.

Box II.2

THE BIOFUELS RACE

Biofuels have emerged as an option for addressing climate change and expanding agricultural development, especially in developing countries. Controversy has arisen, however, about the economic viability of biofuel programmes, and concerns have been voiced about their impact in terms of deforestation, the technological developments needed for their implementation, again especially in developing countries, and how these programmes could drive up food prices and, consequently, poverty rates (World Bank, 2007).

The biomass energy potential of Latin America and the Caribbean, based on the use of surplus farm land, could account for between 17% and 26% of total world energy by 2050. These figures are higher than for any other region in the world, with the exception of Sub-Saharan Africa (depending on the type of production system used). According to production potential and demand estimates, 100% of global demand for transportation fuel by 2050 could be covered by biofuels if all the land considered apt or available for biomass plantations were used to produce transportation fuels. Bioenergy (not just liquid fuels) in Latin America and the Caribbean in particular is projected to have the potential to cover between 120% and 580% of energy demand (Razo and others, 2007a).

It is important to weigh not just the technical potential of biofuels but also their real economic potential. In 2000, the cost of producing biofuels was between 10 and 20 United States dollars per gigajoule (GJ) of energy. It has been estimated that under certain circumstances, by 2050, over 25% of the world's energy needs could be met at a cost of less than 12 dollars per GJ.

Given the large sugar cane surpluses in the region, sugar cane is the main potential source of bioethanol in Latin America and the Caribbean. Ethanol production based on corn, wheat and sorghum is largely concentrated in Argentina, however, which has competitive advantages in these sectors as a major grain producer. Together, on the basis of their exportable surpluses, the countries of the region could produce almost 20 billion litres of bioethanol a year, of which 58% would be obtained from sugar cane, 22% from corn and 18% from wheat. This is approximately equivalent to 26% of average regional gasoline consumption (Razo and others, 2007b).

Latin America and the Caribbean definitely has the potential to be a biofuel-producing region. Some countries, such as Brazil, whose ethanol industry has become highly efficient, are considering expanding their biofuel exports. The possibility of doing so will depend on the policies applied by their trading partners, especially the United States and Europe. In the case of the United States, some 200 domestic support measures for biofuel production costing between US$ 5 billion and US$ 7 billion have been introduced (World Bank, 2007). The biofuel sector has been able to expand in developed countries largely thanks to significant tariff barriers and subsidy schemes. In the European Union, import duties on ethanol range from 40% to 100%. Import duties are far lower in the case of biodiesel (6.5%), which distorts the market. Ethanol and other biofuels can be imported duty-free from least developed countries and the countries of Africa, the Caribbean and the Pacific or under the Generalized System of Preferences (GSP).

---

[11] See [online] http://www.ip-watch.org/weblog/index.php?p=1117.

Box II.2 (concluded)

The most-favoured-nation tariff for ethanol imports in the United States is 2.5%, but imports are subject to a mark-up of 54 cents on the gallon (14.27 cents per litre), except in the case of imports from the member countries of the Caribbean Basin Initiative. This mark-up is due to expire on 31 December 2008 but will probably be extended given the protection it grants corn growers and ethanol producers in the United States. Even when subject to duties, ethanol imported from Brazil reaches the United States market at US$ 2.18 per gallon compared with US$ 2.55 per domestically-produced gallon.

Discrepancies are beginning to emerge within the WTO regarding biofuels, especially within the framework of the Doha Development Round, in which some biofuels form part of the agricultural negotiations (bioethanol) and others do not (biodiesel is classified under industrial chemicals HS 382490). Biofuels have not been included in the list of environmental goods, as Brazil has proposed, because of opposition from developed countries, which means they cannot benefit from the proposed tariff cuts for environmental goods. Meanwhile, on 13 June 2008, the European Union initiated anti-subsidy and anti-dumping investigations into imports of biodiesel from the United States. If these lead to the application of anti-dumping measures or countervailing duties, the case will probably be transferred to the WTO.

Source: Economic Commission for Latin America and the Caribbean (ECLAC), on the basis of C. Razo and others, "Producción de biomasa para biocombustibles líquidos: el potencial de América Latina y el Caribe", Desarrollo productivo series, No. 181, Santiago, Chile, Economic Commission for Latin America and the Caribbean (ECLAC), 2007; C. Razo and others, "Biocombustibles y su impacto potencial en la estructura agraria, precios y empleo en América Latina", Desarrollo productivo series, No. 178 (LC/L.2768-P), Santiago, Chile, Economic Commission for Latin America and the Caribbean (ECLAC), 2007; World Bank, World Development Report, 2008: Agriculture for Development, Washington, D.C., 2007; and Inside US Trade, vol.26, No. 24, 13 June 2008.

Bibliography

Bridges Daily Update (2008), "WTO Mini-Ministerial Evades Collapse, As Lamy Finds 'Way Forward'", No. 6, 26 July.

ECLAC (Economic Commission for Latin America and the Caribbean) (2008), "Balance de temas comerciales en 2007" [online] http://www.eclac.org/comercio/noticias/documentosdetrabajo/8/32098/BAL-COM2007-I.pdf.

___ (2007), Latin America and the Caribbean in the World Economy, 2006. Trends 2007 (LC/G.2341-P), Santiago, Chile. United Nations publication, Sales No. E.07.II.G.85.

Inside U.S. Trade (2008a), vol. 26, No. 22, 30 May.

___ (2008b), vol. 26, No. 17, 25 April.

___ (2007a), vol. 25, No. 48, 7 December.

___ (2007b), "U.S., EU set to unveil C-TPAT, AEO mutual recognition road map", vol. 25, No. 44, November.

___ (2007c), vol. 25, No. 25, 22 June.

Razo, Carlos and others (2007a), "Biocombustibles y su impacto potencial en la estructura agraria, precios y empleo en América Latina", Desarrollo productivo series, No. 178 (LC/L.2768-P), Santiago, Chile, Economic Commission for Latin America and the Caribbean (ECLAC). United Nations publication, Sales No. S.07.II.G.104.

___ (2007b), "Producción de biomasa para biocombustibles líquidos: el potencial de América Latina y el Caribe", Desarrollo productivo series, No. 181 (LC/L.2803-P), Santiago, Chile, Economic Commission for Latin America and the Caribbean (ECLAC). United Nations publication, Sales No. S.07.II.G.136.

World Bank (2007), World Development Report, 2008. Agriculture for Development, Washington, D.C.

WTO (World Trade Organization) (2008), "Revised draft modalities for agriculture" [online] http://www.wto.org/english/tratop_e/agric_e/agchairtxt_july08_e.doc.

Chapter III

Globalization and new trends in international trade

Introduction

Since the beginning of the twenty-first century, profound changes have been underway in the international economy, brought about most noticeably by the advance of globalization, sweeping technological changes and the emergence of new and powerful competitors, such as China, India and, more generally, the countries of the Asia-Pacific region.

The implications of these changes are both varied and complex. The globalization of the financial market, for example, is far outstripping that of the real economy, making real-time operations a more common feature in the world of finance than in production or foreign trade. The subprime mortgage crisis in the United States and its repercussions in the global financial system have revealed the extreme volatility of the world's financial markets and exposed how vulnerable developing economies are even when sound and prudent macroeconomic policies have been implemented. Although the real economy is evolving at a different pace, the changes under way in production and trade are also significant.

In the production sphere, the latest advances in information and communications technologies, telecommunications and transportation are constantly redrawing the border between tradable and non-tradable goods and between manufacturing and services. This favours the creation of global value chains, which have become the archetype for the organization of production in the twenty-first century. Not that the vast majority of the world's enterprises are structured along these lines at the moment. In fact, according to the experts, only 20% of existing companies match this prototype of industrial organization (Castells, 2004). This group, however, includes the world's leading corporations, which are the standard-setters in international business, and at least some of the standards they establish become inserted into the rules of international trade itself.

Barcodes, online connections with suppliers and distributors and innovative online information-sharing and working arrangements, together with processes such as outsourcing, offshoring and insourcing, have made it possible to achieve the flexibility needed to keep up with demand. Logistics have become an integral aspect of production, and the value chain now includes research and development, design, distribution, marketing, post-sales services and the recycling or elimination of the product in addition to production per se (Friedman, 2005).

In order to participate in global value chains, companies need to attain high levels of quality and be backed by modern business services that can ensure timely responses and connectivity. The gradual incorporation of the Internet into management is changing business models, improving productivity and profitability in traditional sectors and generating new businesses, such as the online sale of services, or new business models, such as Google or the free delivery of music over the Internet.

At the same time, the impact of economic growth on the environment and on world climate has become an increasingly prominent feature of national and global debate. Awareness of the issue has grown, and several summit meetings have been devoted to the topic, such as those held in relation to the United Nations Framework Convention on Climate Change. Environmental groups and consumer organizations are gaining political weight, particularly in Europe where their influence ultimately shapes consumer behaviour, and this is having an indirect effect on international trade. The importance of saving energy and protecting the environment is now beginning to crop up more frequently in corporate debates on innovation and competitiveness, and markets in the industrialized countries are demanding greater traceability and higher safety standards in the production and international trade of foodstuffs.

Nobody nowadays disputes the link between energy efficiency, environmental conservation and climate change. The differences arise regarding how to tackle the problem. As a global activity, international trade cannot remain on the sidelines of the issue. A mixed bag of initiatives and theories has begun to take shape although no multilateral rules on the subject have been solidified as yet. This is an unusual moment in history inasmuch as, although the countries of the world acknowledge the magnitude of the problem before them, there is no multilateral framework for providing governance, and it is still unclear whether such a structure could be set up without modifying the current multilateral arrangement for managing the traditional topics of trade and finance.

The international (multilateral) trade system seems to have fallen behind in regard to both the pace of technological progress and the unilateral initiatives taking shape within the new structure that is emerging in the corporate world, which is often more relevant or influential, as far as trade is concerned, than the governments of industrialized countries themselves. The interaction between these two elements, which can be summed up as technological and business development, on the one hand, and the emergence of new issues and institutions, on the other, is highly complex, inasmuch as it brings the requirements arising from technological change itself, such as quality certification, up against business models that take advantage of technological progress to limit competition and protect private business interests, as occurs in the case of the requirement to obtain certification from certain laboratories or companies, for example.

The line between technological progress, the creation of new agencies and institutions and protectionism is a very fine one, and it is easily crossed, particularly if developing countries lack the technical capacity to distinguish between the changes inherent to progress and modernity (to which they will have to adjust) and those that are merely novel ways of doing business that can limit competition or increase the level of protectionism.

This chapter looks at several of these new issues, which have arisen with the advance of globalization and technological and organizational change or in response to the new threats to international harmony, such as terrorism. The first section examines the rules governing trade security, which have gained prominence since the terrorist attacks of 11 September 2003 in the United States. This is followed by a discussion of the application of private-sector standards in trade, which, though voluntary, can affect a country's competitiveness. These include good agricultural practices, safety certifications, International Organization for Standardization (ISO) standards and quality certificates. The last section documents the public-policy debates in the United States and the European Union on the link between trade and labour and on the link between trade and climate change. The analysis is by no means an exhaustive one and focuses mainly on the aspects that could impact the foreign trade of Latin America and the Caribbean.

The trade security norms that are being unilaterally promoted by some countries or recommended by multilateral agencies, such as the World Customs Organization, are creating strong pressure for institutional and operational improvements to be introduced along the whole length of the trade chain. At the same time, the regulatory role that is being played by leading private corporations as regards product quality and the public policies that may be adopted in the main industrialized economies regarding the link between trade and labour and the link between trade and climate change are further straining the competitiveness of the countries of Latin America and the Caribbean and could effectively turn into new barriers to trade that are not covered by any international rules. The region therefore needs to follow events in this arena closely and develop the necessary technical and negotiating capacity both to capitalize on the openings that globalization and technological change offer for enhancing innovation and competitiveness and to avoid the threats posed by the new form of protectionism that is arising in the twenty-first century.

A. Security in international trade

Security and, more specifically, being able to guarantee security as an exporter or a transportation agent has gained considerable importance in recent years thanks to two unrelated phenomena that have been linked together by the force of current international circumstances.

The first is the growing concern regarding food safety and the possible accidental contamination of food supplies. In addition to the number of serious food contamination incidents that have occurred since the 1990s,[1] two factors are now fuelling this concern: in objective terms, the incidence of foodborne diseases has increased in many countries; and in subjective terms, many foodborne pathogens are relatively unknown because the micro-organisms involved or the role that food plays in their transmission was only recently discovered (WHO, 2002).

> "The food chain has undergone considerable and rapid changes over the last 50 years, becoming highly sophisticated and international. Although the safety of food has dramatically improved overall, progress is uneven and foodborne outbreaks from microbial contamination, chemicals and toxins are common in many countries. The trading of contaminated food between countries increases the potential that outbreaks will spread. In addition, the emergence of new foodborne diseases creates considerable concern, such as the recognition of the new variant of Creutzfeldt-Jakob disease (vCJD) associated with bovine spongiform encephalopathy (BSE)." (WHO, 2007b).

The second phenomenon arose in the wake of the attacks of 11 September 2001, which decisively changed the course of foreign policy in many countries, not just the United States. The attacks on the Twin Towers and the Pentagon moved "terrorism" (no agreement has been reached as yet on how to define the term) from the sidelines of international relations to the centre stage, and the regulatory framework for international trade was consequently altered as well.

When foreign policy changes, the trade variables affected by foreign policy change as well, and measures to prevent the international supply chain from being used for terrorism purposes suddenly become a top priority. In response to this new situation, the United States set up the Customs-Trade Partnership Against Terrorism (C-TPAT) in 2002, the World Customs Organization established the Authorized Economic Operator (AEO) programme in 2005,[2] and the Canadian Government developed its Partners in Protection (PIP) process. These and other initiatives around the world all pursue one goal: to protect the supply chain.

One tricky issue that affects both the C-TPAT and the AEO scheme is that they are not wholly compatible with one another. The C-TPAT is a unilateral arrangement in which private companies ask the United States Government to be allowed to join the programme and, by meeting the requirements it imposes, they receive the corresponding benefits. The AEO programme is a multilateral scheme, its implementation depends on the States' wishes, and it is the States that decide the requirements that private operators are subject to and the benefits they receive. So far, the United States has not managed to get C-TPAT members recognized as authorized economic operators by the European Union. The fact that two of the most important trading partners of Latin America and the Caribbean are implementing different security schemes calls for the public sector in the region's countries to assume a guiding role in this area. Latin American and Caribbean businesses and small and medium-sized exporters in particular will need orientation and support, which will mean providing sound information and coordinating public-private initiatives to make prudent decisions regarding which steps to take and what kind of mutual-recognition agreements to pursue.

The international situation has been such that measures to guarantee the security of international cargo have been introduced far and wide over the past six years. These aim to prevent cargo shipments from accidentally transmitting diseases or from unwittingly transporting conventional weapons or biological, chemical or radioactive agents that could be used to destroy the peace and security of States and their citizens.

---

1 The global incidence of foodborne disease is difficult to estimate, but it has been reported that in 2005 alone 1.8 million people died from diarrhoeal diseases. A great proportion of these cases can be attributed to the contamination of food and drinking water. In industrialized countries, the percentage of the population suffering from foodborne diseases each year has been reported to be up to 30%. (WHO, 2007a).

2 The AEO programme has been implemented in Australia, China, Hong Kong (Special Administrative Region), Japan, Malaysia, New Zealand, Republic of Korea, Singapore and the European Union.

These two increasingly important trade factors, food safety and cargo security, are different in kind and have traditionally been tackled with different measures. The new trade security programmes, however, tend to be broader in scope and to address the issue of security along the whole length of the supply chain. They now aim to guarantee not only the integrity of international cargo, but also its correct handling and traceability. This new approach stems from the supposition that "the security of a transport chain depends upon its weakest link." (Commission of the European Communities, 2003).

For simplicity's sake, this analysis will limit itself to examining the AEO programme implemented in the European Union and the C-TPAT established by the United States as these two markets together absorbed over 60% of goods exports from Latin America and the Caribbean in 2005-2007.

1. The Customs-Trade Partnership Against Terrorism (C-TPAT) [3]

The C-TPAT began functioning in mid-2002 as a partnership between customs authorities and import businesses. It offered expedited entry for goods into the United States in return for protection of cargo containers against terrorist acts. Under this mechanism, C-TPAT importers aim to guarantee the security of goods from the moment they leave the factory floor to their arrival at their final destination. C-TPAT was given a solid legal basis by the passing of the Security and Accountability For Every Port Act (or SAFE Port Act) in October 2006. The United States thus unilaterally grants certification within a scheme that is backed by its own national legislation and offers various benefits for importers, such as fewer controls and simpler procedures for clearing merchandise.

Initially, the programme had only seven members (CBP, 2004), but it expanded to cover around 40% of imports to the United States by mid-2005, and an estimated 60% or more by mid-2007. It is hoped that the mechanism will curtail the threat of terrorists using cargo containers to transport bombs, weapons of mass destruction, biological or chemical weapons, or arms components (Hong Kong Trade Development Council, 2005; BancoMext, 2007).

C-TPAT has four goals, which are intended to improve border safety and efficiency: (i) ensure that C-TPAT members improve their supply-chain security; (ii) provide incentives and benefits to expedite the movement of merchandise within the system; (iii) introduce the programme's principles into the international community on the basis of cooperation and coordination; and (iv) support other initiatives and programmes of the United States Customs and Border Protection service.

Operators have to meet several requirements to become a member of the C-TPAT programme according to the activity they engage in. These generally fall into the categories set out in table III.1.

Table III.1
GENERAL REQUIREMENTS OF THE CUSTOMS-TRADE PARTNERSHIP AGAINST TERRORISM [a]

Procedures	Infrastructure	Staff
(1) Appropriate procedures for protection against unmanifested cargo (2) Procedures for denying access to installations (3) Written procedures for assessing business partners (4) Submission of complete, legible and accurate manifests to Customs prior to arrival by a secure means	(5) Physical integrity of the means of transport (6) Railway buildings and yards built with materials that resist unlawful entry (7) Information systems with duly controlled access, protected by individually assigned passwords that are periodically changed	(8) Interviews, employment screening and background checks (9) Training in security and to recognize internal conspiracies

Source: Economic Commission for Latin America and the Caribbean (ECLAC) on the basis of M. Alvarez, "C-TPAT and AEO: new channels for world trade", *FAL Bulletin*, No. 258, Santiago, Chile, Economic Commission for Latin America and the Caribbean (ECLAC), February 2008.
[a] This list is not exhaustive; it summarizes the general requirements of the C-TPAT.

[3] For further details on these programmes, see Alvarez (2008).

Applicants for participation in the scheme are classified into one of three possible tiers that confer different benefits:

- Tier 1 (attestation only): five to eight times fewer inspections than non-members;
- Tier 2 (validation): even fewer inspections, and when one is required, the container is moved to the front of the line;
- Tier 3: no regular security inspections, and infrequent random checks.

The United States Customs and Border Protection (CBP) service conducted a survey of C-TPAT members in 2007. One question asked members to indicate the potential benefits that influenced their decision to join the programme. "Reducing the time and cost of a shipment being released by the CBP" was considered to be the most important benefit members obtain from their participation in the scheme (figure III.1).

Figure III.1
POTENTIAL BENEFITS FROM PARTICIPATION IN THE C-TPAT SCHEME
(Maximum 4 points)

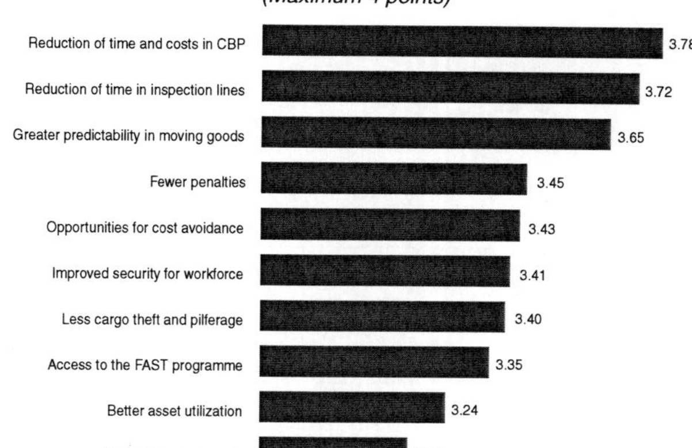

Source: United States Customs and Border Protection (CBP), "Cost/Benefit Survey" [online] www.cbp.gov, August 2007.

2. The Authorized Economic Operator (AEO) programme

The World Customs Organization created the AEO programme in 2005 within the regulatory framework to guarantee and facilitate world trade (SAFE). The programme consists of a series of requirements that customs authorities must impose on economic operators. These measures are aimed at improving security in the supply chain and lowering the risk of accident or deliberate mishandling endangering cargo of any kind. Although the initiative is being promoted by an international agency, its implementation is completely voluntary and financed by the States that choose to adopt it. The requirements and benefits granted under the programme are defined by each State within certain parameters. The final goal is to facilitate international trade through the mutual recognition of authorized economic operators so that operators that are certified by the customs service of one country can have smooth access to a third market that recognizes that certification.

Companies have been able to request AEO certification in the European Union since January 2008. This procedure is intended to be one of the pillars of the new community-wide customs policy and to supersede traditional controls by increasing the role of customs in security matters.[4]

The establishment of the AEO programme within the European Union is set out in *Authorised Economic Operators: Guidelines*. This document defines which entities are considered operators in the international supply chain and what their responsibilities are (European Commission, 2007).[5]

Applicants are awarded one of the three possible AEO certificates and the benefits that go with them:

- Customs simplification certificate: (a) easier admittance to customs simplifications;[6] (b) fewer physical and document-based controls; (c) priority treatment if selected for control; (d) possibility to request a specific place for such control.
- Security and safety certificate: (a) possibility of prior notification; (b) reduced data requirements set for summary entry and exit declarations; (c) fewer physical and document-based controls; (d) priority treatment if selected for control; (e) possibility to request a specific place for such control.
- Customs simplifications and security and safety certificate: combines the benefits of the other two certificates.

There are specific requirements for each type of agent in each certification category as set out in part 3 of the document (see table III.2).

---

4 As explained by Juan José Blanco, Director of Customs and Special Taxes of KPMG (*Expansión*, 2007).

5 These are: manufacturers, exporters, forwarding agents, bailees, customs brokers, shippers and importers.

6 Article 14b (1) of the Community Customs Code as amended (CCIP): "If the holder of an AEO certificate referred to in point (a) or (c) of Article 14a(1) applies for one or more of the authorisations [...], the customs authorities shall not re-examine those conditions which have already been examined when granting the AEO certificate."

Table III.2
REQUIREMENTS MADE OF AUTHORIZED ECONOMIC OPERATORS OF THE EUROPEAN UNION

Procedures	Infrastructure	Company
(1) Customs procedures (2) Procedures as regards backup recovery and fall-back archival options (3) Accounting system (4) Internal control system (5) Information security-protection of computer systems and documentation security (6) Logistics	(7) Volume of business (8) Flow of goods (9) Entry and access to premises (10) Physical security (11) Cargo units (12) Incoming goods (13) Storage of goods (14) Production of goods (15) Loading of goods	(16) Statistics on customs matters (17) Compliance history (18) Financial solvency (19) Security (20) Non-fiscal requirements (21) Security requirements for foreign business partners (22) Personnel security (23) External services

Source: Economic Commission for Latin America and the Caribbean (ECLAC), on the basis of European Commission, *Authorised Economic Operators: Guidelines* (TAXUD/2006/1450), Brussels, 2007.

The AEO programme has certain advantages over the C-TPAT and other similar initiatives. First, the AEO scheme was designed by World Customs Organization, and is therefore universal in kind and not geared just towards the European Union (or any of the States that have implemented it). States are free to implement the programme in different ways within the framework established by the World Customs Organization. Second, countries are urged to mutually recognize each other's national programmes. This means that each programme can be adapted to the needs of each country and facilitate access for its operators to other markets while ultimately increasing the level of security in the international supply chain. However, although the AEO programme is intended to foster mutual recognition of other security programmes, problems have arisen regarding the compatibility of AEO and C-TPAT certificates as certain requirements that are determining factors for obtaining one are not included in the other. This is the case of the "fiscal solvency" requirement for AEO certification, for example (*Inside U.S. Trade*, 2007b).

3. Cost and policy implications

Complying with new trade rules incurs new costs: production processes and procedures have to be constantly adjusted and updated to meet certification requirements, and operators have to spend in order to obtain and maintain accreditation.

Calculating these costs is not easy because they vary according to the level of certification sought and the company's conditions beforehand. The AEO programme of the European Union is fairly new, but C-TPAT has been operating for over five years, and the United States Customs and Border Protection service has conducted a survey of how C-TPAT members view the programme (see table III.3).

Table III.3
AVERAGE ANNUAL IMPLEMENTATION AND MAINTENANCE COSTS OF THE CUSTOMS-TRADE PARTNERSHIP AGAINST TERRORISM PROGRAMME

Specific aspect of C-TPAT	Implementation		Maintenance	
	Companies that incurred expenses	Average expenses in United States dollars	Companies that incurred expenses	Average expenses in United States dollars
Physical security	57.2%	38 471	47.5%	13 141
Internal knowledge and training	52.3%	9 192	45.0%	4 945
Payroll	45.2%	32 986	36.3%	28 454
Cargo security	43.7%	18 443	41.4%	7 110
Staff security procedures	43.2%	11 643	33.1%	5 437
Identification system	41.7%	9 681	35.8%	6 241
Staff monitoring procedures	35.8%	7 079	33.1%	3 723
Electronic communication and database systems	33.7%	24 303	34.4%	8 752
Staff security	19.7%	35 682	22.4%	40 441
Total average annual expenditure		US$ 187 480		US$ 118 244

Source: Economic Commission for Latin America and the Caribbean (ECLAC) on the basis of M. Alvarez, "C-TPAT and AEO: new channels for world trade", *FAL Bulletin*, No. 258, Santiago, Chile, Economic Commission for Latin America and the Caribbean (ECLAC), February 2008.

Table III.3 shows that over half the companies (in seven of nine areas) did not incur any implementation expenses, except in the most sensitive areas of the programme (physical security and internal knowledge of the programme). These kinds of initiatives can have a negative impact on small and medium-sized producers, however, because if they fail to meet the programme requirements, they run the risk of losing markets by being unable to compete with those that do benefit from the programme and are therefore able to get their goods through not only faster, but with greater security guarantees. Competitiveness is now no longer just a matter of product quality and prices: the security factor is becoming increasingly important too.

4. Impact on Latin America and the Caribbean

Security costs have increased considerably with the implementation of these programmes. This new variable should be considered as a fixed cost by companies, however, and not as a one-off expense in the ordinary course of business. Supply-chain security is probably here to stay, and its importance for gaining access to sophisticated markets could be growing.

Authorities in Latin America and the Caribbean now face a new public-policy decision. Even if the security programmes discussed here are implemented, they do not impose any obligatory requirements on operators, and it is up to each country to decide what role the public and the private sector should play in their use. They could decide, for example, that it is up to private enterprises to choose whether to meet the requirements or not and that the public sector should only concern itself with activities at State-run ports. Helping operators obtain security certifications, however, not only improves the stability of exports (thanks to improved security), but also significantly increases the competitiveness of local goods, which in turn generates more growth in the domestic production sector.

Although these programmes establish requirements that must basically be met by the private sector, the public sector also plays an important part in lowering the costs of regulation, coordinating the process and keeping operators informed and hence in facilitating trade. The proliferation of information, programmes and standards can complicate the decision-making process in small and medium-sized firms. In addition to coordinating efforts, the public sector can therefore help by processing information and issuing clear guidelines that exporters can readily understand.

There are some unregulated aspects of international trade in which public policy can make a real difference. By drafting suitable legislation to fill these gaps, resolving information asymmetries and improving coordination among the country's economic operators, the public sector can strengthen national competitiveness. This is a suitable area for concerting regional efforts to increase trade facilitation and set up trade support initiatives. Synergies can be established between governments and business organizations in the region, and information on third markets and the steps being taken in each country can be shared to consolidate more coordinated positions. The region faces both a huge challenge and a huge opportunity as far as cooperation is concerned. The mutual recognition agreements with the main trading partners can be entered into individually or in a more coordinated manner. If the region of Latin America and the Caribbean manages to harmonize standards and set up a network of agreements on the subject within the region itself, it could be in a much stronger position to negotiate with its main training partners and to boost its own intraregional trade.

B. Private-sector standards and their legal status

1. The regulatory role of the private sector [7]

In an attempt to ensure product safety, as well as ethical corporate behaviour as regards the protection of the environment, labour rights and other issues, both the number and level of voluntary quality standards have increased.[8]

Economic operators know that in order to participate in global value chains they need to meet international quality standards and, in order to do that, they need modern business services that can guarantee them connectivity, opportunities and productivity gains. Complying with voluntary private-sector standards can be a passport to the more profitable segments of those chains. On occasions, however, quality certification can turn into an attractive business in itself that has relatively little to do with its initial purpose of ensuring quality along the length of the value chain. The proliferation of private-sector norms, particularly in the food industry, and the growing demand for food quality standards in markets around the world is in fact making it difficult for exporters to meet all the new requirements. This is creating demand for international consultancy services in a market that lacks transparency and has high entry barriers and is consequently dominated by uncompetitive quality-certification services. Worryingly, standards that may have started out as private voluntary initiatives in large international consortiums are tending to become the norm in international markets either through gradual *de facto* multilateralization or through their strong influence on key markets. In either case, the competitiveness of exporters suffers because another factor that unlevels the international playing field comes into play when they run into safety or traceability standards that are, for example, financed by public policy or some form of agricultural protectionism in the destination market.

In some cases, the quality requirements of the private sector are incorporated into government initiatives to standardize quality. This not only encourages the government to assume a regulatory role in the issue, it also affects the voluntary nature of what are private-sector requirements. In practice, through repeated use, these voluntary requirements end up as *de facto* obligations, and it becomes necessary for food production, for example, to take them into account. The agricultural sector and the agro-export sector in particular then find themselves forced to meet a large number of public- and private-sector requirements (table III.4).

The need for professional oversight of the food chain (from the farm to the table) and the dominant presence of multinationals are two of the factors that are most notably shaping the regulatory role of the private sector. The large multinationals in the food business have, jointly or severally, invested increasingly in good agricultural practices and safety certification. The handling of quality in the food sector is also being influenced by the concentration of distribution channels in import markets and the establishment of retailer associations and organizations or alliances that bring together companies operating either within a specific subsector or at similar stages in the food chain. When standards and certifications are recommended by such associations, it is much easier to coordinate their adoption en masse by suppliers.

7 For further details, see Salles de Almeida (2008).

8 The World Trade Organization Agreement on Technical Barriers to Trade distinguishes between technical regulations whose application is obligatory and those drawn up by public or private entities whose application is voluntary. This work refers to the norms agreed to by private entities whose application is voluntary and makes no distinction between norms and standards. The WTO Agreement on the Application of Sanitary and Phytosanitary Measures makes no distinction between measures whose application is mandatory and those whose application is voluntary. This has generated speculation about whether measures adopted by private entities are covered by this agreement, and the issue has yet to be resolved.

Table III.4

EXAMPLES OF THE STANDARDS AFFECTING THE REGION'S MAIN EXPORTS [a]

Product	Private-sector standards (voluntary)	Public-sector standards (obligatory)
Meats	EUREP-GAP Safe Quality Food standards (SQF) QF 1000/2000 of the British Retail Consortium (BRC) ISO 9000, ISO 14000 (environmental standards) ISO 22000 (food safety) Appellation of origin Geographical identification	Hazard Analysis and Critical Control Points (HACCP) Good agricultural practices Good manufacturing practices Traceability Sanitary certification
Fish/seafood	Good agricultural practices (for example, Best Aquaculture Practices standards, Codes of Practice for Responsible Shrimp Farming, both of the Aquaculture Certification Council) "Naturland Standards for Organic Aquaculture"	HACCP Good agricultural practices Good manufacturing practices Traceability United States Department of Agriculture (USDA) standards for organic products Sanitary certification
Fruit	Fairtrade Ethics protocols EUREP-GAP SQF 1000/2000 International Federation of Organic Agriculture Movements (IFOAM), ISO 65, others (organic farming) ISO 9000, ISO 14000 (environmental standards) ISO 22000 (food safety) Appellation of origin Geographical identification	HACCP (Juices) Traceability Production system Integrated Fruit Production Good agricultural practices Good manufacturing practices Sanitary certification Bioterrorism Protocol of the Food and Drug Administration (FDA) of the United States USDA standards for organic products
Cereals and oilseeds	IFOAM, ISO 65, others (organic farming) ISO 9000, ISO 14000 (environmental standards) ISO 22000 (food safety) Good manufacturing practices	Labelling Preserved identification Genetically modified organisms (GMO) Traceability Good agricultural practices (residues) Good manufacturing practices Sanitary certification FDA Bioterrorism Protocol (United States) USDA standards for organic products
Processed foods	Fair Trade Organic farming ISO 9000, ISO 14000 (environmental standards) ISO 22000 (food safety) Good manufacturing practices of BRC Ethics protocols Appellation of origin Geographical identification.	Labelling GMO identification Traceability Good manufacturing practices FDA Bioterrorism Protocol (United States) HACCP

Source: Juliana Salles de Almeida, "Normas privadas: el nuevo desafío de las exportaciones de los países en desarrollo", *Comercio internacional series*, No. 85 (LC/L.2861-P), Santiago, Chile, Economic Commission for Latin America and the Caribbean (ECLAC), 2008. United Nations publication, Sales No. S.08.II.G.06

[a] Norms demanded in the United States and Europe.

2. The role of the private sector in the most important safety and quality systems in place today

Concerns regarding food safety and the sustainability of food production have led several private and public institutions, in collaboration with the various actors in the food chain, to promote and implement good agricultural practices and good manufacturing practices in the production and management of food. Good agricultural practices refer to the production, processing and transportation of products of agricultural origin and aim to ensure the safety of food items and protect the environment, as well as the persons working in their production. In the case of animal products, good agricultural practices also cover animal welfare.[9]

Table III.5 presents an illustrative list of the topics covered by the main codes of good practice. The use of good agricultural practices is being increasingly promoted by the private sector through the implementation of formal codes of practice and indicators that have been drawn up by food manufacturers and retailers in response to new consumer demands for healthy food products that are obtained through sustainable farming practices. The Euro-Retailer Produce Good Agricultural Practices (EurepGAP), which was created by the European retail sector, is the most widely applied code of practice today.

[9] The FAO has drawn up a definition that states that "the concept of Good Agricultural Practices is the application of available knowledge to the use of the natural resource base in a sustainable way for the production of safe, healthy food and non-food agricultural products, in a humane manner, while achieving economic viability and social stability" (FAO, 2006).

Table III.5
THE MAIN TOPICS COVERED BY CODES OF GOOD PRACTICE

Good agricultural practices	Good manufacturing practices
Growing and handling conditions	Buildings and installations
Installations	Water use and management
Pest control	Waste and garbage handling
Quality assurance	Hygiene during processing
Food hygiene	Personnel (training, education, hygiene)
Water use and management	Equipment and utensils (cleanliness and hygiene)
Responsible handling of agrochemicals and fertilizers	Cooling, washing and disinfection processes
Use of organic fertilizers	Production process control (sanitary control)
Vector and pest control	Reception, treatment and packaging
Personnel issues (working conditions and welfare and health conditions of agricultural workers)	Pest control in packaging
	Storage conditions
Harvest activities	Labelling
Waste and garbage handling	Documentation and record keeping
Environmental protection measures	Distribution (reception operations, transportation)
Traceability	
Documentation and record keeping	
Transportation	

Source: Juliana Salles de Almeida, "Normas privadas: el nuevo desafío de las exportaciones de los países en desarrollo", *Comercio internacional series*, No. 85 (LC/L.2861-P), Santiago, Chile, Economic Commission for Latin America and the Caribbean (ECLAC), 2008. United Nations publication, Sales No. S.08.II.G.06

The EurepGAP chapter on fruit and vegetables is one of the most extensively implemented codes of practice in Argentina and Chile. This private set of standards has become an important international point of reference for guaranteeing the safety of farm produce and high-quality fruits and vegetables and has replaced or assimilated various regional standards for certain groups of products and for fruit and vegetable retailers. The EurepGAP protocol has also incorporated rules regarding the Hazard Analysis and Critical Control Points (HACCP) system, maximum residue levels and traceability.

There are other codes of practice in addition to EurepGAP, such as USGAP, JapanGAP and ChinaGAP. Private organizations have also created codes of good aquaculture practices. These codes all contain directives aimed at promoting practices that are environmentally, economically and socially sustainable and ensure the safety, quality and traceability of food products.[10] Large multinationals have also adopted codes of good practices, such as the Sustainable Agriculture Initiative, co-founded by Groupe Danone, Nestlé and Unilever in 2001. This initiative aims to ensure decent living conditions for farmers, respect for the environment and socially responsible labour practices.

3. Good practices in Latin America

Chambers of commerce, together with associations of agricultural producers and exporters, have joined forces in several countries in the region to launch good agricultural practice initiatives in diverse sectors. These initiatives have progressed most in the countries in which fruit and food exports are not only significant, but also can compete with the highest international standards. In Argentina, over 40 entities came together to create the Forum of the Agroindustrial Chain Argentina, which publishes a manual on good agricultural practices.[11] In Chile, private entities constituted a National Commission for Good Agricultural Practices, which advises the Ministry of Agriculture on the formulation of agricultural policies that promote the incorporation of good agricultural practices.[12] The Commission has created its own code on the basis of the recommendations laid down in the EurepGAP.

[10] The principles underlying these codes of good practices include: (1) operating practices that are sustainable in the long term and have acceptable ecological effects that avoid the unnecessary destruction of mangroves and other environmentally significant flora and fauna; (2) installation, design and management practices that conserve water resources, including subterranean sources of fresh water, and minimise the effects of waste on the quality of surface and subterranean water; (3) cooperation in research and educational activities to improve the environmental compatibility of aquaculture; (4) efforts to ensure local communities benefit by promoting the diversification of the local economy, job creation, contributions to the tax base and tax infrastructure, and respect for small artisanal fishing, forestry and agricultural operations, among others.

[11] Available online at http://www.foroagroindustrial.org.ar.

[12] More details are published on the website of the National Commission for Good Agricultural Practices http://www.buenaspracticas.cl/.

Chile is one of the countries that has made the greatest headway in this regard and, through its interesting public-private sector dynamic, has developed more good practice codes than any other country in the region.[13] One of its major trade initiatives, ChileGAP, was developed by the Fruit Growers Federation of Chile (FEDEFRUTA) and, after a lengthy accreditation process involving a series of analyses and audits by foreign agencies, has been approved as equivalent to the EurepGAP.[14]

Mexico has taken steps to implement MexicoGAP, while Uruguay is starting to bring its practices in the beef-cattle and sheep farming sectors into line with the Integrated Farm Assurance protocol of EurepGAP through its Certified Natural Meat Program. In Argentina, producers already have a lengthy experience with good agricultural practices in terms of phytosanitary controls and efficient and rational fertilizer use, direct seeding and rational soil use (Foro de la Cadena Agroindustrial Argentina, 2005).

Three important pieces of legislation on good agricultural practices have been passed in Argentina: resolution 71/99 of the Ministry of Agriculture, Livestock, Fisheries and Food, and resolutions 530/01 and 510/02 of the National Agrifood Health and Quality Service on aromatics and fruit, respectively. The content of these resolutions and those adopted in other countries in the region is similar to the stipulations of the EurepGAP code. Two more sets of regulations that will tend to make good agricultural practices obligatory in Argentina have been put forward. One is a proposal submitted by the National Food Institute for the implementation of good agricultural practices for fruit, vegetables and aromatics, and the other is a proposal to include good agricultural practices for beekeeping in the Argentine Food Code.[15] These initiatives reflect the pressure that governments are under to adopt private-sector standards.

The Brazilian Agricultural Research Enterprise, which is connected to the Ministry of Agriculture, Livestock and Food Supply in Brazil, has played a central role in spreading information and providing training on good agricultural practice techniques in different segments of agriculture. This organization has drafted a series of concrete technical guidelines for melons, mangoes, fruit and vegetables and farm, dairy, beef, pork and poultry products on the basis of good agricultural practices that have been tried and tested by small-, medium- and large-scale farmers. It has also given courses on the most important products in the Brazilian export basket, including training in good agricultural practices for beef farming and the safe production of fruit and vegetables.

4. Standards of practice regarding social responsibility

Several organizations promoting the concept of fair trade have sprung up in the last few years. Among other initiatives, this has led to the issue of private certificates (in the form of labels) guaranteeing that a product was produced according to the criteria that these organizations advocate. There are currently twenty such fair trade labelling initiatives operating around the world, most of them in Europe and North America. Their aim is to regulate the use of certification marks in their respective countries. Fairtrade Labelling Organizations International (FLO) is the umbrella organization for these initiatives. Its role is to provide direct support to certified producers and to define the criteria for fair trade.[16] Currently, the FLO, in compliance with the international ISO standard for certification agencies, inspects and certifies around 508 producer associations in over fifty African, Latin American and Asian countries.

---

13 The National Commission for Good Agricultural Practices of Chile has developed technical good agricultural practice regulations for the following farming sectors: beef cattle, dairy cattle, sheep, goats, laying hens, broiler chickens, pigs, potatoes, wheat, corn, rice, fruit, vegetables and berries. The manuals can be consulted at www.buenaspracticas.cl.

14 For further details, consult http://www.chilegap.com/.

15 For further details, consult http://www.foroagroindustrial.org.ar.

16 The FLO has two operations units: FLO-CERT GMBH and FLO e.V. FLO-CERT GMBH ensures that producers, wholesalers and retailers comply with the FAIRTRADE Standards. FLO e.V. defines the International FAIRTRADE Standards, facilitates and develops the organization's commercial activities and promotes fair trade. Futher details are available at http://www.fairtrade.net.

5. The impact of private-sector standards on trade

For the countries of the region, the adoption of private-sector standards, as well as obligatory official ones, poses both a challenge and an opportunity, as compliance with such norms has become a de facto requirement for selling agricultural products in markets in which both environmental awareness and the demand for quality are rising. Fulfilling private-sector standards can open doors to numerous markets and thus create new trade opportunities. The same standards can pose a barrier to trade, however, especially for developing country suppliers, because meeting them means incurring additional costs. They can also conceal an unjustified attempt to protect domestic producers when they go beyond the scientifically sustainable requirement established in the WTO Agreement on the Application of Sanitary and Phytosanitary Measures of the World Trade Organization (WTO). In general terms, the proliferation of private-sector standards has raised concern among agricultural exporters in developing countries and the least advanced countries. WTO draws a distinction between the content- and the compliance-related concerns about private-sector standards, which are summarized in table III.6.

Table III.6

CONCERNS REGARDING PRIVATE-SECTOR STANDARDS

Content-related concerns	Compliance-related concerns
Multiplication of private standards systems in and among markets	Costs of third-party certification, especially for small and medium-sized enterprises and farmers in developing countries
Fuzzy line between official sanitary and phytosanitary measures and private standards	Some private systems demand certification by specific certification agencies
The relationship between private standards and the international standardization institutions mentioned in the WTO Agreement on Sanitary and Phytosanitary Measures	The lack of equivalence among systems results in certification inspections having to be repeated
Scientific justification for some of the limitations placed on production processes and methods	The certificates are not recognized or accredited certification agencies do not operate in developing countries

Source: World Trade Organization (WTO), "Private standards and the SPS Agreement" (G/SPS/GEN/746), Committee on Sanitary and Phytosanitary Measures, 24 January 2007.

Although quality systems are included on both the public and the private sectors' agendas in Latin America and the Caribbean, small and medium-sized farmers have serious difficulties applying the sanitary and phytosanitary quality systems that export markets demand. These difficulties are related to: (i) the high costs of certification (table III.7); (ii) the lack of infrastructure; (iii) the lack of technology or inadequate technology; (iv) unawareness of, or insufficient training in, the requirements that need to be met; (v) inadequate legal frameworks; (vi) sociocultural factors; (vii) the failure of small producers to organize themselves and link up with production chains; (viii) inadequate training and information for small-scale farmers; (ix) the minimal implementation of systems to guarantee safety and quality; and (x) insufficient access to credit, which hampers the implementation of innovation and technology transfer programmes (Salles de Almeida, 2008).

Developing countries face three major challenges as far as good agricultural practices in particular are concerned. The first is how to guarantee that the more widespread use of good agricultural practices to ensure food safety and the sustainability of domestic production does not run counter to the interests of small-scale farmers. The second is how to handle the risk of farmers becoming overburdened by the growing number of disperse good agricultural practice initiatives and the multiple codes and regulations, which, though not legally binding, in practice determine whether goods gain access to markets. The third is related to the increase in production, certification (see table III.7), processing and marketing costs that informed consumers may be willing to absorb, but which consumers in developing countries and the least advanced countries may not.[17]

17 Other problems stem from the lack of procedures for tackling: (a) the need for adequate inspection of processes; (b) the certification of exports or the assurance of the integrity and phytosanitary safety of shipments between certification and shipment; (c) the lack of operations manuals (on quality management, process safety, etc.); (d) the absence of internal auditing systems to ensure service quality; and (e) the inadequacy of laboratory facilities and equipment.

Table III.7
COSTS OF PRIVATE CERTIFICATION THROUGH THE AQUACULTURE CERTIFICATION COUNCIL
(United States dollars)

Certification	Application fee	Initial inspection fee	Value of the certificate	Annual renewal of the certificate
Processing Plant Certification	500	5 000	2 000 – 12 000 (depending on the volume exported)	5 000 (inspection) + 2 000 – 12 000 (2 000 per metric ton exported)
Shrimp Farm Certification	500	3 000	500 – 4 000 (depending on production volumes)	3 000 (inspection) + 500 – 4 000 (depending on production volumes)
Shrimp Hatchery Certification	500	3 000	500	3 000 (inspection) + 500 (certificate)
Total	1 500	11 000	3 000 – 16 500	14 000 – 27 500

Source: Juliana Salles de Almeida, "Normas privadas: el nuevo desafío de las exportaciones de los países en desarrollo", *Comercio internacional series*, No. 85 (LC/L.2861-P), Santiago, Chile, Economic Commission for Latin America and the Caribbean (ECLAC), 2008. United Nations publication, Sales No. S.08.II.G.06

Studies show that producers would be willing to raise quality standards even if this entails higher costs provided that the requirements are incorporated into national legislation and the certification process is simplified (Díaz, 2005). This would mean increasing the requirements both for exports and for goods sold on the domestic market, and thus eliminating the export bias. National standards are usually less demanding, however, because international agreements on sanitary and phytosanitary measures require standards to be based on scientific proof, which requires investment in research. To avoid having to do this, governments can adopt the standards set by the three international agencies that specialize in this task: the Food and Agriculture Organization (FAO)/World Health Organization Codex Alimentarius Commission, the World Organisation for Animal Health and the FAO Commission on Phytosanitary Measures. These organizations draw up the most demanding scientifically-based standards. Adhering to these standards not only raises the quality of goods traded internally but also reduces the risk of running up against barriers to entering third markets. In order to encourage the adoption of these standards, countries receive support from the corresponding organizations, as well as help from other countries, such as in the Sanitary and Phytosanitary Measures Initiative of the Americas.[18]

In all the topics discussed so far (security, good practices and private-sector quality standards), it is possible to find protectionist distortions or at least opportunities for them. It is therefore important for Latin America and the Caribbean to handle these matters through its regional institutions and to increase its technical and institutional readiness to put forward common positions on issues that are becoming increasingly relevant in international trade.

6. The debate in international organizations

The main international forums to address this topic are the WTO Committee on Sanitary and Phytosanitary Measures (the "SPS Committee") and the UNCTAD Consultative Task Force on Environmental Requirements and Market Access for Developing Countries. At the regional level, FAO has conducted studies and seminars on the impact of some specific regulations, such as the EurepGAP and the certification of organic products, among others.

The impact of private-sector standards on trade was first broached in June 2005 in the SPS Committee when Saint Vincent and the Grenadines complained that the private-sector standards applied to bananas were more rigid than the international ones, which was creating difficulties for small-scale farmers. The complaint was backed by several other developing countries, mainly from Latin America and the Caribbean.[19]

18 This initiative was developed by the Inter-American Institute for Cooperation on Agriculture and the United States Department of Agriculture and with the collaboration of six countries that serve as a steering committee (Argentina, Brazil, Canada, Chile, United States and Mexico). Thirty-four countries participate in the initiative: 6 providers of cooperation and 28 direct beneficiaries (Alvarez, 2008).

19 The countries that backed this complaint were: Argentina, Belize, Cuba, Dominica, Ecuador, Egypt, Indonesia, Jamaica, Kenya, Mexico, Peru and South Africa.

The European Commission alleged that it was not in a position to intervene because the EurepGAP requirements, though more rigid than international standards, were in keeping with community legislation on food safety. It maintained that private-sector organizations responded to consumer demands and suggested that the countries that felt that their interests were being affected should bring their concerns to the attention of the non-governmental organization in question. This was the first occasion on which the SPS Committee discussed how governments should proceed when the standards imposed by the private sector were stricter than those prescribed by the State.

The main trade-related issues raised within the WTO framework refer to the relationship between private and international standardization agencies (private-sector standards are generally more rigid than international ones). Discussions have also been held on the nature of the unnecessary trade restrictions private standards can impose, especially on small-scale farmers, as well as on the measures governments could take to ensure private organizations comply with the Agreement on Sanitary and Phytosanitary Measures and the implications for other WTO areas, such as technical barriers to trade. The possibility of authorities accepting different measures that offer the same level of protection in terms of food safety, animal health and plant preservation is under consideration, with a view to helping developing countries with less advanced technology protect the health and safety of farm produce. In other words, the use of "equivalent" measures is under study. The need to clarify aspects of article 13 on the application of the Agreement on Sanitary and Phytosanitary Measures and the activities undertaken by institutions not affiliated with the central government or by non-governmental entities operating within a territory has been analysed. Finally, concerns have been voiced about the lack of transparency of private-sector rules as there is no requirement for WTO to be notified of their application.

Another point of discussion is the role of the State in the certifications market. Increasingly, people are asking whether the public sector should oversee the certification systems used by private agents. Some maintain that governments should indeed intervene in the matter and should both audit private certification processes and sanction errors or fraud. The technical and financial complexity of this task, however, is beyond the capacity of many governments in the region. Controlling the certification processes through autonomous technical entities specifically created for this purpose in the form of accreditation agencies, for example, would therefore seem to be a more viable option. Public policy needs to define the rules of the game, boost competition and transparency and ensure that the recognized independent certification agencies perform their function and eventually draw up and propose new standards for incorporation into national legislation according to the needs of each country, sector or administration (Salles de Almeida, 2008).

This is another potential area for cooperation among the region's governments. They could share information on the main restrictions their products face in the industrialized markets as a result of private-sector standards that undermine their competitiveness. Collective action could be taken towards entering into joint negotiations with the governments or private associations of industrialized countries or to carry out subregional trade-facilitation projects that would enable the countries of the region to keep up with the most important trends underway in the various aspects of quality certification at the international level.

C. Trade and labour

The relationship between trade and labour rights has been gaining importance, in tandem with the relationship between trade and the environment, since the end of the 1980s. Both topics have been on the international agenda for far longer, however. This section will focus mainly on the links between trade and labour. Even prior to the creation of the International Labour Organization, there had been concern about the problems that some industrial sectors could face as a result of the adoption of certain labour standards in developed countries. Attempts have been made to include the issue in the international trade agenda since as far back as the 1950s. At the end of the Uruguay Round of the General Agreement on Trade and Tariffs (GATT), the United States and France unsuccessfully proposed the insertion of labour standards in the WTO agenda.[20] To date this has not happened.

20 Labour standards are understood to refer to the protection of the following: (a) the right of association; (b) the right to organize and to collective bargaining; (c) the prohibition of any form of forced or compulsory labour; (d) the minimum age for admission to employment and the elimination of the worst forms of child labour; and (e) acceptable working conditions regarding minimum wages, working hours and occupational health and safety.

In November 1971, the GATT Council of Representatives agreed to set up a Group on Environmental Measures and International Trade (also known as the "EMIT" group). This group never functioned owing to the other topics on the GATT agenda at the time, but served as a basis for the creation of the WTO Committee on Trade and Environment in 1991, which has been examining the links between the two issues. The current mandate of the Doha Round contemplates holding talks on the relationship between the WTO rules in force and the specific trade obligations established in multilateral agreements on the environment.

The generalized systems of preferences offered by the developed countries to the developing ones have contemplated the inclusion of conditionality clauses regarding compliance with certain labour, environmental and intellectual property standards. The incorporation of these issues into trade agreements to force compliance with environmental and labour standards by applying the trade sanctions established in dispute settlement mechanisms has always been a highly complex and polemic issue and is currently not feasible at the multilateral level.[21]

At the bilateral level and in the free trade agreements promoted by the United States, however, obligations regarding trade, environmental and labour standards have been established within the framework of the approval process for the North American Free Trade Agreement (NAFTA). The United States proposed the negotiation of two parallel agreements, one on the environment[22] and another on labour issues, each with their own provisions and dispute settlement mechanism. Subsequently in 1997, Canada and Chile negotiated relatively similar cooperation agreements based on the same model.

Owing to objections from environmental and labour groups to the outcome of the NAFTA model, the labour and environmental provisions incorporated into subsequent trade agreements were made subject to a single dispute settlement mechanism. The free trade agreement between the United States and Jordan, which was concluded in 2000 and entered into effect in 2001, was the first to use this new model. The Trade Promotion Authority that the United States Congress granted President George W. Bush in 2002 contemplated labour provisions and identical dispute settlement systems as well as countervailing measures in case of non-compliance.[23] These were incorporated into the free trade agreements signed with Chile and Singapore and reproduced in the Dominican Republic - Central America - United States Free Trade Agreement (CAFTA-DR).

The evidence on the impact of trade liberalization on labour markets is mixed, with the empirical literature often finding difficulty in capturing the relationship between liberalization and labour market dynamics (wages, elasticities, employment), as well as sometimes finding unexpected results that lead to new theoretical frameworks.

Recent reviews of the literature on the topic reveal that existing studies support the view that trade liberalization on average increases employment and income. They also point, however, to reallocation and other adjustment costs that have to be addressed with social policy instruments. Greater trade liberalization has mixed effects on wage inequality between high-skilled and low-skilled workers, while providing an incentive for greater productivity across all sectors. The empirical evidence also shows that the impact of lower barriers to trade differs significantly across countries as an appreciation of domestic policy structure is key to understanding the relationship between liberalization and labour markets.

As indicated in the work of Reina and Zuluaga (2008) and in keeping with theory-based expectations, studies have found that trade liberalization tends to shift labour demand to labour-abundant countries, which can reduce wage inequalities in the developing world. The authors also point out that this is only a minor effect, however, because technological changes play a more significant role in this process. Jensen and Lee (2007) present evidence to show that, while salary premiums in Asia have indeed declined in line with the expectations mentioned above, Latin America has seen an increase in the spread between high-skilled and low-skilled wages. Possible explanations include: China winning the lower-skilled segment of the production market while the advantage of Latin America and the Caribbean shifts towards the medium-skilled segment; the abundance of natural resources in Latin America and the Caribbean; greater foreign direct investment (FDI) flows that have resulted in more demand for high-skilled labour; pre-liberalization tariff schedules that protected industries employing lower-skilled labour; and the dynamics of competition at the product level. In addition, the fact that higher-income countries trade mainly among themselves limits the effect of any shifts in labour demand.

There are strong concerns that the rise of Asia, and of China in particular, and its impact on labour markets will result in lower employment growth in other regions. The empirical evidence over the last couple of decades shows, however, that, despite growth in trade and FDI,

21 See a general discussion in Hoekman and Kostecki (2001).

22 The agreement on environmental cooperation recognizes that it is up to the countries to determine their level of environmental protection and their environmental policies, as well as to draw up environmental legislation. The main (but not sole) substantial commitment is to ensure compliance with that legislation.

23 See a discussion on recent developments in this area in Elliot (2004).

no drastic change in the aggregate employment situation has been recorded. These concerns are possibly justified on the basis that relatively rapid improvements in China and India should in theory imply a deterioration in other regions (including Latin America and the Caribbean), but there is no evidence of a systematic relationship between liberalization and the long-term employment situation. Macroeconomic events and labour legislation are found to have a greater impact on employment.

An analysis of the impact of trade on the distribution of economic activity also produces interesting results. According to the survey conducted by Jansen and Lee (2007), empirical studies find that greater trade openness promotes the reallocation of economic activity from less-productive to more-productive companies across all sectors, while unemployment levels are not found to be correlated with trade openness. There is also evidence that salaries in export-oriented industries decline following liberalization. The findings of studies looking for a link between trade liberalization and either labour market turbulence or increases in the own-price elasticity of labour demand, however, have been inconclusive.

Trade liberalization has been shown to have a positive impact on income and growth in the long run, at the same time that short-term negative effects were found to be weaker than expected. In the case of liberalization in Latin America and the Caribbean in the 1990s, only modest changes in the composition of employment and in labour displacement were detected. According to Reina and Zuluaga (2008), the evidence suggests that the short-term impact of trade liberalization on employment depends largely on the structure of labour markets and the regulatory framework in place. It is also important to mention that while the literature is not able to answer whether short-term effects occur via employment or salary channels, the studies agree that the overall impact is slight. These same models also reveal that FDI is highly positive for incomes in both the short and the long run (Reina and Zuluaga, 2008).

Surveys show that openness is found to be generally beneficial, but the best mix of trade and domestic-oriented policies designed to counter negative short-term effects has yet to be identified (Reina and Zuluaga, 2008; Jensen and Lee, 2007). In particular, policies are needed to facilitate the transition of workers between industries, create a safety net for affected sectors, redistribute income as needed, provide education opportunities and address bottlenecks in the response on the supply side, such as in investment in infrastructure and the availability of financing.

In terms of the impact on individual sectors, there is evidence that specific sectors gain from trade liberalization. In a study of the impact of different liberalization proposals, Polaski (2006) shows that lowering of tariffs and non-tariff barriers by 36% in developed countries and by 24% in emerging economies benefits the rural sector.[24]

The new political configuration in the United States is awarding greater importance to labour (and environmental) issues in the legislature's discussions of free trade. This became patently clear in the debates on the agreements with Colombia, Peru and Panama, in which changes had to be introduced to incorporate stricter environmental and labour standards. This trend is likely to continue given the economic slowdown that is expected in the wake of the financial crisis. The growing presence of China as a competitor is moreover fuelling initiatives to link trade to labour standards. The region needs to fine-tune its technical and its political position regarding these issues because the links between trade and labour, as well as the links between trade and the environment, rightly or wrongly, will be taking up more and more of the international agenda from now on.

D. Climate change, trade and the multilateral trading system

The recent debate on the repercussions of climate change is beginning to permeate multiple facets of economic affairs. In the realm of international trade, the situation is being diagnosed and positions are beginning to be assumed, more noticeably in Europe and the United States than anywhere else at the moment. The talks to review the Kyoto Protocol meanwhile are highlighting the need for countries to implement tax and trade policies that combat the effects of climate change. This section presents and comments upon some of the initiatives that are under discussion in the United States Congress and the European Union, paying special attention to how they might come

24 This is the so-called "Hong Kong scenario" which arose as a result of the ministerial talks on Hong Kong (Special Administrative Region of China) in December 2005. The proposal also established that the least developed countries would not lower their tariffs. All agricultural and industrial export subsidies would be eliminated.

into conflict with the multilateral WTO trade rules. The conclusions stress how important it is for the Latin America and the Caribbean to address these issues and establish a regional standpoint that will enable the region to act in a coordinated manner at international forums.

Climate change has become one of the most important challenges that the international community will have to address in the coming years. The trading system is the main focus of attention due to possible tensions arising from the conflict between trade-related proposals for tackling climate change and the core principles of international trade (non-discrimination, elimination of quantitative restrictions and non-arbitrary discrimination). Unlike other international instruments that address environmental issues, the Kyoto Protocol, which was negotiated under the United Nations Framework Conference on Climate Change, does not contain specific trade-related measures to ensure implementation even though the commitments may impact countries' competitiveness and their access to markets.[25]

Governments around the globe are drafting climate-change-related legislation in order to fulfil their international obligations, in particular in the context of the Kyoto Protocol. If enacted legislation does not take into account the core WTO principles, WTO members will probably be forced to resolve their differences in the context of the dispute settlement mechanism, which would increase the cost of cooperation and intensify opposition to the functioning of the rules-based multilateral system (Hufbauer, 2008).

Climate change concerns will influence domestic and international agendas, creating new challenges for cooperation among countries and greater tension if conflicting views on how to address its impact are not resolved. Initiatives to tackle trade-related climate change using "border adjustments measures" are emerging in developed countries (Brewer, 2007).

During 2007 and early 2008, domestic legislative initiatives were put forward in the United States and the European Union to address climate change problems and to improve the implementation of international commitments. These proposals may affect international trade by introducing measures to preserve the competitiveness of domestic industries vis-à-vis imports.

An examination of these proposals reveals an interesting paradox. Those under consideration in the United States, which has not signed the Kyoto Protocol, in addition to being unilateral, tend to be more restrictive than those of the European Union, where priority is awarded to environmental subsidies and adjusting the regulatory framework of the World Trade Organization to meet the challenges posed by climate change. The unilateral measures the United States is contemplating, moreover, could conflict with WTO rules and impose high costs on exports from Latin America and the Caribbean to the United States market. This would be particularly unfair given that, in addition to being bound by the Kyoto Protocol, the region only accounts for 6% of global carbon emissions. If the region fails to gear up properly for this debate and the subsequent negotiations, it will probably find itself once again arriving too late to do anything and in a few years' time hence having to comply with global standards that take neither its interests, nor its particularities nor its viewpoint into account. It is therefore essential for Latin America and the Caribbean to start discussing the topic within the region and to exchange experiences, technical analyses and information with a view to agreeing on a regional position on the matter. If the region fails to rise to this challenge in a timely fashion, the playing field of international trade may become even more uneven and adverse to the interests of developing countries, who will be saddled with energy and environmental standards that will stunt the development of their competitiveness.

1. The handling of climate change in the United States and the European Union

(a) Impact of United States climate change legislation on the trade prospects of Latin America and the Caribbean

In the United States, climate-change-related legislation will most likely impact commerce by imposing an additional cost on certain imports. The most advanced legislation in this regard is the Lieberman-Warner Climate Security Act of 2007 (S. 2191), or ACSA. It proposes a cap-and-trade system for firms in the electrical, industrial, and fuel and non-fuel chemicals sectors in the United States that surpass a stipulated level of greenhouse gas emissions. While the legislation is aimed primarily at domestic producers, there is great concern on the part of both industrial representatives and labour unions that the additional abatement costs will result in United States firms losing competitiveness in the

[25] With the exception of the emission-trading system. For instance, the Montreal Protocol does contain trade-related measures to ensure implementation (Cosbey and Tarasofsky, 2007).

face of imports from countries that do not have similar environmental constraints. In order to placate these fears, the ACSA bill includes a section that requires products entering the United States after 2020 to meet certain environmental requirements. This has the potential to impact trade flows from Latin America and the Caribbean.

Under the proposed legislation, when certain conditions are met —trading in products associated with greenhouse gas emissions (primary products or pollution-equivalent manufactured products) that originate in countries that are not least-developed, that emit a certain amount of global greenhouse gas emissions and whose manufacturers have not yet taken sufficient action to reduce emissions— companies importing into the United States market must purchase International Reserve Allowances before the product is allowed entry. This extra cost, which is the equivalent of a tariff on certain imports, would diminish both the profitability of Latin American and Caribbean exports and the demand for these products in the United States. The International Reserve Allowance captures the value of the tariff within the United States, partly offsetting the losses to United States consumers, but without providing any such relief to international firms. If Latin American and Caribbean firms are not well prepared to either avoid or absorb these additional costs, regional commercial activity will lose competitiveness both relative to United States producers and to other suppliers around the world.

(i) The impact on trade

It is difficult to estimate the potential impact of this legislation on the region since many of the important details are left to be developed by the United States Environmental Protection Agency (EPA) and by the Executive Branch. The methodology, price, rules, banking and other details of the International Reserve Allowance mechanism are to be established by the EPA in the future. The list of products subject to this legislation is only partially known (some specific primary goods are mentioned), while the Executive Office of the President is responsible for devising the methodology to determine which other products will be covered. The proposal aims to include goods whose manufacturing generates a substantial quantity of greenhouse gas emissions and goods that are closely related to another good whose cost of production in the United States is affected by the ACSA. In this regard, the Executive Office's interpretation of "substantial", "closely related", and the calculation of the impact of the ACSA on each industry in the United States will determine the list of products covered. In addition, the Executive Office is required to certify that a country has taken comparable steps to reduce greenhouse gas emissions, as well as to determine the country's status as a least developed country and whether it emits at least 0.5% of global greenhouse gas emissions.[26]

Since a number of very important variables are left to be determined in the future, any analysis of the potential impact of this legislation on Latin America and the Caribbean must rely on some bold assumptions. Recognizing this limitation, this analysis assumes that only imports of the products explicitly mentioned in the legislation are subject to the ACSA requirements, namely: iron, steel, aluminium, cement, bulk glass and paper. This sets a lower boundary for this variable. It is also assumed that none of the countries of Latin America and the Caribbean are able to take "comparable steps" and that each country's global share of greenhouse gas emissions in 2006 will remain the same through 2020.

Table III.8

PROJECTED SHARE OF GLOBAL GREENHOUSE GAS EMISSIONS OF SELECTED LATIN AMERICAN COUNTRIES IN 2020

Brazil	2.82%
Mexico	2.28%
Argentina	1.04%
Venezuela (Bolivarian Rep. of)	0.93% (above the 0.5% threshold)
Colombia	0.48%
Chile	0.24%
Peru	0.22%
Bolivia	0.15%
Uruguay	0.13%
Ecuador	0.12%

Source: United States Environmental Protection Agency (EPA), Oak Ridge National Laboratory Forecast and calculations of the Economic Commission for Latin America and the Caribbean (ECLAC).

A quick calculation of exports to the United States of goods originating from the Latin American and Caribbean countries that are expected to be subject to the legislation (those that produce over 0.5% of global greenhouse gas emissions, are not least developed countries and export the products mentioned above) shows that over US$ 9.1 billion or 3.4% of their trade with the United States in 2006 would be subject to the additional cost.[27] Excluding the Bolivarian Republic of Venezuela (due to its concentration on oil exports), the proportion jumps to 3.8% of the total exports of Brazil, Mexico, and Argentina to the United States.

---

26 See "S.2191—110: America's Climate Security Act of 2007", [online] http://www.govtrack.us/congress/bill.xpd?bill=s110-2191, [date of reference: 23 April 2008].

27 This number is the total for the broad product categories mentioned above since the precise list of affected product codes is not available. Only four countries emit more than 0.5% of global greenhouse gas emissions: Argentina, Brazil, Mexico and the Bolivarian Republic of Venezuela. No countries in Latin America and the Caribbean (except Haiti) are considered least developed countries by the United Nations.

Table III.9 illustrates the potential impact of the legislation on affected industries in the 33 countries of the region. Over 30% of these industries' exports to the United States market are likely to be subject to the proposed measures.

Table III.9
POTENTIAL IMPACT ON LATIN AMERICAN EXPORTS TO THE UNITED STATES OF PRODUCTS SUBJECT TO ACSA REQUIREMENTS, 2006
(Millions of United States dollars, and percentages)

	Iron+Steel	Aluminium	Cement	Glass	Paper	Total
Mexico	2 285	845	98	1 160	1 103	5 491
Brazil	2 589	507	12	23	242	3 373
Venezuela (Bol. Rep. of)	0	3	0	0	1	4
Argentina	72	175	0	8	17	273
Total (4 countries)	4 947	1 529	110	1 191	1 363	9 140
Total Latin America and the Caribbean (33 countries)	16 898	6 031	452	1 996	4 680	30 056
Four countries relative to Latin America and the Caribbean: total exports to the United States	29.3%	25.4%	24.2%	59.7%	29.1%	30.4%

Source: Economic Commission for Latin America and the Caribbean (ECLAC), on the basis of official figures.

Another potential impact is the additional leverage that such legislation would give to United States negotiators. It is easy to envision a case whereby the threat of inclusion in a list of non-compliant products or countries could be used to strengthen a negotiating position.

(ii) United States policy trends

The ACSA bill is not the only bill introduced in 2007 that proposes greenhouse gas emission controls (via cap and trade schemes) and includes an offsetting international trade component. The United States' Senate bill 1766 (S. 1766) introduced by Senators Bingaman and Specter is very similar to the ACSA bill discussed above in that it proposes that foreign importers must purchase greenhouse gas emission allowances as an alternative to offsetting tariffs. The S. 1766 bill targets the United States' top five sources of imports, which currently include Mexico.

Generally, the topic of climate change has intersected with international trade issues, and this combination in United States policy is likely to lead to a significant number of agreements over the medium term that will impact international trade in Latin America and the Caribbean.

(b) Emerging proposals in the European Union

(i) The European Parliament

On 29 November 2007, the European Parliament issued a resolution on trade and climate change calling on the European Council and the Commission of the European Communities to work towards building a consensus on a post-2012 framework through broader engagement and the inclusion of key parties currently outside of the Kyoto Protocol, notably the United States and Australia.[28]

According to the European Parliament, increasing trade should be regarded as a positive factor for economic growth and citizens' well-being once the problems relating to climate change have been taken into account. At the same time, there are concerns, however, regarding the substantial contribution that increased trade is making to climate change, and general considerations are that trade policy must therefore provide part of the solution.

As far as WTO is concerned, the European Parliament seeks to ensure that the Dispute Settlement Body acts in accordance with Article XX of the General Agreement on Tariffs and Trade, "which allows its members to take measures, including protectionist measures, necessary to protect human, animal or plant life or health or relating to the conservation of exhaustible natural resources". Also, the resolution suggests amending the WTO Agreement on Subsidies and Countervailing Measures in order to reintroduce a clause providing for the non-action ability of certain environmental subsidies. The European Parliament proposes to examine WTO-compatible mechanisms and climate-friendly trade policies in order to address the issue of third countries which are not bound by the Kyoto Protocol and to make more explicit provision for such possibilities in future versions of the Protocol. According to the resolution, trade protection measures should be taken only when alternative measures would be ineffective in achieving a given environmental objective. Finally, when trade remedies are revised, they should take into account the feasibility of introducing environmental factors in order to avoid environmental dumping of products originating from countries that do not ratify the post-Kyoto protocol.

It has been proposed that commitments to the social and environmental aspects of trade and sustainable development and to the effective implementation of multilateral environmental agreements be included in the European Union's negotiations of trade agreements with partners in Asia and Latin America.

---

[28] European Parliament non-legislative resolution of 29 November 2007 on trade and climate change (2007/2003(INI)) [online] http://www.europarl.europa.eu/oeil/FindByProcnum.do?lang=2&procnum=INI/2007/2003. Australia has since ratified the Protocol.

(ii) The European Council and the Commission of the European Communities

In March 2007, the European Council set precise and legally binding targets on greenhouse gas emissions and energy consumption. Among them are two targets worth mentioning:

- A reduction of at least 20% of greenhouse gas emissions by 2020 compared with 1990. This figure may even rise to 30% if an international agreement for the period beyond 2012 is put into place that commits other developed countries to "comparable emission reductions and economically more advanced developing countries to contributing adequately according to their responsibilities and respective capabilities".
- 20% of European Union energy consumption by 2020 covered by renewable energies.

According to these objectives, the Commission of the European Communities, on 23 January 2008, proposed a decision addressing specific measures that will strengthen and implement new policies in the European Union member States (Commission of the European Communities, 2008).

The proposal is based on the following principles:

- The targets must be met, and proposals must be effective and credible and have mechanisms for monitoring and compliance;
- The efforts required from different member States must be fair and take into account financial abilities to address the necessary investments, and proposals must be flexible to take into account different starting points and circumstances;
- The costs must be minimized, using a tailor-made design for keeping the costs of change, as well as the consequences for global competitiveness, employment and social cohesion, at the forefront of efforts in this regard;
- Member States must look beyond 2020 to make deeper cuts in greenhouse gases to meet the target of halving global emissions by 2050 by stimulating technological development and using available tools to encourage innovation and create a competitive edge in clean energy and industrial technologies; and
- A comprehensive international agreement to cut greenhouse emissions must be sought.

According to the Commission of the European Communities, an international agreement is needed in order to address the concerns of energy-intensive industries, such as ferrous and non-ferrous metal, pulp and paper, and mineral-based industries, and the impact of increased electricity prices on certain sectors. In the absence of such an agreement or of significant unilateral action by competitors in energy-intensive sectors, the European Union will take action to ensure a level playing field. Such action will be taken when certain criteria are met "to show that the extra costs could not be passed on without a significant loss of market share to less carbon-efficient competitors outside the European Union. Sectors meeting these criteria would be given some or all of their Emission Trading System allowances free of charge. This would be followed up by a review looking at the impact of international negotiations, which could lead to proposals such as adjusting the proportion of free allowances or requiring importers to enter Emission Trading System auctions to purchase allowances alongside European competitors, as long as such a system was compatible with WTO commitments" (Commission of the European Communities, 2008).

According to the Commission of the European Communities, the overall cost to the European economy of reaching all the goals considered is estimated "at just under 0.5% of GDP by 2020".

2. Domestic policies and potential problems in the context of WTO rules

The WTO rules system addresses a number of issues that may conflict with certain measures contemplated by international climate change instruments. For instance, two key rules are most-favoured-nation (Article I) and national treatment (Article III) of the General Agreement on Tariffs and Trade (GATT) that provide for non-discrimination among WTO members and between imported and national products and may be in conflict with certain climate-change-related policies that provide for differentiation among countries and products. Related to these provisions is the principle of non-discrimination of like products. Also the general prohibition of quantitative restrictions, except in specific circumstances (Article XI), may conflict somewhat with carbon-content-related measures. Measures that are not consistent with GATT provisions may be adopted under Article XX on General Exceptions.

Although in recent findings both the WTO panels and the Appellate Body have handed down recommendations that were welcomed by the environmental community, a number of untested issues have also arisen as potential areas of conflict (Green, 2005). Furthermore, some important WTO agreements have not been interpreted in the context of the Dispute Settlement Understanding, raising new concern of potential conflict stemming, for example, from the General Agreement on Trade in Services (GATS) and its relationship with the treatment of emission reductions and the Agreement on Technical Barriers to Trade.

Another area of potential conflict is related to the key concepts and definitions used in relation to the principle of non-discrimination: "like product", "like services" and "like services providers". Like-product analysis is directly related to the assessment of the treatment of a product. If products are "like", they shall be treated no less favourably than any other like product. In order to determine the "likeness" of two products, panels have adopted a non-closed list of four criteria: (a) the properties, nature and quality of the products; (b) the end-uses of the products; (c) consumers tastes and habits: and (d) the tariff classification of the products (Green, 2005). These criteria raise a number of questions about their practical application in the context of climate change. For example, whether two products that differ in terms of efficient energy consumption or the emission of greenhouse gases can be considered "like" (Green, 2005). Also, there is the more general question of whether two goods produced by different processes that have different environmental impacts can be considered "like".

Once likeness is determined, the question is whether the treatment accorded is "less favourable". In order to assess this, the panel must test if the measure changes the conditions of competition in favour of the domestic producer. Another question that has arisen is whether any less favourable treatment will be covered by GATT or only measures that have protectionist intents. The analysis of the measure will presumably require a form of discretionary balancing and, explicitly or implicitly, will examine the measure's regulatory purpose, which will limit the choice governments have to implement climate change initiatives (Green, 2005).

3. International agreements and WTO rules

Exploring the linkages between the Kyoto Protocol and WTO agreements is a complex issue. Although the Protocol does not contain specific trade-related provisions, there is a potential problem in the relationship between parties and non-parties to this agreement. Annex I of the Protocol lists the countries that are subject to Kyoto commitments and whose industrial and energy sectors will be subject to expensive adjustments. These obviously suffer a competitive disadvantage relative to the same sectors of non-parties, but trade measures to offset this competitive disadvantage in trade with non-parties and non-Annex I parties may raise concerns regarding their compatibility with WTO rules. This problem has not emerged yet, however. (Cosbey and Tarasofsky, 2007).

Emissions trading serves as a way to hold countries with high emissions accountable for the damage they cause. Under the trading scheme, industrialized countries are set emissions targets. Those countries that stay under their limits can sell their remaining capacity to countries that are over their limits —this mechanism creates the so-called "carbon market".

The cost of these "excess capacities" is high in order to put pressure on countries to comply with their targets and to promote alternative sources of energy with lower emissions. One of the major problems of this emissions 'stock-market' is the difficulty of monitoring countries' actual emissions and of setting up accounting procedures and expert review teams to keep track of their development.

In general, experts consider that tradable emissions allowances are neither goods nor services and are therefore not directly covered by WTO rules. However, if emissions were to be considered "goods" by WTO definition, then the exclusive right to trade them among Annex I parties (those parties who have committed to cutting greenhouse gas emissions) may violate the most-favoured nation principle of WTO by discriminating against non-Annex I trading partners.

On the other hand, emissions allowances inevitably have a financial value and could be considered to be negotiable instruments under GATS and specific financial services commitments, in which case they might be subject to WTO rules (Green, 2005; Cosbey and Tarasofsky, 2007).

Nevertheless, there are aspects of the emissions trading regime that may be in conflict with some WTO rules. For example, the allocation of emissions permits that do not reflect their market value may be considered subsidies under the Subsidies Agreement (Cosbey and Tarasofsky, 2007).

If goods do not face the same domestic taxes in all countries, then a unilateral carbon tax may only have the effect of giving away market share of domestic business to foreign competitors, and, in the end, global carbon emissions may be unaffected. A solution would be to team up carbon taxes with a border-tax adjustment —imported goods pay the same taxes as domestic goods, and exported domestic goods are refunded the taxes they paid. Border-tax adjustments for these sorts of taxes are permitted under GATT, but the extent to which they can apply to energy inputs is unclear and raises debates as to whether WTO permits distinctions based on the method by which a good is produced, rather than just the product as such (Cosbey and Tarasofsky, 2007).[29]

Efficiency standards that are constructed with the aim of favouring domestic industries might run afoul of the WTO Agreement on Technical Barriers to Trade. Although this agreement, unlike the SPS agreement, does not mandate a scientific basis for decisions, Article 2.2 states that when assessing risks "relevant elements of consideration are, inter alia: available scientific and technical information related processing technology or intended end-uses of products". This aspect raises concern among environmentalists regarding the cost associated with regulation in the sphere of climate change, where scientific evidence is subject to strong debate. In the context of the European Commission-asbestos case, the Appellate Body stated in its finding that a "Member is not obliged, in setting health policy, automatically to follow what, at a given time, may constitute a majority scientific opinion" (Green, 2005). This conclusion has provided some comfort to WTO critics.

Domestic regulation dealing with product characteristics will fall under the WTO Agreement on Technical Barriers to Trade. For example, mandatory requirements relating to fuel efficiency or greenhouse gas emissions, as well as labelling requirements, will fall within the scope of the Agreement. This means that they must be non-discriminatory and not be prepared, adopted or applied with a view to, or with the effect of, creating unnecessary obstacles to international trade.

Another issue that has arisen among experts is the extent to which non-product-related process and production methods are covered by GATT and the Agreement on Technical Barriers to Trade. Process and production method requirements based on energy efficiency or emissions will not be found to comply with GATT. Nevertheless, it is possible, though still under debate and a matter of interpretation, that they will be considered legitimate measures to differentiate among like products (Green, 2005).[30]

It is obvious that, as far as climate change and trade obligations are concerned, the international rules have yet to be clearly defined. The debate has already started in the United States and the European Union, and initiatives that could clash with the current multilateral trade framework are beginning to take shape. At the same time, openings for international and regional cooperation are also emerging. Latin America and the Caribbean cannot afford to remain a bystander in this debate. The region may not be a major producer of greenhouse gas emissions, but it is a significant repository of the world's biodiversity and should pay attention to the international forums where trends originate among academia before being picked up on by the media and eventually enshrined in unilateral or multilateral legal instruments. This is one area in which coordinated regional efforts could level the global playing field more by making sure that the needs of developing countries are taken into account and that the cooperation mechanisms set up to help countries gradually adjust to any new requirements are compatible with the overarching goals of sustainable development and do not have a negative impact on trade.

29 A comprehensive analysis can be found in Pauwelyn (2007).

30 Another aspect is whether, when assessing "likeness", difference in consumers' perceptions should be taken into account.

Table III.10

WTO RULES AND CLIMATE CHANGE POLICY OPTIONS

Measures to address climate change that may restrict imports		Justified under GATT articles?				
		Article I (Most favoured nation)	Article II (Tariff schedules	Article III (National treatment)	Article XI (Quotas)	Article XX (Exceptions)
Import restriction applied to penalize "foreign emitted carbon" (measure applied only to imports)	Import ban (quantitative restriction)				Violated because quotas are prohibited except in specific circumstances	**Yes.** If any provision or restriction on imports can be justified under Article XX, it is permitted even though it violates other GATT rules Whether a trade-restrictive measure is determined to be "necessary" under Article XX requires consideration of three factors: (1) how trade-restrictive the challenged measure is; (2) the value of what the measure is designed to protect; (3) the contribution of the measure to the objective However, even "necessary" trade-restrictive measures should not discriminate between trading partners or against imports by comparison with domestic goods
	Additional or punitive tariff	Violated if tariffs are discriminatory among WTO members	Violated because tariff commitments are based on bindings			
	Anti-dumping or countervailing duties	No permitted. Under present GATT rules, even if the exporting country does not restrict its carbon emissions, the social cost of carbon cannot be labelled as dumping or a subsidy. The failure to impose a carbon tax or otherwise internalize the full price of carbon does not currently give other WTO members the right to impose penalty duties on imports				
	Carbon tax	Permitted as long as the taxes do not discriminate among WTO members		Not violated. Carbon taxes can be justified as an "internal tax" under GATT Article III:2 and thus can be adjusted at the border		
Competitive provision applied as an extension of the domestic climate policy of the United States (measure applied both to domestic production and imports)	Cap-and-trade system	Permitted as long as the taxes do not discriminate among WTO members		Not violated. The cost of purchasing carbon credits can be justified as an "internal tax" or "other internal charge of any kind" under GATT Article III:2 and thus can be adjusted at the border		
	Quantitative carbon regulation	Permitted as long as the taxes do not discriminate among WTO members		Not violated. Article III permits regulations as long as they are not discriminatory. However, there is a "product" versus "process" issue. Even if a carbon regulation can not be adjusted at the border by imposing a tax under GATT rules, extension of the regulation to imports could be justified under the Agreement on Technical Barriers to Trade		

Source: Gary Clyde Hufbauer, "Climate Change: Competitiveness Concerns and Prospects for Engaging Developing Countries", testimony before the Subcommittee on Energy and Air Quality, United States House of Representatives, 2008, on the basis of J. Pauwelyn, "U.S. Federal Climate Policy and Competitiveness Concerns: The Limits and Options of International Trade Law", *Working Paper*, No. 07-02, Nicholas Institute for Environmental Policy Solutions, Duke University, 2007.

E. Conclusions

The situation described in this chapter poses both enormous challenges and opportunities for the region. The countries of Latin America and the Caribbean need to work together as effectively as possible to identify regional and global support mechanisms that will enable them to find constructive ways to handle the changes that the new international scenario is demanding with regard to trade security, quality standards and certification, private-sector standards and the links between trade and labour, trade and the environment and trade and climate change.

The challenge facing the region is huge. New requirements in any of the aforementioned areas could seriously hamper the competitiveness of the region's exports if they become obligatory or if protectionist elements are incorporated into their design for the supposed purpose of "equalizing conditions for competition" with local production in industrialized countries, as sometimes occurs in the area of labour rights, environmental protection and, more recently, climate change. In the case of climate change, the arsenal of initiatives is so vast that it ranges from tariff surcharges (or their equivalent through the requirement to acquire international emissions rights), to new types of subsidies, trade remedies (safeguards and antidumping measures) or even, in regard to emission requirements, "equal conditions" regardless of each region's relative contribution to global greenhouse emissions. It is a shame that the argument for creating "equal conditions for competition" is not applied more enthusiastically to the export subsidies and domestic support measures currently distorting world trade in agriculture. The region must start preparing itself for the debates that lie ahead. These issues are going to find their way into international negotiations sooner than expected, and it is absolutely imperative that the region comes to the table with a clear idea of the objectives, the lines of defence and the main alliances involved. Multilateral organizations also face a significant challenge in this respect inasmuch as they will have to perform on-going diagnoses of the situation and put forward informed and up-to-date proposals that will both safeguard the interests of the developing countries and defend multilateral forums as the best-positioned instances for providing governance in these complex globalization issues.

Bibliography

Alvarez, M. (2008), "C-TPAT and AEO: new channels for world trade", *FAL Bulletin*, No. 258, Santiago, Chile, Economic Commission for Latin America and the Caribbean (ECLAC), February.

BancoMext (2007), "Estiman que 60% de la mercancía importada por EU es vía C-TPAT" [online] www.buyinmexico.com.mx, July.

Bergsten, F., R. Keohane and J. Nye (1975), "International economics and international politics: a framework for analysis", *International Organization,* vol. 29, No. 1.

Brewer, Thomas L. (2007), *U.S. Climate Change Policies and International Trade Policies: Intersections and Implications for International Negotiations*, Washington, D.C., Georgetown University Press, November.

Canale, Felipe and Marta Pardo Leal (2006), "Estudio técnico-legal sobre las capacidades fitosanitarias de los países miembros del organismo internacional regional de sanidad agropecuaria (OIRSA)", *FAO Legal Papers Online series,* No. 50 [online] http://www.fao.org/legal/prs-ol/lpo50es.pdf, January.

Castells, Manuel (2000), "La factoría", No. 12, June-September [online] http://www.lafactoriaweb.com/articulos/castells12.htm.

CBP (United States Cusoms and Border Protection) (2007), "Cost/Benefit Survey" [online] www.cbp.gov, August.

___ (2004), "Securing the Global Supply Chain" [online] www.cbp.gov, November.

Commission of the European Communities (2008), "Communication from the Commission to the Council, the European Parliament, the European Economic and Social Committee and the Committee of the Regions: 20 20 by 2020. Europes climate change opportunity" (COM(2008) 30 final) [online] http://eur-lex.europa.

eu/LexUriServ/LexUriServ.do?uri=COM:2008:0030:FIN:EN:PDF.

___ (2003), "Communication from the Commission to the Council, the European Parliament, the European Economic and Social Committee and the Committee of the Regions on enhancing maritime transport security" (COM(2003) 229 final), Brussels.

Cosbey, Aaron and Richard Tarasofsky (2007), *Climate Change, Competitiveness and Trade*, Chatham House.

Díaz, Alejandra (2005), "Las nuevas medidas de seguridad y sus efectos en las exportaciones agrícolas", Mexico City, ECLAC subregional headquarters in Mexico, unpublished.

ECLAC (Economic Commission for Latin America and the Caribbean) (2007), *Latin America and the Caribbean in the World Economy, 2006. Trends 2007* (LC/G.2341-P/E), Santiago, Chile. United Nations publication, Sales No. E.07.II.G.85.

Elliot, Kimberly Ann (2004), "Labor standards and the FTAA", *Integrating the Americas: FTAA and Beyond*, Antoni Estevadeordal, Dani Rodrik, Alan M. Taylor and Andrés Velasco (eds.), Harvard University.

European Commission (2007), *Authorised Economic Operators: Guidelines* (TAXUD/2006/1450), Brussels.

Expansión.com (2007), "El certificado aduanero crea oportunidad de negocio" [online] www.Expansión.com, 18 May.

Fairtrade Labelling Organizations (FTO) (2007), "Generic Fairtrade Standards for Hired Labour", March.

FAO (Food and Agriculture Organization of the United Nations) (2006), *Resultado de la Conferencia electrónica: las buenas prácticas agrícolas (BPA). En búsqueda de la sostenibilidad, competitividad y seguridad alimentaria (19 de julio - 9 de agosto de 2004)*, Santiago, Chile, FAO Regional Office for Latin America and the Caribbean.

___ (2003a), "Item 6: A Framework for Good Agricultural Practices", Committee on Agriculture, seventeenth session, Rome, 31 March to 4 April [online] www.fao.org/unfao /bodies/coag/coag17/coag17-e.htm.

___ (2003b), *Summary Analysis of Relevant Codes, Guidelines, and Standards Related to Good Agricultural Practice. Background paper for the FAO Expert consultation on GAP*, FAO GAP Working Paper series, No. 2, Rome.

___ (2002), "Food Quality and Safety Systems - A Training Manual on Food Hygiene and the Hazard Analysis and Critical Control Point (HACCP) System" [online] http://www.fao.org/docrep/w8088e/w8088e00.htm.

___ (2000), *Impact of Technical Obstacles and Non-Tariff Barriers on Agricultural Trade in Latin America and the Caribbean* (LARC/00/2), Twenty-sixth FAO Regional Conference for Latin America and the Caribbean, Mérida, 10-14 April.

FAO/EMBRAPA (Food and Agriculture Organization of the United Nations/ Brazilian Agricultural Research Enterprise) (2002), *Guideliness for Good Agricultural Practices*, Brasilia.

Friedman, Thomas (2006), *The World is Flat. A Brief History of the Twenty-first Century*, Farrar, Strauss and Giroux.

Foro de la Cadena Agroindustrial Argentina (2005), *Buenas prácticas agrícolas. Diagnósticos y propuestas: el primer eslabón*, Buenos Aires, October.

Green, Andrew (2005), "Climate change, regulatory policy and the WTO. How constraining are trade rules?", *Journal of International Economic Law*, vol.8, No. 1.

Hoekman , Bernard y Michel M. Kostecki (2001), T*he Political Economy of the World Trading System: The WTO and Beyond*, Oxford University Press.

Hong Kong Trade Development Council (2005), "Issue 02" [online] www.tdctrade.com, February.

Hufbauer, Gary Clyde (2008), "Climate Change: Competitiveness Concerns and Prospects for Engaging Developing Countries", testimony before the Subcommittee on Energy and Air Quality, United States House of Representatives, Committee on Energy and Commerce.

Humphrey, John (2006), *Global Value Chains in the Agrifood Sector*, Vienna, United Nations Organization on Industrial Development (UNIDO).

Inside U.S. Trade (2008a), vol. 26, No. 22, 30 May.

___ (2008b), vol. 26, No. 17, 25 April.

___ (2007a), vol. 25, No. 48, 7 December.

___ (2007b), "U.S., EU set to unveil C-TPAT, AEO mutual recognition road map", vol. 25, No. 44, November.

___ (2007c), vol. 25, No. 25, 22 June.

Jaffee, S. (2003), "From Challenge to Opportunity: Transforming Kenya's Fresh Vegetable Trade in the Context of Emerging Food Safety and Other Standards in Europe", *Agricultural and Rural Development Discussion Paper*, No. 2, Washington, D.C., World Bank.

Jansen, Marion and Eddy Lee (2007), *Trade and Employment: Challenges for Policy Research*, Geneva, International Labour Office/Secretariat of the World Trade Organization.

Pauwelyn, Joost (2007), "U.S. Federal Climate Policy and Competitiveness Concerns: The Limits and Options of International Trade Law", *Working Paper*, No. 07-02, Nicholas Institute for Environmental Policy Solutions, Duke University.

Polaski, S. (2006), *Winner and Losers: Impact of the Doha Development Round on Developing Coutnries*, Washington, D.C., Carnegie Endowment fo International Peace.

Razo, Carlos and others (2007a), "Biocombustibles y su impacto potencial en la estructura agraria, precios y empleo en América Latina", *Desarrollo productivo series*, No. 178 (LC/L.2768-P), Santiago, Chile, Economic Commission for Latin America and the Caribbean (ECLAC). United Nations publication, Sales No. S.07.II.G.104.

___ (2007b), "Producción de biomasa para biocombustibles líquidos: el potencial de América Latina y el Caribe", *Desarrollo productivo series*, No. 181 (LC/L.2803-P), Santiago, Chile, Economic Commission for Latin America and the Caribbean (ECLAC). United Nations publication, Sales No. S.07.II.G.136.

Reina, Mauricio and Sandra Zuluaga (2008), "Comercio y pobreza: análisis comparativo de la evidencia para América Latina", *Comercio internacional series*, No. 87 (LC/L.2903-P), Santiago, Chile, Economic Commission for Latin America and the Caribbean (ECLAC). United Nations publication, Sales No. S.08.II.G.39.

Salles de Almeida, Juliana (2008), "Normas privadas: el nuevo desafío de las exportaciones de los países en desarrollo", *Comercio internacional series*, No. 85 (LC/L.2861-P), Santiago, Chile, Economic Commission for Latin America and the Caribbean (ECLAC). United Nations publication, Sales No. S.08.II.G.06.

Santacoloma, Pilar (n/d), "Costs and managerial skills in organic certified products", Rome [online] http://www.fao.org/docs/eims/upload/229934/2005_12_doc10.pdf.

Sanz, Carlos and others (2004), *Plan Nacional para la Implementación de Buenas Practicas Agrícolas*, Bogotá, Ministerio de Agricultura y Desarrollo Rural, Dirección de Desarrollo Tecnológico y Protección Sanitaria, December.

UNCTAD (United Nations Conference on Trade and Development) (2005), Trade, environment and development (TD/B/COM.1/70), Trade and Development Board, Commission on Trade in Goods and Services, and Commodities, 7 January.

___ (1999), Report of the Expert Meeting on Examining trade in the agricultural sector, with a view to expanding the agricultural exports of the developing countries, and to assisting them in better understanding the issues at stake in the upcoming agricultural negotiations (TD/B/COM.1/EM.8/2), February.

WHO (World Health Organization) (2007a), "Food safety and foodborne illness", *Fact Sheet*, No. 237, March.

___ (2007b), *World Health Report, 2007. A Safer Future: Global Public Health Security in the 21st Century,* Geneva.

___ (2002) "Foodborne diseases, emerging", *Fact Sheet*, No. 124, January.

World Bank (2007), *World Development Report, 2008. Agriculture for Development*, Washington, D.C.

WTO (World Trade Organization) (2007), Private standards and the SPS Agreement (G/SPS/GEN/746), Geneva, 24 January.

Chapter IV

Integration and trade initiatives

Introduction

The international agenda calls for more cooperation among the countries of Latin America and the Caribbean if they are to improve their position in the global economy. This cooperation is needed not only in terms of competitiveness and innovation, but also regarding issues related to trade and security, climate change and energy efficiency. New reforms, investments and management approaches will be needed, as well as coordination among customs, ports and the many external trade agencies, in order to satisfy the requirements of the main markets. In all such areas, the governments of the region need to agree on positions and speak with one voice in international negotiation forums, while at the same time making the necessary efforts at home to tie this in with new business opportunities and increased competitiveness. All of these tasks would benefit from broad and unified markets and gradual convergence in a series of related public policies. The region needs to raise the degree and quality of integration in order to implement those national strategies for international integration that have the greatest impact on the challenges of growth and equity.

With considerable uncertainty dogging the international context, and especially exports to the United States, strenuous efforts are being made within integration schemes to move forward with community commitments on trade facilitation. One example is the adoption of a unified customs document and the harmonization of customs regimes within the Andean Community. Similarly, the Council of Ministers for Economic Integration (COMIECO) of the Central American Common Market (CACM) approved and updated a series of technical regulations on standardization measures, metrology and authorization procedures, as well as sanitary and phytosanitary measures and procedures.

Efforts have also been made to boost trade strategies aimed at increasing regional interdependencies. Examples include the promotion of the South American Community of Nations (UNASUR), the Mesoamerican Integration and Development Project (Mesoamerica Project), formerly the Puebla-Panama Plan (PPP), as well as efforts by countries that make up the Latin American Pacific Basin Initiative to generate synergies in trade relations with countries of the Asia-Pacific region (especially China, India and countries of the Association of South-East Asian Nations (ASEAN)). Lastly, countries of the Caribbean (in 2007) and of Central America and the Andean Community (in 2008) have been involved in trade negotiations with the European Union (see chapter V).

The failure of the Doha Round means there is now more political time available for regional integration. The Government of Mexico is seeking to unify its trade agreements with Central American countries to allow accumulation of origin. Mexico and Central America are in turn requesting accumulation of origin in their agreements with European Union partners, which will promote business partnerships that can take advantage of Mesoamerican and European markets. Brazil is promoting negotiations between MERCOSUR and Central America, and is organizing a Latin American Summit on Integration in December. The 11 economies that make up the Latin American Pacific Basin Initiative (Colombia, Costa Rica, Chile, Ecuador, El Salvador, Guatemala, Honduras, Mexico, Nicaragua, Panama and Peru) are preparing a joint proposal for the governments of the Asia-Pacific region to include accumulation of origin in agreements between them. These good tidings would have even greater repercussions if Brazil's prominent role in the Doha negotiations and the international recognition of Mexico and Brazil as members of G5 (along with China, India and South Africa) were to boost integration, strengthen links between Mexico and Central America and South America and facilitate convergence on the basis of realistic foundations that are compatible with the global economy's demands for innovation and competitiveness.

A. Current situation and recent progress

Intraregional trade flows are still small compared to total exports in Latin America and the Caribbean, standing at around 18% in 2006-2007. However, the situation varies greatly among countries. In some cases, such as Mexico, around 5% of exports go to the region, while in countries such as Bolivia and El Salvador the figure is over 60%.[1] Furthermore, trade density within integration schemes in the last five years amounts to no more than 15% in MERCOSUR and 10% in the Andean Community, while in the Central American Common Market (CACM) the figure is about 30% if maquila is included and 18% otherwise.[2]

In 2007, intraregional trade again registered double-digit growth, although the rise was lower than in previous years. This was nonetheless sufficient to push up the ratio of intraregional exports to 19%. In the first quarter of 2008, intraregional exports continued to expand, offsetting to some extent the contraction in exports to the United States. All groups show an upward trend in comparison with the first quarter of 2007 (see table IV.1).

The low ratios of intraregional trade show that its potential is underused, especially in certain subregional schemes. Progress has also been limited in the formation of intraregional production chains linked to integration schemes, which could take advantage of preferential access to markets outside the region as provided in trade agreements. Deeper integration would be a key factor in attracting investment in such production chains, especially for smaller countries. However, the persistence of non-tariff restrictions, the absence of clear rules and the corresponding lack of legal certainty do little to boost investment.

In recent years, the international expansion of certain companies has resulted in an increase in foreign investment, especially in Argentina, Brazil, Chile and Mexico. Latin American investment abroad stood at US$ 40 billion in 2006 and US$ 20.6 billion in 2007.[3] Trans-Latins have become an increasingly significant phenomenon, and currently account for around 8% of inflows of foreign direct investment (FDI) to Latin America and the Caribbean,[4] especially in the sectors

1 ECLAC (2008c), table 2.2.2.45.

2 Estimates from ECLAC.

3 The difference is due to a specific operation by Brazil in 2006 (ECLAC, 2008b).

4 Given the problems with data, the information provided reflects magnitudes and trends (rather than precise figures).

of natural resources and natural-resource-based manufactures, food and beverages and commerce and services (with this last sector representing approximately half of the total). However, for Central America and the Dominican Republic, trans-Latins represent 20% of total FDI, or almost 40% if United States investment is removed from the equation. It is interesting to note that, in the case of services, FDI is the principal means for suppliers to offer services abroad. The Mexico telecoms company América Movil, Telmex and retailer Cencosud of Chile offer examples of this.

Table IV.1

LATIN AMERICA AND THE CARIBBEAN: TOTAL EXPORTS BY SUBREGIONAL INTEGRATION SCHEME, 1990–2007

(Millions of current dollars and percentages)

	1990	1995	1998	2002	2003	2004	2005	2006	2007	Jan-Mar 2007	Jan-Mar 2008[a]
Latin American Integration Association (LAIA)											
Total exports (1)	112 694	204 170	251 345	319 807	346 145	427 835	506 557	602 803	675 139	154 001	189 416
Exports to LAIA (2)	13 589	35 471	43 118	36 164	40 872	56 777	72 979	91 757	107 586	22 664	29 678
Percentage intrasubregional exports (2:1)	12.1	17.4	17.2	11.3	11.8	13.3	14.4	15.2	15.9	14.7	15.7
Andean Community											
Total exports (1)	31 751	39 134	38 896	52 177	54 716	74 140	100 089	126 112	139 102	29 596	44 213
Exports to Andean Community (2)	1 312	4 812	5 504	5 227	4 900	7 604	10 313	12 719	12 909	2 622	4 012
Percentage intrasubregional exports (2:1)	4.1	12.3	14.2	10.0	9.0	10.5	10.3	10.1	9.3	8.9	9.1
Southern Common Market (MERCOSUR)											
Total exports (1)	46 403	70 129	80 227	89 500	106 674	134 196	162 512	188 188	221 498	46 749	56 718
Exports to MERCOSUR (2)	4 127	14 199	20 322	10 197	12 709	17 319	21 134	26 626	33 051	6 807	9 415
Percentage intrasubregional exports (2:1)	8.9	20.2	25.3	11.4	11.9	12.9	13.0	14.1	14.9	14.6	16.6
Central American Common Market (CACM)											
Total exports b (1)	4 480	8 745	14 987	17 006	18 117	19 767	21 849	24 493	26 036	6 795	7 257
Exports to CACM (2)	624	1 451	2 754	2 871	3 110	3 506	3 912	4 429	5 217	1 218	1 305
Percentage intrasubregional exports (2:1)	13.9	16.6	18.4	16.9	17.2	17.7	17.9	18.1	20.0	17.9	18.0
Caribbean Community (CARICOM)											
Total exports (1)	4 118	5 598	4 790	5 732	6 712	7 880	15 949	18 709	19 872	5 734.3	5 666.2
Exports to CARICOM (2)	509	843	1 031	1 220	1 419	1 810	2 091	2 427	2 793	693.9	775.2
Percentage intrasubregional exports (2:1)	10.3	14.2	18.6	17.2	16.5	17.4	13.1	13.0	14.1	12.1	13.7
Latin America and the Caribbean											
Total exports c (1)	130 214	227 922	280 065	347 610	376 590	472 444	568 798	679 713	761 959	167 356	203 061
Exports to Latin America and the Caribbean d (2)	18 727	45 180	56 644	53 424	59 635	79 952	99 839	121 923	144 211	30 600	39 063
Percentage intraregional exports (2:1)	13.9	19.8	20.2	15.4	15,8	16.9	17.6	17.9	18.9	18.3	19.2

Source: Economic Commission for Latin America and the Caribbean (ECLAC), on the basis of official figures from the respective subregional groupings and the International Monetary Fund (IMF), *Direction of Trade Statistics.*

[a] Preliminary figures.

[b] Figures include maquila trade.

[c] Includes LAIA, CACM, the CARICOM countries, Panama, Cuba and the Dominican Republic.

[d] Includes intrasubregional trade in the Andean Community, MERCOSUR, CACM, CARICOM and trade between Chile and Mexico and the rest of the region, as well as trade between groups, plus exports from Cuba, Panama and the Dominican Republic to other countries in the region.

Although this emerging process of internationalization is one of the most noteworthy features of regional economic events, unfortunately it is not linked with integration decisions. Any effort to deepen integration must seek to strengthen links with the regional actors of internationalization for the sake of both the expansion of companies involved and the relevance and effectiveness of the integration process (see section E).

Despite the significant conceptual and instrumental renewal —which ECLAC termed "open regionalism"— in the 1990s and a sharp rise in intraregional trade since the end of that decade, progress in integration processes has been uneven. Some schemes have maintained the drive for renewal, others have developed new initiatives to complement existing ones (such as UNASUR), while yet others have lost momentum following rapid initial progress.

In Central America, regional integration has received fresh impetus. One milestone in this process was the Plan of Action for Central American Economic Integration, signed in 2002 by the governments of the subregion as a mechanism for transitioning from CACM to a customs union. Other important measures have included the creation of a regional dispute settlement mechanism and the establishment of integrated customs houses to speed up the movement of merchandise. Lastly, in February 2007 Central American countries signed the Protocol to the Treaty on Investment and Trade in Services, which is in the process of being ratified. The Protocol takes an ambitious approach to bringing trade in services and investment into Central American integration.

In Central America, free trade agreements with partners outside the region (United States) and the possible association agreement with the European Union are all helping to modernize the subregion's integration scheme and tackle the new issues within interregional as well as intraregional relations.

Integration has intensified in the Caribbean as well, albeit not at the pace some of the countries had hoped. The Caribbean Common Market came into force with a membership of 12 countries and in mid–2007 the subgroup of Eastern Caribbean countries also agreed to set up an economic union. In December 2007, the Caribbean Forum of the African, Caribbean and Pacific Group of States (CARIFORUM), which includes the Dominican Republic, concluded negotiations for an association agreement with the European Union, which is a significant step forward for this group of countries.

A number of achievements have been made in South America, with the Andean Community's social development programmes and the MERCOSUR Structural Convergence Fund, while efforts continue towards the development of single customs codes and the full implementation of the common external tariff. However, market constraints, problems stemming from asymmetries among certain members and the way in which bilateral differences have been handled bear witness to major ongoing institutional weaknesses.

B. Main initiatives in integration schemes

1. Andean Community

Trade between the four member countries of the Andean Community expanded by 13% in 2007, giving an intraregional trade ratio of just 9.3%: the lowest out of all the subregional integration schemes. If the Bolivarian Republic of Venezuela is considered part of the group, for the purposes of trade, intra-Andean trade rose by barely 3% that year as a result of the huge decline in exports from Bolivia and the Bolivarian Republic of Venezuela to the rest of the subregion.

Advances were made in trade facilitation among members in the second half of 2007 and the first six months of 2008. In July 2007, the Andean Community adopted Decision 670 on the creation of a unified customs document, which will be implemented alongside the harmonization of customs regimes from 1 June 2009 (see Decisions 670 and 671 of the *Gaceta judicial del Acuerdo de Cartagena,* 2007).

Other results have been achieved in terms of standardization, mutual recognition and conformity assessment and technical regulation activities. Measures have also been taken to harmonize formats and procedures for presentation and recognition of Compulsory Sanitary Notification in member countries.

Talks are still under way on setting up the Andean services market. In July 2007, representatives of the countries examined several options for moving ahead with the liberalization of the market for professional services, financial services and television, among others. Some progress has been made towards defining a regime to regulate the liberalization of financial services community-wide. This regime should be completed by 30 September 2008, according to Decision 659 of December 2006, which was formulated to govern these proceedings. In addition, following intensive joint technical and diplomatic lobbying, the Andean countries persuaded the world's top telecommunications body to extend by three years the time frame for the launch of the Andean Community's satellite network. The deadline for the satellite network is now 18 September 2010, thereby removing the risk of losing the satellite position for the time being.

In conjunction with experts from the Pan American Health Organization (PAHO), the World Health Organization (WHO) and the Secretary General of the Andean Community, the statistical offices of the countries' Ministries of Health are carrying out a study on harmonizing health indicators, in order to ensure proper follow-up for projects implemented under the Community's Integrated Plan for Social Development.

The Andean Council of Ministers of Foreign Affairs set up the Consultative Council for the Indigenous Peoples of the Andean Community to replace the Roundtable on the Rights of Indigenous Peoples, in an attempt to increase the participation of indigenous peoples in the subregional integration process.

The statistical institutes of member countries will extend the harmonization programme beyond economic indicators to include social, environmental and security indicators.

The United States extended the Andean Trade Promotion and Drug Eradication Act (ATPDEA) until December 2008. As a condition of approval of its free trade agreement with the United States, the Government of Peru had to amend the previously negotiated chapters on labour and the environment to take account of the May 2007 legislative agreement of the United States Congress on trade agreements (ECLAC, 2007a, p. 117), incorporating commitments that are more binding on domestic legislation and relate to the International Labour Organization (ILO) Declaration on Fundamental Principles and Rights at Work, adopted in 1998. It was also made obligatory to sign seven agreements on the environment and undertake to implement any multilateral agreements signed. These amendments were approved by the Peruvian Congress. At the request of the Government of Peru, the Andean Community reformulated Decision 486 on intellectual property to adopt a more flexible approach to the matter and combine protection of intellectual property rights with multilateral requirements and standards. In its new form, Decision 486 enables Peru to comply with commitments undertaken as part of the free trade agreement with the United States. Colombia will need to implement similar reforms if the United States Congress gives the green light to the free trade agreement with the country. Bolivia did not give its support to this new community legislation and indeed continues to reject it. The Bolivian authorities have, in fact, stated their intention of seeking to derogate and annul the decision by legal means before the Andean Court of Justice. All this has eroded Bolivia's already deteriorated relations with its Andean Community partners.

The Government of Bolivia trusts that the country can become a full member of MERCOSUR without having to relinquish full membership of the Andean Community, and can thus act as a bridge between the two integration schemes. This is another situation that the authorities of the Andean Community must consider.

Negotiations to admit Panama as an associate member of the Andean Community are ongoing. Such a step would be expected to raise the profile of logistics and business services on the Andean agenda, given Panama's interesting achievements in those areas.

2. Caribbean Community (CARICOM)

Although the governments of the CARICOM member countries formally declared their interest in advancing towards the CARICOM Single Market and Economy (CSME) in 2006, the formation of a single economy remains delayed.

As some of the group's main members, including Jamaica, are not in a position to meet these requirements, monetary union remains a distant proposition. For the moment, monetary integration is suspended owing to a lack of economic convergence.

The single market implies the free movement of goods, services, capital and skilled workers in the region; the right to set up businesses without restriction; and the implementation of a common tariff[5] and single trade policy. The aim of CSME is therefore to supplement the existing free trade area by suspending all quantitative restrictions and other trade barriers between member countries. Preparations are also under way for a common regional investment programme to facilitate the transition towards the free movement of capital.

The single economy also refers to deeper integration requiring macroeconomic coordination, harmonization of policies, laws and regulations in various economic areas, and the development of regional sectoral programmes in agriculture, industry and transport. CSME is expected to be implemented in two phases.

The first phase (2008-2010) will focus on consolidating the single market and preparing for the single economy. The main pillars will include a broadening of the categories of professionals allowed to move freely, full implementation of the free movement of service providers, approval of the CARICOM investment regime, setting up of a regional stock market, preparation of a regional development strategy and creation of a regional development fund. This phase is also expected to see agreement among the central banks on the unit of common currency.

In the second phase (2011-2015), the partners will seek to complete the single economy by harmonizing tax systems, the financial climate and fiscal and monetary policies; setting up the CARICOM monetary union; and implementing the regional competition policy, intellectual property regime and common sectoral policies in agriculture, energy, transport, small and medium-sized enterprises and tourism.

Some of the major regional institutions to have been set up under the umbrella of CARICOM include the Regional Negotiating Machinery (CRNM) for extraregional negotiations, the Caribbean Court of Justice for the settlement of disputes relating to the application of the CARICOM treaty, the Caribbean Regional Technical Assistance Centre (CARTAC) and the Caribbean Disaster Emergency Response Agency (CDERA). In January 2008, the CARICOM Competition Commission was established.

The group has also provided for macroeconomic coordination, with regular meetings of Ministers of Finance and Governors, as well as biannual publications of the Caribbean Centre for Monetary Studies (CCMS) on performance and convergence of the Caribbean economies.

Caribbean integration does not concern itself particularly with asymmetry among CARICOM members. However, the Economic Partnership Agreement recently concluded between CARIFORUM and the European Union contains elements of differentiated treatment. For instance, a distinction is made between less developed countries (LDCs) and more developed countries (MDCs), which affects the level of liberalization in service sectors.

In July 2008, the twenty-ninth Annual Summit of the Caribbean Community concluded in Antigua and Barbuda. At the close of the meeting, major concerns were expressed over non-fulfilment of some important decisions. Qualified spokespersons have described the state of integration as being at a standstill, shackled by the failure to give legislative approval to the Caribbean Community Act, which was put forward in 1992 and which would make CARICOM decisions automatically effective in all member countries (Girvan, 2008). According to this author, countries need to surrender some of their sovereignty to the regional bloc, otherwise its cohesion will be weakened. In this respect, Guyana and Suriname recently joined UNASUR, while Dominica, Saint Vincent and the Grenadines and Antigua and Barbuda joined the Bolivarian Alternative for Latin America and the Caribbean (ALBA) and the Peoples' Trade Treaty (TCP).

In May 2008, the Organisation of Eastern Caribbean States (OECS)[6] presented the draft of the new OECS treaty, which outlines the details of the drive for OECS to become an economic union. At the same time, focus groups were set up to raise public awareness about the content and scope of the initiative. During the 26 years OECS has been in existence, employment and labour migration have been included among the issues considered key for deepening integration (OECS, 2008).

5 The common tariff was adopted in 1994, but its implementation has been extremely slow. Only 11 of the 15 countries involved apply the common tariff. As a result, the average external tariff dropped from 20% in the 1990s to 10% at present. However, there is considerable scope for exceptions at the national level that hamper the application of the common tariff.

6 The member countries of OECS are Antigua and Barbuda, Montserrat, Saint Kitts and Nevis, Saint Lucia and Saint Vincent and the Grenadines.

3. Central American Common Market (CACM)

Intraregional trade continues to grow every year as a percentage of total trade, and in 2007 amounted to US$ 5.2 billion or 20% of the total (the highest percentage of intraregional trade among all the integration schemes of Latin America and Caribbean). At the same time, CACM has successfully consolidated its exports to third markets, especially those with which the group —or individual countries within in— have concluded free trade agreements (United States, Mexico, Panama, Canada, Dominican Republic, Chile and CARICOM). As of December 2007, 70% of the subregion's exports enjoyed tariff preferences through such agreements, and this is expected to rise to over 80% when the Agreement of Association is concluded with the European Union.

Costa Rica has ratified the Dominican Republic - Central America - United States Free Trade Agreement (CAFTA-DR),[7] but intellectual property legislation and a legal framework on competition matters still need to be approved in order for the public institutions to operate under a market regime. By mid-August 2008 the Costa Rican legislature had passed a dozen complementary laws and has until the end of the year to approve the remaining pieces of legislation. The process of legislative approval includes two plenary votes, signature by the executive body and publication in the official legal journal.

The countries of CACM have signed a framework agreement for the establishment of a customs union. Panama has stated its intention to join this union as well as the Central American Integration System (SICA). All the countries of Central America, except Costa Rica, have announced their decision to negotiate a free trade agreement with CARICOM.

Another relevant factor in Central America is the growing presence of China in the trade of Central American countries. In 2007, China was the fifth largest seller to Central America (4.9% of total imports), and its fourth largest buyer (5.3% of total exports) (SIECA, 2008). Having established diplomatic relations with China, the government of Costa Rica is now exploring the possibility of trade negotiations with the Asian giant, which would pose a new long-term challenge to Central American countries in terms of their capacity to conduct joint negotiations with main trading partners.

New trade-facilitation measures have been promoted in order to make the most of the buoyant internal market and strengthen export competitiveness. For instance, the Council of Ministers for Economic Integration (COMIECO) approved, udpated and amended a series of technical regulations on standardization measures, metrology and authorization procedures, as well as on sanitary and phytosanitary measures and procedures. To make all these measures viable, the Council also amended the Uniform Central American Customs Code (CAUCA) and its regulations. Both instruments were approved in April 2008 and will enter into force on 25 August 2008.

In addition to the progress made so far in the establishment of a customs union and in the areas of trade liberalization and tariff harmonization, improvements have been made to customs administration in the subregion through the increasing application by government authorities of the CAUCA and its regulations (RECAUCA) and the use of the corresponding registries (for sanitary measures, pesticides, natural products, official national laboratories, etc.). Furthermore, merchandise clearance and valuation procedures have been streamlined. Integrated and peripheral customs have been set up within the customs territory to speed up the passage of merchandise and people in transit, and the costs and times involved in completing customs procedures have been reduced. Peripheral customs have been set up in El Salvador (the port of Acajutla and the port of Cutuco), in Guatemala (Tecún Umán, Puerto Quetzal, Santo Tomás de Castilla and Puerto Barrios), in Honduras (Puerto Cortés) and in Nicaragua (Peñas Blancas). A project is also underway to create a unified customs information system for Central America within the framework of European Union-Central American cooperation to make it possible to track merchandise circulating within the Central American customs territory and ensure the transparent handling and fair distribution of fiscal income. Steps are also being taken to harmonize sanitary and phytosanitary measures as well as the institutional-juridical framework (Schatan and others, 2008).

At the thirty-second regular meeting of the Heads of State and Government of the Central American Integration System (SICA), held on 27 June 2008 in San Salvador, delegates discussed the social aspects of integration, food security and advances in the integration process. As far as social issues are concerned, participants reviewed and

[7] CAFTA-DR was finalized by the United States in 2005. The Senate ratified the Agreement on 30 June and the Chamber of Representatives did so on 27 July. President George W. Bush signed the Agreement into law on 2 August 2005. The Central American countries completed the legislative process between December 2004 and October 2005. The first country to legally adopt the Agreement was El Salvador (17 December 2004), followed by Honduras (3 March 2005), Guatemala (10 March 2005), the Dominican Republic (6 September 2005) and Nicaragua (10 October 2005).

enhanced the Strategic Social Agenda of Central America. They also examined the impact of higher food prices on food security and social indicators in Central America, and arranged coordination measures to improve food and nutritional security for the most vulnerable groups. Some of these measures consist of plans to increase production and productivity of basic grains and a programme of the Central American Bank for Economic Integration (CABEI) to allocate funds to boost the subregion's food production and storage capacity.

Some interesting advances have been made in terms of economic and trade integration: (i) entry into force of the Treaty on Investment and Trade in Services between Costa Rica, El Salvador, Guatemala, Honduras and Nicaragua; (ii) legislative approval by Guatemala of the Convention on Mutual Assistance and Technical Cooperation between Central American Tax and Customs Administrations and the Convention on the Reconciliation of Domestic Taxes Applicable to Trade in the Customs Union; and (iii) the ratification by El Salvador of the Framework Convention for the Establishment of the Central American Customs Union (INTAL, 2008).

Following joint negotiations with the United States, the group of Central American countries is now in talks with the European Union, with a view to obtaining additional improvements to the existing Generalized System of Preferences (GSP-Plus) (see chapter V).

Another development of note is the tightening of links between Mexico and Central America. In late June 2008, countries attending the tenth summit meeting of the Tuxtla Mechanism for Dialogue and Coordination renamed the Puebla-Panama Plan (PPP) as the Mesoamerican Integration and Development Project (Mesoamerica Project). The main projects carried out so far have been in transportation infrastructure, energy, telecommunications and trade facilitation. In some cases, these were pre-existing initiatives that were reformulated for inclusion in the Mesoamerica Project. Transportation infrastructure projects have received the most backing and resources.

In addition to awarding priority to improving the interconnections of road, electricity, telecommunications and biofuel infrastructure, the Mesoamerica Project aims to promote the public-private partnership mechanism and the creation of a Mesoamerican Fund for infrastructure pre-investment and investment preparation. Lastly, as another priority objective, countries also considered it a good time to begin negotiations on the convergence of existing trade agreements, with a view to moving towards a Mesoamerican association agreement.

4. Southern Common Market (MERCOSUR)

The main progress made by this scheme was the launch of the Technical Unit of the MERCOSUR Structural Convergence Fund (FOCEM), which has been operational since 2007. Between that date and early July 2008, resources of up to US$ 130 million were allocated to areas the countries considered priorities (MERCOSUR secretariat, 2007; Chiaradía, 2008).

In the second half of 2007, the MERCOSUR strategy to combat desertification, land degradation and drought effects was made public. The strategy comes under the framework of the United Nations Convention to Combat Desertification (which has been in force since 1996), and in particular Annex III, the Regional Implementation Annex for Latin America and the Caribbean. According to data recently reported by MERCOSUR members and associates, aggregate estimates (not including Bolivia and Uruguay) of areas susceptible to or in the process of desertification and drought amount to almost 3.8 million square kilometers, which is just over 28% of the mainland territory of the subregion's countries.

National assessments and other available data suggest that agricultural productivity is falling as a result of land degradation, at annual rates of between 3% and 7% of the sector's gross output.[8] The details on the scale of desertification and drought and their impact on GDP, and the estimated escalation of such phenomena, show that urgent action is required to tackle the issue comprehensively.

On 1 July 2008, the Presidents of the MERCOSUR member and associate countries met at the thirty-fifth meeting of the Common Market Council in San Miguel de Tucumán. Delegates at the meeting approved five major road infrastructure projects in selected regions of Paraguay.[9] As well as facilitating access to drinking water and sanitation services, these projects encourage SMEs to become involved in the development of production

8 The document argues that the investment required to prevent degradation is less than the costs that would result from degradation, which confirms the findings of studies carried out in other areas.

9 These projects have been given priority and were studied by the Technical Unit of FOCEM. They represent projected outlays of US$ 18.5 million on the part of FOCEM.

linkages and infrastructure works (Chiaradía, 2008; Alvarez, 2008). Participants also approved the Productive Integration Programme, which aims to link national agencies associated with business and production development, provide research and development support, and develop and transfer human resources.

In the social sphere, the multinational project on social economics for regional integration is taking shape. The aim of the project is to strengthen labour-market and social inclusion in MERCOSUR. In the area of mobility and migration, countries reached an agreement on travel documents of member and associated countries of MERCOSUR, which enables citizens to move around the subregion using one legal document that does away with the need for a passport.

On the international stage, the Pro Tempore MERCOSUR secretariat is in contact with ASEAN countries, with a view to establishing a political dialogue between the two regions. MERCOSUR also maintains an active dialogue with the Russian Federation and, following several years of negotiation, concluded a Services Agreement with Chile (signed in Tucumán in July 2008) which, broadly speaking, establishes market access and national treatment conditions for professional services, business services, engineering, distribution, transport and tourism. This is the first extraregional services agreement concluded by MERCOSUR.

In December 2007, MERCOSUR signed a free trade agreement with Israel and hopes to conclude a similar agreement with the countries of the Southern African Customs Union (SACU). Despite joint coordination meetings with European Union representatives, talks on an association agreement with the European bloc remain at a standstill.

The Government of Brazil, in its capacity as holder of the Pro Tempore Presidency of MERCOSUR, is to host a Latin American Summit in Salvador, Bahía, in December 2008. The aim is to assess the state of regional integration schemes and ways in which they might be strengthened. In September, technical staff of MERCOSUR and the Central American Integration System (SICA) will meet to explore the possibility of a trade agreement between MERCOSUR and Central America. The failure of WTO negotiations will probably add impetus to attempts to breathe new life into regional integration.

C. Mexico: regional integration and trade initiatives

The Mexican authorities have been implementing an active trade policy aimed at concluding new bilateral and regional integration agreements. The country has signed 12 free trade agreements that are currently in force, seven partial scope agreements and one framework agreement with MERCOSUR. The objective of this strategy is to diversify markets and forge deeper and better political and trade relations with various actors in the international arena. The main activities revolve around participation in the Group of Five (G5), the harmonization of rules with trading partners and promotion of the Puebla-Panama Plan (PPP), now called the Mesoamerica Project.

1. Group of Five (G5)

Mexico plays an important role in the architecture of global international relations, which has been strengthened by its active participation in forums such as the Group of Five (G5). The other emerging nations that make up the G5 are Brazil, China, India and South Africa, and they have established a formal dialogue with the Group of Eight (G8) (which brings together the seven most industrialized countries plus the Russian Federation), in what is termed the "Heiligendamm Process". The G5 thus seeks to present the concerns of developing countries to the developed economies that make up the G8.

Given that Mexico is the only country that is a member of both the Organisation for Economic Co-operation and Development (OECD) and G5, it can play an important role as moderator between the two groups. This is partly why the European Union proposed a strategic association with Mexico. Mexico's role may be particularly important in issues such as climate change, food security, energy security, development cooperation and migration.

2. Convergence of trade agreements between Mexico and Central America

Another significant decision of the tenth summit meeting of the Tuxtla Mechanism for Dialogue and Coordination was to begin negotiations to achieve convergence between trade agreements in force with Central American countries, with a view to reaching a Mesoamerican association agreement. The aim of the agreement would be to untangle the "spaghetti bowl" of trade agreements involving Mexico and Central American countries. This decision goes beyond the negotiation of clauses on regional accumulation of origin, as it would result in the convergence and standardization of all agreement disciplines, thereby simplifying their administration and application.

However, the convergence of trade agreements is not only on the agenda of the Central American countries and Mexico. Convergence is also an issue for other regional forums, such as the Latin American Pacific Basin Initiative, which at its most recent meeting set up a group (coordinated by Mexico) to discuss the most appropriate means of forming an institutional structure that would respect its flexible nature as a forum for political dialogue and consultation.

3. From the Puebla-Panama Plan to the Mesoamerica Project

Another regional integration process in which Mexico is actively involved is the Puebla-Panama Plan (PPP). The Plan came into being in 2001 as a mechanism for coordinating integration and cooperation efforts between Mexico and the countries of the Central American isthmus. The agreement was extended to Colombia in 2006.

In late 2006, the PPP member countries agreed to strengthen the Plan and began a restructuring process that concluded in the first half of 2008. Besides many changes to the organizational structure, the way of working has been changed from a model based on initiatives, to a scheme built around projects (with the portfolio streamlined from 102 to 22 projects and programmes). Following these structural changes, the Heads of State of member countries relaunched the Plan at the tenth summit meeting of the Tuxtla Mechanism for Dialogue and Coordination in June 2008, renaming it the Mesoamerican Integration and Development Project, or Mesoamerica Project.

The Mesoamerica Project has made progress in several areas, especially transport, energy, telecommunications and trade facilitation. The most important transport projects include the construction of a Mesoamerican network of highways, known as RICAM, to improve over 13,000 kilometres of road between Mexico and Panama, and the modernization of customs and border crossings between the region's countries. In the energy sector, there are three projects under way to integrate electricity transmission between Mexico and Colombia using over 2,500 kilometres of power lines. With respect to biofuel, three pilot biodiesel plants are being built in Guatemala, El Salvador and Honduras, with the support of Colombia. In the sphere of telecommunications, there is a project to enhance digital connectivity in the Mesoamerican region by improving broadband infrastructure and harmonizing the regional regulatory framework in this area.

As for trade facilitation, the Mesoamerica Project includes measures to reduce transit time at borders and speed up the flow of merchandise. A pilot system at a border bridge between El Salvador and Honduras became operational this year. Steps have also been taken to modernize facilities at customs and border crossings between Mexico and Belize and Mexico and Guatemala, while there also plans to modernize the facilities at other crossings such as those between El Salvador and Honduras, El Salvador and Guatemala, and Costa Rica and Panama.

This new phase of Mesoamerican cooperation also seeks to provide impetus to issues such as the Mesoamerican public health system, a territorial information system for disaster risk reduction, as well as a Mesoamerican strategy on environmental sustainability, renewable energies and competitiveness.

D. Latin American Pacific Basin Initiative

The Forum of the Latin American Pacific Basin Initiative (ARCO) started out as an initiative to deepen trade agreements and trade facilitation in the Latin American countries of the Pacific Basin. The Forum aims to broaden economic cooperation and political dialogue among those countries, not only to build strength in the regional sphere but also to present a coordinated front to the Asia-Pacific region, in keeping with recommendations put forward by ECLAC (see ECLAC, 2007a, chapter II and chapter V of this report).

The representatives of countries participating in the Forum have agreed to consolidate the growing number of understandings based on common interests, by establishing a formal body for political dialogue and consultation. The member countries are Chile, Colombia, Costa Rica, Ecuador, El Salvador, Guatemala, Honduras, Mexico, Nicaragua, Panama and Peru. Up to October 2008, four meetings had been held, and four working groups had been set up on the following subjects:

(i) Trade convergence and integration;
(ii) Trade facilitation, infrastructure and logistics;
(iii) Investment promotion and protection and;
(iv) Economic and technical cooperation for competitiveness.

At its third meeting, the Forum recognized the work of the groups and issued them with further instructions. The working group on trade convergence and integration was tasked with identifying ways of moving towards common rules on accumulation of origin, which is a major issue for the region. That group was also asked to conduct a more detailed analysis of trade and integration agreements in force in the Latin American Pacific Basin, with an emphasis on issues concerning technical barriers to trade, sanitary and phytosanitary measures, customs procedures, trade facilitation, trade defence measures, dispute settlement, services, investment and government procurement.

The Working Group on Economic and Technical Cooperation for Competitiveness was tasked with encouraging the exchange of successful experiences of public-private partnerships to boost competitiveness and identify international best practices in terms of science, technology and innovation policies. Both topics are at the heart of ECLAC proposals for improving regional competitiveness (ECLAC, 2008a). This group is also responsible for assessing the best way of using technical cooperation offered by Asia-Pacific countries to improve production patterns, innovation, the incorporation of technology, education and the development of human resources.

The other two groups continue to work on technical cooperation between investment-promotion agencies; regulatory frameworks for investment, negotiations, dispute settlement between investors and the State and the fiscal treatment of investment; analyses of the regional situation in terms of infrastructure and logistics (including an inventory of alternative and renewable energy projects); transport and communications; and telecommunications.

The dynamism of the Forum may give the region impetus in key areas for deepening intraregional trade. The possibility of establishing accumulation of origin among the agreements in effect between the Forum's 11 Latin American countries could also provide a renewed impetus for regional integration efforts. Similarly, the Forum offers the ideal setting for joint initiatives aimed at forging closer links with the Asia-Pacific region (Rosales and Kuwayama, 2007).

E. UNASUR and the drive towards integration

In mid-2008, the Andean and MERCOSUR countries, plus Chile, Guyana and Suriname, concluded the Constitutive Treaty of the South American Union of Nations (UNASUR), an ambitious project for regional integration and union in the political, economic, financial, social, cultural, energy and infrastructure sectors. According to the preamble of the Treaty, UNASUR aims to eliminate socio-economic inequality, achieve social inclusion and civil-society participation, strengthen democracy and reduce asymmetries.[10] UNASUR is the result of several years of work that began in Cuzco in December 2004 and continued at the summits of Brasilia (September 2005), Cochabamba (December 2006) and Margarita (April 2007). Leaders

10 Article 3 of the South American Union of Nations Constitutive Treaty lists 21 specific objectives.

agreed to set up four bodies: (i) the Council of Heads of State and Government; (ii) the Council of Ministers of Foreign Affairs; (iii) the Council of Delegates; and (iv) the General Secretariat. Once the Constitutive Treaty has been signed, it must be ratified by the countries, which is expected to take some time.

It was agreed to establish the headquarters of the General Secretariat in Quito, and rotate the Pro Tempore Presidency among all the Member States for one-year periods, with the first year corresponding to Chile. The formation of the General Secretariat and the appointment of the Secretary-General and the Secretariat's technical team remain pending. The former President of Ecuador, Rodrigo Borja, resigned as Secretary-General as a result of disagreement over the way the process is being conducted (CELARE, 2008).

Table IV.2
INTRAREGIONAL TRADE MATRIX, 2007
(Millions of dollars and percentages)

	Andean countries	MERCOSUR	Chile	South America	Intraregional exports (%)
Andean countries	**12 812**	**4 752**	**2 991**	**20 582**	**14.4**
Bolivia	427	2 171	58	2 656	54.9
Colombia	5 720	558	376	6 675	23.2
Ecuador	2 580	111	658	3 352	24.2
Peru	1 881	1 068	1 693	4 645	16.9
Venezuela (Bol. Rep. of)	2 204	844	206	3 254	4.8
MERCOSUR	**14 074**	**33 065**	**8 763**	**55 989**	**24.9**
Argentina	3 513	12 483	4 185	20 191	36.1
Brazil	10 221	17 353	4 264	31 902	19.9
Paraguay	233	1 983	206	2 422	71.8
Uruguay	107	1 247	108	1 474	32.8
Chile	**3 374**	**4 401**	**0**	**7 778**	**11.4**
Guyana	**3**	**1**	**1**	**14**	**2.1**
Suriname	**47**	**30**	**0**	**96**	**8.6**
South America	**30 310**	**42 250**	**11 755**	**84 459**	**19.3**

Source: Economic Commission for Latin America and the Caribbean (ECLAC), on the basis of official figures from the respective subregional grouping and the International Monetary Fund (IMF), *Direction of Trade Statistics*.

Exports to other South American countries are highly significant for small and medium-sized countries such as Bolivia, Colombia, Ecuador, Paraguay and Uruguay, as well as for the larger ones including Argentina and Brazil. This explains efforts made to achieve convergence between the subregion's two largest customs unions —the Andean Community and MERCOSUR— on the one hand, and Chile, Guyana and Suriname, on the other.[11] Such a process would be based on liberalization agreements previously concluded by member countries (Economic Complementarity Agreements: ECA 23, ECA 35, ECA 36; ECA 58 and ECA 59) (see Vaillant, 2007 and LAIA, undated).

UNASUR may be a suitable forum for tackling sensitive issues that have not been resolved within the Andean Community or MERCOSUR. For instance, the issues of physical infrastructure and energy complementarity could more easily be accommodated within the wider geographical coverage corresponding to UNASUR, in which interests could be balanced more readily. The Regional Infrastructure Integration in South America (IIRSA) initiative could also benefit from a more subregional focus (Nogueira, 2008; Peña, 2008; LAIA, 2008).

A certain degree of frustration at South American experiences of integration is part of the legacy inherited by UNASUR, although its very creation reflects the political will to push ahead with integration. This will is manifested in a long list of objectives, although the general nature of the objectives poses a serious challenge

11 This is the first time that Guyana and Suriname have been part of a South American integration scheme, as they have traditionally been part of the Caribbean Community (CARICOM).

when it comes to defining the concrete actions needed to achieve them. Its limitations aside, the Economic Complementarity Agreements deposited with LAIA, MERCOSUR and the Andean Community are probably the most suitable institutional basis on which UNASUR can build. It is telling, however, that the Treaty makes no reference to free trade areas, customs unions or convergence of existing trade agreements between South American countries.

In terms of institutional design, UNASUR is more deliberative than executive. The General Secretariat fulfills functions of administration and legal representation. The Union will operate by consensus and its rules will only be binding once they have been incorporated into the countries' national legislations. Lastly, member countries may be indefinitely exempt from the partial or total application of some or all of the policies, institutions, organizations or programmes approved by the majority of other countries. This allows for flexible combinations of variable geometry and different speeds in designing and implementing commitments, which contributes to the overall effectiveness of the process. However, this modality may also dilute commitment to the most important initiatives.

The aims of UNASUR go beyond the combination of infrastructure and trade integration that has characterized South American schemes since 2000. The objectives this time are wider and considerably more ambitious, probably inspired by the European model: with emphasis on development issues such as equity and poverty reduction, as well as integration in terms of energy, finance, infrastructure and industry and convergence in social issues (such as access to social security and health services). One major challenge will be to balance these ambitious objectives with the limited coverage of the institutional structure, legal instruments and financial resources of UNASUR. In other words, the challenge is to reconcile the European model of solidarity-based integration (which reinforces social cohesion and seeks to gradually reduce asymmetries among members), with the lack of community institutions and structural financing that have made such achievements possible in the European context.

The main challenge facing the UNASUR authorities is probably to define a strategy for globalization and the integration of South America into the world economy that is accepted by all its members. The Union's procedures will have to be harmonized with those of existing integration schemes (such as the Andean Community and MERCOSUR) that already have a broad range of legal and trade commitments. This task calls for political dialogue and tact, to avoid duplication of labour or conflict between the work of UNASUR and that carried out by the Andean Community, MERCOSUR and government agencies working on integration issues. In practical terms, this means competing with those organizations and with government agencies for scarce human, financial and logistical resources and political priority that the subregion assigns to integration (INTAL, 2008).

In order to reconcile the gradual and flexible approach taken by UNASUR with the need to satisfy expectations of integration it is necessary to concentrate on a small number of tasks that can yield short-term results. Such achievements would make it possible to scale up the list of objectives, engage private actors, strengthen coordination with other ongoing initiatives and win prestige as a pillar of coordination and governance for different integration efforts, even in terms of trade, infrastructure and cooperation.

Coordination between UNASUR and MERCOSUR (the main subregional actor) is crucial. Indeed, MERCOSUR cannot be the only trade integration forum in South America, given that the subregion has various tariff regimes that exist alongside each other (MERCOSUR, Andean Community, Chile and CARICOM), while issues of energy and financial integration involve all South American economies (*La Nación*, 2008). Given the importance of MERCOSUR (and its largest member, Brazil) within South America, the quality of the UNASUR-MERCOSUR link will be decisive. Complementarity between the two will strengthen the integration process, while any overlap or dilution of efforts will undermine both (Peña, 2008).

Without such coordination, it will be difficult for UNASUR to influence actual integration processes. If MERCOSUR fails to motivate productive investment decisions to take advantage of the wider market, neither organization will have an impact on changing production patterns in its members. If, on the other hand, MERCOSUR were to opt for flexible institutions and predictable policies, including processes of variable geometry and multiple speeds (Peña, 2008), and were to work on achieving compatibility between its own and Chile's extraregional trade agreements (Amadeo, 2008), this could enhance interaction and feedback between MERCOSUR and UNASUR.

F. Latin American investment, trade in services and internationalization

Unlike in the 1960s, 1970s and 1980s, when the bulk of FDI in Latin America and the Caribbean was destined for the manufacturing sector, since the mid-1990s and specifically in more recent years, growth in FDI in general and in intraregional FDI in particular has been fuelled by the boom in commercial services in the region and the increased transnationalization of a large number of companies.

The empirical evidence reveals that a high level of integration has been attained in the business sector largely through the investment and commercial activities of the region's main economic groups in both the goods and the services sectors. The region is witnessing a real de facto integration process that is being driven by the common need to transnationalize in order to generate the economies of scale required for success in today's global markets.

The large network of free trade agreements and regional integration schemes in Latin America, which could be described as de jure integration, could benefit from this situation, which has received little attention at the subregional and regional levels. To date, there has been little discussion on the role of private agents in regional integration; indeed, they have been seen as secondary actors. A more effective integration drive depends on a stronger engagement of private agents and on closer public-private coordination in defining the next steps on the road to regional integration.

1. Importance of intraregional investment in services

A breakdown of intraregional FDI by origin and destination (when this can be obtained) shows that, in the case of MERCOSUR and the Andean Community (including the Bolivarian Republic of Venezuela), the bulk of this FDI is invested within the same group (52.1% and 61.1%, respectively).[12] The second largest proportion is invested in countries from the other group (MERCOSUR-Andean Community) and accounts for 20% of the total FDI of both groups. If Chile and its reciprocal FDI with MERCOSUR and the Andean Community are added to the equation, the subregional FDI accumulated among the countries of South America represents around 46% of total intraregional FDI in the region.[13]

Within Central America, intrasubregional FDI makes up 47% of the subregion's total investments in Latin America (with Costa Rica, Honduras and El Salvador as the main origin and destination countries).

In South America, as well as among Central American countries and Panama, intraregional FDI has become an important means of increasing business integration, especially in sectors previously reserved for national capital (such as telecommunications, electricity, banking and finance). Greater integration has also been achieved in new or non-traditional sectors, such as electronics, tourism, manufacture of medical equipment, construction services for real-estate projects and commerce. Mexico and Chile have invested heavily in the region, especially in areas that are geographically close, with Chilean investment in Argentina and Peru and Mexican investment in Central America and the Caribbean (although Mexican businesses also have a strong presence in South America, especially in Brazil and Argentina).

About 61.4% of intraregional investment goes to services, which is thus the main destination by sector. Within services, slightly over 73% of those investments are in the categories of energy, telecommunications, banking and finance and retail commerce (Durán and Pellandra, 2008).

The main investors in services are companies from Argentina, Brazil, Chile and Mexico: Telmex, América

[12] This section is based on a study now being developed on the link between investment and services at the regional level. It is based on official information from the balance of payments from 1990-2007 and on secondary sources such as the financial press and official company information (Durán and Pellandra, 2008).

[13] This figure rises to 60% if Panama is excluded from the total.

Móvil, Banco Itau, Banamex, Inverlat, Lan Airlines, Copa Airlines, Cencosud and Falabella, among others. For these, direct investment is an important way of increasing exports of services to other countries. There is also a second group of international players that are not necessarily directly involved in services but that obtain much of their revenues from operations abroad. Some of these are: Grupo Bimbo, GRUMA, CEMEX, Vitro, Petrobras, Techint, Arcor and Grupo Votorantim.

(a) Brazil

Brazil's services exports represented US$ 23.744 billion in 2007, which accounted for more than 20% of the total exported by Latin America and the Caribbean, and over 30% of the total exported by South America. The service exports of Brazil are the fastest-growing in the region, as they doubled between 2003 and 2007, at an annual average growth rate of 22.8% (the highest in the region). This performance reflects the dramatic surge in exports of "other services", which in 2006 corresponded to 56.7% of total service exports (above the world average of 49.7%).

Some of the factors behind the impressive buoyancy of Brazilian service exports in recent years are set out below:

(i) The expansion of industrial exports to South America, which has led to a gradual rise in investment abroad and the setting up of services companies in other countries of the subregion. As Brazil's export supply has diversified, companies have had to match their clients' needs and offer after-sales services in other countries, thus boosting outward investment. Thus, the globalization of manufacturing companies generates incentives for the globalization of certain services, especially financial, ICT, logistics and professional services. Some enterprises, such as Banco Itaú, Unibanco, the São Paulo Stock Exchange (BOVESPA), the Brazilian Mercantile and Futures Exchange (BM&F), Datasul, Microsiga, CPM, TAM and Varilog, now have regionally integrated operations. In addition, Brazilian legal firms and consultancy and auditing services have built up a competitive presence in the subregion.

(ii) Brazil has a competitive edge in certain segments, arising from factors particular to its economy's recent development, not necessarily connected to the internationalization of other sectors. This is true of various branches of information technology, engineering and construction. Three Brazilian construction companies figure among the world's top 225 export constructors and the region's largest firms: Norberto Odebrecht, Andrade Gutierrez and Camargo Correa Construções e Comércio.

(iii) Brazil has a competitive advantage over its industrialized rivals in certain service niches in terms of being able to detect and manage the political and economic risk of South American economies. Examples of this are found, among others, in infrastructure projects and construction services, air transport, software and financial services.

(b) Uruguay

In 2006, Uruguay's exports of services totalled US$ 1.285 billion, which represented 22.6% of the country's total exports (the highest proportion among South American countries). Over the last 20 years, Uruguay has become a logistics platform where international enterprises centralize their merchandise inventories for regional distribution. The country has evolved from a mere transit point into a hub for other areas of logistics, incorporating value added through mini-manufacturing production units and building up genuine regional distribution centres that coordinate all stages of orders, from regional clients to suppliers within the region and beyond.

Uruguay has a privileged geographical location at the ocean mouth of the Río de la Plata Basin, which places it on the region's main cargo route, and its coastal conditions are ideal for ports. The country's political stability and institutions, backed up by the quality of its human resources and advances in infrastructure, offer secure conditions for the development of services associated with the logistics industry. In this context, Uruguay began to develop logistics operations based on such legal regimes as the Free Zones Act and the Ports Act, which provided a framework for trade, industrial and service activities that has made Montevideo the first Atlantic-coast terminal in South America to offer free circulation of merchandise without the need for formal procedures or authorization. The surge in trade following the creation of MERCOSUR then increased the logistics requirements of export companies.

The most recent step taken to support the sector was the development of the logistics and transport cluster in the context of the Programme to Support the Competitiveness and Promote the Exports of Small and Medium-Sized Enterprises (PACPYMES) of the Ministry of Industry, Energy and Mining, with the assistance of the European Union. The cluster includes maritime, road, rail and air transport services, terminal operators, logistics and warehouse operators and customs agents. The logistics cluster now encompasses almost 9,000 firms working with the various public agencies involved with the movement and storage of goods and related services. The sector represents around 6% of GDP and has become a natural exporter of services, making intensive use of skilled and semi-skilled labour.

(c) Central America

The main Central American enterprises with a subregional presence are from El Salvador, Guatemala and Costa Rica. Those three countries represented 80% of total intrasubregional capital stock as of December 2007. The main destinations of subregional investment flows are Honduras and Costa Rica. Economic groups and the major alliances between them have played an important part in the Central American integration process.

Central American economic groups tend to have highly diversified operations and activities in financial services, transport and tourism, construction, commerce and industry. The common denominator is that the largest investments are mainly in services and commerce. Increased foreign competition in the wake of trade liberalization increased pressure on local markets and opened up new opportunities for regional accumulation, thus fomenting a pro-liberalization business culture and facilitating the natural expansion of the main national groups into the regional market (Segovia, 2005). Some of the large groups engaging in intra-Central American operations are TACA and Poma in El Salvador and La Fragua, Pantaleón, Gutierrez-Bosch (owners of the Pollos Campero company) and Castillo in Guatemala. The large players in Costa Rica are the Uribe family (owners of the Corporación de Supermercados Unidos), Grupo Durman Esquivel and la Nación. Other equally important regional investors are the Pellas and Zamora families, who own companies in banking and financial services, as well as assets in other sectors.[14]

CAFTA-DR has sped up the processes of internationalization by promoting business alliances and company mergers aimed at taking advantage of the expanded subregional market and increased access to the North American market, while also scaling up business in preparation for competition from North American and European companies that may set up in Central America.

G. Proposals for the future

It is an established fact that the challenges of integration are not confined to trade and market expansion. There is also a broad agenda of infrastructure, energy and logistics issues, as well as cooperation in areas including macroeconomics, migration, social cohesion and the environment. This agenda needs the engagement of the private sector, which should be treated as an important actor in the integration process. Increasing coordination between the public and business sectors is a fundamental pillar of the integration process and a task that remains pending.

Generally speaking, recent developments as regards foreign investment and international positioning by Latin American enterprises have not resulted from specific public policies or measures arising from integration commitments. This vital process could be strengthened by integration initiatives in the framework of trade agreements and trade facilitation measures. As well as increasing the credibility of dispute settlement mechanisms, trade agreements promote convergence of regulatory frameworks in the services sector and may even be updated to include chapters on trade in services. Trade facilitation measures include investment in logistics and infrastructure and the harmonization of regulations, as well as mobility of technical and professional workers and the gradual harmonization of tax and financial procedures (CNI, 2007).

In many countries, the current integration process coincides with more ambitious, broader and deeper approaches to liberalization than in the past. This is reflected in aspects of trade that either featured only partially in previous integration models (as with investment) or not at all (as in the case of services). One of the most radical changes in approaches to integration is that several Latin American and Caribbean countries have sought to conclude trade agreements with their main trading partners (especially the United States, the European Union and, more recently, Asia).

The past three decades have seen rapid changes in technology and in the world economy, as well as the emergence of new competitors and markets (China and India, along with the rest of the Asia-Pacific region). This has dramatically altered the world map of trade, comparative advantages and investment location, and will continue to do so.

It is in this global context of new opportunities and challenges that the state of integration falls short of the mark. Indeed, integration schemes do not figure in major

14 A number of studies provide a detailed picture of intraregional FDI and the main economic groups in Central America. See Segovia (2005), Pérez and Berrios (2001) and Rosenthal (2005, 2006).

business decisions and integration is not at the heart of political agendas; when it does appear, it amounts to little more than statements of intention. Against that backdrop, it should come as no surprise that the possible ways of integrating into the world economy are increasing. The sharp structural and policy differences among the countries of the region are well known. Structural differences refer to size, production structures, export capacities, comparative advantages, structure of main destination markets and degree of complementarity or substitution with the main agricultural products of industrialized economies that heavily subsidize exports or support domestic producers. Policy differences relate to the role that each country aspires to play in the regional and world economy, the strength of its economy and institutions and, hence, its bargaining power and alliance structure —all of which is reflected in trade policy and trade negotiations.

It is therefore vital to acknowledge and reconcile the different visions that have emerged, so as to preserve the aim of integration. Integration has to be built up from diverse realities, with a view to achieving new schemes that can make an expanded regional market more attractive. The time is ripe to update the notion of "open regionalism" by reinforcing the complementarity between integration into the world economy and subregional or regional integration schemes. This would not only broaden access to the main markets for products intensive in natural resources and cheap labour, but would also encourage the development of technology- and knowledge-intensive activities, including the incorporation of value added in natural-resource-based products.

Integration schemes urgently need to be endowed with elements of development and policy coordination that do not form part of free trade agreements concluded with partners from outside the region. Although the preferability of integration depends precisely on this endowment, the serious political and technical efforts it would require have thus far not materialized. Of course, integration is about more than trade, and more attention must indeed be paid to the social dimension (especially in a continent blighted by social inequality). However, this cannot be at the cost of delaying or compromising the economic and trade aspects of integration, but should rather reinforce the complementary nature of the commercial and social dimensions. With this in mind, efforts should be redoubled to build subregional value chains that enable members to export to third markets, with measures to encourage the inclusion of less developed countries in those chains. This appears a suitable form of "open regionalism" that combines growth, the quest for third markets and social cohesion and in which structural support for reducing asymmetries among member countries promotes the development of a competitive export supply in less developed members. Otherwise, the social dimension is seen merely as a compensatory mechanism, rather than one that offers access to growth opportunities, which would amount to expecting integration to make up for national inequalities —which no country has been able to achieve within its own borders.

The current phase of globalization demands competitiveness and innovation in exchange for a place on the new world map of production, trade and comparative advantages. To gain ground in international value chains, competitiveness and innovation must be combined with wide and unified markets built upon a convergence of rules, disciplines and regulations, as well as the legal certainty to facilitate long-term decisions and international alliances. To ensure that this open regionalism provides a more solid link between competitiveness and social cohesion, public policy must make greater efforts to encourage more SMEs to venture into export activities.

In South America, trade issues tend to be controversial. But this should not be an obstacle to progress in other, perhaps more urgent, areas. A joint approach to strengthening ties with the Asia-Pacific region (through multinational ministerial and business missions) would help to promote project portfolios in infrastructure, energy, banking, tourism and logistics, with mutual advantages for both regions. Coordinating the strategies of trans-Latins to promote subregional and regional value chains would link integration with the international expansion decisions of the main regional economic actors. Partnership for innovation and competitiveness also needs to be strengthened as a matter of urgency. Technology centres in joint business and research activities can be linked to generate synergies and build up a critical mass from the limited human resources that the region assigns to these matters that are so crucial for the future. There is also a great opportunity for regional cooperation in trade facilitation measures involving several countries, such as the modernization of customs, ports, infrastructure, logistics and ICT interoperability and connectivity. In all of these areas, unilateral courses of action are a poor second best, as they ignore the possibilities offered by coordinated action among countries, the advantages of expanded markets and policy convergence.

Bibliography

Álvarez, Carlos (2008), "Quinto informe de actividades del Presidente de la Comisión de Representantes Permanentes del MERCOSUR" [online] http://www.mercosurpresidencia.org/pdf_es/cumbre_tucuman_2008/Informe_trabajo_CRPM.pdf.

— (2007), "Cuarto informe de actividades del Presidente de la Comisión de Representantes Permanentes del MERCOSUR" [online] http://www.mercosurpresidencia.org/pdf_es/cumbre_montevideo_2007/Informe_Semestral_CRPM.pdf.

Amadeo, Eduardo (2008), "¿Quo vadis, Mercosur?", *La Nación*, 20 May.

Andean Community (2007), "Decisions 669-671. Year XXIV", No. 1520, Lima, 16 July.

Calderón, Álvaro (2007), "Chile: direct investment abroad and internalization of conglomerates", *Global Players from Emerging Markets: Strengthening Enterprise Competitiveness through Outward Investment* (UNCTAD/ITE/TEB/2006/9), Geneva, United Nations Conference on Trade and Development (UNCTAD).

— (2006), "The expansion model of the major Chilean retail chains", *CEPAL Review*, No. 90 (LC/G.2323-P), Santiago, Chile, Economic Commission for Latin America and the Caribbean (ECLAC), December.

CELARE (Latin American Centre for Relations with Europe) (2008), *Newsletter*, No. 208, 27 June-3 July.

Chiaradía, Alfredo (2008), "Resultados de la Presidencia Pro Tempore Argentina. I semestre 2008", *Informe de la Presidencia Pro Tempore Mercosur* (MERCOSUR/XXXV CMC/DI), No. 01/08, Tucuman, 30 June.

CNI (National Confederation of Industry) (2007), "Os intereses empresariais brasileiros na América del Sul. Informe de la Confederação Nacional da Indústria", unpublished.

Durán, J.E and A. Pellandra (2008), "Perfil exportador y competitividad de los servicios comerciales en América Latina y el Caribe", unpublished.

ECLAC (Economic Commission for Latin America and the Caribbean) (2008a), *Structural Change and Productivity Growth, 20 Years Later. Old problems, new opportunities* (LC/G.2367(SES.32/3)), Santiago, Chile, May.

— (2008b), *Foreign Investment in Latin America and the Caribbean, 2007* (LC/G.2360-P), Santiago, Chile, March.

—(2008c), *Statistical Yearbook of Latin America and the Caribbean, 2007* (LC/G.2356-P/B), Santiago, Chile. United Nations publication, Sales No.E/S.08.II.G.1.

—(2007a), *Latin America and the Caribbean in the World Economy, 2006. Trends 2007* (LC/G.2341-P), Santiago, Chile. United Nations publication, Sales No. E.07.II.G.85.

—(2007b), *Foreign Investment in Latin America and the Caribbean, 2006* (LC/G.2336-P), Santiago, Chile. United Nations publication, Sales No. E.07.II.G.32.

—(2006), *Foreign Investment in Latin America and the Caribbean, 2005* (LC/G.2309-P), Santiago, Chile. United Nations publication, Sales No. E.06.II.G.44.

El Periódico (2008), "Los 'súper' se unen para competir con Wal-Mart", 12 May.

Foro del Arco del Pacífico Latinoamericano (2008), "Declaración de Cancún", Cancun, 13-14 April.

—(2007a), "Declaración de Cali", Santiago de Cali, 30 January.

—(2007b), "Declaración de Lima", Lima, 20- 21 August.

Girvan, Norman (2008), *Towards a Single Development Vision and the Role of The Single Economy*, University of the West Indies (UWI).

INTAL (Institute for the Integration of Latin America and the Caribbean) (2008), *INTAL Monthly Newsletter*, No. 144, July.

La Nación (2008), "Entrevista a M. Aurelio García", 20 May.

LAIA (Latin American Integration Association) (n/d) official website [online] http://www.aladi.org/

—(2008), "Seguimiento de las actividades en el marco de la Iniciativa para la Integración de la Infraestructura Regional Sudamericana (IIRSA), el Plan Puebla-Panamá (PPP), la Unión de Naciones Sudamericanas (UNASUR) y la Iniciativa de Transporte del Hemisferio Occidental (ITHO)", *Informe del primer semestre* (ALADI/SEC/di 2160), 15 June.

MERCOSUR Secretariat (2007), *Informe anual de actividades de la Secretaría del MERCOSUR*, Montevideo, December.

Nogueira, Uziel (2008), "Union of South American Nations: challenges and opportunities", *INTAL Monthly Newsletter*, No. 142, May.

OECS (Organisation of Eastern Caribbean States) (2008), *The Organisation of Eastern Caribbean States: Draft of the New Treaty*.

OEI (Organization of Ibero-American States for Education, Science and Culture) (2008), "Acta de la trigésimo quinta reunión del Consejo del Mercado Común (MERCOSUR)", San Miguel de Tucumán, 1 July [online] http://www.oei.es/noticias/spip.php?article2981—.

Peña, Felix (2008), "¿En que se diferenciaría UNASUR de un Mercosur ampliado?" [online] http://www.felixpena.com.ar/index.php?contenido=negociaciones&neagno=informes/2008-06-unasur-mercosur-ampliado.

Pérez, Felipe and Luisa Nelly Berrios (2001), *Características e impacto de la inversión costarricense en Nicaragua durante el período 1990-2001*, Central American Institute of Business Administration (INCAE)/Latin American Centre for Competitiveness and Sustainable Development (CLACDS), August.

PACPYMES (Programme to support the competitiveness and promote the exports of small and medium-sized enterprises), *Informe de transporte y logística*, Montevideo.

Rosales, Osvaldo and Mikio Kuwayama (2007), "Latin America meets China and India: prospects and challenges for trade and investment", *CEPAL Review*, No. 93 (LC/G.2347-P), Santiago, Chile, Economic Commission for Latin America and the Caribbean (ECLAC).

Rosenthal, Gert (2006), "La inversión extranjera directa en Centroamérica, 1990-2004: un bosquejo", *Inversión extranjera en Centroamérica*, Grettel López C. and Carlos E. Umaña A. (eds.), San José, Central American Bank for Economic Integration (CABEI).

___ (2005), "Logros y límites de la integración regional: Centroamérica", document presented at the seminar Integration Perspectives in Latin America and the Caribbean at the Beginning of the 21st Century 40 years since the creation of INTAL, Buenos Aires, 24 August.

Schatan, Claudia and others (2008), "Integración regional e integración con Estados Unidos. El rumbo de las exportaciones centroamericanas y de República Dominicana", *Estudios y perspectivas series*, No. 93 (LC/MEX/L.831/Rev.1), Mexico City, ECLAC subregional headquarters in Mexico. United Nations publication, Sales No. S.08.II.G.7.

Segovia, Alexander (2006), "Integración real y grupos centroamericanos de poder económico. Implicaciones para la democracia y el desarrollo regional", *ECA: estudios centroamericanos*, No. 691-692.

SGCAN (General Secretariat of Andean Community) (2008), "Informe de labores junio 2007 a mayo 2008. Informe de la Secretaría General de la Comunidad Andina ante el XXX Consejo Andino de Ministros de Relaciones Exteriores en Reunión ampliada con la Comisión", *documento informativo* (SG/di 889), 16 June.

SIECA (Secretariat for Central American Economic Integration) (2008), *Estado de situación de la integración económica centroamericana*, Guatemala, July.

Summit of Heads of State and Government of the countries members of the Tuxtla Mechanism for Dialogue and Coordination (2008a), "Declaración de Villahermosa", Villahermosa, Tabasco, 28 June.

___ (2008b), "El PPP: avances, retos y perspectivas. Informe ejecutivo", Villahermosa, Tabasco, 28 June.

Tavares, Marcia (2006), "Trans-latins. Trends and issues", document presented at the meeeting Emerging multinationals: who are they, what do they do, what does it mean?, Organisation for Economic Co-operation and Development (OECD), 27 March.

UNCTAD (United Nations Conference on Trade and Development) (2007), *Global Players from Emerging Markets: Strengthening Enterprise Competitiveness through Outward Investment* (UNCTAD/ITE/TEB/2006/9), Geneva.

Vaillant, Marcel (2008), "Oportunidades de una economía pequeña y remota en el mundo global: Uruguay como exportador de servicios", Santiago, Chile, Economic Commission for Latin America and the Caribbean (ECLAC), unpublished.

___ (2007), "Heterogénea evolución de la integración económica en América del Sur: entre la complementariedad y el conflicto", *Comercio internacional series*, No. 83 (LC/L.2777-P), Santiago, Chile, Economic Commission for Latin America and the Caribbean (ECLAC), August. United Nations publication, Sales No. S.07.II.G.113.

Valls Pereira, Sennes (2008), "Diversifying and upgrading services trade in Brazil", Santiago, Chile, Economic Commission for Latin America and the Caribbean (ECLAC), unpublished.

Chapter V

The European Union and Latin America and the Caribbean: from preferences to reciprocity

Introduction

Forging stronger economic and commercial ties with the European Union is an important item on the regional trade agenda. At the end of 2007, talks between the European Union and the Caribbean concluded with the signing of an Economic Partnership Agreement (EPA), while around the same time negotiations were launched for a similar agreement with the countries of Central America and of the Andean Community. After eight years, the negotiations with MERCOSUR are still ongoing even though little significant progress has been made. In mid-2008, the European Commission announced its intention to negotiate a Strategic Partnership agreement with Mexico, which will upgrade relations between the parties. If all these negotiation processes are brought to a successful conclusion by the end of 2010, 13 economies of Latin America will have Association Agreements with the European Union (19 if MERCOSUR concludes its talks and the Bolivarian Republic of Venezuela becomes a member of MERCOSUR). Regional integration efforts therefore need to adjust to a new reality: if all this goes ahead, the countries of the Caribbean, Central America, Andean Community and MERCOSUR, as well as Mexico and Chile, will be covered by agreements with the European Union, which all share a similar framework.

The year 2007 marked a fundamental shift in the relationship between the European Union and the Caribbean countries and brought important advances in the consolidation of European-Latin American relations. The European Union launched trade negotiations with Central America and the Andean countries and concluded the negotiation of an EPA with the CARICOM countries, Haiti and the Dominican Republic, i.e., with the so-called Caribbean Forum of African, Caribbean and Pacific States (CARIFORUM). The EPA paves the way for a progressive and reciprocal expansion of market access in goods, as well as the liberalization of services and investment, which poses serious challenges for the CARIFORUM countries but also offers opportunities for diversifying exports to reduce their dependency on the United States as their principal market. The intensification of trade relations between the two regions is in part driven by the fact that the preferential treatment traditionally given to many of the region's countries is not sustainable in the long run as it contradicts the principles of the World Trade Organization (WTO). The negotiation, implementation and adjustment to a reciprocal agreement is not an easy process for the economies of Latin America and the Caribbean, in particular the smaller and less developed ones, since the disappearance of the one-sided preferences and adaptation to the new trading environment require them to boost their productive capacities and lower trading costs in order to be able to compete globally.

Although the European Union is still the Latin American and Caribbean region's second most important trading partner after the United States, since 1990 it has been gradually losing ground (see figure V.1). Imports from the European Union as a share of total Latin American and Caribbean imports declined from 20% in 1990 to approximately 14% in 2006. In the same period exports to the European Union declined from 25% to 13%. Meanwhile, Asia-Pacific has been gaining momentum as the region's trading partner. In particular, since 2001 more Latin American and Caribbean imports have originated in the Asia-Pacific region rather than in the European Union, and the share of Asia-Pacific imports is rising steadily (for further details, see ECLAC, 2007, chapter V). If the current trend continues, by 2010, as much as 30% of Latin American and Caribbean imports could come from the Asia-Pacific region.

Figure V.1
LATIN AMERICA AND THE CARIBBEAN: SHARE OF THE UNITED STATES, EUROPEAN UNION AND THE ASIA-PACIFIC REGION IN THE REGION'S EXPORTS AND IMPORTS

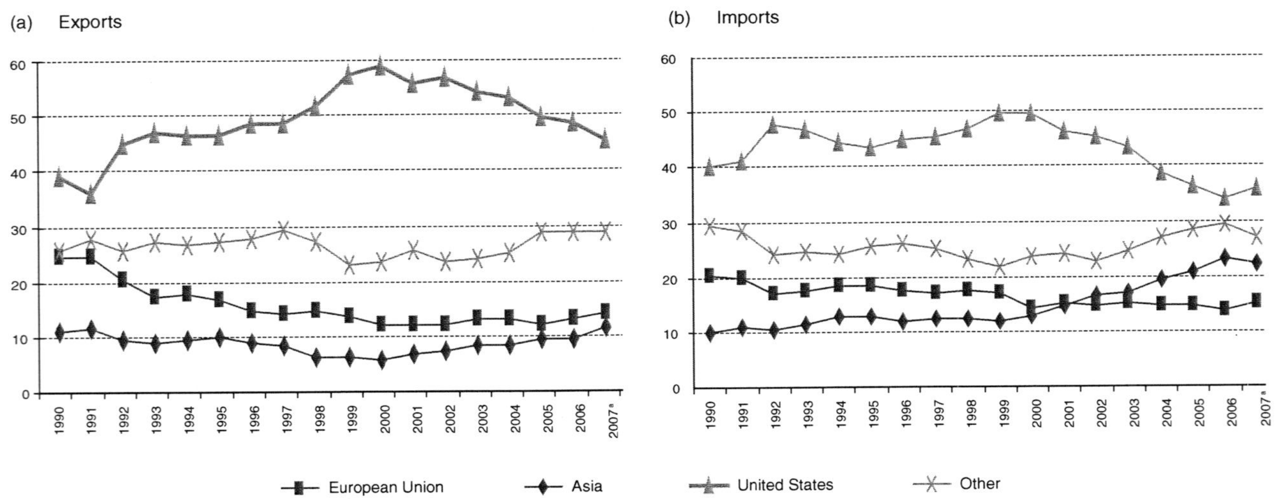

Source: Economic Commission for Latin America and the Caribbean (ECLAC), on the basis of United Nations Commodity Trade Database (COMTRADE).
ª Projection.

Intensification of economic relations between the European Union and its partners in Latin America and the Caribbean region through trade liberalization is a chance for the European Union to regain some of the ground it has been losing. For Latin America and the Caribbean expansion of trade in goods with the European Union would mean capitalizing on the comparative advantages that the region already possesses, although additional negotiations will be needed for sensitive products such as bananas. Table V.1 lists the principal export products from the region to the European Union by bloc and shows that exports are still highly concentrated in commodities, such as bananas, bovine meat, coffee, copper, gas and coal, iron and steel, petroleum and soybeans. On the other hand, as trade barriers come down, agreements with the European Union could provide opportunities for diversifying region's export base and developing services exports, an issue of particular importance for the Caribbean countries.

All the ongoing and recently completed negotiations between the European Union and Latin American and Caribbean countries pursue the conclusion of an agreement based on three pillars: political dialogue, cooperation and the reciprocal liberalization of trade in goods and services. The first two pillars may prove to be just as important for growth and development of the Latin American and Caribbean region as trade, since an association with the European Union would provide an important political support to the integration process within the region's blocs and financial assistance for carrying out important reforms and measures complementary to trade policy, in particular in the area of trade facilitation. Faced with substantial differences in levels of development and progress in regional integration among the economies involved, and considering its own strategic objectives in each subregion, the European Union essentially adopted a multi-speed approach, with different completion targets for the agreements in each case.

Table V.1

TOP EXPORTS FROM SUBREGIONS IN LATIN AMERICA AND THE CARIBBEAN TO THE EUROPEAN UNION (27 COUNTRIES), 2004-2006

Product Name	% of total goods exports	Product Name	% of total goods exports
Central American isthmus [a]		**CARIFORUM**	
Parts and accessories for computers	19.1	Cruise ships, yachts and excursion boats	27.9
Bananas	18.3	Aluminium oxide	9.0
Electronic integrated circuits and microassemblies	17.7	Rum	8.8
Coffee	9.2	Natural gas and other petroleum gases	8.7
Cruise ships, yachts and excursion boats	8.0	Sugar	6.3
Pineapples	7.1	Petroleum oils	6.2
Crustaceans: fresh, frozen or prepared	2.2	Bananas	5.6
Fish: fresh, frozen or prepared	1.9	Ferro-alloys	3.3
Melons and watermelons	1.9	Acyclic alcohols	1.9
Other	14.6	Medical appliances	1.2
Total	100.0	Crustaceans: fresh, frozen or prepared	1.2
		Other	19.9
		Total	100.0
MERCOSUR		**Andean Community** [b]	
Soybean and soybean oil	20.1	Bananas	20.2
Iron and steel	12.7	Coal	15.9
Bovine meat	4.3	Copper	10.3
Coffee	3.5	Coffee	7.9
Wood pulp	3.2	Zinc	5.0
Fruit juices	2.7	Fish: fresh, frozen or prepared	4.4
Motor vehicles and their parts	2.6	Ferro-alloys	4.0
Aluminium	2.5	Crustaceans: fresh, frozen or prepared	3.3
Petroleum oils	2.3	Cut flowers	2.3
Copper	1.8	Tin	1.5
Tobacco	1.5	Other	25.2
Other	42.9	Total	100.0
Total	100.0		

Source: Economic Commission for Latin America and the Caribbean (ECLAC), on the basis of United Nations Commodity Trade Database (COMTRADE).
[a] Includes Panama.
[b] Does not include the Bolivarian Republic of Venezuela.

A. Patterns of inter-regional trade

Exports to the European Union, the second largest trading partner of CARIFORUM, make up 21% of all exports from the subregion. These exports grew faster between 2000 and 2006 than exports to the United States. At the same time, the share of exports to the new member States in Central and Eastern Europe expanded from a mere 0.1% to approximately 2% in 2004 and onwards. In particular, high growth was recorded in exports to Poland, which in 2006 became the fifth-largest market for the CARIFORUM States in the European Union[1]. The breakdown by product reveals that cruise ship tourism and yachting account for a large proportion of the subregion's exports to the European Union: 27.9% of total exports in the period 2004-2006. Other important products are rum, sugar and bananas, which together accounted for 20.7% in the same period, as well as alumina (9%), natural gas (8.7%) and petroleum oils (6.2%) (see table V.1). The composition of exports changed substantially over time: the proportion of primary goods in CARICOM exports to both the European Union and the world expanded from slightly over 20% in 2000 to over 40% in 2006. The bulk of this increase may be attributed to the expansion of natural gas exports from Trinidad and Tobago, which represented 28% of all CARICOM exports to the European Union in 2006, up from only 8% in 2000.

The European Union is also the second most important trade and investment partner of Central America, after the United States. According to the Statistical Office of the European Communities EUROSTAT, the inflow of European Union foreign direct investment (FDI) into the Central American countries amounted to 28.9 billion euros (€) in 2006. Almost 20% of Central American goods exports went to the European market in 2006. Although this subregion exports twice as much to the United States market as to Europe and imports three times more from the United States, between 2000 and 2006 its trade flows with the European Union grew more rapidly than with the United States. Exports to Europe almost doubled over that period, from US$ 3.6 billion to US$ 7.2 billion, while exports to the United States grew by a modest 20%. On the other hand, the share of imports from the European Union in the total imports of Central America has been stable for the past six years at approximately 10% of total. Central America's exports to the European Union consist predominantly of agricultural products and other commodities. Primary goods accounted for 70% of all exports from the Central American Common Market to the European Union in 2006 (see table V.2). Although this represents a substantial change since 1990, when primary goods constituted 92% of all merchandise exports to European Union, the proportion of these goods in Central American exports to the European Union was still much higher than their share of total exports from the subregion, which was only one third in 2006. Coffee and bananas constitute the bulk of agricultural exports from Central America to the European Union. These two products accounted for 27.5% of total exports to the European Union in the period 2004-2006 (see table V.1). Computer parts and accessories represented 19.2% of exports and electronic integrated circuits accounted for 17.6%. Central American imports from European Union are concentrated in machinery, chemicals, ships, boats, vehicles and fuels.

The European Union accounts for approximately 16% of the Andean Community trade with the world and as such is this Community's second largest trading partner after the United States. In 2006, 18% of Andean exports went to Europe and 13% of imports came from the European Union. As in the case with Central America, Andean countries export twice as much to the United States as to European Union; however exports to the European market grew faster during the period 2000-2006 than those to the United States. Andean Community exports predominantly agricultural and mining products to the European market. Bananas accounted for 20% of all exports to Europe between 2004 and 2006 (see table V.1). Coal represented 16% (exported only by Colombia), while zinc and copper (both exported predominantly by Peru) accounted for 10% and 5%, respectively. Coffee (68% of it from Colombia) constituted 8% of subregional exports to the European Union. Together, these five products accounted for over half of European imports from the Andean Community. Although primary goods constitute the bulk of Andean exports to the world and to the European Union (73% and 67% of total exports in 2006, respectively), the share of industrial products in the group's exports to European Union has been increasing over time: it grew from 28% in 1990 to 34% in 2006. On the other hand, the Andean countries import mostly manufactured goods from European Union, in particular machinery and chemicals.

1 After Spain, United Kingdom, Germany and France.

Trade flows between the European Union and MERCOSUR are double those between the European Union and the Caribbean, Central American and Andean countries put together. The potential implications of a trade deal between the two blocs for the economies involved are therefore stronger than in the other cases. Unlike the other Latin-American blocs, MERCOSUR trades more with the European Union than with the United States: about a quarter of total MERCOSUR exports are destined for the European Union and a quarter of its imports come from that source. At the same time, MERCOSUR also trades more than other subregions with the rest of the world: in 2006 59% of its exports went to countries outside the European Union and the United States. Approximately half of that amount went to other Latin American countries. MERCOSUR exports to the European Union are concentrated in traditional products in agriculture and the mining sector. In agriculture, exports are dominated by soybean (20%), followed by bovine meat (4.3%) and coffee (3.5%) (see table V.1). The five most important products accounted for 44% of European imports from MERCOSUR. In 2006, primary products represented almost one third of the products exported by MERCOSUR to the European Union, a much higher share than their share of exports to the world, which was 24% (see table V.2).

Table V.2

STRUCTURE OF MERCHANDISE EXPORTS FROM LATIN AMERICA AND THE CARIBBEAN BY DESTINATION AND CATEGORY

(Percentages)

	European Union			World		
	1990	2000	2006	1990	2000	2006
	Latin America and the Caribbean					
Primary products	44.1	36.2	39.2	42.9	24.3	32.3
Manufactures	55.7	63.6	60.6	56.5	75.1	66.6
Other goods	0.2	0.3	0.2	0.7	0.6	1.2
Total	100.0	100.0	100.0	100.0	100.0	100.0
	Central American Common Market					
Primary products	92.4	63.7	70.2	56.6	36.1	33.1
Manufactures	6.6	36.2	29.8	39.9	63.7	66.8
Other goods	1.1	0.1	0.1	3.5	0.2	0.1
Total	100.0	100.0	100.0	100.0	100.0	100.0
	CARICOM					
Primary products	23.4	21.2	43.7	27.8	23.4	42.6
Manufactures	72.8	78.5	56.2	72.0	76.5	57.2
Other goods	3.8	0.3	0.1	0.2	0.1	0.2
Total	100.0	100.0	100.0	100.0	100.0	100.0
	MERCOSUR					
Primary products	30.5	29.8	32.6	23.1	22.4	23.9
Manufactures	69.5	70.0	67.2	76.1	75.7	74.2
Other goods	0.0	0.3	0.1	0.9	1.9	1.8
Total	100.0	100.0	100.0	100.0	100.0	100.0
	Andean Community					
Primary products	72.1	65.0	66.5	73.1	56.7	72.9
Manufactures	27.7	35.0	33.5	26.7	43.3	27.0
Other goods	0.2	0.0	0.0	0.2	0.0	0.1
Total	100.0	100.0	100.0	100.0	100.0	100.0

Source: Economic Commission for Latin America and the Caribbean (ECLAC), on the basis of official country data.

Note: Following ECLAC's definition of primary and manufactured goods, primary products include unprocessed agricultural output, crude oil, gas, coal, minerals and metal ores. Manufactures include processed resource-based products (agricultural, metals and fuels).

B. CARIFORUM: the sealed deal?

Working on a tight schedule to meet the deadline of 1 January 2008, the negotiations of the EPA and the agreement was eventually signed on 15 October 2008 between the European Commission and CARIFORUM concluded formally on 16 December 2007 and the agreement was eventually signed on 15 October 2008. The new agreement replaced the system of preferences granted under several Lomé agreements and the 2001 Cotonou Agreement between the European Union and the African, Caribbean and Pacific (ACP) countries. The urgency to conclude the negotiations before 2008 was dictated by the temporary status of this non-reciprocal trade regime (the corresponding WTO waiver that was set to expire on 31 December 2007). Since under the Cotonou agreement most exports from CARIFORUM entered the European Union duty-free, the main advantage of the EPA for CARIFORUM lies in making preferential market access permanent and WTO compatible, rather than in securing additional market access.

Consistent with the European Union's comprehensive approach to partnerships with developing countries, the EPA covers all relevant areas of trade and trade-related cooperation and goes beyond market access to include customs and trade facilitation, technical barriers to trade, sanitary and phytosanitary measures, investments, competition, innovation and intellectual property, public procurement and environment and social aspects of trade, among others. As such, the EPA sets up a new reciprocal trading system between the European Union and the CARIFORUM countries, while the other two dimensions —political dialogue and cooperation in a broader sense— continue, for the time being, to be covered by the Cotonou agreement.[2]

The implementation of a comprehensive trade agreement with the European Union poses serious challenges for the CARIFORUM states. Except for the Dominican Republic, which is signatory to the CAFTA-DR agreement with the United States, this is the first time that the countries are engaged in a reciprocal trade liberalization scheme vis-à-vis a major and economically superior partner. The major asymmetries in size, level of development and economic power that exist between the European Union and the CARIFORUM countries imply that the costs of adjustment to the new trading environment borne by the CARIFORUM economies will be much higher than those of the European Union. The EPA addresses this issue with two sets of instruments: (i) asymmetric liberalization of investments as well as trade in goods and services and (ii) development cooperation and technical assistance, as will be discussed further in the chapter.

Asymmetric liberalization is embedded in the European Union's commitment to remove tariffs and quotas on all goods starting 1 January 2008, with the exception of rice and sugar, which have phase-out periods until 2010 and 2015, respectively. In addition, the agreement commits the European Union to eliminating export subsidies on all agricultural products for which CARIFORUM has agreed to eliminate tariffs.

The trade barriers to goods imports in CARIFORUM are to be dismantled gradually, with tariffs being liberalized in phases of 5, 10, 15, 20 and 25 years. A three-year moratorium has been established for tariff reductions in all categories of items coming into the subregion,[3] meaning that liberalization will actually commence on 1 January 2011. CARIFORUM countries agreed to slash the tariffs on a total of 61.1% of their imports (by value) over 10 years, 82.7% over 15 years and 86.9 % over 25 years (European Commission, 2008). In the agricultural sector, most products have either been excluded from liberalization or are subject to long transition periods (20 or 25 years). The main exclusions apart from agricultural products (meat, poultry, dairy, certain fruits and vegetables and some prepared foods) are certain chemicals, furniture and other manufactured products. A special "infant industry clause" has also been agreed to, which allows CARIFORUM countries to apply safeguard measures to protect a growing industry for a limited period of time. Under the EPA, CARICOM States will grant the Dominican Republic the same treatment they give the European Union, and vice versa.

The EPA contains specific provisions on sugar and bananas, which together constituted 14% of the total value of exports to the European Union from the subregion in 2006. The EPA specifies that on top of the existing 410,000 tons Tariff Rate Quota (TRQ) allocation for sugar, CARIFORUM will receive an additional quota of 60,000 tons: the Dominican Republic 30,000 tons, and the CARICOM sugar-producing countries 30,000

2 As such, the EPA covers one of the five pillars covered by the Cotonou Agreement: The political dimension, participatory approach, development strategies (a strengthened focus on poverty reduction), the new trade framework and financial cooperation. The Cotonou Agreement was concluded for a twenty-year period from 2000 to 2020.

3 With the exception of motor vehicles, spare parts and gasoline.

tons to be shared among them, for the period up to the end of September 2009.[4] Additionally, the two sides agreed that any quota shortfalls can be reallocated among the Caribbean States. On the downside, a number of manufactured products that contain sugar are excluded from the "cumulation" clause of the rules of origin.[5] The European Union has committed to reviewing and reducing the list of the products exempted from the clause within three years. Bananas gain full duty-free and quota-free access to the European Union market from the moment the agreement enters into force. The preferential market access for Caribbean producers is thus now granted under a WTO-compatible regional trade agreement (see box V.1). The EPA also contains a comprehensive joint declaration on bananas, which commits the European Union to providing funding to assist the industry during the adjustment period. In the case of rice, duty-free and quota-free access will be granted by the European Union in 2010. In the meantime, CARIFORUM countries will receive quotas of 187,000 tons in 2008 and 250,000 tons in 2009, which can be exported under a zero tariff (compared to the € 65/ton duty currently paid). The current quota allocated to Guyana and Suriname is 145,000 tons. This is a significant achievement in particular for Guyana, whose rice exports accounted for 15% of the total value of its exports to the European Union between 2004 and 2006.

Box V.1

THE END OF THE BANANA WAR?

The preferential access granted by the European Union to its former colonies in the ACP region through a system of quotas and tariffs has been the source of a bitter argument between Europe and Latin American exporters for over a decade. Despite various reforms to the European Union's import regime for bananas, complaints have been filed by both Latin American nations (most notably Ecuador) and the United States since 1996, claiming that that the regime violates WTO rules. The WTO has repeatedly ruled against the European Union's MFN import tariffs (the latest was set at € 176 per ton in 2006) and the preferential quotas given to ACP producers. In the most recent case, Ecuador, the principal exporter of bananas to the European Union and the world's largest producer, claimed to have lost US$ 131 million in the first 15 months of the tariff's existence. On 7 April 2008, a WTO Panel report concluded that "The preference granted by the European Communities to an annual duty-free tariff quota of 775,000 tons of imported bananas originating in ACP countries constitutes an advantage for this category of bananas, which is not accorded to like bananas originating in non-ACP WTO Members, and is therefore inconsistent with Article I:1 of GATT 1994" (WT/DS27/RW2/ECU). On 19 May 2008, WTO again ruled against the European Union in a similar case initiated by the United States. The European Union's reaction was to argue that since 1 January 2008, following the expiration of the WTO waiver for the Cotonou preferences, the preferences granted by the European Union to the ACP have been covered by new trade arrangements, including the full regional EPA with CARIFORUM and a number of interim agreements with certain countries or regions in Africa and the Pacific.

In the latest round of multilateral negotiations, a group of Latin American countries attempted to link the banana issue to the negotiations on tropical products within the Doha round with a view to obtaining a substantial cut in the current tariff of € 176 per ton. Negotiating banana tariffs as part of tropical products would result in faster, steeper multilateral tariff cuts. This proposal was met with a resistance from the ACP members, which are pushing for bananas to be classified as so-called preference products that are subject to longer implementation periods. Such a move would help to soften the blow ACP countries could face from the erosion of the current preferences. During the last round of multilateral talks in July 2008 the European Union had agreed to cut its most favoured nation (MFN) tariffs on bananas to € 114 by 2016, with an initial cut to € 148 in 2009. In exchange, the Latin American countries were expected to agree not to challenge the European Union's preferential access to banana imports from ACP countries and to drop existing lawsuits. However, since the round collapsed once again, failing to deliver a Doha breakthrough, this offer was taken off the table. On the other hand, there is some hope that a stand-alone agreement on bananas will be achieved. In the meanwhile, on August 28 the European Union filed an appeal in an attempt to overturn the recent WTO rulings on discrimination against Latin American countries.

Between 2004 and 2006, 22% of European banana imports came from Ecuador and an additional 42% came from Colombia, Costa Rica and Panama, while 6% came from the CARIFORUM countries. Bananas accounted for 18% and 20% of total exports by value from Central America and the Andean countries, respectively. In CARIFORUM, the share of bananas in total exports to the European Union was 5.6%.

---

4 The expansion of tariff-rate quotas (TRQs) is intended to partly offset the negative effect of the reform of the European Union's sugar regime, which gave ACP sugar growers higher prices than other exporters. Following the gradual dismantling of the minimum price granted to the ACP countries by the Sugar Protocol, only a few countries in the subregion will remain competitive in the world market. In the Caribbean, the countries that will continue to produce and export sugar are Guyana, Jamaica and Belize, and those are the countries that will benefit from higher export quotas as of 2009.

5 The cumulation clause allows exporters to obtain preferential market access for products that incorporate inputs originating in other Caribbean states as well as other ACP countries.

Box. V.1 (concluded)

DISTRIBUTION OF EU'S IMPORTS OF BANANAS BY ORIGIN, 2004-2006

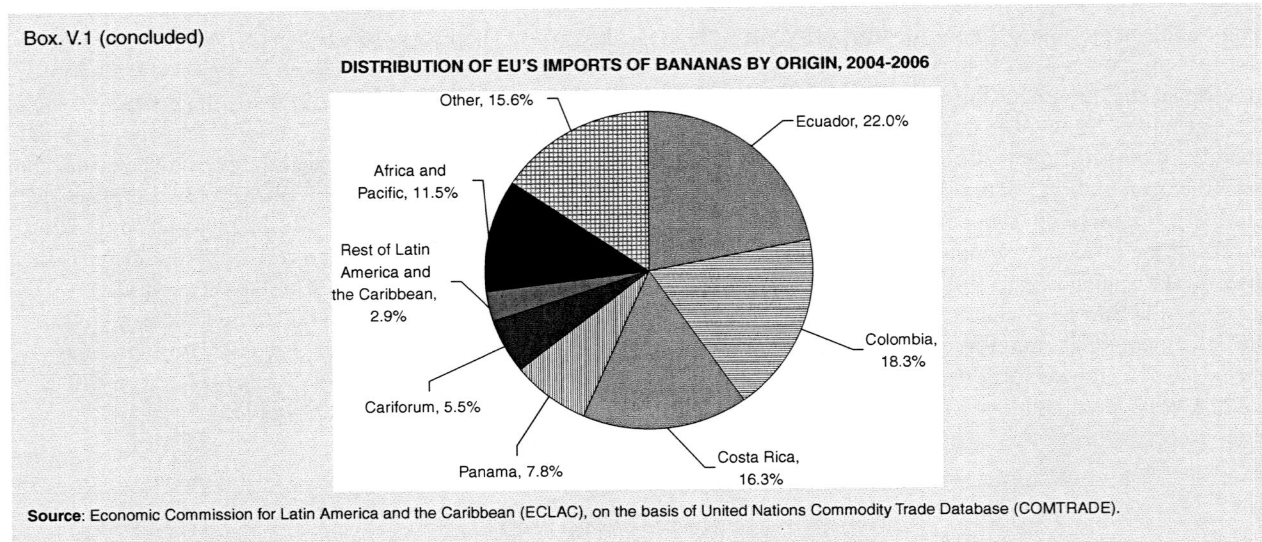

Source: Economic Commission for Latin America and the Caribbean (ECLAC), on the basis of United Nations Commodity Trade Database (COMTRADE).

The Caribbean region is the only ACP region that is a net exporter of services. Services constitute the bulk of exports in most Caribbean countries, generating US$ 8.7 billion in export revenues in 2005,[6] which corresponded to 24.8% of the subregion's GDP. The most important services sectors are tourism, which accounts for two thirds of services exports, followed by transportation (10.4%) and business services (6.3%).[7] According to the World Tourism Organization, in 2005, the tourism sector generated US$ 5.9 billion in receipts in CARICOM member countries and US$ 3.5 billion in the Dominican Republic. Gaining better access to the European services market was therefore a priority for the CARIFORUM countries.

The EPA handles the services trade through sets of provisions covering three subjects: commercial presence, the cross-border supply of services and the temporary presence of natural persons. Public services, utilities and other sensitive sectors have been excluded from liberalization. Although there is certain asymmetry in the scope of the liberalization of services between the European Union and CARIFORUM, the obligations assumed by the CARIFORUM countries under the EPA go well beyond the commitments of the developing countries in the WTO.[8] One potential problem in this is that, by giving national treatment to European Union service providers, CARIFORUM has limited the scope of its regulatory capacity in the services sector, which could hamper its ability to deploy policies to protect or encourage local service suppliers as part of a broader development strategy.

The EPA has been hailed by the European Union as a major achievement for CARIFORUM States regarding temporary employment possibilities for Caribbean professionals in Europe. Some 29 European sectors have been opened up to allow professional employees of CARIFORUM firms not established in Europe or contractual service suppliers to temporarily supply services in the European Union. In addition, 11 sectors have been opened up to allow self-employed CARIFORUM professionals to enter the European Union for temporary work. However, by and large, these commitments remain within the scope of the European Union's schedule under the General Agreement on Trade in Services (GATS) or its services offer within the Doha Agenda (South Centre 2008). Moreover, in the absence of established mutual recognition procedures for the technical qualifications of professionals,[9] the de facto barriers to the movement of persons could prevail. The EPA mentions requirements regarding professional qualifications and university

6 International Monetary Fund (IMF), Balance of Payment Statistics Database (BOP) [online] http://www.imfstatistics.org/BOP/logon.aspx.

7 United Nations Service Trade Statistics Database [online] http://unstats.un.org/unsd/servicetrade.

8 According to the initial press releases (for example, "The EPA: fact vs. fiction" [online] http://www.crnm.org/epa_fact_fiction1.htm), the European Union has made liberalization commitments in 94% of the sectors, while the corresponding figures for CARIFORUM are 75% for the so-called "more developed countries" and 65% for the "lesser developed" CARIFORUM countries, although at this point it is not clear how these percentages are calculated. The current commitments of CARICOM countries in the General Agreement on Trade in Services (GATS) affect only 8.4% of all services sectors on average.

9 The EPA provides for the encouragement of the relevant professional bodies in their respective territories to start negotiations no later than three years after the entry into force of the EPA and to jointly develop and provide recommendations on mutual recognition, among others, in the following disciplines: accounting, architecture, engineering and tourism.

education as prerequisites for work permits. In addition, in various sectors, economic needs tests apply. The real value of these commitments to the professionals from the CARIFORUM countries will therefore become apparent only when the EPA is fully operational. In sum, the net benefits of the EPA for CARIFORUM services providers will depend on whether the EPA provisions go beyond the access that will be granted to developing countries once the European Union GATS offer locks in, although it appears that the differences are minimal.[10] This additional access has to be weighed against the costs of compliance with the obligations imposed by the EPA on the CARIFORUM economies.[11] It should be noted that the ACP countries are not required to negotiate a services agreement with the European Union to achieve WTO compatibility.

The EPA does contain other instruments that have the potential to contribute to its declared development objectives. The commitments in the area of competition include prohibition of anti-competitive business practices, including the commitment to establish appropriate legislation, which is currently either weak or nonexistent in most Caribbean countries. In the area of trade facilitation, the private sector in the CARIFORUM countries will benefit from transparency, predictability and less red tape as the countries adopt a single administrative document (SAD) or its electronic equivalent, which will replace the numerous documents currently needed to process imports and exports. In the area of cooperation, the development cooperation agreement contains clauses on promoting private-sector and enterprise development, enhancing technological and research capabilities in the CARIFORUM States and developing CARIFORUM innovation systems. To support these initiatives and to help CARIFORUM to export successfully to European Union markets, the European Union has pledged financial and non-financial support in a number of priority areas, such as customs modernization and infrastructure development.

The process of implementation and adjustment to the EPA in CARIFORUM will require substantial efforts in trade facilitation in order to benefit fully from expanded market access. The success of the EPA in achieving its declared development objectives by repositioning the export base of CARIFORUM away from primary products towards goods with greater value-added as well as services hinges critically on those countries' ability to address the challenges of improving the efficiency of revenue collection, restructuring vulnerable sectors, harnessing the business climate to attract capital and boost competitiveness, strengthening domestic and regional institutions and enhancing regional integration. In particular, developing the services sector, for which market access opportunities are expanding, is a major priority.

The countries will need significant resources to bolster their internal capacities to face these challenges. The European Union has pledged to increase its trade-related assistance, although this is not something that is an inherent part of the EPA. Financing pertaining to development cooperation and specifically to the implementation of the EPA is subject to the rules of the Cotonou Agreement, in particular the programming procedures of the European Development Fund (EDF).[12] Under the tenth EDF for the period 2008-2013, an estimated € 165 million will be allocated to the Regional Indicative Program for the Caribbean, which will be used to fund strengthening of regional cooperation and integration, with implementation of the Caribbean Single Market and Economy as a major priority as well as to address vulnerabilities and social issues and EPA implementation.

In order to channel these resources, in the EPA, the parties commit to establish a regional development fund two years from the date of signature of the agreement. Thus, the distribution of this pledged support among the countries and the specific programmes are yet to be determined. In addition, the European Union's national indicative programmes for the Caribbean countries are also oriented towards activities linked to trade: five programmes will target competitiveness, three programmes will contribute to governance and public administration reforms and three others will focus on infrastructure. These amount to € 454 million or 75% of the sum of approximately € 600 million set aside for the national programmes (European Commission, 2008). The EPA also contains a declaration stating the link with the expansion of the Aid-for-Trade funding. Under the European Union's Aid-for-Trade Strategy, European Union Member States are committed to reach an annual amount of € 1 billion by 2010 in trade-related assistance, with a range of 50%, of which 22% is available for ACP countries. In the EPA the European Union states its intention "to ensure that an equitable share of Member States' Aid

[10] A further analysis of the implications of the commitments regarding the movement of natural persons, as well as other services provisions, for the CARIFORUM countries requires a comparison of the annexes to the EPA and the European Union's updated schedule of commitments in the GATS. Services negotiations in the context of the Doha round are currently in progress and no official revised offers from the European Union are yet available.

[11] Apart from services liberalization, the EPA establishes a set of obligations in the areas of investment, competition, government procurement, trade facilitation and intellectual property rights, as well as sector-specific regulations in the services sectors, such as tourism, financial services and telecommunications.

[12] p. 22 of the Economic Partnership Agreement between the CARIFORUM states and the European Community.

for Trade commitments will benefit the Caribbean ACP States, including for funding programs related to the implementation of this Agreement".[13]

Nevertheless, the basic premise of the EPA is that trade is the primary vehicle for stimulating development. The European Union maintains that the EPA will spur development by expanding trade, strengthening regional integration and attracting investment: "The Caribbean EPA aims at achieving development objectives through the establishment of a trade partnership based on the promotion of regional integration, the gradual integration of CARIFORUM countries into the world economy, capacity building in trade policy and trade related issues, supporting the conditions for increased investment and economic growth." (European Commission, 2008). Critics of the EPA argue, on the other hand, that development orientation of the EPA is too weak, since trade and investment liberalization by itself is not sufficient to deliver development, and that the provisions regarding delivery of assistance are too vague. Moreover, the EPA does not go far enough to address the differences in economic power and levels of development among CARIFORUM States through special and differential treatment for less developed countries (see for example Girvan, 2008).

The EPA was signed on 15 October 2008 by the European Union and all CARIFORUM member states except Guyana and Haiti. Guyana has raised its concerns about the agreement, citing as the main reasons insufficient market access in the European Union for its vital products: sugar, rum and rice, and the potential impact of the EPA on its trade balance and balance of payments as the main reasons. Guyana also indicated that it was considering signing a "goods and services agreement" only, leaving out the so-called Singapore issues, such as government procurement, investments and competition. The opposition to the deal was reaffirmed by Guyana's President, Bharrat Jagdeo, in his address to the United Nations General Assembly (sixty-third session) on 23 September 2008. Nevertheless, Guyana finally signed the agreement, while Haiti requested more time to analyse the terms, since its current priority is to recover from the natural disasters it has suffered.

C. Central America: the fast track

The negotiations of the Association Agreement between the European Union and Central America (Costa Rica, El Salvador, Guatemala, Honduras and Nicaragua) were formally launched in October 2007. The principal objectives of the negotiations are to enhance the political dialogue between the blocs, to intensify and improve cooperation in a vast variety of areas and to enhance and facilitate bi-regional trade and investment. At this stage, Panama participates as an observer only since it is not a member of the Secretariat for Central American Economic Integration (SIECA).[14] The talks have been dynamic: four rounds of negotiations have already been held, progress has been made in establishing certain cooperation agreements, and proposals on trade in goods and services have been exchanged and discussed. As regards political dialogue, agreements on democracy, good governance, human rights and the information society have already been reached.

The parties have agreed that tariff dismantling will take place in the following phases: immediately and then 3, 5, 7 and 10 years after the agreement enters into force. A special category for products without a defined liberalization schedule and products subject to tariff-rate quotas applies. It was agreed that trade liberalization will cover both goods and services and that liberalization of investments will also be negotiated. In addition, the usual trade-related areas will be covered: trade facilitation, competition rules and public procurement. The parties have exchanged the initial liberalization offers on trade in goods and are in the process of negotiating them. The current offer by Central America affects 80% of the tariff lines. The European Union is asking for 90% of the Central American market to be liberalized in exchange for consolidation of the preferences granted by the European Union under the GSP-plus arrangement.[15] The European Union offer currently on the table includes duty-free

[13] p. 397 of the Economic Partnership Agreement between the CARIFORUM states and the European Community.

[14] Panama has concluded bilateral free-trade agreements with El Salvador, Honduras and Costa Rica and is currently negotiating with Nicaragua and Guatemala. Panama can participate fully in the negotiations with the European Union only after it signs the protocol of accession to SIECA and becomes part of the Central American customs union, since the European Union approach is to negotiate agreements with country blocs.

[15] On 1 January 2006, GSP-plus replaced the 'drugs regime' of the GSP, providing special incentives to the countries of the Central American isthmus to promote sustainable development and good governance.

access for all products that enter with zero tariff under the GSP-plus arrangement, with the exception of 30 products. The exceptions include ethanol and frozen shrimp, both of importance to Central America. From the viewpoint of Central America, GSP-plus should be the starting point for further liberalization rather than an end.

The most intense period in terms of negotiating the core commitments of the future agreement will be 2008 and 2009. Several important trade issues still need to be settled, including access to the European Union market for sensitive products such as sugar, bananas, ethanol and shrimps and Central American tariffs on European cars, electronics and pharmaceutical products. These issues were to be addressed during the fifth round of negotiations, which was scheduled to take place early in October in Guatemala. The European Union is concerned with what it considers to be an insufficient offer from Central America regarding investments and market access in telecommunications. Moreover it has signalled that it would be flexible in the definition of the rules of origin for certain goods produced in Central America, such as textiles and plastics.

The parties agreed that the negotiations should be concluded during 2009. It may, however, become difficult to achieve that goal, given the typical complications associated with the asymmetry principle of the negotiations and the sensitivity of agriculture in both the European Union and Central America.

D. The Andean Community: pausing to rethink the process

Similar to the Central American case, European Union-Andean trade relations are currently dominated by GSP preferences: first through the 'drugs regime' and, since 2006, through GSP-plus arrangements. The negotiations of the Association Agreement commenced in September 2007, with the standard objective "to enhance the political dialogue between both regions, to intensify and improve their co-operation in a vast variety of areas and to enhance and facilitate bi-regional trade and investments".[16]

In the area of cooperation, the parties have agreed to place emphasis on economic and social development, in particular poverty reduction, social cohesion and the welfare of underprivileged groups. In trade, the parties have so far only exchanged views on the structure of the trade part of the agreement and discussed the general objectives, as well as directives and guidelines for trade subgroups. The initial tariff offers were made during the third round in April 2008. During these talks, the parties barely touched upon trade, however, and postponed negotiations of the tariff schedules until the fourth round.

A temporary boost to the process was provided by the Summit of Heads of State and Government from Latin America and the Caribbean and from the European Union, hosted by Peru in May 2008. Apart from the formal outcomes that focused on collaborative efforts in poverty reduction and sustainable development, the talks involved a discussion on three topics more closely related to bi-regional negotiations: investment, rule of law and flexibility of the negotiations. Flexibility is particularly important in the Andean case, where the countries are characterized not only by different levels of development, but also by different degrees of readiness to move forward with the negotiations. The idea of a flexible framework that would let the Andean countries negotiate with the European Union along independent tracks was put forward by the Governments of Peru and Colombia, the countries that are most eager to conclude the Association Agreement. Ecuador and Bolivia, on the other hand, have expressed their reservations with regard to the trade talks. Bolivia has in fact indicated that it will opt out of the negotiations on a number of topics: trade in services, right of establishment and movement of capital, public procurement and intellectual property.

These differences in attitude among the members of the Andean Community make the establishment of a common position vis-à-vis the European Union extremely difficult and have seriously hampered the negotiating process. In particular, there is still an ongoing debate within the bloc on issues such as the extent of trade liberalization, intellectual property rights, public procurement and sustainable development. As a result, in July the European Union, citing the lack of a common Andean position in presenting offers on trade in goods as cause, announced the suspension of the fourth round

---

16 European Union, "EU and the Andean Community launch negotiations for Association Agreement", Press release (IP/07/834), Brussels, 14 June 2007.

of negotiations, and effectively placed the talks on hold. In September, frustrated with the lack of progress, the Governments of Colombia and Peru formally asked Brussels to pursue bilateral negotiations with them. Referring to "different visions" within the Andean region, Colombian President Alvaro Uribe urged the European Commission President Jose Manuel Barroso to advance simultaneously with the negotiation of bilateral trade agreements between each of the Andean countries and the European Union and expressed the hope that the negotiations could be concluded in the first half of 2009.[17]

In a final attempt to resolve their differences, the Andean countries convened in mid-October at an extraordinary summit meeting in Guayaquil, Ecuador, at which they agreed to ask the European Union for fresh talks to restart the negotiations and to consider the possibility of negotiating jointly, but at different speeds.

E. MERCOSUR: stop-and-go

Eight years have passed since the formal launch of the negotiations between MERCOSUR and the European Union. Progress has been painstakingly slow, leaving various pledges to complete the negotiations by a certain date unfulfilled. Following a pause of almost a year, the negotiations were resumed at a ministerial meeting in 2005 in the hope that the Association Agreement would be completed by 2006. However, another series of meetings made little progress in achieving consensus in critical areas. Once again the negotiations stalled, and the prospects of concluding them in the near term seem bleak as the principal concerns remain unsolved. The talks have been hampered by some of the same issues impeding the Doha round: reforms of the European Union's farm support system and access for European manufacturing goods and services to the Southern Cone markets. Moreover, the current approach pursued by the European Union Commission in bilateral agreements, which pushes for commitments beyond those negotiated in the WTO in the areas of public procurement, investments and intellectual property rights, does not go down well with the MERCOSUR countries and poses additional obstacles. On the other hand, as the Doha round may be revived in 2008, the European Union and MERCOSUR have both signalled their willingness to press ahead and to make another attempt at reaching an agreement on trade. At the end of 2007, the parties announced that they would resume talks in May 2008. They have recently pushed the date towards the second half of the year, however. Much work remains to be done, and in light of previous complications it seems unlikely that the negotiations will be concluded before 2010.

It is also possible that the European Union will focus on developing a special relationship with Brazil, parallel to the negotiations with MERCOSUR. Brazil could become an important hub for the European Union's economic relations with Latin America and could act as an engine for deeper regional integration in MERCOSUR. In May 2007, the European Union Commission proposed a strategic partnership to strengthen its ties with Brazil, focusing on trade and investment as issues of particular bilateral relevance. Other areas for proposed joint action included strengthening multilateralism and cooperation on global challenges such as tackling poverty and inequality, environmental issues (particularly climate change), energy, regional stability in Latin America and integration within MERCOSUR. These topics were discussed at the first European Union-Brazil Summit, held in Lisbon in July 2007.

[17] Colombia Reports, "Europe too slow on trade deals, say Colombia and Peru", 22 September 2008 [online] http://colombiareports.com/colombian-news/economy/1329-europe-too-slow-on-trade-deals-say-colombia-and-peru.html.

F. A strategic partnership with Mexico

Mexico and the European Union are heading towards a strategic partnership, in other words, a relationship that goes beyond the bounds of the bilateral free trade, cooperation and political agreements that make up the European Union-Mexico Economic Partnership, Political Coordination and Cooperation Agreement that has been in effect since 2000. The parties agreed to pursue the proposed strategic partnership at the Summit of Heads of State and Government from Latin America and the Caribbean and from the European Union held in Lima in May 2008. In July 2008, the European Commission submitted the proposal to the European Parliament under the title "Towards an EU-Mexico Strategic Partnership". It must now be presented to the Council of Ministers of the European Union, and the process is expected to be concluded by the end of the year.

In the eight years since the entry into force of the Free Trade Agreement (FTA) between the European Union and Mexico, Mexican exports to the European Union have risen 170%, from US$ 5,157 million in 1999 to US$ 13,943 million in 2007. Imports meanwhile rose 162% from US$ 12,928 million in 1999 to US$ 33,839 million in 2007. Mexico's trade deficit with the European Union remains high even though exports have expanded more than imports. This deficit is expected to shrink as cooperation efforts within the framework of the association agreement begin to bear fruit. These currently consist of measures aimed at strengthening small and medium-sized Mexican companies through the Mexico-EU Comprehensive Support Programme for Small and Medium Enterprises (PIAPYME by its Spanish acronym) and activities conducted as part of the capacity building project of the Mexico-European Union Free Trade Agreement (PROTLCUEM by its Spanish acronym), which covers topics such as treaty administration, sanitary and phytosanitary issues, and customs.

European investment in Mexico grew 105% between 1999 and 2007 and mostly went to the manufacturing and financial services sectors. Flows came mainly from Spain, the Netherlands, the United Kingdom and Germany (see figures V.2 and V.3). The European Union has thus become Mexico's second largest trade and investment partner, after the United States.

The European Union hopes Mexico will become its fifth strategic trading partner after the United States, China, the Russian Federation and Brazil. Its interest in Mexico stems largely from the country's strategic geographical and political position in the Americas. The strategic partnership would expand upon the trade commitments already established within the FTA and the cooperation agreements signed between Mexico and the European Union regarding other topics. Under the new partnership arrangement, both parties would commit to pursuing decisions regarding the main issues on the international agenda, including political, security, environmental, energy, economic and social matters.

Figure V.2

MEXICO: TRADE FLOWS AND FDI INFLOWS FROM THE EUROPEAN UNION, 1999-2007

(Millions of United States dollars)

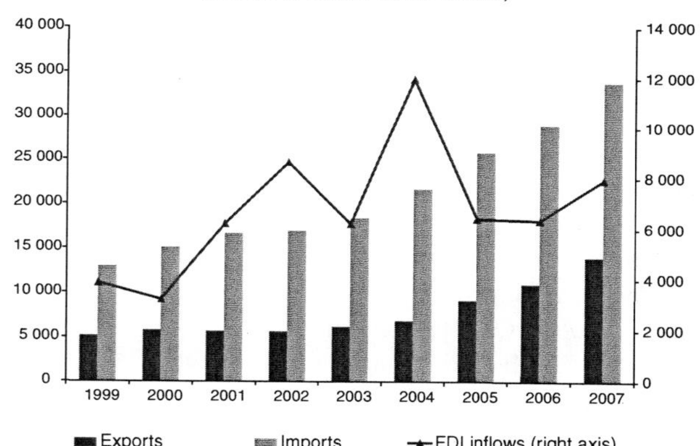

Source: Secretariat of Economic Affairs of Mexico.

Figure V.3

MEXICO: GROWTH IN TRADE FLOWS AND FDI INFLOWS FROM THE EUROPEAN UNION, 1999-2007

(Millions of United States dollars)

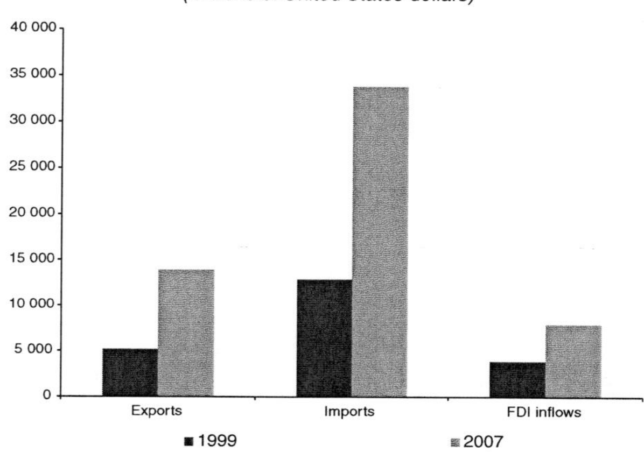

Source: Secretariat of Economic Affairs of Mexico.

The scope of the negotiations between Mexico and the European Union may extend even further given that partnership negotiations are simultaneously under way with other subregions, and additional synergies to those originally proposed in each agreement are now being sought. One notable example of this is the request submitted by Mexico and Central America to the European Union via the Tuxtla Dialogue and Agreement Mechanism for origin cumulation among the countries of the subregion in the case of certain products. If this proposal is accepted, new clauses would be inserted into the two agreements with the European Union in order to allow Central American inputs to be incorporated into Mexican products without these losing the preferences they benefit from in the European Union. The same would apply to Central American exports to the European Union that contain Mexican inputs (tenth Summit of Heads of State and Government of the Tuxtla Dialogue and Agreement Mechanism, Villahermosa, 28 June 2008).

The possibility of cumulation of origin was already contemplated in the Economic Partnership Agreement between Mexico and the European Union of 2000 but was never formalized. In this agreement, both parties committed to encourage cooperation with Central America and the Caribbean and to award priority to initiatives promoting intraregional trade. The possibility of origin cumulation between Central America and Mexico would strengthen intraregional trade and production linkages and improve regional value chains.

G. The principal issues affecting European Union-Latin American negotiations

Progress in negotiations with the European Union has been uneven across the subregions because in each case, both the benefits of a potential agreement and the obstacles on the path towards it are different. The economic implications of a potential agreement depend on the specific characteristics of the economies, the political landscape and the trade patterns of each bloc, in particular on the sectors that are considered to be "sensitive". One of the thorniest issues in the negotiations with Central American and Andean countries is the trade in bananas. The battle in the WTO over the European most-favoured-nation (MFN) banana tariffs, one of the longest-running trade disputes in history, created a rift between the European Union and some of the major exporters (see box V.1), a problem that will need to be addressed. In the Central American case, banana exports are currently being negotiated as a separate issue, and this will most likely happen in future negotiations with CAN.

Textiles and apparel is another trade sector that is of great importance to both Central America and the Andean countries. Market access for this sector to the European Union will be one of the major issues during the negotiations on trade in goods. When the European Union textile quotas were eliminated in 2005 as the Agreement on Textiles and Clothing (ATC) expired, the textile industry in Latin American counties suffered heavily from the fierce competition posed by China and other Asian countries, which have an enormous advantage over Latin America in terms of manufacturing costs. Chinese textile exports to the European Union soared, squeezing the garment industry in Mexico and Central America. Adjustment to quota expiration is a serious concern for Central American producers, as well as for Colombia and Peru, which will push for maximum preferences for the textile and apparel industry and possibly for investments and assistance to boost the competitiveness of the sector. Fully duty-free and quota-free market access, such as that granted to the Dominican Republic under the CARIFORUM EPA, would help the countries in the region to retain some of their competitive edge vis-à-vis China.

Another issue that the Andean and Central American textile industry will have to cope with is rules of origin. If these are set too stringent, they could preclude preferential exports of a large proportion of the textiles produced in these countries, since typically the content of United States inputs is very high, in particular in the export processing zones of Central America.

Furthermore, in Central America, the European requirement for ratification of the Statutes of Rome of the International Criminal Court in Central America could constitute a possible political impediment to advancement in the negotiations. So far only Panama, Costa Rica and Honduras have ratified the Statutes intended to prosecute and judge human rights violations and crimes against humanity. The other Central American countries do not acknowledge the Court.

In the Andean region, there are major differences in the countries' readiness to negotiate and to open up their markets. Peru and Colombia are very active and are pushing for a quick conclusion of the negotiations, while Bolivia and Ecuador are exerting more caution. Bolivia has already put limits on the scope of the agreement it would be willing to accept. It has indicated that it would keep its natural-resource-based sectors (agriculture, mining and gas) outside the reach of the agreement, as well as public procurement and intellectual property. According to the President of Ecuador, Rafael Correa, Ecuador is not ready to negotiate a comprehensive agreement either and would instead proceed "sector by sector, product by product and with mutual benefits".[18] An additional hurdle to the completion of the talks was indirectly posed by the recent tightening of immigration regulations by the European Union.[19] Colombia and Peru in particular have therefore suggested allowing greater flexibility in the negotiations so that Bolivia and Ecuador can opt out of certain provisions and the talks can move ahead. Faced with the indeterminate postponement of the negotiations, Peru is insisting on talks proceeding on a country-by-country basis. It will be attempted to reach a final outcome to the negotiations at a forthcoming meeting between the Andean Community and the European Union, further to agreements adopted at the recent summit of Presidents held in Guayaquil.

In the case of MERCOSUR, the prolonged standstill in the negotiations is in part due to the European Union's insistence on MERCOSUR becoming a "real common market", a requirement that has proven to be difficult to fulfil. The integration process in MERCOSUR has been uneven at best owing to continued trade disputes among the MERCOSUR members. But an even larger problem is the failure of the European Union and MERCOSUR to agree on market access in agriculture, a sector where MERCOSUR is highly competitive. Sugar has been a point of disagreement between the European Union and Brazil in the past. However, given the major reform of the European Union's sugar policy and the resulting reduction of both production and exports, it should no longer pose a serious obstacle. Furthermore, the Brazilian ethanol industry will benefit from the European policies that encourage the use of biofuels.[20] The future European Union-MERCOSUR agreement could include a scheme for managing European ethanol imports from Brazil through a TRQ system.

H. Prospects for 2008 and 2009

The region is entering into a qualitatively new phase of economic and trade relations with the European Union, its second most important trading partner. Expansion of commercial ties with the European Union will be crucial for reducing dependency on the United States market, in particular for Central America and the Caribbean, now that the slowdown in the United States economy is likely to have a negative effect on the region. Latin American and Caribbean countries should therefore prioritize the negotiations with the European Union and push for a reasonable timeframe for concluding them.

During the Summit of Heads of State and Government from Latin America and the Caribbean and from the European Union in May 2008 it was reaffirmed that the countries will "actively pursue" the negotiations of association agreements, and that the target for concluding them with Central America and the Andean countries is 2009. This seems like a plausible deadline for the negotiations with Central America. In the case of the Andean community, however, various issues that could complicate the talks have surfaced during 2008. The Central American Common Market is far more advanced than Andean Community in its own integration process, in particular in the establishment of a customs union, and the Central American countries are acting with a unified voice vis-à-vis the European Union. By contrast, the progress in the negotiations with the Andean Community will continue to be hampered by the ideological differences

18 *Diario La Hora*, Guatemala, 14 May 2008 [online] http://www.lahora.com.gt/notas.php?key=30501&fch=2008-05-14.

19 On 18 June 2008, the European Parliament adopted a so-called "return directive" that allows illegal migrants to be detained for up to 18 months and face a five-year travel ban after being deported. The new directive was widely criticized by the governments in the region as a violation of human rights. Ecuador, which has a large pool of immigrants in the European Union, was particularly critical and threatened to suspend the trade talks.

20 A 2003 European Commission directive established the replacement of 2% of petrol or diesel by substitute fuels in 2005 and of 5.75% in 2010 as an indicative objective for the European Union. Several car makers have recently announced the launch of ethanol-powered vehicles. To encourage the development of lower-carbon fuels and biofuels, in 2007 the European Union Commission proposed new standards that will oblige suppliers to reduce the greenhouse gas emissions caused by the production, transport and use of their fuels by 10% between 2011 and 2020.

and conflicts within the bloc itself, slow progress in the implementation of the integration agenda and the various degrees of preparedness to negotiate. The situation with MERCOSUR is also complicated, but for pragmatic, rather than political reasons, and the talks hinge on the progress made in the Doha round. The Summit declaration states that the negotiations with MERCOSUR will be completed "as soon as the conditions allow". As such, a breakthrough before 2010 is unlikely.

Still, the prospects for negotiations in 2008 and 2009 offer some interesting opportunities for the countries of Latin America and the Caribbean to shape the future of economic relations with Europe, provided sufficient progress is made in regional integration and assuming that each bloc manages to come up with coherent positions on the most critical topics. Alternatively, a far greater flexibility should be allowed in the negotiations, permitting countries to opt out of certain areas of negotiations or to adjust the degree of liberalization. One possibility would be to let countries opt out of some of the provisions initially and join the full agreement at a later stage. The application of the variable geometry and flexibility principles that allow the asymmetries within blocs to be addressed would speed up the negotiation process for those countries that are ready to enter into an agreement.

The prospects of an association agreement with the European Union play a catalytic role in consolidating and deepening the integration process within the region itself. First, the European Union has made it clear that it will only negotiate bloc to bloc, even if some degree of flexibility in the negotiations is introduced. Second, an association agreement would go beyond market access in goods and services. The European Union has always emphasized economic cooperation as an integral part of an association process and has consistently provided political and financial support to further integration in the region. The strategic partnerships embedded in the association agreements are typically supported by cooperation programmes in specific areas and technical assistance with a strong focus on regional integration, especially in the areas of trade facilitation, the convergence of rules and the strengthening of regional institutional capacity.[21] The availability of financial and political support for regional economic integration from the European Union would provide an important external boost to regional integration. However, to truly succeed, the impetus needs to come from the region itself. In order to compete successfully in the European Union market, as well as globally, the countries of Latin America and the Caribbean need to make a greater effort to enhance the systemic competitiveness of the region through greater cooperation in key trade-related areas. The convergence of rules and procedures at the regional level, collaborative efforts to facilitate trade and the development of regional institutional and physical infrastructure are important instruments of regional economic integration that will help the region to adjust to, and benefit from rapid shifts in global trading rules.

Another issue is that once the agreements with the European Union enter into force, the countries within each subregional integration scheme will automatically assume similar liberalization commitments towards each other as they do towards the European Union, as happened in the case of CARIFORUM. The provisions of such an agreement would almost certainly go well beyond those contained in today's regional integration schemes in Latin America, as they would cover liberalization of services and investments and contain important regulatory commitments, for example, regarding intellectual property rights and competition policy. This means that it may become easier for the countries of Latin America, to incorporate these critical issues into their regional integration processes.

---

[21] Thus, the current Regional Strategy for Central America focuses on strengthening the institutional system for the process of Central American integration; reinforcement of the regional economic integration process and strengthening regional security. In the Caribbean region, the European Union's assistance programme has the implementation of the Caribbean Single Market and Economy as one of its main objectives. The Regional Strategy for the Andean Community highlights establishment of a fully functioning Andean Common Market and facilitation of European Union-Andean Community negotiations for an association agreement. Finally, in December 2007 the EU approved an assistance packaged for € 50 million providing support in order to strengthen MERCOSUR institutions.

Bibliography

Condon, Bradly J. (2007), "The EU - Mexico FTA", Working Paper, Autonomous Technological Institute of Mexico (ITAM)/Department of Business Administration, Bond University, 22 January.

CRNM (Caribbean Regional Negotiating Machinery) (2008), "The EPA at a glance", July.

___ (2007), "What's in the EPA for the private sector?", *Private Sector Trade Note*, 19 December.

Diario Oficial de México (2000), "Decreto Promulgatorio del Acuerdo de Asociación Económica, Concertación Política y Cooperación entre los Estados Unidos Mexicanos y la Comunidad Europea y sus Estados Miembros", Mexico City, 26 June.

ECLAC (Economic Commission for Latin America and the Caribbean) (2007), *Latin America and the Caribbean in the World Economy, 2006. Trends 2007* (LC/G.2341-P), Santiago, Chile.

European Commission (2008), "Cariforum-EU Economic Partnership Agreement: An Overview", Information Paper, April.

Girvan, Norman (2008), "Caribbean integration and global Europe: implications of the EPA for the CSME" [online] http://normangirvan.info, August.

Mori, Antonella (2005), "Trade liberalisation and cooperation: Is the EU approach towards Latin America working well?", first draft, Washington, D.C., Inter-American Development Bank, 30 September.

ODI/ECDPM (Overseas Development Institute/European Centre for Development Policy Management) (2008), "The new EPAs: comparative analysis of their content and the challenges for 2008" [online] www.ecdpm.org/pmr14.

South Centre (2008), "The EU-Cariforum EPA on Services, Investments and E-Commerce – Implications for other ACP countries", May.

Working Group on European Union-Mercosur Negotiations (2007), "EU-Mercosur Trade Negotiations: 'Make or Brake'", The MERCOSUR Chair Annual Seminar, 25 January.

Chapter VI

Latin America and the Caribbean and Asia-Pacific in search of closer trade and investment relations

Introduction

Although trade and investment between Latin America and the Caribbean and the Asia-Pacific region have recovered since the Asian crisis and are continuing to expand, thanks especially to the recent upsurge in trade flows with China, biregional economic links generally remain weak and show little diversification. For most of the countries in Latin America and the Caribbean, the Asia-Pacific region is still a largely unexploited market despite its impressive record in areas such as growth, international trade, foreign direct investment (FDI), technology upgrading and innovation capacities, as well as its continuously expanding foreign reserves. The present dynamic aggregate demand of the countries of the Asia-Pacific region, especially China, offers Latin America and the Caribbean unprecedented production and export opportunities, both in commodities and in manufactures. The Latin American and Caribbean region's authorities should thus redouble their efforts to identify and capitalize on such new opportunities to enhance their countries' potential complementarities with the Asia-Pacific region.

A number of important events have been organized in recent years to address the nature and scope of cooperation between the two regions. However, these initiatives have stopped short of institutionalizing high-level political talks or implementing plans and programmes aimed at strengthening economic, political and cultural ties. There is a lack of awareness about the importance of biregional trade and investment, and there have been few coordinated strategies between countries or regional groupings for seeking closer trade and investment links with the Asia-Pacific region. Approaches to that region by Latin America and the Caribbean have thus far been sporadic and piecemeal, and have chiefly been confined to the conclusion of bilateral free trade agreements.

Until recently, Asia-Pacific regional integration has centred around its burgeoning intraregional trade flows, which are being driven by the increasing production and trade complementarities of the different countries' manufacturing sectors. Intra-industry trade (IIT) (i.e., cases where a country both imports and exports similar but not identical products) has expanded significantly as the specific advantages of production and marketing chains are exploited more effectively. This de facto (market-led) integration process in the Asia-Pacific region is now being reinforced by de jure (government-led) integration, and strong production and trade relations are being complemented by free trade agreements of various types aimed at consolidating such links.

To take full advantage of Asia's trade and investment dynamic, Latin America and the Caribbean must, as a matter of urgency, reorient and realign its relations with the Asia-Pacific region in order to sustain its commodity exports while producing more value added and more technologically complex manufactures for that market. The strategy in this regard should be to: (i) promote the Latin American and Caribbean region's participation in Asian supply chains with a view to boosting the value added and technology/knowledge content of its exports (including its exports of natural-resource-based products (the de facto approach); and (ii) implement instruments such as free trade agreements in order to address market-access problems (the de jure approach). The public and private sectors must both be prepared to allow their companies to build ties with successful Asian firms by forming part of the supply chains for their production and distribution units, including those of the natural-resource-based manufactures that are currently being exported to the Asia-Pacific region.

The call for greater biregional business alliances also applies to Asia-Pacific countries, which are global players in the market for technology-intensive goods and other sectors such as footwear, textiles and apparel, and electronics. Asia-Pacific competes directly with North American, European and Latin American firms in the Latin American market. The strategic position of the Asia-Pacific region in relation to other suppliers suggests that, in order to secure an even larger share of the Latin American and Caribbean market, Asia-Pacific countries need to strengthen their links with Latin American and Caribbean economies by building up alliances and promoting various forms of mutually beneficial business cooperation. Achieving this goal will require a deeper knowledge, on their part, of Latin American and Caribbean markets.

A. Latin America and the Caribbean and Asia-Pacific in the world economy

The regions of Latin America and the Caribbean and Asia-Pacific encompass widely diverse countries in terms of population, economic scale, geographical location, stage of development, and cultural backgrounds, although the more densely populated and highly developed countries are concentrated in the Asia-Pacific region. According to estimates for 2007, these regions together account for more than 2.5 billion inhabitants, or 60% of world population: 51% in Asia-Pacific and 9% in Latin America and the Caribbean. China alone accounts for 21% of the world total, while India's share is about 18%.

Total Asia-Pacific GDP in current prices is estimated at US$ 11,134 billion for 2007, or more than 20% of world GDP, while Latin America and the Caribbean contributes approximately 6%. Measured in terms of purchasing power parity (PPP), these region's relative share of world output is even greater at close to 28% and 8%, respectively. Moreover, in terms of PPP, the GDP of Asia-Pacific surpasses that of the United States or the European Union (see table VI.1).[1] In sum, regardless of the measure considered, Asia-Pacific, especially developing Asia, is already a formidable regional grouping worldwide.

Asia-Pacific's share of world GDP has increased at an impressive rate. Among the countries in that region, China stands out; despite the downscaling of the PPP by IMF in 2008, that economy still accounts for almost 11% of world output. The rest of developing Asia represents another 10% of world output when measured in PPP. Asia-Pacific as a whole is projected to sustain high growth rates and to increase its share of world total in the near future.

[1] Asia-Pacific includes both developed and developing countries of vastly different economic strengths, and as a result, the region's combined GDP is unequally distributed; four countries, Japan, China, Republic of Korea and Australia each accounted for slightly more than 18% and 20% of world output in 2007, as measured in nominal dollars or purchasing power parity, respectively.

Table VI.1

SHARE OF LATIN AMERICA AND THE CARIBBEAN AND ASIA-PACIFIC IN WORLD GDP

(Percentages of world total in current dollars and purchasing power parity)

	1985		1990		1995		2000		2005		2007		2010 (projections)	
	Nominal	PPP	Nominal	PPP	Nominal	PPP	Nominal	PPP	Nominal	PPP	Nominal	PPP	Nominal	PPP
European Union	24.5	28.0	31.4	27.3	31.0	26.2	26.7	25.3	30.6	23.4	31.0	22.7	30.0	21.4
United States	32.7	23.1	25.4	22.8	25.0	23.1	30.8	23.6	27.7	22.3	25.5	21.3	22.6	19.7
Asia-Pacific [a]	18.4	18.5	19.8	20.4	25.4	23.6	23.3	24.3	20.9	26.7	20.5	28.0	22.0	30.2
Japan	10.6	8.5	13.3	9.1	17.9	8.8	14.7	7.7	10.2	7.0	8.1	6.6	7.7	6.2
Australia	1.3	1.2	1.4	1.2	1.3	1.2	1.2	1.2	1.6	1.2	1.7	1.2	1.7	1.1
New Zealand	0.2	0.2	0.2	0.2	0.2	0.2	0.2	0.2	0.2	0.2	0.2	0.2	0.2	0.2
Developing Asia [b]	6.4	8.6	4.8	10.0	6.1	13.4	7.3	15.1	8.9	18.4	10.5	20.0	12.3	22.8
Newly industrialized Asian economies [c]	1.6	2.1	2.4	2.6	3.5	3.4	3.4	3.6	3.2	3.7	3.1	3.7	3.1	3.8
Republic of Korea	0.7	1.0	1.2	1.3	1.8	1.7	1.6	1.8	1.8	1.8	1.8	1.9	1.7	1.9
China	2.4	2.9	1.7	3.6	2.5	5.7	3.8	7.2	5.0	9.6	6.0	10.8	7.4	12.7
India	1.7	2.5	1.4	2.8	1.2	3.2	1.5	3.7	1.7	4.2	2.0	4.6	2.2	5.2
Latin America and the Caribbean	5.8	9.0	5.0	8.3	5.9	8.8	6.3	8.6	5.6	8.2	6.4	8.3	6.8	8.3
Africa	2.2	3.1	1.8	2.9	1.4	2.7	1.4	2.7	1.8	3.0	2.0	3.1	2.3	3.3
Central and Eastern Europe	3.0	4.7	2.4	4.3	1.9	3.8	2.1	3.7	2.9	3.9	3.4	4.0	3.5	4.1
Commonwealth of Independent States	6.8	7.7	6.9	7.6	1.4	4.0	1.1	3.6	2.2	4.2	3.1	4.5	4.5	4.8
Middle East	2.8	3.6	1.9	3.2	1.6	3.4	2.0	3.5	2.3	3.7	2.6	3.8	3.1	4.0
World	**100.0**	**100.0**	**100.0**	**100.0**	**100.0**	**100.0**	**100.0**	**100.0**	**100.0**	**100.0**	**100.0**	**100.0**	**100.0**	**100.0**

Source: Economic Commission for Latin America and the Caribbean (ECLAC), on the basis of International Monetary Fund (IMF), World Economic Outlook Database [online], April 2008.

[a] Asia-Pacific consists of developing Asia plus Australia, Japan and New Zealand.

[b] For the definition of developing Asia, see International Monetary Fund (IMF), *World Economic Outlook*, 2008, Washington, D.C., April 2008.

[c] Newly industrialized Asian economies consist of Hong Kong SAR, Republic of Korea, Singapore and Taiwan Province of China.

The importance of Asia-Pacific is becoming abundantly clear, not only with regard to production and world trade, but also in terms of global finance. The countries in this region are the main economies sustaining the increasing current account deficits of the United States (US$ 740 billion in 2007) and the European Union (US$ 220 billion) (see figure VI.1). The current account surplus of Japan, China and the Asian newly industrialized economies (Hong Kong SAR, Republic of Korea, Singapore and Taiwan Province of China) in 2007 was US$ 213 billion, US$ 361 billion and US$ 102 billion, respectively. The sum of the surpluses recorded by Japan, China, Asian newly industrialized economies and ASEAN (5), US$ 727 billion, was practically enough to cover the current account deficit of the United States in that year. China's surplus alone was greater than that of the Middle East, which stood at US$ 275 billion. Latin America and the Caribbean reported a surplus of US$ 16 billion in that year.

The countries of developing Asia, including the newly industrialized economies, are also significant net capital importers from a wide cross-section of sources worldwide. In 2007, this region was the largest importer of capital as a group among the developing countries and the economies in transition. In 2007, net capital inflows into emerging Asia totalled US$ 194 billion. This figure includes net private direct investment of US$ 91 billion, net private portfolio investment of US$ 18 billion and other private capital flows of US$ 85 billion. Official outflows amounted to US$ 38 billion and the variation (reduction) in reserves was US$ 669 billion.

Not only China and Japan but also the newly industrialized economies (NIEs), and to a lesser extent, ASEAN, provide the United States with cheap savings, keep interest rates low and accumulate international reserves through the purchase of Treasury bonds, thus helping to finance its current account deficit. As at February 2008, Japan and China held US$ 587 billion and US$ 487 billion, respectively, in United States Treasury bonds, (see figure VI.2). Nine of the top 27 holders of United States Treasury securities (mainly T-bonds and notes) are of Asian origin. Not only Japan and China but also Hong Kong SAR, Republic of Korea, Singapore, Taiwan Province of China and Thailand, appear among the top 20. The major holders in Latin America are Brazil and Mexico, the former being the fourth largest, with a sum of US$ 147 billion. The Caribbean financial centres, as a group, hold just over US$ 100 billion.

Figure VI.1
BALANCES ON CURRENT ACCOUNT, BY REGION AND COUNTRY, 2007
(Billions of dollars)

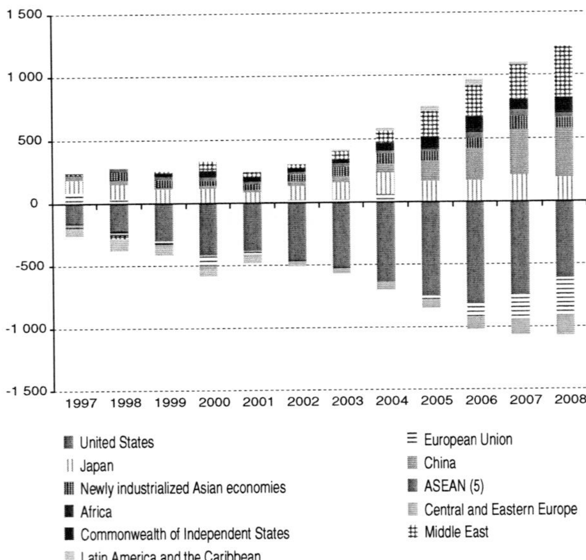

Source: Economic Commission for Latin America and the Caribbean (ECLAC), on the basis of International Monetary Fund (IMF), World Economic Outlook Database [online] http://www.imf.org/external/pubs/ft/weo/2008/01/weodata/WEOApr2008all.xls.

Note: ASEAN (5) includes Indonesia, Malaysia, Philippines, Thailand and Viet Nam and excludes Singapore, which is included among the newly industrialized Asian economies (Hong Kong SAR, Republic of Korea, Singapore and Taiwan Province of China).

Figure VI.2
TOP 27 FOREIGN HOLDERS OF UNITED STATES TREASURY SECURITIES, FEBRUARY 2008
(Billions of dollars)

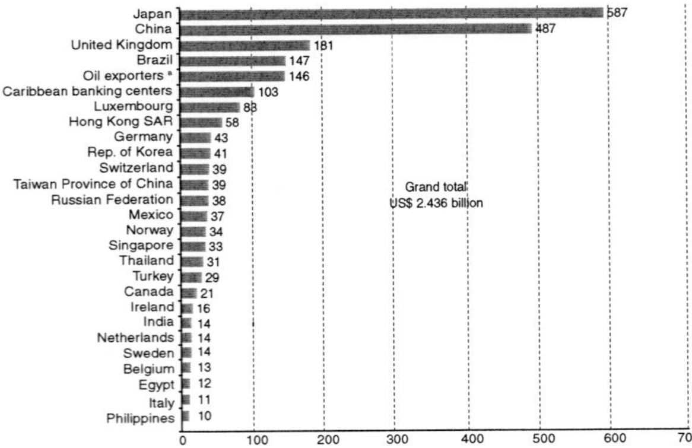

Source: United States Department of the Treasury [online] www.ustreas.gov.
[a] Include Algeria, Bahrain, Bolivarian Republic of Venezuela, Ecuador, Gabon, Indonesia, Iran, Iraq, Kuwait, Libya, Nigeria, Oman, Qatar, Saudi Arabia and the United Arab Emirates.

Asian countries are also the major holders of foreign reserves worldwide: Asia, including Japan, accounts for 60% of world reserves minus gold. The share of China alone was roughly 24% at the end of 2007, at US$ 1.53 trillion (see table VI.2). The seven Latin American countries (Argentina, Bolivarian Republic of Venezuela, Brazil, Chile, Colombia, Mexico and Peru) accounted for 9% of the world stock of foreign reserves. The amount in the hands of Chinese authorities is continuing to rise: as of March 2008, Chinese reserves exceeded US$ 1.682 trillion, surpassing those of Japan (US$1.016 trillion). While capital inflows to Asia, particularly portfolio inflows, have often been seen as temporary, current account surpluses tend to endure and have a lasting effect on the exchange rate.

Table VI.2
STOCK OF FOREIGN RESERVES (MINUS GOLD), DECEMBER 2007 [a]
(Billions of dollars and percentages)

	Stock	Percentage world share
Asia	2 917	45.2
China	1 530	23.7
India	267	4.1
Republic of Korea	262	4.1
Taiwan Province of China	270	4.2
Other Asia [b]	587	9.1
Latin America [c]	400	6.2
Central Europe [d]	121	1.9
Russian Federation	464	7.2
Middle East [e]	149	2.3
Total emerging markets (8)	4 051	62.8
Japan	953	14.8
Total world	6 446	100.0

Source: Economic Commission for Latin America and the Caribbean (ECLAC), calculations on the basis of information from International Monetary Fund (IMF), International Financial Statistics.
[a] Cumulative sum for 2007, in billions of United States dollars. Aggregates are the sum of the economies' reserves.
[b] Hong Kong SAR, Indonesia, Malaysia, Philippines, Singapore and Thailand.
[c] Argentina, Bolivarian Republic of Venezuela, Brazil, Chile, Colombia, Mexico and Peru.
[d] The Czech Republic, Hungary and Poland.
[e] Kuwait, Libya, Oman, Qatar and Saudi Arabia.

Countries in both regions are highly integrated into the international trading system. Asia-Pacific accounted for 28% of world merchandise exports and 23% of world services exports in 2007, respectively (see figure VI.3 and table VI.3). Meanwhile, the corresponding shares for Latin America and the Caribbean were approximately 6% and 3%, respectively, in that year. At present, Asia-Pacific trade is almost four and a half times as great as that of Latin America and the Caribbean.[2] As analysed later, this dynamic growth has resulted in strong intra-Asia-Pacific

[2] World merchandise exports and imports stood at US$ 13.57 trillion and US$ 13.94 trillion in 2007, respectively, an increase in value of approximately 15% over 2006. With respect to services, which represent almost 20% of world trade in goods and services, the Asian shares are also high although their share of exports of services is slightly lower than their share of total exports.

trade, which accounted for 11.0% of world exports and 12.8% of world imports in 2006.

In 2007, China became the world's second largest exporter of goods, surpassing the United States. The four newly industrialized Asian economies contributed 7% of world exports and imports, while the ASEAN group's total exports and imports amounted to US$ 863 billion and US$ 773 billion, respectively, exceeding the total of Latin America and the Caribbean as a group. The share of Latin America and the Caribbean still remains below 6%.

Figure VI.3

SHARE OF LATIN AMERICA AND THE CARIBBEAN AND ASIA-PACIFIC IN WORLD MERCHANDISE EXPORTS AND IMPORTS, 2007

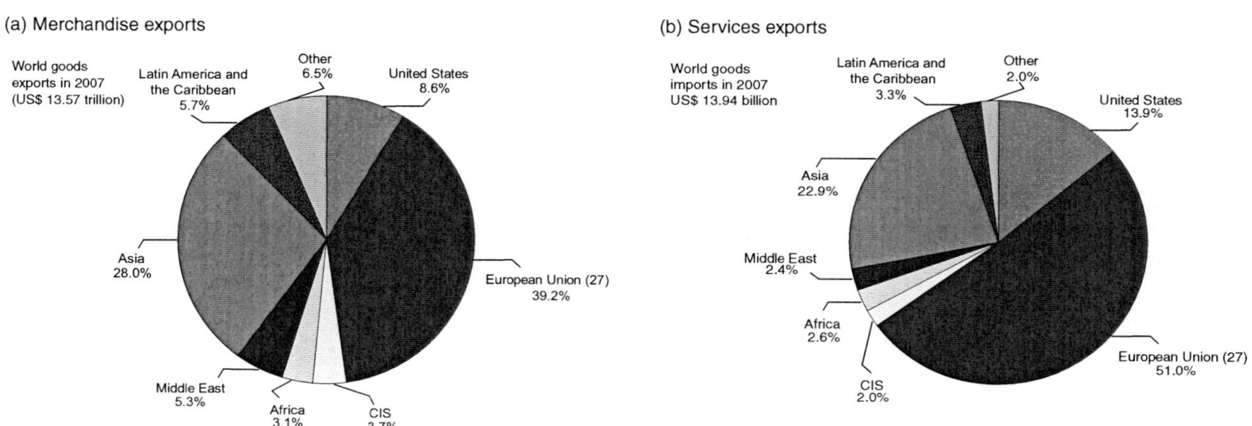

Source: World Trade Organization (WTO), "World Trade 2007, Prospects for 2008", Press Release (Press/520/rev.2), 17 April 2008.

Table VI.3

SHARE OF ASIAN AND LATIN AMERICAN COUNTRIES IN WORLD TRADE, 2007

(a) Merchandise exports

Countries/regions	Value (billions of dollars)	Share in total of Asia plus Latin America and the Caribbean	World share
Asia	3 798	83.2	28.0
Japan	713	15.6	5.3
China	1 218	26.7	9.0
Republic of Korea	372	8.1	2.7
Taiwan Province of China	246	5.4	1.8
Singapore (domestic exports)	156	3.4	1.1
India	145	3.2	1.1
Other Asia	1 194	26.1	8.8
Latin America and the Caribbean	768	16.8	5.7
Brazil	161	3.5	1.2
Mexico	272	6.0	2.0
Other Latin American and Caribbean countries	335	7.3	2.5
Asia and Latin America and the Caribbean	4 566	100.0	33.6
World	13 570	...	100.0

(b) Services exports

Countries/regions	Value (billions of dollars)	Share in total of Asia plus Latin America and the Caribbean	World share
Asia	745	87.3	22.9
Japan	136	15.9	4.2
China	127	14.9	3.9
Newly industrialized economies [a]	243	28.5	7.5
India	86	10.1	2.6
Other Asia	153	17.9	4.7
Latin America and the Caribbean	108	12.7	3.3
Brazil	23	2.7	0.7
Mexico	17	2.0	0.5
Other Latin American and Caribbean countries	68	8.0	2.1
Asia and Latin America and the Caribbean	853	100.0	26.2
World	3 260	...	100.0

Source: World Trade Organization (WTO), "World Trade 2007, Prospects for 2008", Press Release (Press/520/Rev.1), 17 April 2008.
[a] Newly industrialized economies comprise Hong Kong SAR, Republic of Korea, Singapore and Taiwan Province of China.

The share of Asia-Pacific countries in world merchandise exports continued to increase in the past two decades, from 18.0% in 1985-1990 on average to 20.6% in 1991-1995 and 22.5% in 2001-2006. The share of Latin America and the Caribbean rose slightly, to stand at just over 5% in the present decade, with the most remarkable performance coming from Mexico. With respect to Asia-Pacific, China's expansion has been the most noteworthy, while the shares of the three developed economies in the region, Australia, Japan and New Zealand, show a decline (see figure VI.4).

Figure VI.4
CHANGES IN SHARE OF WORLD TRADE BETWEEN 1991-1995 AND 2001-2006

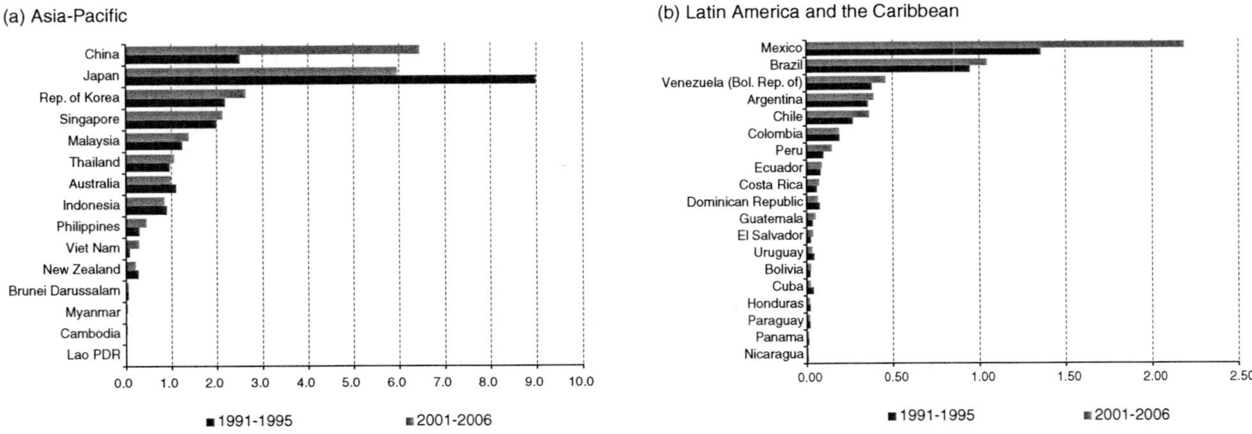

Source: Economic Commission for Latin America and the Caribbean (ECLAC), on the basis of World Bank, World Development Indicators [online database].

The importance of trade development is illustrated by the recovery process from the sharp recessions experienced around the years 1997-1999 in both regions. Asia bounced back rapidly after the dot.com calamity in 2001 and maintained and increased both inter-and intraregional exports and imports; those of Latin America and the Caribbean, which recovered at a more moderate pace, stagnated in 2000. The Asian financial crisis had a significant impact on intraregional trade in Latin America.

Developing countries have been absorbing an increasing share of world FDI —about 35% of world totals, up from 25% in 1990. In the 1970s, Latin America accounted for 40% of FDI inflows into developing countries. In the second half of the 1990s, when national firms were privatized, Latin America once again became one of the major choices for investors. Developing Asia has since taken over from Latin America as the destination of choice for foreign investors, and absorbed about half of the FDI flowing into developing countries in the first half of the 1990s and more than 40% in the second half of the decade.

According to the UNCTAD database, inward FDI into Asia-Pacific (15) has increased steadily over the years, averaging US$ 110 billion per year during 2000 and 2006, almost twice the amount recorded during the 1990s. More than half of this total was invested in China. Meanwhile, Australia, Singapore and other ASEAN countries, together with the Republic of Korea, have emerged as important FDI recipients (see table VI.4). As of 2006, cumulative FDI in Asia-Pacific exceeded US$ 1.2 trillion, equivalent to 10% of world FDI stock. The corresponding figures for Latin America and the Caribbean are also impressive: an annual average inflow of about US$ 63 billion in the current decade.

Inward FDI to Latin America and the Caribbean increased by 1.5% compared with 2005 to stand at US$ 72.4 billion. Mexico, the leading recipient, attracted as much as US$ 19.0 billion, reflecting an increase of 20.8%, while investment in Brazil expanded by 24.7% to US$ 18.8 billion. An interesting trend relating to Latin American FDI is that the sources of inward FDI have recently become more diversified, with investment from Spain, the major investor in the region, on the decline, while investment in resources-related industries and service-related operations, financed mainly by firms of the region itself, is on the rise, resulting in the emergence of trans-Latins. Their stock at the end of 2006, estimated at US$906 billion, represented 7.6% of the world total. In short, FDI flows into Asia-Pacific, especially to China and ASEAN, are continuing to increase. Latin America and the Caribbean's share of total inflows to developing countries is gradually shrinking, with higher concentrations of that share being invested in Brazil, Mexico and Chile.

Table VI.4
STOCK OF INWARD FDI TO ASIA-PACIFIC AND LATIN AMERICA AND THE CARIBBEAN, 1980, 1990, 2000 AND 2006
(Billions of dollars)

	1980	1990	2000	2006	World (percentage)
Asia-Pacific (15)	51.7	180.5	681.1	1 200.5	10.0
Australia	24.8	73.6	111.1	246.2	2.1
Brunei Darussalam	0.0	0.0	3.9	9.9	0.1
Cambodia	0.0	0.0	1.6	3.0	0.0
China	1.1	20.7	193.3	292.6	2.4
Indonesia	4.7	8.9	24.8	19.1	0.2
Japan	3.3	9.9	50.3	107.6	0.9
Lao People's Democratic Republic	0.0	0.0	0.6	0.9	0.0
Malaysia	5.2	10.3	52.7	53.6	0.4
Myanmar	0.0	0.3	3.9	5.0	0.0
New Zealand	2.4	7.9	24.9	63.1	0.5
Philippines	1.3	3.3	12.8	17.1	0.1
Republic of Korea	1.3	5.2	38.1	71.0	0.6
Singapore	5.4	30.5	112.6	210.1	1.8
Thailand	1.0	8.2	29.9	68.1	0.6
Viet Nam	1.4	1.6	20.6	33.5	0.3
Latin America and Caribbean	35.0	105.0	480.6	906.1	7.6
Argentina	5.3	8.8	67.6	58.6	0.5
Bolivia	0.4	1.0	5.2	4.8	0.0
Brazil	17.5	37.2	103.0	221.9	1.8
Chile	0.9	10.1	45.8	80.7	0.7
Colombia	1.1	3.5	11.0	44.8	0.4
Costa Rica	0.5	1.3	2.7	6.8	0.1
Cuba	0.0	0.0	0.1	0.1	0.0
Dominican Republic	0.2	0.6	1.7	5.6	0.0
Ecuador	0.7	1.6	7.1	16.1	0.1
El Salvador	0.2	0.2	2.0	4.4	0.0
Guatemala	0.7	1.7	3.4	4.9	0.0
Honduras	0.0	0.3	1.4	3.0	0.0
Mexico	-2.0	22.4	97.2	228.6	1.9
Nicaragua	0.1	0.1	1.4	2.7	0.0
Panama	2.5	2.3	6.7	12.8	0.1
Paraguay	0.2	0.4	1.3	1.6	0.0
Peru	0.9	1.3	11.1	19.4	0.2
Uruguay	0.4	0.7	2.1	4.4	0.0
Venezuela (Bolivarian Republic of)	1.6	3.9	35.5	45.4	0.4
Caribbean a	3.8	7.5	74.5	139.6	1.2
Developing countries	140.4	364.8	1 778.9	3 545.0	29.5
World	551.2	1 779.2	5 810.2	11 998.8	100.0

Source: Economic Commission for Latin America and the Caribbean (ECLAC), on the basis of official information from the database of the United Nations Conference on Trade and Development (UNCTAD).

[a] Anguilla, Antigua and Barbuda, Aruba, Bahamas, Barbados, British Virgin Islands, Cayman Islands, Dominica, Grenada.

B. Trade and investment links between Latin America and the Caribbean and Asia-Pacific

1. An overview of biregional trade

Trade between Latin America and the Caribbean and the Asia-Pacific region has recovered after two years of stagnation (1998-1999) following the Asian crisis, and is expanding steadily. The Asia-Pacific region[3] has also become a very important trading partner for Latin America and the Caribbean, particularly in terms of the latter's imports. In 2006, exports to the Asia-Pacific region from Latin America and the Caribbean[4] amounted to US$ 58.2 billion, representing 8.9 % of the region's total exports; while Asia-Pacific imports totalled US$ 126.9 billion with a 22.3% share. In the same year, the United States' share of exports from Latin America was 48.6%, while the European Union (27 member States) accounted for 13.4%. With respect to imports, the United States and the European Union (27) provided 34.3% and 13.3% respectively of the region's imports. As a trading partner for Latin America and the Caribbean, the Asia-Pacific region is thus much more important as a source of imports than as a destination for exports, and this has generated a growing trade deficit with that region since 1992, amounting to US$ 69 billion in 2006.

The importance of Asia-Pacific as an export market is not the same for all Latin American and Caribbean countries. The MERCOSUR countries with the exception of Paraguay have relied heavily on that market since the beginning of the present decade. On the other hand, the Asia-Pacific share of trade with the Andean Community expanded in the mid 1990s, but has since declined, dropping to 5% or less in 2007. The exception, Peru, continues to export substantial volumes to that region. Exports from Central American countries to Asia-Pacific have been flat, accounting for less than 4% of their total shipments, except in the case of Costa Rica which ships more than 20% of its total exports to that market.

In contrast, following a sharp contraction in 1998 as a consequence of the Asian crisis, Chile's exports to the region have been picking up steadily and accounted for 40% of the country's total in 2007. Brazil, the largest exporter to Asia-Pacific in absolute terms, saw its share rise to 16% in the same year. Interestingly, in the case of Mexico, the relative importance of Asia-Pacific remains low; the bulk of exports from Mexico and the Central American countries are sold to the United States, the main trading partner for these countries. The latter have, however, signed trade agreements with a number of Asia-Pacific countries, in an effort to diversify into this market. Asia-Pacific has not been a major destination for exports from the Caribbean countries, Jamaica being an important exception.

Behind this dynamic trade between the two regions, China is playing an increasing role in both exports and imports, rapidly displacing Japan as Asia-Pacific's main trading partner with Latin America and the Caribbean since the start of the decade, notwithstanding Japan's slight recovery in recent years on the export side (ECLAC, 2007b). In addition, the ASEAN group (5) has gained a share similar to that of the Republic of Korea as a source of imports for Latin America and the Caribbean and as a destination for exports originating there.

An analysis by regions and sectors by technological intensity finds that almost half of all Asia-Pacific exports went to other countries within that same region in 2006, while other markets such as the United States, the European Union and Latin America and the Caribbean were secondary export destinations (see table VI.5). What is most striking is that, regardless of export destination, the Asia-Pacific export basket consists primarily of manufactures, especially products in the medium- and high-technology categories. Patterns of intra-Asia-Pacific

3 Unless indicated otherwise, the Asia-Pacific region encompasses the group of 12 countries and territories consisting of Australia, China, Hong Kong SAR, Indonesia, Japan, Malaysia, New Zealand, the Philippines, Republic of Korea, Taiwan Province of China, Singapore and Thailand. For statistical reasons, the figures cited here do not include the other members of ASEAN (Brunei Darussalam, Cambodia, Lao People's Democratic Republic, Myanmar and Viet Nam).

4 Unless indicated otherwise, Latin America and the Caribbean consists of 33 of the countries in the region.

trade show that "high" and "medium" technology products already account for roughly 60% of the total and are continuing to gain ground. These categories of products, together with other manufactures, also account for a significant (albeit lower) proportion of total exports traded intraregionally within Latin America and the Caribbean (approximately 43%).

In contrast, trade between the two regions is typically inter-industrial, with Latin America and the Caribbean exporting basically primary products to Asia-Pacific, which, in turn, exports relatively high-technology manufactures to Latin America and the Caribbean. In general, the share of manufactures of differing technological intensity (low, medium or high) is very small and contrasts starkly with the structure of Latin American intraregional trade, which includes a high component of medium-technology products. This contrasting production and trade specialization by the two regions seems to be partially responsible for a low level of reciprocal foreign direct investment.

Table VI.5
LATIN AMERICA AND ASIA-PACIFIC TRADE BY REGION AND PRODUCT, BY TECHNOLOGICAL INTENSITY, 2006
(Percentages)

Products by technological intensity	Export matrix by region and sector								Export distribution by region and sector							
	Latin America and the Caribbean [a]	United States	European Union [b]	Asia-Pacific (12) [c]	China	Japan	Others	Total	Latin America and the Caribbean [a]	United States	European Union [b]	Asia-Pacific (12) [c]	China	Japan	Others	Total
Asia-Pacific																
Primary products	0.1	0.5	0.6	4.5	0.8	1.7	1.3	7.0	3.0	2.6	4.3	9.3	9.2	21.1	8.2	7.0
NRB manufactures	0.3	1.4	1.4	7.6	1.4	1.3	2.0	12.6	7.1	7.8	9.5	15.5	15.8	16.7	13.2	12.6
Low-technology manufactures	0.6	3.9	2.8	6.3	0.7	1.5	3.3	17.0	17.0	22.0	19.5	12.9	8.0	19.4	21.8	17.0
Medium-technology manufactures	1.6	6.2	4.3	12.3	2.7	1.3	6.1	30.6	45.1	34.7	29.9	25.3	30.5	16.4	39.8	30.6
High-technology manufactures	0.8	5.5	4.8	16.3	2.9	1.8	2.4	29.9	23.3	30.9	33.4	33.5	32.8	23.2	15.9	29.9
Other transactions	0.1	0.3	0.4	1.3	0.2	0.1	0.7	2.9	4.1	1.8	2.9	2.6	2.5	1.0	4.8	2.9
Total	3.6	17.9	14.5	48.7	8.7	7.9	15.3	100.0	100.0	100.0	100.0	100.0	100.0	100.0	100.0	100.0
Latin America and the Caribbean																
Primary products	3.5	12.6	5.8	5.6	2.2	1.7	7.3	34.8	20.9	26.5	46.1	58.5	61.8	73.0	54.5	34.8
NRB manufactures	4.0	5.7	3.6	2.3	0.8	0.4	2.5	18.1	23.7	12.0	28.9	23.8	22.8	17.8	18.7	18.1
Low-technology manufactures	1.9	5.1	0.7	0.3	0.1	0.0	0.4	8.4	11.5	10.7	5.2	3.5	3.7	1.0	2.7	8.4
Medium-technology manufactures	5.5	14.2	1.9	0.9	0.2	0.1	1.3	23.8	33.0	29.7	15.0	8.9	6.9	6.3	10.0	23.8
High-technology manufactures	1.6	9.2	0.5	0.5	0.2	0.0	0.6	12.5	9.8	19.3	4.4	5.1	4.8	1.8	4.5	12.5
Other transactions	0.2	0.9	0.0	0.0	0.0	0.0	1.3	2.4	1.2	1.8	0.3	0.1	0.0	0.1	9.6	2.4
Total	16.7	47.8	12.5	9.6	3.6	2.3	13.4	100.0	100.0	100.0	100.0	100.0	100.0	100.0	100.0	100.0

Source: Economic Commission for Latin America and the Caribbean (ECLAC), on the basis of United Nations Commodity Trade Database (COMTRADE).
[a] Latin America and the Caribbean consists of 33 countries in the region.
[b] The European Union includes 15 countries.
[c] Asia-Pacific includes Taiwan Province of China and Hong Kong SAR.

2. Country concentration

Exports by the Latin American and Caribbean region to Asia-Pacific, including India, are highly concentrated in just a few countries. During the period 2004-2006, on average, five countries accounted for almost 92% of all Latin American and Caribbean exports to Asia-Pacific: Brazil (35%), Chile (28%), Argentina (14%), Mexico (9%) and Peru (7%). These shares have not changed substantially over the last two decades (Kuwayama, 2001). Within the region, Mexico and the MERCOSUR countries, particularly Brazil, are major importers from Asia-Pacific. The most striking feature of regional imports from the Asia-Pacific region is the rapidly increasing share of Mexico, which represented roughly 53% of total imports from that region during this period, compared with 25% at the beginning of the 1990s.

Mexico has become the largest importer from all the Asian partners (i.e., Japan, China, Republic of Korea, ASEAN, combined share of Australia and New Zealand, and India). The North American Free Trade Agreement (NAFTA) is considered to be the major factor behind this dynamism. In fact, in terms of imports, China has become Mexico's second trading partner after the United States. Meanwhile, the share of the rest of Latin American and Caribbean countries is very small. As a result, in geographical terms, regional imports from Asia-Pacific are even more concentrated than its exports: these countries, namely, Mexico and Brazil, account for nearly 70 % of the total. Chile and Peru play a much less substantial role as importers from Asia-Pacific than as exporters to that region.

As shown in figure VI.5, some countries of the region rely heavily on Asia-Pacific, including India, as a trading partner, especially for their imports. In general, China accounts for a significant share of both exports and imports, while Japan is more visible in imports. Nonetheless, the share of the Republic of Korea and that of the ASEAN group (5) are moderately high for some countries.

Figure VI.5
SHARE OF ASIA-PACIFIC, INCLUDING INDIA, IN TOTAL LATIN AMERICAN AND CARIBBEAN EXPORTS AND IMPORTS, AVERAGE 2004-2006
(Percentages)

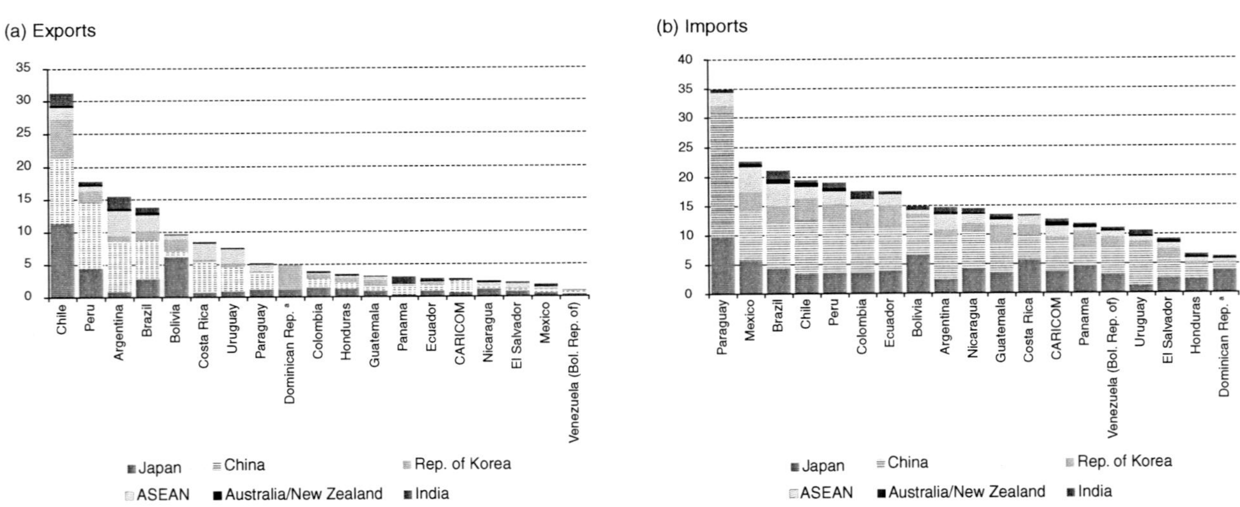

Source: Economic Commission for Latin America and the Caribbean (ECLAC), on the basis of United Nations Commodity Trade Database (COMTRADE).
[a] The figures for the Dominican Republic relate to 2001.

From the Asia-Pacific perspective, however, Latin America and the Caribbean has not been a major trading partner: during 2004 and 2006, on average, only 2.3% of total Asia-Pacific exports were shipped to the region, while only 2.7% of imports originated here (see figure VI.6).[5] Moreover, there has been no significant change in these shares over the last two decades (Kuwayama, 2001). For all the geographical groupings (Japan, China, Republic of Korea and the ASEAN group (5)) for which data are available, the share of Latin America and the Caribbean in total exports and imports of Asia-Pacific does not usually exceed 4%. Significant differences exist between countries, however. In average terms, Latin America and the Caribbean's imports from Republic of Korea represent 3.9% of that country's exports, higher than its share in any other Asia-Pacific country's export market. As a provider for Asia-Pacific import markets, Latin America and the Caribbean accounts for a higher proportion of China's imports (4%) than its share of any other Asia-Pacific country's import market. Latin America and the Caribbean account for an extremely small percentage of the total exports and imports of the smaller economies in Asia-Pacific, such as those of ASEAN.

In sum, regional trade is becoming more balanced among Asian exporter countries. Whereas Japan was the main trading partner (both supplier and buyer) from the region in the 1980s and 1990s, in recent years, China, Japan, Republic of Korea and ASEAN have each accounted for a substantial share of Latin American and Caribbean trade. China is now the dominant partner for both exports and imports, although in terms of imports into Latin America and the Caribbean from Asia-Pacific, its penetration is unparalleled.

Figure VI.6
THE LATIN AMERICAN AND CARIBBEAN REGION'S SHARE IN TOTAL ASIA-PACIFIC EXPORTS AND IMPORTS, AVERAGE 2004-2006
(Percentages)

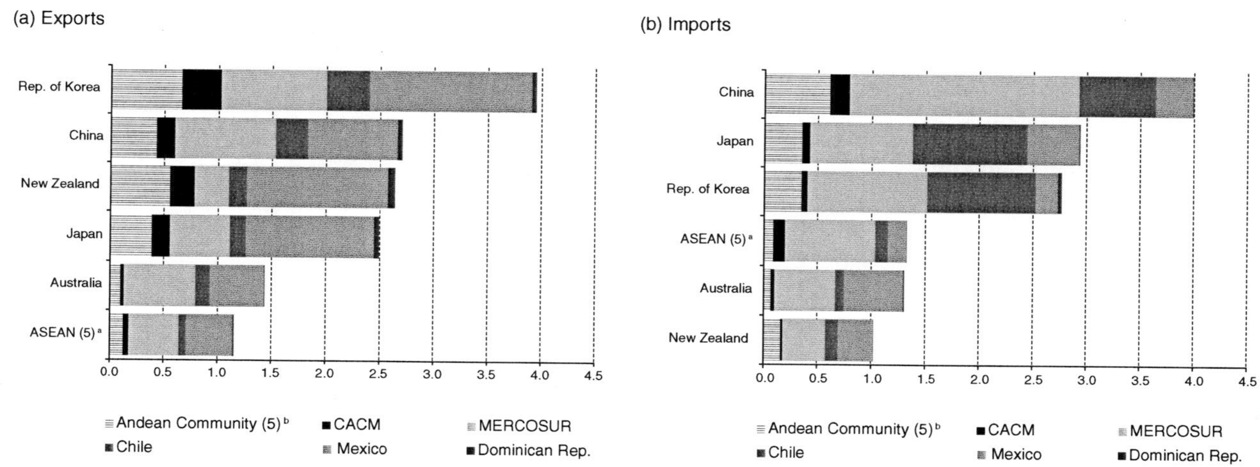

Source: Economic Commission for Latin America and the Caribbean (ECLAC), on the basis of United Nations Commodity Trade Database (COMTRADE).
[a] ASEAN (5) consists of Indonesia, Malaysia, Philippines, Singapore and Thailand.
[b] For the purposes of the present study, the Bolivarian Republic of Venezuela is included in the Andean Community.

5 In this analysis, data are derived from official figures reported by Asia-Pacific countries. Therefore, the trade flows calculated from the Asia-Pacific side do not correspond to those shown in the earlier sections of this report, which are based on trade data in which the countries of Latin America are used as reporters.

3. Product concentration

The principal regional exports to Asia-Pacific are primary commodities and natural resource-based manufactures. Of the products shipped by the region to ASEAN (5)+3 (Japan, China and the Republic of Korea), those with the highest export values in 2006 are highly concentrated in natural resources and resource-based processed products (ECLAC, 2008). However, whereas the region has such a high concentration in a just a handful of products, ASEAN (5)+3 has achieved a high level of diversification of supply sources, sufficient to prevent the countries of the region from having strong bargaining power with respect to these products. There is significant competition with several developed economies and with neighbouring developing Asia-Pacific countries in mining, agricultural, fishery and forestry products, in respect of which Latin America traditionally enjoys comparative advantages.

It is important to note, however, that the list includes a number of new products, such as fishery products and pig meat, along with high-technology manufactures, including electronic microcircuits and telecommunications equipment and data-processing machinery. The presence of these manufactures products indicates that Latin America is gradually beginning to gain a foothold in the supply-chain networks existing in the Asia-Pacific region.

In stark contrast with this trend, Asia-Pacific exports to the region consist mainly of manufactures. They range from labour-intensive products to motor vehicles and electronics. The top 30 products imported by Latin America and the Caribbean from ASEAN (5)+3 in 2006 accounted for 54% of the value of total Latin American and Caribbean imports from Asia-Pacific in that year. Another interesting feature of these 30 products is the importance of Asia-Pacific and North American countries as exporters to the Latin American region. Despite the predominant role of the United States as the principal exporter of many products, Asia-Pacific has a strong market presence. Also noticeable is the presence of some Latin American countries, namely Mexico and Brazil, as alternative sources of imports for passenger motor vehicles and parts, and several electric and non-electronic products, which reflects the increasing importance of Latin America in intraregional trade and the relevance of intra-industry trade in manufactures.

The above confirms that Asia-Pacific countries are strong players in the market for technology-intensive goods. In several other sectors, such as footwear and textiles and apparel and electronics products, the region competes directly with Latin American countries in the Latin American market and third-country markets. The strategic position of Asia-Pacific in relation to other suppliers suggests that to secure an even higher share of the Latin American market, Asia- Pacific countries need to strengthen their links further with Latin American economies by building up alliances and promoting various types of business cooperation. Achieving this goal in turn requires a deeper knowledge of Latin American markets. Meanwhile, the strong position of the United States and several Latin American countries in many manufactured product groups underlines the challenges for Asia-Pacific countries in maintaining or expanding their market shares under existing free trade agreements with the United States or the European Union. In the absence of a similar international trade arrangement with Asia-Pacific countries, these agreements with the North could lead to a relative deterioration in market-access conditions for Asia-Pacific exports to Latin America and the Caribbean.

C. Divergent patterns of de facto integration in and between the two regions

As many Asian experts point out (e.g., ADB, 2007; Kawai and Wignaraja, 2007; World Bank, 2007; Ando and Kimura, 2005), trade ties between Asia-Pacific economies are increasingly characterized by burgeoning intra-industry trade (IIT), based on the increasingly complementary production and trade components of the different countries' manufacturing sectors. This type of trade has expanded significantly as the specific advantages of productive and marketing chains have been exploited more effectively. The Asia-Pacific region thereby has become "factory Asia" for the rest of the world. IIT has entailed an increasingly broad and complementary group in which development is disseminated in concentric circles, thanks to intra-industry regional trade and intraregional foreign direct investment (FDI). In addition, this process of de facto (market-led) integration in Asia-Pacific is now being supported by de jure (government-led) integration, and strong production and trade relations are being complemented by free trade agreements of various types that aim to consolidate those links. In view of these trends, Latin America and the Caribbean needs to strengthen its trade links to make its production more complementary with that of Asia-Pacific, and establish trade and investment partnerships, in addition to trade agreements, which would provide new access to these markets and help them integrate into Asian production and export chains.

1. Limited but increasing Intra-Industry Trade (IIT) between the two regions

A key element in the structuring of Asia-Pacific over the last decade relates to technological development and the possible fragmentation of the production chain, which triggered a sharp increase in Asian intraregional trade. The intra-Asian trade coefficient for the countries of ASEAN+3 plus Hong Kong SAR and Taiwan Province of China, grew from 43% in the early 1990s to 55% in 2006 (see table VI.6). This indicator surpasses the level of intraregional trade attained by the countries of the North American Free Trade Agreement (NAFTA), and is rapidly approaching that displayed by the European Union. Trade among members of ASEAN (10) has increased and surpasses the 16%, 9% and 11% attained by MERCOSUR, the Andean Community and the Central American Common Market (CACM), respectively, in 2006. This expansion of intra-Asian trade has been driven partly by the robust growth of intra-firm and intra-industry trade, thanks to the construction of a complex network of vertical supply chains by transnational corporations, in which China plays a fundamental role as both origin and destination.

Intra-Asia-Pacific trade has been characterized by a strong and increasing presence of products categorized as being of "high" and "medium" technology-intensity and which account for more than 59% of the total (see table VI.5). However, this overall picture of the region as a world export platform of medium- and high-technology intensity manufactures masks the wide diversity that exists among Asia-Pacific countries (see table VI.7). Primary products and natural resource-based manufactures account for a significant proportion of exports from Australia, Brunei Darussalam, Indonesia, New Zealand and Viet Nam. Countries such as China, Japan, Malaysia, Philippines, Republic of Korea, Singapore, and to a lesser degree, Thailand, determine the overall picture of Asia-Pacific as the world factory for manufactures worldwide. The low-technology sector, which includes textiles and apparel, is still a significant segment of manufactures exports for several countries in that region.

Table VI.6

ASIAN INTRAREGIONAL TRADE, BY GEOGRAPHICAL GROUPING [a]

(Percentages of the region's total trade)

Region	1980	1985	1990	1995	2000	2003	2006
Within ASEAN (10)	17.9	20.3	18.8	24.0	24.7	26.6	27.2
Within ASEAN+3	30.2	30.2	29.4	37.6	37.3	39.0	38.3
Within ASEAN+3+Hong Kong SAR+ Taiwan Province of China	34.1	37.1	43.1	51.9	52.1	55.4	54.5
Memo: European Union (27)	61.5	60.0	66.8	66.9	66.3	68.1	65.8
NAFTA	33.8	38.7	37.9	43.1	48.8	47.4	44.3
MERCOSUR	11.1	7.2	10.9	19.2	20.7	14.7	15.7
Andean Community (5) [b]	...	3.3	5.4	12.4	10.8	10.8	9.1
CACM	...	n.a.	12.1	15.6	17.5	17.6	...

Source: Economic Commission for Latin America and the Caribbean (ECLAC), on the basis of United Nations Commodity Trade Database (COMTRADE).

[a] The share in intraregional trade is defined as the percentage of intraregional trade with respect to total trade of the region in question, based on export data. It is calculated as follows: Xii /{(Xiw + Xwi)/2}, where Xii refers to exports that originate and remain within region i, Xiw represents exports from region i to the world, and Xwi represents world exports to region i. A higher percentage indicates a higher level of dependency on intraregional trade.

[b] The Andean Community (5) includes the Bolivarian Republic of Venezuela.

Table VI.7

ASIA-PACIFIC: EXPORT STRUCTURE BY TECHNOLOGICAL INTENSITY, BY COUNTRY, 2006

(Percentages)

Asia-Pacific countries	Primary products	Natural resource-based manufactures	Low-technology manufactures	Medium-technology manufactures	High-technology manufactures	Total
Australia	61.2	18.5	3.6	10.6	6.2	100.0
Brunei Darussalam [a]	96.6	0.2	1.9	0.9	0.5	100.0
Cambodia [b]	3.0	0.8	95.0	0.9	0.2	100.0
China	3.1	9.5	31.8	22.1	33.4	100.0
Indonesia	36.2	24.7	17.3	13.2	8.6	100.0
Japan	0.4	8.8	7.9	57.5	25.3	100.0
Malaysia	12.9	15.3	8.8	17.7	45.3	100.0
New Zealand	42.8	32.6	8.0	11.2	5.4	100.0
Philippines	3.8	9.8	9.2	12.0	65.1	100.0
Republic of Korea	0.6	13.2	11.0	39.7	35.5	100.0
Singapore	1.1	21.0	5.8	19.1	53.0	100.0
Thailand	11.4	17.8	15.6	28.7	26.5	100.0
Viet Nam [b]	45.0	6.6	36.8	6.1	5.5	100.0

Source: Economic Commission for Latin America and the Caribbean (ECLAC), on the basis of United Nations Commodity Trade Database (COMTRADE)

[a] The figures for Brunei Darussalam refer to 2006 only.

[b] The figures for Cambodia and Viet Nam refer to 2004 only.

Equal to or greater than 25%.

Greater than 15%, but less than 25%.

The expansion and deepening of supply chain networks in Asia-Pacific is observed in a wide range of industrial sectors that include not only manufactures but also natural resource-based products. A detailed analysis of the structure of intraregional trade in this region shows that of the 20 main products exported to the world in 2006,[6] four product categories, namely, electric machinery, apparatus and appliances, office machinery and automatic data-processing equipment, road vehicles, and precision machinery, figure among the most important products exported within the region (see table VI.8). For example, close to 45% of total exports in electrical machinery takes place within the Asia-Pacific region. Indeed, this sector accounted for almost 18% of total intraregional trade in that year.[7] These sectors have been particularly dynamic in China; but, in general, export growth in all East and South-East Asian groupings far outpaced that of world trade in these products.

6 Products are classified at the two-digit level of the Standard International Trade Classification – SITC, Rev. 2).

7 This finding is consistent with conclusions of other studies on Asian intraregional trade. The Asian Development Bank (ADB, 2007) shows that at the global level, and for certain Asian groupings, the four machinery sectors in the two-digit Harmonized System (HS 84, 85, 86-89 and 90-91) all display high growth rates.

Table VI.8
ASIA-PACIFIC INTRAREGIONAL TRADE [a]
(Millions of dollars and percentages)

Rank	Product description	Value of intra-Asia-Pacific exports (millions of dollars)			Share of intra-Asia-Pacific exports in total regional exports (percentages)			Share in total of intraregional trade (percentages)		
		1990	2000	2006	1990	2000	2006	1990	2000	2006
1	Electrical machinery, apparatus and appliances	17 283	101 690	178 240	31.7	42.1	44.5	9.3	20.4	17.5
2	Petroleum, petroleum products and related materials	22 634	37 556	84 938	71.5	68.6	71.4	12.2	7.5	8.3
3	Office machines and automatic data-processing machines	5 638	42 623	72 760	14.1	29.3	27.7	3.0	8.5	7.1
4	Telecommunications and sound recording and reproducing apparatus	8 571	25 651	56 365	17.5	26.9	23.7	4.6	5.1	5.5
5	Iron and steel	9 136	15 730	43 760	49.1	53.5	50.8	4.9	3.2	4.3
6	Road vehicles (including air cushion vehicles)	10 002	18 422	40 319	13.5	15.7	17.5	5.4	3.7	4.0
7	General industrial machinery and equipment, n.e.s. and machine parts, n.e.s.	7 219	14 858	33 299	35.4	35.1	36.6	3.9	3.0	3.3
8	Non-ferrous metals	4 838	10 524	32 180	56.5	53.7	57.1	2.6	2.1	3.2
9	Organic chemicals	3 478	11 362	32 121	39.8	44.6	49.9	1.9	2.3	3.2
10	Machinery specialized for particular industries	7 482	15 513	30 433	39.1	41.0	40.4	4.0	3.1	3.0
11	Artificial resins, plastic materials and cellulose	2 908	11 394	27 072	42.4	48.2	50.6	1.6	2.3	2.7
12	Professional, scientific and controlling device instruments	1 842	6 975	26 705	24.6	31.0	40.0	1.0	1.4	2.6
13	Articles of apparel and clothing	5 066	18 054	26 685	19.1	30.0	22.9	2.7	3.6	2.6
14	Metalliferous ores and metal scrap	3 445	5 873	26 044	42.3	50.6	67.3	1.9	1.2	2.6
15	Miscellaneous manufactured articles	3 923	13 367	25 822	19.0	26.1	26.3	2.1	2.7	2.5
16	Textile yarn, fabrics, made-up articles, n.e.s. and related products	6 267	16 575	23 677	27.1	36.7	31.2	3.4	3.3	2.3
17	Gas, natural and manufactured	5 914	10 295	20 207	93.1	78.2	77.6	3.2	2.1	2.0
18	Manufactures of metal, n.e.s.	3 078	7 278	18 839	31.3	32.6	31.5	1.7	1.5	1.9
19	Power generating machinery and equipment	3 623	9 074	17 979	29.3	33.0	37.6	2.0	1.8	1.8
20	Coal, coke and briquettes	3 466	5 138	15 286	59.6	54.8	51.4	1.9	1.0	1.5
	Other	49 202	119 294	205 736	...	...	...	26.7	20.2	18.1
	Total	185 015	498 824	1 018 260	...	...	...	100.0	100.0	100.0

Source: Economic Commission for Latin America and the Caribbean (ECLAC), on the basis of United Nations Commodity Trade Database (COMTRADE).
[a] Standard International Trade Classification (SITC), Rev.2 (two-digit level).

East Asia, especially the ASEAN+3 economies and Taiwan Province of China, is one of the most important IIT hubs in the world. According to the most recent calculations made by the Asian Development Bank (ADB, 2007), the last decade witnessed high and rising coefficients of IIT in natural-resource-related sectors and also among technology- and human-capital-intensive sectors. Roughly half of the growth in IIT seen in East Asia between 1990 and 2003 is attributable to an expansion of trade in the components and machine parts sector (Ando and Kimura, 2005) which has registered the fastest growth. East and South-East Asia thus jointly assume the mantle of "Factory Asia".

At a greater level of detail, roughly 60% of trade in machinery and transport equipment and in parts and components in Asia-Pacific takes place intraregionally (see figure VI.7),[8] following a significant increase since the early 1990s. Latin America and the Caribbean, however, has much less intraregional trade in parts and components, though trade in machinery and transport equipment registered a slight increase. IIT performance in these sectors has been much poorer in the region, even for the NAFTA countries, which have seen a slight decline in intraregional trade in parts and components. To attract greater investment into the region, Latin American countries need to promote supply chain networks in these sectors.

Figure VI.7
INTRAREGIONAL TRADE IN MACHINERY AND TRANSPORT EQUIPMENT AND IN PARTS AND COMPONENTS,[a] 1990 AND 2006
(Percentages)

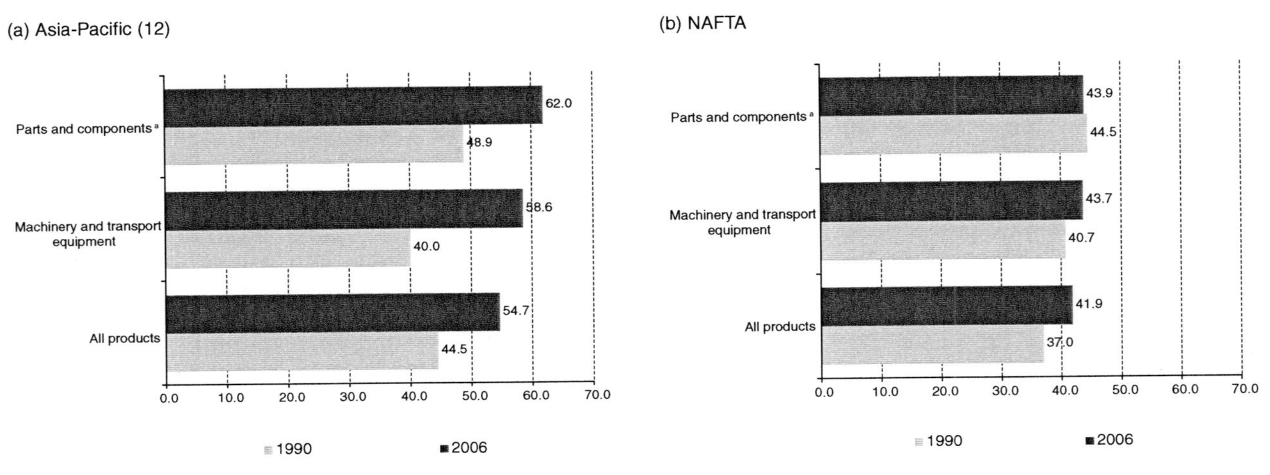

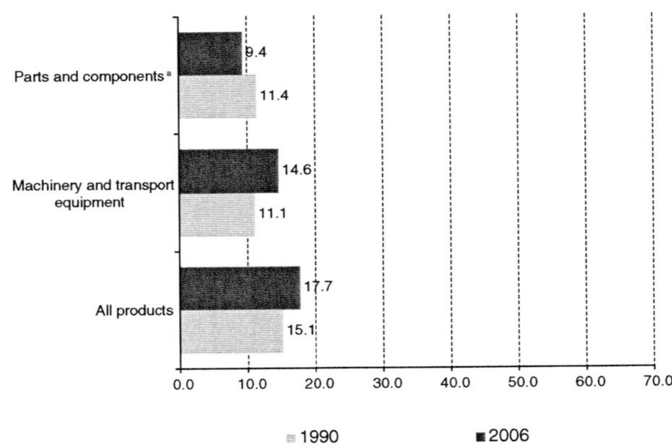

Source: Economic Commission for Latin America and the Caribbean (ECLAC), on the basis of United Nations Commodity Trade Database (COMTRADE).
[a] The sector of machinery and transport equipment is defined as those products belonging to SITC code 7 (Rev. 2), while the definition of parts and components (51 groups of products classified at the 3 to 5 digits) are those that are not finished goods of the same SITC code 7 product category.

8 Machinery and transport equipment is the largest and most buoyant segment of manufactures exports, accounting for 37% of world merchandise exports and 53% of world manufactures exports in 2006. Notably, 24% of world exports in machinery and transport equipment originate in Asian countries (WTO, 2008).

Despite their image as exporters of primary products and natural-resource-based manufactures, when examined at the national level, the Latin American export structure is quite diverse (ECLAC, 2006). In fact, manufactured goods, especially in the low- and medium-technology categories, account for significant proportions of exports by Argentina, Brazil, Mexico, Colombia, and Costa Rica and, to a lesser degree, El Salvador and Guatemala. Substantial intra-industry trade flows take place among the member countries of MERCOSUR, the Andean Community and the Central American Common Market countries.

The trade of Asia-Pacific is relatively similar to that of Latin America in terms of product composition, with road vehicles, petroleum, iron and steel and several machinery products figuring among the top 20 products (see table VI.9). These 20 products accounted for over 76% of total intraregional trade in Asia-Pacific in 2006. The coincidence of major intraregional trade products in Asia-Pacific and Latin America might suggest that bi-regional trade opportunities exist in these products.

Table VI.9
LATIN AMERICA AND THE CARIBBEAN: INTRAREGIONAL TRADE [a]
(Millions of dollars and percentages)

Rank	Product description	Value of intra-Latin American exports (millions of dollars)			Share of intra-Latin American exports in total regional exports (percentages)			Share in total intraregional trade (percentages)		
		1990	2000	2006	1990	2000	2006	1990	2000	2006
1	Road vehicles (incl. air cushion vehicles)	838	5 416	14 314	16.9	15.4	25.1	5.2	10.6	14.1
2	Petroleum, petroleum products and related materials	2 530	8 530	12 448	8.6	15.3	9.7	15.8	16.6	12.3
3	Non-ferrous metals	539	1 698	5 186	6.6	15.2	14.7	3.4	3.3	5.1
4	Telecommunications and sound recording equipment	93	945	4 660	18.2	4.5	13.0	0.6	1.8	4.6
5	Iron and steel	771	1 659	4 593	13.2	21.9	25.6	4.8	3.2	4.5
6	Artificial resins, plastic materials, cellulose	462	1 852	3 659	37.1	56.8	51.7	2.9	3.6	3.6
7	Metalliferous ores and metal scrap	493	835	3 569	9.4	8.9	9.4	3.1	1.6	3.5
8	Gas, natural and manufactured	288	662	3 086	57.1	94.3	90.3	1.8	1.3	3.0
9	Cereals and cereal preparations	834	2 179	3 083	46.1	58.9	50.9	5.2	4.2	3.0
10	Electrical machinery, apparatus and appliances	367	1 426	3 018	27.4	5.0	8.9	2.3	2.8	3.0
11	Paper, paperboard, pulp and related articles	319	1 622	2 456	26.0	52.4	49.1	2.0	3.2	2.4
12	Machinery specialized for particular industries	289	657	2 350	28.1	24.9	28.6	1.8	1.3	2.3
13	Medicinal and pharmaceutical products	175	1 465	2 146	50.4	67.6	65.4	1.1	2.9	2.1
14	General industrial machinery and equipment	406	1 142	2 136	27.5	16.3	16.1	2.5	2.2	2.1
15	Miscellaneous manufactured articles	371	1 319	2 065	30.2	20.0	22.0	2.3	2.6	2.0
16	Textile yarn, fabrics, made-up articles	426	1 479	1 902	21.7	31.0	37.6	2.7	2.9	1.9
17	Essential oils and perfume; toilet and cleansing preparations	132	953	1 881	45.5	55.4	58.4	0.8	1.9	1.9
18	Manufactures of metal, n.e.s.	341	1 044	1 872	31.0	19.3	22.1	2.1	2.0	1.8
19	Organic chemicals	464	995	1 820	26.4	30.0	24.4	2.9	1.9	1.8
20	Chemical materials and products, n.e.s.	290	917	1 508	49.5	58.9	57.4	1.8	1.8	1.5
	Other	5 585	14 478	23 639	...	...	...	34.9	28.3	23.5
	Total	16 013	51 273	101 391	...	...	...	100.0	100.0	100.0

Source: Economic Commission for Latin America and the Caribbean (ECLAC), on the basis of United Nations Commodity Trade Database (COMTRADE).
[a] Standard International Trade Classification (SITC), Rev.2 (two-digit level).

However, in the case of Latin America and the Caribbean, natural-resource-based products account for a larger proportion of the total intraregional trade basket; in addition to petroleum-related products, there are substantial amounts of non-ferrous metals, natural gas, cereals, paper and paper products, chemicals and essential oils. Almost half of these products are exported within the region. The coefficients for machinery products are generally low, while those for medicinal and pharmaceutical products, another high-technology item, are quite high at 65%. There is also a substantial amount of intraregional trade in textiles and apparel.

A brief analysis of trends in IIT between 1990 and 2006 in Asia-Pacific and Latin American countries, both intraregionally and with other regions of the world, indicates that there have been substantive changes over the years, especially in Asia-Pacific. This conclusion was based on Grubel Lloyd Index (GLI) calculations,[9] which indicated that:

- IIT has expanded over the years in both regions, from 0.13 to 0.20 in Latin America and from 0.22 to 0.36 in Asia Pacific;
- The strongest hikes in IIT coefficients are observed in Asia-Pacific;
- The IIT coefficients for bi-regional trade, though increasing, remain very low, not surpassing 0.05 and 0.07; and
- Each region's IIT coefficient with the European Union and, most strikingly, the United States, has increased substantially.

Of the four patterns of IIT (see table VI.10), in more than 93% of the sectors analysed, most trade flows between the Asia-Pacific region and Latin America are inter-industrial rather than intra-industrial in nature, i.e., trade consists of exchanging primary or natural-resource-based products for manufactures. However, this general pattern, which is based on regional averages, hides considerable variations in trade among the countries or groups of countries within each region and between countries from both regions.

Table VI.10

ASIA-PACIFIC AND LATIN AMERICA AND THE CARIBBEAN: INTRA-INDUSTRY TRADE WITHIN EACH REGION AND WITH OTHER REGIONS, 1990, 1995, 2000 AND 2006

(Grubel Lloyd index)

	Intra-Asia-Pacific/ America		Extra-Asia-Pacific/ Latin America	
Regions/countries	Latin America and the Caribbean	Asia-Pacific	European Union (27)	United States
1990				
Latin America	0.13	0.03	0.08	0.23
Asia-Pacific	0.04	0.22	0.19	0.30
1995				
Latin America	0.22	0.04	0.10	0.37
Asia-Pacific	0.04	0.30	0.26	0.37
2000				
Latin America	0.27	0.06	0.12	0.44
Asia-Pacific	0.07	0.36	0.27	0.39
2006				
Latin America	0.20	0.05	0.13	0.39
Asia-Pacific	0.07	0.36	0.26	0.27

Source: Economic Commission for Latin America and the Caribbean (ECLAC), on the basis of United Nations Commodity Trade Database (COMTRADE).

Among the four regional groupings (Latin America and the Caribbean, Asia-Pacific, the United States and the European Union) considered, Asia-Pacific's intraregional IIT shows the highest GLI, while its IIT with Latin America is by far the lowest. Countries such as China, Japan, Malaysia, Philippines, the Republic of Korea, Singapore and Thailand each maintain a high GLI with each of their major trade partners. Australia and New Zealand also show a relatively high GLI with each major trade bloc (ECLAC, 2008). The preliminary findings cited here support the existing literature on the role that China and other emerging Asian countries are beginning to play in Asian regional integration (Wakasugi, 2007; IMF, 2007;[10] Ando, 2005; Kinoshita, 2004; Fukao, Ishido and Ito, 2003; Durking and Kryegier, 2000). One of the explanations for this dynamic lies in the "fragmentation" or "slicing-up" of the production processes across national boundaries, promoted by various types of business associations (FDI, joint ventures and others) and intra-firm trade.

9 This analysis of intra-industry trade (IIT) between Latin America and the Caribbean and Asia-Pacific is based on the methodology by Grubel and Lloyd, (1975) that measures the degree of trade flows in the same sector between countries/regions. It is calculated as follows:

$$GLI_t = 1 - \frac{\sum_i |X_{it} - M_{it}|}{\sum_i (X_{it} + M_{it})}$$

where X_{it} and M_{it} are exports and imports of the product in question in the year t. The coefficient can take a value between 0 and 1. The coefficient moves closer to 1 as the proportion of IIT increases. In this exercise, in order to capture substantive changes and differentiate the depth of IIT, three levels of GLI are adopted: first level: GLI > 0.33; second: GLI > 0.10 <0.33; and third: GLL < 0.10. The calculations are performed at the 3-digit SITC level, disaggregated into 233 product groups.

10 It should be noted that the findings of the recent IMF report *Regional Perspectives for Asia Pacific countries 2007* provides GLIs that are much higher than the GLIs of the present report and other studies (0.35 in the IMF study). The difference between the two derives from the fact that the IMF study disaggregates at the 2 digit levels, while the present report adopts the production classification based on SITC at the 3 digit levels.

What is striking is that the overall GLI for trade between the two regions in 2006 is quite low, not surpassing 0.07 (see table VI.10). When examined from the viewpoint of Asia-Pacific, in most cases the IIT matrix shows this type of trade as almost non-existent, with a GLI below 0.10. However, some bilateral flows are found, indicating emerging IIT, albeit at an incipient stage (see table VI.11). In general, Mexico's trade with Asia-Pacific shows higher GLIs than that of other Latin American countries. Argentina, Brazil, Costa Rica and other Central American countries are beginning to show some degree of IIT, though not yet consistently among all the Asian trade partners. On the Asia-Pacific side, Singapore and Australia are moving into IIT with Latin America and the Caribbean. In sum, there has been a breakthrough from a complete inter-industry trade type to a trade structure that is a little more intra-industry oriented.

Moreover, the products driving IIT between the two regions are principally high-and medium-technology goods involving electrical apparatus, parts and accessories, microcircuits, automatic data processing machines, measuring, checking, controlling instruments, pharmaceutical products, and others in which Asia-Pacific countries have made strong inroads at the global level. Products incorporating medium technology also include a variety of plastics products, motor vehicles and their parts and engines, as well as a number of products which fall under the category of general machinery. The low-technology products include textiles, yarn and iron and steel products (ECLAC, 2008).

The forgoing seems to indicate that several Latin American firms have begun to insert themselves in several Asian supply/value chains in recent years. The emergence of IIT across the two regions involving an increasing number of countries and sectors suggests that there are interesting opportunities and possibilities to expand such trade in the future. There are certain sectors in the manufacturing industry where bi-regional IIT can be promoted. However, in order to exploit these opportunities, closer entrepreneurial contacts are needed, including FDI and other types of business association, as well as the signing of free trade agreements among the countries in both regions.

Table VI.11

INTRA-INDUSTRY TRADE RELATIONS OF SOME LATIN AMERICAN AND CARIBBEAN COUNTRIES WITH ASIA-PACIFIC, 2006

(Grubel Lloyd indices)

Countries \ Partners	Australia	China	Indonesia	Japan	Malaysia	New Zealand	Philippines	Rep. of Korea	Singapore	Thailand	Viet Nam
Argentina	0.08	0.03	0.02	0.02	0.01	0.17	0.00	0.03	0.13	0.02	0.01
Bolivia	0.01	0.01	0.00	0.00	0.01	0.00	0.00	0.00	0.02	0.00	0.00
Brazil	0.07	0.08	0.05	0.06	0.02	0.14	0.02	0.05	0.18	0.05	0.06
Chile	0.08	0.01	0.00	0.00	0.01	0.02	0.03	0.01	0.02	0.01	0.00
Colombia	0.18	0.02	0.02	0.01	0.00	0.03	0.01	0.00	0.13	0.07	0.06
Costa Rica	0.05	0.10	0.02	0.55	0.19	0.01	0.38	0.09	0.36	0.10	0.01
Dominican Republic	0.12	0.03	0.00	0.04	0.08	0.01	0.01	0.03	0.27	0.03	...
Ecuador	0.05	0.01	0.01	0.00	0.08	0.02	0.03	0.01	0.19	0.01	0.00
El Salvador	0.00	0.01	0.01	0.00	0.00	0.00	0.00	0.00	0.00	0.01	0.00
Guatemala	0.02	0.03	0.03	0.01	0.01	0.00	0.02	0.02	0.03	0.04	0.00
Honduras	0.00	0.10	0.00	0.00	0.00	0.00	0.00	0.01	0.00	0.02	0.00
Mexico	0.15	0.27	0.09	0.16	0.24	0.03	0.11	0.09	0.56	0.37	0.02
Nicaragua	0.00	0.00	0.00	0.00	0.00	0.00	0.00	0.00	0.00	0.00	0.10
Panama	0.11	0.00	0.00	0.00	0.00	0.00	0.00	0.17	0.00	0.00	0.00
Paraguay	0.00	0.00	0.00	0.00	0.00	0.01	0.04	0.00	0.00	0.00	0.00
Peru	0.10	0.01	0.01	0.01	0.00	0.02	0.34	0.02	0.02	0.02	0.00
Uruguay	0.04	0.03	0.11	0.00	0.01	0.05	0.00	0.06	0.03	0.00	0.00
Venezuela (Bolivarian Republic of)	0.07	0.01	0.01	0.00	0.03	0.00	0.00	0.00	0.00	0.02	0.00

Source: Economic Commission for Latin America and the Caribbean (ECLAC), on the basis of United Nations Commodity Trade Database (COMTRADE).

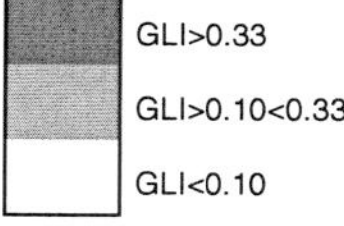

2. Intraregional FDI, key to intraregional and intra-industry trade

In recent years, the Asian newly industrialized economies, namely the Republic of Korea, Taiwan Province of China and Hong Kong SAR and, to a lesser extent, the ASEAN countries have become significant investors in emerging Asian countries. For instance, in Thailand and Viet Nam, firms from Asian NIEs are the most dominant investors. Hong Kong SAR is by far the largest investor in China. FDI by firms in the Asian NIEs has become much more significant, representing 29% of total FDI inflows to ASEAN (9) and 54% of total inflows to China. In addition, more recently, firms from the middle-income ASEAN countries, such as Malaysia and Thailand, have begun to invest in other ASEAN countries and in China (Kawai and Wignaraja, 2007).

(a) The case of Japan

Japan's external trade grew significantly in 2007 in relation to the previous year's levels, with exports expanding by 10.1% and imports by 7.2%. The country's Asian neighbours continue to be key partners as both destinations and origins for its foreign trade (see figure VI.8), with a similar trade structure being maintained during the present decade (see table VI.12). Asia-Pacific countries (excluding India) supplied over 48% of Japan's imports and absorbed an even larger proportion (almost 50%) of its exports. Among neighbouring Asian countries, China and ASEAN (10) stand out, especially in terms of imports, since they account for over 20% and 14% of total imports, respectively. Japan's imports from ASEAN (10) surpassed those coming from the either United States or the European Union. Latin America and the Caribbean remains a relatively minor market; representing 4.9% as an export destination and 3.9% as an origin for Japan's imports.

A large proportion of the goods that Japan imports from its Asian neighbours consists of electronic machinery and other manufactured products of general use. This characteristic is clearly visible not only in its imports from China and the Asian NIEs (4) (Hong Kong SAR, Republic of Korea, Singapore, and Taiwan Province of China), but also in its trade with the members of ASEAN (4). The only sector in which Latin America and the Caribbean has a strong presence in Japan's imports is crude materials (see table VI.13).

Figure VI.8
JAPAN'S FOREIGN TRADE IN 2007, BY COUNTRY/REGION
(Percentages)

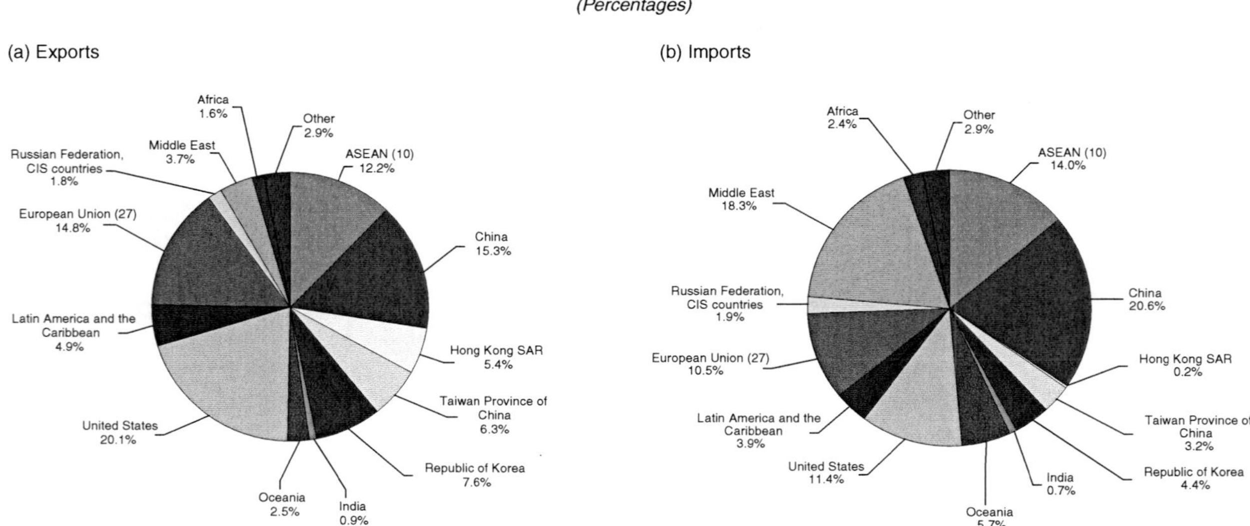

Source: Economic Commission for Latin America and the Caribbean (ECLAC), on the basis of official figures from the Japan External Trade Organization (JETRO) [online] http://www.jetro.go.jp.

Table VI.12
JAPAN'S TRADE AND OUTWARD FOREIGN DIRECT INVESTMENT BY COUNTRY, TERRITORY AND REGION

Country/territory/region	Foreign trade (2004-2006 annual average)		Cumulative OFDI end 2006 (based on balance of payments, net, in millions of dollars)	
	Share in exports (percentage)	Share in imports (percentage)	Stock end of 2006	Share (percentage)
Asia	48.1	44.3	107 653	23.9
China	13.6	20.7	30 316	6.7
Asian NIEs [a]	24.0	9.9	39 042	8.7
Taiwan Province of China	7.2	3.6	6 328	1.4
Republic of Korea	7.8	4.8	10 669	2.4
Hong Kong SAR	6.0	0.3	7 776	1.7
Singapore	3.1	1.3	14 270	3.2
ASEAN (4) [b]	8.7	11.5	34 313	7.6
Thailand	3.6	3.0	14 839	3.3
Indonesia	1.4	4.1	7 457	1.7
Malaysia	2.1	2.9	7 763	1.7
Philippines	1.5	1.5	4 253	0.9
ASEAN (10)	12.4	14.2	49 837	11.1
India	0.6	0.6	2 315	0.5
Latin America and the Caribbean	4.3	3.2	39 291	8.7
Oceania	2.5	5.3	13 794	3.1
Middle East	2.8	16.7	2 038	0.5
Africa	1.4	2.1	2 701	0.6
United States	22.5	12.6	156 411	34.8
European Union (25)	15.0	11.4	118 852	26.4
Other	3.4	4.4	8 941	2.0
Total	100.0	100.0	449 680	100.0
Total year average (millions of dollars)	582 734	494 750	...	...

Source: Economic Commission for Latin America and the Caribbean (ECLAC), on the basis of official figures from the Japan External Trade Organization (JETRO) [online] http://www.jetro.go.jp.
[a] The regional groupings are: Asian NIEs (Hong Kong SAR, Rep. of Korea, Taiwan Province of China, and Singapore).
[b] ASEAN (4) (Indonesia, Malaysia, Philippines and Thailand).

Japan's role as an investor and as a recipient of worldwide OFDI is quite small: based on balance-of-payments statistics, Japanese OFDI represented 3.5% of total world OFDI in 2006 (US$ 50.2 billion), while its inward FDI experienced a slight contraction (net outflow of US$ 6.8 billion). However, East and South-East Asia are very important as destinations for this type of Japanese investment. In terms of Japan's cumulative FDI stock at the end of 2006, Asia as a group accounted for 24% of the total, while the European Union (27) and the United States represented 35% and 26%, respectively.

Table VI.13

JAPAN'S IMPORTS, BY REGION AND SECTOR, AVERAGE FOR 2005-2007

(Millions of dollars and percentages)

	United States	European Union (27)	Asian NIEs (4)	ASEAN (4)	China	Latin America and the Caribbean	Other	World (million of dollars)	Share (%)
Total	11.8	10.7	9.5	11.3	20.7	3.5	32.5	573 005.2	100.0
Food and direct consumers	23.8	10.7	4.9	8.8	16.1	9.0	26.6	49 764.7	100.0
Industrial supplies	5.7	7.3	5.8	12.0	7.6	4.7	56.8	283 654.6	100.0
Crude materials	7.9	5.2	3.5	20.5	4.2	24.2	34.6	36 392.8	100.0
Mineral fuels	0.7	0.1	2.6	11.4	1.9	0.2	83.1	154 902.9	100.0
Industrial chemicals	20.5	33.9	11.9	5.9	12.9	4.2	10.6	40 895.2	100.0
Metals	5.3	7.3	15.1	4.2	14.6	7.5	46.1	25 508.9	100.0
Textiles	5.1	12.9	13.0	10.4	49.3	0.5	8.8	4 751.9	100.0
Capital equipment	21.4	12.8	19.0	12.8	29.7	1.1	3.3	144 328.6	100.0
Non-electrical machinery	20.0	14.6	13.6	10.5	37.2	1.0	3.0	53 908.3	100.0
Electric equipment	17.3	8.7	25.2	16.3	28.2	1.0	3.4	65 924.3	100.0
Transport equipment	46.9	21.0	6.3	9.3	11.2	1.1	4.1	11 417.7	100.0
Consumer non-durable goods	9.6	14.4	2.0	3.3	65.5	0.3	5.0	38 411.7	100.0
Textile products	1.1	6.9	1.8	3.3	81.3	0.3	5.4	24 562.2	100.0
Consumer durable goods	7.0	22.9	8.0	9.9	43.2	1.1	7.9	43 319.4	100.0
Household equipment	5.3	26.0	7.6	4.9	52.6	0.5	3.0	1 452.9	100.0
Domestic electrical equipment	1.6	3.7	4.2	26.1	63.2	0.4	0.7	7 209.5	100.0
Passenger cars	7.1	76.9	0.5	0.8	0.2	2.3	12.3	7 811.3	100.0
Motorcycles and bicycles	12.5	11.1	18.1	5.5	51.7	0.1	1.0	1 473.0	100.0
Toys and musical instruments	6.4	5.1	4.7	4.6	77.8	0.1	1.3	6 437.5	100.0
Others	16.9	10.0	28.9	16.4	15.8	1.1	10.9	13 526.2	100.0

Source: Economic Commission for Latin America and the Caribbean (ECLAC), on the basis of official figures from the Japan External Trade Organization (JETRO) [online] http://www.jetro.go.jp.

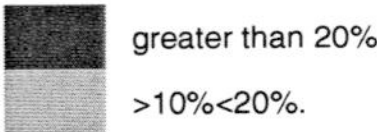

greater than 20%.

>10%<20%.

Among the Asian countries, ASEAN (10) as a group was the largest recipient with an 11% share. In 2006, over 34% of Japan's OFDI went to Asia, breaking down as follows: China (12.3%), Hong Kong SAR (7.8%), Malaysia (5.9%), Thailand (4.0%), Republic of Korea (3.0%), Taiwan Province of China (3.0%), Indonesia (1.5%) and India (1.0%). Asia's combined share in Japanese OFDI in 2006 outweighs that going to the United States (18.5%) and is closer to the level going to the European Union (35.7%). Latin America and the Caribbean received US$ 2.5 billion of Japanese investment, a significant decline from the previous year (JETRO, 2007).

Considering investment by individual sectors, the electronics machinery (14.0%), transport equipment (17.1%), precision machines (2.8%), and chemicals and pharmaceuticals (8.8%) segments were the most favoured in the manufacturing sector. In terms of the cumulative stock during the period 1989-2004, Japan's OFDI in Asia was concentrated in the manufacturing sector, which accounted for 66% of investment projects and 59% of invested value. Meanwhile, non-manufacturing sectors absorbed less than 40% in terms of both number of projects and invested value. The predominant sectors in manufacturing were electrical and transport equipment, which are characterized by high levels of intra-industry and intra-firm trade. The three services sectors (trade, finance and insurance, and services) were also important recipients. The natural-resource-related sectors (farming and forestry, fishery and mining) received roughly 10% of the total. Asia's predominance as a destination, on the one hand, and the importance of the manufacturing sector, on the other, points to the role played by that sector as the key economic integration hub for Japan in Asia-Pacific.

Japan's OFDI in Latin America and the Caribbean contrasts starkly with the case of Asia noted above (ECLAC, 2008). Japanese OFDI in the manufacturing sector accounted for only 14% of its investment in the region, with the transport sector contributing almost 5% of the total invested value. The combined share of the two subsectors (i.e, electrical and electronics and transport equipment) that were the strongest in Asia amounted to only 7%. Across sectors, the largest recipient was the finance and insurance sector, which absorbed roughly 47% of total Japanese OFDI, followed by transportation with a share of 25%. Surprisingly, the natural-resource-based industries were not a significant recipient of FDI from Japan, with the exception of mining. In fact, in terms of investment value, Asia received more in each of the three natural-resource based subsectors than Latin America during the 15-year period in question.

The number of Japanese affiliates operating overseas reached some 16,000 worldwide in 2006, according to a recent survey conducted by the Ministry of Economy, Trade and Industry (METI) of Japan. These affiliates operated in a wide range of industries, and do not include those in the financial and insurance or real estate industries (see table VI.14). Roughly 58% of these (9174 firms) were located in Asia, 20% in China alone. Some 13% were operating in the three NIEs (Taiwan Province of China, Republic of Korea and Singapore), and another 17% in ASEAN (4). The corresponding figures for North America and the European Union were much lower, 18% and 14% of the total, respectively. At the same date, there were some 800 affiliates of Japanese firms operating in Latin America and the Caribbean, representing 5% of the worldwide total, a smaller number than those in Singapore. Brazil, Mexico and Argentina were the principal hosts for these firms.

Table VI.14

NUMBER OF JAPANESE AFFILIATES, BY COUNTRY/REGION, 2006

(Number of companies)

	World	United States	European Union	Latin America and the Caribbean	Brazil	Mexico	Asia	China	NIEs (3) [a]	ASEAN (4) [b]
Total	15 850	2 623	2 258	823	194	140	9 174	3 139	2 044	2 715
Manufacturing	8 048	1 221	835	251	107	81	5 449	2 156	959	1 761
Foods	393	79	25	17	8	2	246	125	21	78
Textiles	399	17	19	14	8	1	347	216	18	82
Wood and pulp	144	11	10	5	3	...	84	37	3	36
Chemicals	1 089	180	151	23	7	6	704	237	194	216
Petroleum and coal	35	6	3	2	2	...	19	6	6	6
Iron and steel	203	44	8	10	5	1	135	51	18	58
Non-ferrous metals	221	28	10	3	3	...	175	55	26	77
General machinery	848	133	124	33	12	12	527	234	113	136
Electric machinery	665	83	69	14	6	5	484	223	94	119
Communication equipment	1 183	140	121	36	12	17	866	293	175	280
Transport equipment	1 375	305	157	69	28	28	771	258	96	335
Precision machinery	273	39	44	8	6	2	174	70	36	31
Other manufacturing	1 220	156	94	17	7	7	917	351	159	307
Non-manufacturing	7 802	1 402	1 423	572	87	59	3 725	983	1 085	954
Farming and forestry	114	13	10	22	7	...	37	9	4	18
Mining	142	21	21	21	4	1	19	4	3	10
Construction	269	28	14	7	5	1	205	33	35	117
Communications	385	94	47	9	5	...	218	107	48	39
Transportation	1 006	100	155	190	9	8	496	148	119	149
Wholesale	3 763	669	796	160	41	33	1 812	449	604	354
Retail	503	91	125	11	2	3	229	52	86	50
Services	939	187	142	49	9	6	494	136	130	152
Other non-manufacturing	681	199	113	103	5	7	215	45	56	65

Source: Economic Commission for Latin America and the Caribbean (ECLAC), on the basis of information from the Ministry of Economy, Trade and Industry (METI) of Japan, "Kaigai jigyo katsudo kihon chosa" (Basic trend survey of overseas business activities) No. 36, 2007.

[a] NIEs (3) include Republic of Korea, Singapore and Taiwan Province of China.

[b] ASEAN (4) includes the Indonesia, Malaysia, Philippines and Thailand.

By industry, roughly 50% of Japanese affiliates were engaged in activities related to the manufacturing sector. Chemicals, communications equipment and transport equipment were the top three sectors, followed by general and electric machinery, whose production bases have been primarily found in Asia. In Latin America and the Caribbean, some 570 affiliates were operating in the non-manufacturing sector, mainly in transportation and wholesale activities, and some 250 in manufacturing, about 70 of them in the production of transport equipment. The number of affiliates operating in natural-resource-related sectors was relatively small. Japan's overwhelming presence in and around the machinery industry in Asia reflects the buoyant and complex supply chains networks that have been developing in that region.

Japan's OFDI was concentrated in the ASEAN countries in the 1990s. It later shifted towards China and is now reverting to other Asian countries. The centre of gravity of Japanese OFDI continues to be the United States, Asia and the European Union. The performance of Japanese subsidiaries in Asia is especially notable in terms of the number of firms, sales, profits, and number of employees. Japanese OFDI in Latin America and the Caribbean yields exceptionally good profit rates, though it represents a small share of the world total in terms of number of firms, employees and sales. Almost 13% of total current profits of Japanese overseas subsidiaries originate from those operating in Latin America and the Caribbean. China has not necessarily been the hub for profits and sales of Japanese multinationals' operations (ECLAC, 2008).

Another characteristic of the overseas operations of Japanese firms is their strong export orientation. This applies especially to manufacturing production bases in Asian countries. While more than 90% of total sales by the subsidiaries operating in the United States are made in local markets, in Europe, a high proportion is exported to third countries in addition to domestic sales. In the case of Asian countries, sales to third markets combined with sales to Japan (reverse-imports by Japan) account for about 50% of total sales. Japanese companies in Asia typically seek profits by all three avenues; domestic sales, exports and reverse-imports. In contrast, the grouping of other non-Asian countries, which includes Latin America and the Caribbean, shows a very low export orientation. Substantially higher export-orientation figures are observed for the four industrial categories, namely industrial machinery, electrical machinery, transport equipment and precision instruments, especially in ASEAN and China, where there are high ratios of intra-industry and intra-firm trade.

In sum, Asia-Pacific has grown extremely important in the transnationalization of Japanese enterprises, since it has become their largest market in terms of trade and FDI, especially in the manufacturing sector. Asia-Pacific offers factor endowments that enable Japanese firms to be internationally competitive and profitable. These firms have adopted a different corporate strategy in Asia-Pacific than in other regions of the world. Asia-Pacific, including China, provides Japan with an efficient platform for export to third countries within and outside the Asia-Pacific region.

(b) The case of China

The FDI received by China from the three leading sources —Japan, ASEAN and the Republic of Korea— increased significantly, especially following China's accession to the World Trade Organization (WTO) in 2001. Those three sources represented on average about 20% of total FDI during 2002 and 2007, a non-negligible figure given that: (i) the United States and the European Union accounted for about 6% and 7%, respectively, of total FDI during the period; (ii) the percentage corresponding to Taiwan Province of China was 4.5%; and (iii) almost 33% of FDI entering China comes from Hong Kong SAR in the form of triangulation. In fact, the ASEAN countries are an important source of FDI for China even though most of this originates in Singapore (between US$ 2 and US$ 3 billion per year). In short, the most important actors in China's recent transformation into the world's third-largest FDI recipient worldwide after the United States and Germany have been its Asian neighbours (see table VI.15).

Latin America and the Caribbean is a very minor source of Chinese FDI, except for a huge amount of such investment coming from Cayman Islands and Virgin Islands. According to the Economist Intelligence Unit (EIU, 2008), the share of the eight Latin American countries considered has accounted for less than 0.1% in recent years, with between US$ 70 and US$ 80 million each year. Among the countries of Latin America, Brazil and Argentina, Mexico and Chile are the largest investors in China. Peru, Colombia and the Bolivarian Republic of Venezuela also invest in China, but more sporadically and on a smaller scale.

Foreign-owned firms operating in China, or Foreign Invested Enterprises (FIEs), are major drivers of that country's external trade, rapidly displacing the State enterprises and collectives (see figure VI.9). In 2007, such firms are reported to have exported US$ 696 billion, equivalent to 57% of total exports, and imported US$ 559 billion, close to 59% of total imports (Ministry of Commerce of China, n/d). Detailed information on 2006 indicates that the goods made by FIEs from 10 selected Asian countries accounted for 45% of China's total FIE exports and 62% of its imports (see figure VI.10). In contrast, FIEs of United States or European origin accounted for 24% and 18% of total FIE exports, respectively. Firms originating in the Hong Kong SAR were by far the largest FIE exporters, accounting for 20% of China's total FIE exports. Exports by firms of Japanese origin established in China exceeded US$ 61 billion, and these were followed by exports worth US$ 25 billion by firms from the Republic of Korea and US$ 14 billion in exports by firms from Taiwan Province of China. Firms originating in the five countries of ASEAN (Philippines, Indonesia, Malaysia, Singapore and Thailand) accounted for US$ 37 billion in exports, equivalent to 6.5% of the total exported by FIEs operating in China. The contribution to Chinese exports made by United States or European firms is quite small compared to that of their Asian competitors.

Table VI.15

MATERIALIZED FOREIGN DIRECT INVESTMENT IN CHINA (NON-FINANCIAL SECTORS), AVERAGE 2002-2007

(Millions of dollars and percentages)

Country/Region	2002	2003	2004	2005	2006	2007	Average 2002-2007	Share
Total	52 742.9	53 504.7	60 630.0	60 324.7	65 821.0	74 767.8	61 298.50	100.0
10 Asian economies/ regions	32 411.2	33 889.8	37 271.2	35 336.3	36 279.4	41 383.4	36 095.21	58.9
Hong Kong SAR	17 860.9	17 700.1	18 998.3	17 948.8	21 307.2	27 703.4	20 253.12	33.0
Indonesia	121.6	150.1	104.5	86.8	106.9	134.4	117.39	0.2
Japan	4 190.1	5 054.2	5 451.6	6 529.8	4 759.4	3 589.2	4 929.04	8.0
Macao SAR	468.4	416.6	546.4	600.5	677.7	637.0	557.76	0.9
Malaysia	367.9	251.0	385.0	361.4	45.1	397.3	301.28	0.5
The Philippines	186.0	220.0	233.2	188.9	14.2	195.3	172.95	0.3
Singapore	2 337.2	2 058.4	2 008.1	2 204.3	2 463.0	3 184.6	2 375.94	3.9
Republic of Korea	2 720.7	4 488.5	6 247.9	5 168.3	3 993.2	3 678.3	4 382.83	7.1
Thailand	187.7	173.5	178.7	95.9	148.6	89.5	145.65	0.2
Taiwan Province of China	3 970.6	3 377.2	3 117.5	2 151.7	2 229.9	1 774.4	2 770.23	4.5
European Union	3 191.8	3 930.3	4 239.0	5 193.8	5 439.5	3 838.4	4 305.46	7.0
Germany	928.0	857.0	1 058.5	1 530.0	2 003.0	734.0	1 185.07	1.9
North America	6 011.9	4 762.0	4 554.8	3 515.4	3 441.7	3 012.8	4 216.44	6.9
United States	5 423.9	4 198.5	3 941.0	3 061.2	3 000.0	2 616.2	3 706.80	6.0
Selected free ports	8 176.4	7 628.7	9 901.7	13 237.8	16 534.3	22 625.6	13 017.43	21.2
Cayman Islands	1 179.5	866.0	042.6	1 947.5	2 131.8	2 570.8	1 789.71	2.9
Virgin Islands	6 117.4	5 777.0	6 730.3	9 021.7	11 677.3	16 552.4	9 312.67	15.2
Western Samoa	879.5	985.7	128.9	1 360.8	1 619.8	2 169.9	1 357.42	2.2
Others	8 963.5	8 055.9	9 218.0	6 556.8	7 567.9	6 920.5	7 880.40	12.9

Source: Economic Commission for Latin America and the Caribbean (ECLAC), on the basis of official figures from the Ministry of Commerce of China, "Invest in China" [online] http://www.fdi.gov.cn.

Figure VI.9

CHINESE EXPORTS BY TYPE OF ENTERPRISE, 1997-2006

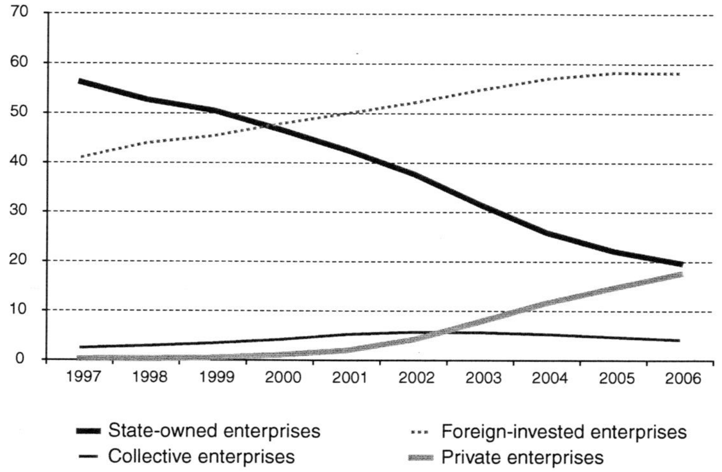

Source: Economic Commission for Latin America and the Caribbean (ECLAC), on the basis of official figures from the Ministry of Commerce of China, "Invest in China" [online] http://www.fdi.gov.cn.

At the same time, the presence of Asian firms is highly influential in China's import orientation. Firms from the 10 selected Asian countries imported US$ 291 billion in 2006, accounting for 62% of China's total FIE imports (see figure VI.10). Firms from the United States and the European Union represented just 7% and 10%, respectively. The predominant firms in China's FIE imports are Japanese, Korean, Taiwanese, Malaysian, Singaporean, Philippine and Thai. These firms import large volumes of components and inputs from their parent companies in their countries of origin, reflecting the high level of intra-industry trade as mentioned above.

Figure VI.10
CHINESE EXPORTS AND IMPORTS BY FOREIGN-OWNED FIRMS, 2006
(Millions of dollars and percentages)

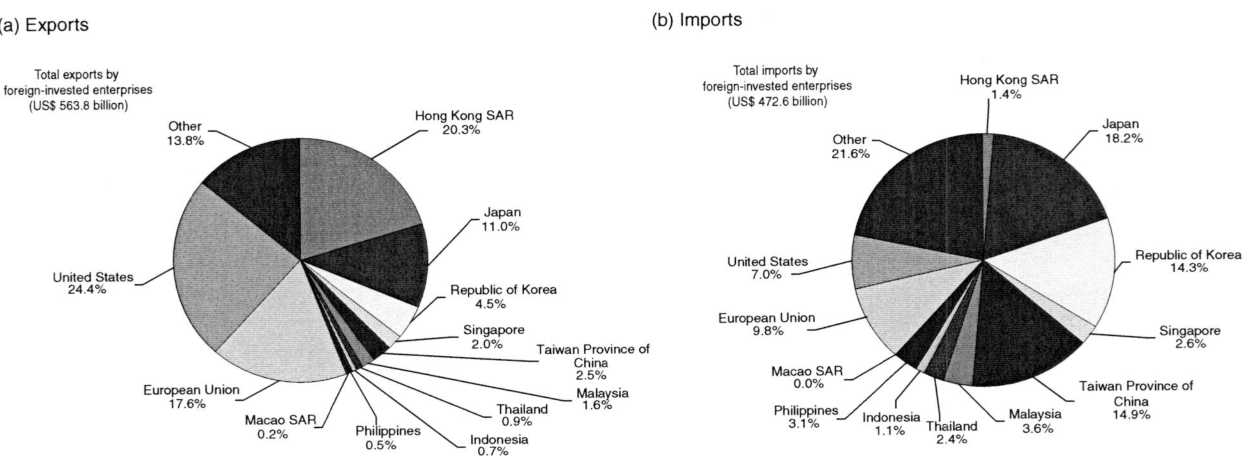

Source: Economic Commission for Latin America and the Caribbean (ECLAC), on the basis of official figures from the Ministry of Commerce of China, "Invest in China" [online] http://www.fdi.gov.cn.

While China has been a major net recipient of FDI over the past two decades, lately it has been investing abroad itself. In fact, among developing countries, it is now the world's sixth-largest source of OFDI among developing countries. As of late 2006, non-financial Chinese companies held a stock of US$ 75 billion abroad, of which US$ 17 billion was invested in 2006 (see table VI.16). Notwithstanding its relatively small role, China is emerging as a leading investor among developed and developing countries, with investments comparable to those of the Republic of Korea (see figure VI.11). According to the Chinese authorities, overseas-invested enterprises realized an internal sales turnover of US$ 274.6 billion, registered total tax payment of US$ 2.82 billion abroad and employed 630,000 workers (including 268,000 foreign local staff).

Table VI.16
CHINA'S OUTWARD FOREIGN DIRECT INVESTMENT, FLOWS AND STOCK, 2006
(Billions of dollars and percentages)

Indicator	Outflows 2006		Stock as of 2006	
	Amount	Percentage	Amount	Percentage
Total	21.16	100	90.63	100
Non-financial outward direct investment	17.63	83.3	75.02	82.8
Financial outward direct investment	3.53	16.7	15.61	17.2

Source: Economic Commission for Latin America and the Caribbean (ECLAC), on the basis of Ministry of Commerce of China, *2006 Statistical Bulletin of China's Outward Foreign Direct Investment.*

Figure VI.11
CHINA'S OUTWARD FOREIGN DIRECT INVESTMENT STOCK COMPARED WITH THAT OF DEVELOPED COUNTRIES, 2006
(Billions of dollars)

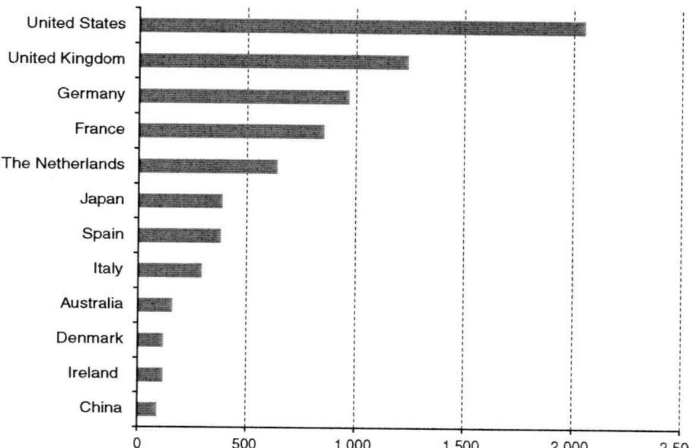

Source: Economic Commission for Latin America and the Caribbean (ECLAC), on the basis of Ministry of Commerce of China, *2006 Statistical Bulletin of China's Outward Foreign Direct Investment.*

Regarding destination, close to 90% of non-financial OFDI has been directed towards the economies in Latin America and the Caribbean and Asia (see table VI.17). Of China's non-financial OFDI flow in 2006, which is valued at US$ 17.6 billion, Latin America and the Caribbean received US$ 8.5 billion, or 48%, which went mainly to the Cayman Islands and the British Virgin Islands. Asia received US$ 7.7 billion, or 43.4%, mainly in the Hong Kong SAR, Singapore, Saudi Arabia, Mongolia, Iran, Indonesia, Laos, Kazakhstan, and Viet Nam. Measured by stock at the end of 2006, Brazil, Mexico and Argentina figure as the largest recipients of China's OFDI, along with several Asian countries such as Singapore, Malaysia and the Republic of Korea.

Despite high expectations on the part of Latin American and Caribbean countries, Chinese investments are slow to materialize, even though a significant number of large Chinese firms have begun to operate in several countries in the region (see table VI.18). These companies are present not only in the natural-resource-related sectors but also in manufacturing. Access to natural resources, expansion in overseas markets (market-seeking) and improvement of production and administration efficiency (efficiency-seeking) are considered to be the three main stimuli for China's OFDI in Latin America in recent decades. An increasing number of large State-owned companies operating in natural resources and manufacturing, ranked by MOFCOM in 2006 as the 30 largest Chinese companies in terms of OFDI stock, have invested in the region.

Table VI.17
DESTINATIONS OF CHINESE OUTWARD FOREIGN DIRECT INVESTMENT
(Billions of dollars)

Rank	Country/Region	Billions of dollars
1	Hong Kong SAR	42.27
2	Cayman Islands	14.09
3	British Virgin Islands	4.75
4	United States	1.24
5	Republic of Korea	0.95
6	Russian Federation	0.93
7	Australia	0.79
8	Macau SAR	0.61
9	Sudan	0.50
10	Germany	0.47
11	Singapore	0.47
12	Mongolia	0.32
13	Kazakhstan	0.28
14	Saudi Arabia	0.27
15	Zambia	0.27
16	Viet Nam	0.25
17	Algeria	0.25
18	Thailand	0.23
19	Indonesia	0.23
20	Japan	0.22

Source: Economic Commission for Latin America and the Caribbean (ECLAC), on the basis of Ministry of Commerce of China, *2006 Statistical Bulletin of China's Outward Foreign Direct Investment.*

Table VI.18

MAJOR CHINESE COMPANIES OPERATING OR HAVING INVESTED IN LATIN AMERICA

Sector	Natural resources																Services	
	Petroleum and gas				Mining							Fisheries			Forestry	Agriculture	Transportation	
Investor	China National Petroleum Corporation	China Petrochemical Corporation	China National Offshore Oil Corporation	Sinochem Corporation	China Minmetals Corporation	Shanghai Baosteel Group	Sinosteel Corporation	China Non-ferrous Metal Mining & Construction Group	Shougang Group	Yankuang Group (Coal)	China Metallurgical Group Corporation	China National Fisheries Corp.	Shandong Zhonglu Oceanic Fisheries Company Limited	Shanghai Fisheries General Corp.	Shanghai Anxin Floors Co. Ltd.	Xintian SA	China Shipping Group	China Ocean Shipping Group
Argentina			✓								✓	✓	✓	✓			✓	✓
Bolivia					✓													
Brazil		✓	✓		✓	✓	✓								✓		✓	✓
Chile					✓									✓			✓	✓
Colombia	✓	✓															✓	
Cuba				✓												✓	✓	
Ecuador	✓	✓		✓													✓	
Mexico	✓	✓	✓													✓	✓	
Peru	✓		✓		✓			✓	✓								✓	✓
Venezuela (Bol. Rep. of)	✓	✓	✓							✓							✓	
Uruguay										✓							✓	

Sector	Manufacturing																	IT
	Construction	Textiles	Pulp and Paper	Motorcycles			Automobile				Telecommunication	Electronics						
Investor	Sichuan Railway Corporation	Sinatex SA	Rotomex Yuncheng SA	Jin Ling	China Jialing Industrial Co.	Nanjing Jincheng Automovil, S.A.	Chery	Faw	Zonda	Geely	Huawei Technologies	TTE (TCL Thomson)	Beiyang Electronic S.A.	SVA	Hisense	Chunlan	Gree	Lenovo
Argentina						S					S	S		S		M		
Bolivia											S							
Brazil					M						M	S		M			M	
Chile				M		S					S							
Colombia						M					S							
Cuba											S							
Ecuador											S							
Mexico		✓	✓					M	M*	M*	S	M			M			M
Peru											S		S					
Venezuela (Bol. Rep. of)	✓										S							
Uruguay							M											

Source: Economic Commission for Latin America and the Caribbean (ECLAC), on the basis of official figures from the Ministry of Commerce of China.

Note: M indicates investment in the establishment of a manufacturing company.
M* indicates an investment that has been authorized but not executed.
S indicates services.
The company names shaded in grey refer to those companies that are among the 30 leading Chinese companies in terms of outward FDI as ranked by the Ministry of Commerce of China.

In the manufacturing sector, Chinese industries, including textiles, paper, automobile, electronics, IT, and telecommunications enterprises, have selected Mexico or member countries of MERCOSUR as their first production base in Latin America. On the one hand, Mexico, Brazil, Uruguay and Argentina are considered a stepping stone to enter and expand in the dynamic markets covered by trade agreements such as NAFTA and MERCOSUR. On the other hand, Mexico can provide an easier entrance not only to the United States but also Central American and Caribbean countries. In addition, production in MERCOSUR can facilitate the access to other Latin American countries.

By sector, Latin America has increasingly attracted Chinese OFDI in automobiles, electronics, and telecommunications. China's automobile companies are establishing production bases in Latin America to reduce production costs and acquire new markets, faced with strong competition from foreign companies in domestic markets and the continuing appreciation of the Chinese currency. In electronics, there are three contributing factors: (i) domestic demand has been sluggish and domestic competition has decreased profits, hence, Chinese electronics companies are seeking new markets in Latin America where a large middle class is emerging; (ii) most of the antidumping cases brought against Chinese products in the region refer to white goods, so the establishment of a production base in the region can help Chinese companies attenuate such trade conflicts; and (iii) Chinese companies do not currently have the capacity to establish production bases in developed countries, so Latin America and Africa have become popular destinations for China's OFDI.

(c) The case of the Republic of Korea

After coming to a standstill in the aftermath of the Asian financial crisis, the Republic of Korea's outward FDI began to pick up and as of June 2007, the cumulative figure exceeded US$ 82 billion and was spread over more than 120,000 projects worldwide (www.koreaexim.go.kr). Asia accounted for 72% in terms of the number of projects undertaken and 49% in terms of the value of executed FDI. This is substantially higher than the share corresponding to the United States or Europe. In Asia, in addition to China, the main recipients of FDI from the Republic of Korea are the ASEAN 10, including several developing countries such as Viet Nam and Indonesia, which have emerged as major recipients. Meanwhile, Japan and Taiwan Province of China have received a relatively smaller share of Korean FDI. Latin America and the Caribbean have received more than 7% of the stock (US$ 6.7 billion) with their share of projects amounting to 2.5% (more than 3,000 projects).

Among destinations for outward FDI from the Republic of Korea, China occupies a predominant place both in terms of the number of projects and in terms of the volume of investments carried out. Official data for the country show that as of March 2008 China had absorbed roughly 65,000 projects (50% of the total), and that investment undertaken amounted to US$ 23 billion, 24% of the overall amount invested. The fact that the amount of Korean investment in China per firm is relatively small is a good indicator of the significant role played by Korean SME investors in China.

The Republic of Korea's cumulative net outward FDI by industry as at March 2008, shows the manufacturing sector in a dominant position with 48% of the total, followed by wholesale and retail trade (17%), mining (9%) and other sectors including services (25%). The firms in the manufacturing sector have been the driving force behind Korean FDI overseas, the main objective of which is to support overseas production facilities and secure markets for sales (Yoon, 2007).

In terms of countries, the tax haven countries such as Bermuda, Cayman Islands and British Virgin Islands have been major recipients of Korean outward FDI in the region accounting for almost half of Korean FDI stock in Latin America and the Caribbean. Apart from these countries, Brazil (13%), Mexico (9%) and Peru (9%) have been major recipients of Korean FDI in the region (see table VI.19). As of March 2008, five Central American countries (Honduras, Guatemala, El Salvador, Costa Rica and Nicaragua, in that order) received almost 5% of total actual FDI inflows from the Republic of Korea into the region, amounting to US$ 300 million (Ex-Im Bank of Korea (n/d)).

In terms of sectors, Korean FDI inflows into Latin America and the Caribbean are concentrated in a few major industries: manufacturing (24%), mining (30%), agriculture and fisheries (2%) and services and commerce (44%). The initial focus on natural resources has gradually shifted to manufacturing activities, especially electronics (38% of investing firms), textiles and apparel (34%), iron and steel, and petroleum undertaken by large Korean firms, with Korean SMEs playing a relatively larger part in the textiles and apparel sectors (for some countries in the region, see table VI.19). Therefore, the scope of Korean investment in the region has still been limited to relatively simple functions such as securing supplies of natural resources, gaining access to markets or establishing imported-component-driven export platforms to supply the United States market with final products (ECLAC, 2007a).

Table VI.19

KOREAN FDI RECEIVED BY SOME LATIN AMERICAN COUNTRIES, BY SECTOR, 2004-2007 CUMULATIVE

(In 1 000 dollars)

	Manufacturing	Wholesale and retail trade	Natural resources	Construction	Other services	Total
Argentina	771	500	7 109	0	0	8 380
Honduras	20 941	0	0	0	0	20 941
Colombia	247	26 725	0	0	0	26 972
Guatemala	17 676	0	0	17 059	0	34 735
Chile	5 927	35 895	0	508	0	42 330
Panama	2 000	86 975	0	4	173 700	262 679
Peru	950	17 000	254 422	235	0	272 607
Mexico	145 187	128 657	0	2 144	1 123	277 111
Brazil	290 679	33 567	210 015	2 450	33 184	569 895

Source: Economic Commission for Latin America and the Caribbean (ECLAC), on the basis of information from Export-Import Bank of Korea [online] http://www.koreaexim.go.kr.

Figure VI.12

STOCK OF KOREAN FDI IN LATIN AMERICA AND THE CARIBBEAN, 1980-MARCH 2008

(Percentages)

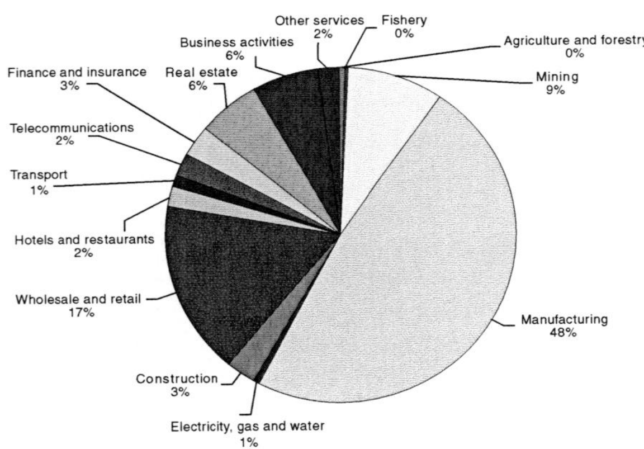

Source: Economic Commission for Latin America and the Caribbean (ECLAC), on the basis of information from Export-Import Bank of Korea [online] http://www.koreaexim.go.kr.

Note: Data for 1980 is a cumulative figure from 1968 to 1980.

In general terms, the Korean FDI channelled into Latin America and the Caribbean seems to serve little as a transmission vehicle for bringing the industrial and technological successes of the Korean economy to the region. This concern has been expressed in one of the conclusions by the Mexico-Korea 21st Century Commission (2005), which states: "[...] Given the lack of integration in Mexico's production chains, particularly in the maquiladora industry, Korea and Mexico should engage in a programme to develop the supporting industry in Mexico. There is no doubt that such a programme would offer benefits to both countries, since Mexican exports would have more domestic value added, and Korean investments in Mexico would benefit from the availability of timely, cheaper, world quality local inputs." (ECLAC, 2007a). In this regard, it is interesting that several chapters of Japan's Economic Partnership Agreement (EPA) with Mexico contemplates, the adoption of technical cooperation measures for improving Mexican industrial capacities and international competitiveness, objectives that do not usually appear in the typical free trade agreement with the United States.

In the 1990s, the main motivation for large Korean firms was to take advantage of the large size of the Chinese market and save on labour costs, which were beginning to rise in the home country. In the current decade, SMEs are accompanying large firms in seeking to exploit the potential offered by the Chinese market. The manufacturing sector is the largest recipient of Korean FDI, followed by construction. Given the current idle capacity in Korean industry, the suspicion is that the boom in FDI to China may be generating an industrial vacuum in the country of origin, as has been happening also in Japan. Also quite notable is the relatively high share of ASEAN (10) as Korean FDI destinations; close to 13% of Korean FDI stock abroad has been accumulated in these Asian countries, especially in Viet Nam and Indonesia, much more than the amount directed to Japan or Taiwan Province of China (Yoon, 2007).

(d) The case of ASEAN

Total trade among ASEAN members in 2006 —combined imports and exports of US$ 352 billion— was more than double the group's trade with each of its two most important trading partners, the United States and Japan, (valued, in each case, at US$ 161 billion); these two partners shared second place, each accounting for

11.5% of total trade with ASEAN (see figure VI.13(a) and VI.13(b)). In the case of both imports and exports, these three entities (ASEAN, Japan and United States) were followed by the European Union, China, Republic of Korea, Australia, and India. Intra-ASEAN trade (exports as well as imports) accounted for as much as 25% of total flows in 2006, surpassing the figures registered by the various Latin American and Caribbean integration schemes (ASEAN Secretariat (n/d)).

The third main source of FDI for ASEAN (in terms of flows) are the other ASEAN countries. The cumulative stock of FDI entering the grouping in 2002-2006 was US$ 170 billion, of which 26% came from the European Union, 18% from Japan, 11% from ASEAN itself, and 8% from the United States. Apart from these countries, the Republic of Korea, Taiwan Province of China and China, represented 2.0%, 1.4%, and 1.3%, respectively, of the total amount invested during the period. The Cayman Islands (1.8%) and unidentified countries of Central America and South America (2.3%) appear among the 10 leading foreign investors in ASEAN (see figure VI.13c and VI.13d). In addition, Australia and India accounted for an appreciable volume of FDI during this period, with amounts of US$1.4 billion and US$ 295 million respectively. As in the case of China, FDI obtained both from neighbours (within ASEAN) and from Japan, China and the Republic of Korea is a major source of financing for business projects (see the ASEAN website). About a third of the Association's FDI comes from within ASEAN+3.

Singapore and Thailand are the leading countries in terms of FDI flows among ASEAN members, followed at some distance by Malaysia and Indonesia. The first two of these countries accounted for about 65% of the total investment among ASEAN members in the period 2004-2006. In the ASEAN countries, the main sectors targeted by investors have been communications equipment (23%), food and beverages (18%), and paper and paper products (Hiratsuka, 2006).

Figure VI.13
ASEAN TRADE AND FDI BY SELECTED PARTNER (COUNTRY/TERRITORY/REGION), 2006
(Percentages)

(a) Exports

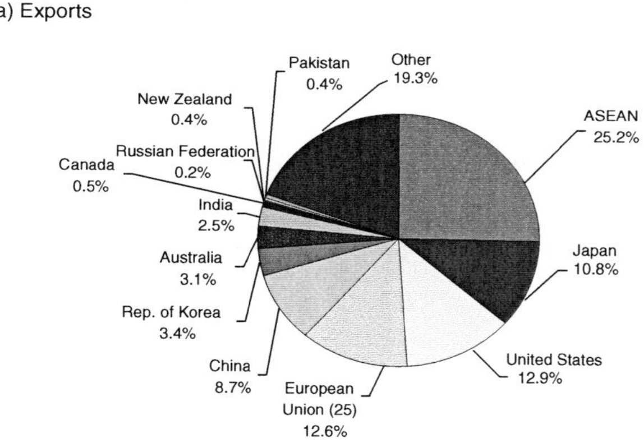
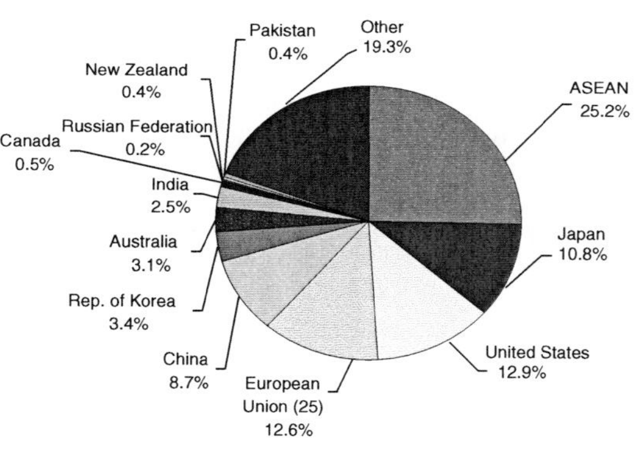

(b) Imports

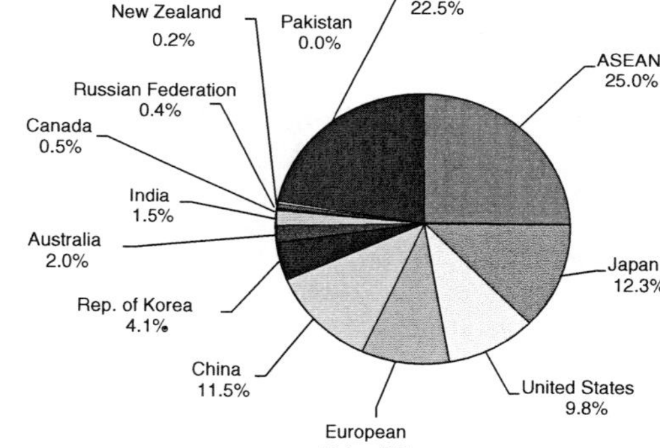

(c) Top ten sources of ASEAN FDI inflows, [a] 2002-2006

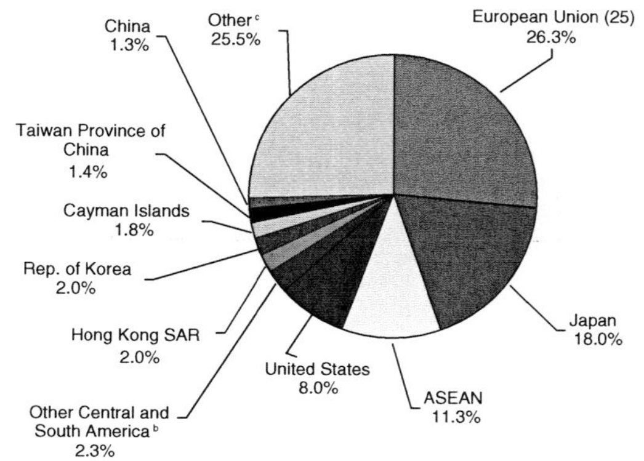

(d) ASEAN FDI inflows, by ASEAN countries, 2004-2006

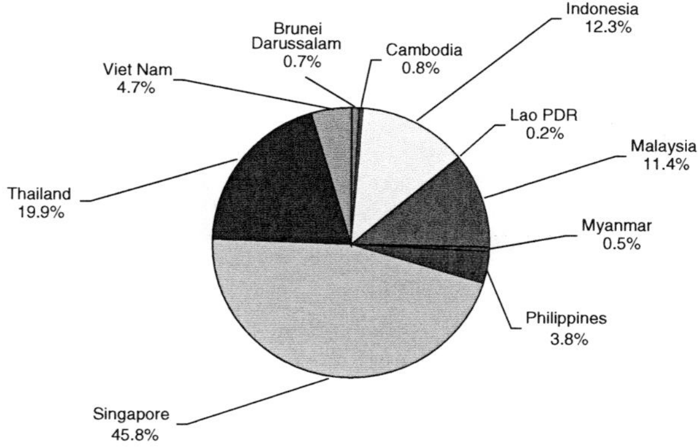

Source: Economic Commission for Latin America and the Caribbean (ECLAC), on the basis of information from ASEAN Secretariat.
[a] Identified on the basis of cumulative inflows from 2002-2006.
[b] Includes countries in Central America and South America other than Argentina, Brazil, Mexico and Panama.
[c] Includes inflows from all other countries, including the Russian Federation, as well as total reinvested earnings in the Philippines (local banks only) for 2002-2006.

3. China as an Asian export platform

Over the past two decades, the share of Asia-Pacific in China's total imports has been increasing; in 2006 roughly 62% of its imports originated in this region. Latin America and the Caribbean's exports to China, consist mainly of primary products and resource-based manufactures, a similar export basket to that coming from Africa and the rest of the world. In this regard, Latin America and the Caribbean competes directly with other regions as a supplier of commodities and processed products (see box VI.1 for an analysis of the increasing competition between the region and Africa as exporters of commodities and recipients of Chinese investment abroad). In comparison, the United States and countries of the European Union export primarily medium- and high-technology manufactures to this destination. The most striking feature of China's import structure is that Asia-Pacific, the leading source of Chinese imports, exports primarily manufactures. Its share of Chinese imports of manufactures exceeds those of the United States and the European Union.

Box VI.1

LATIN AMERICA AND THE CARIBBEAN AND AFRICA COMPETE OPENLY AS COMMODITY SUPPLIERS TO CHINA AND RECIPIENTS OF CHINESE INVESTMENTS ABROAD

In contrast to the early 1990s when official development assistance (ODA) dominated China's relations with Africa, at present, trade and investment links play an increasingly important role in those relations. In fact, China has become a major market, financier, investor, contractor and builder for Africa in addition to being a donor.

Bilateral trade between China and Africa has been growing rapidly: in 2000 and 2007, China's exports to Africa soared from US$ 5.0 billion to US$ 37.2 billion, and its imports from that region from US$ 5.6 billion to US$ 36.3 billion. Meanwhile, China's exports to and imports from Latin America and the Caribbean jumped from US$ 7.2 billion to US$ 51.5 billion and from US$ 5.4 billion to US$ 51.1 billion over the seven year period. In 2007, Africa's share in total Chinese imports stood at 4%, while that of Latin America and the Caribbean was 6%. China has become Africa's third largest trading partner after the United States and the European Union. Thanks to the commodity export boom, Africa's terms of trade with China improved by 80% to 90% during the present decade. Although Latin America still retains its relative position as one of China's major commodity suppliers, Africa is rapidly closing the gap.

China's trading pattern with Africa is quite similar to that with Latin America and the Caribbean, although primary products weigh more heavily in Africa's export basket to China than in that of Latin America and the Caribbean. Africa's principal export products to China are crude oil (71% of total China's imports from Africa in 2006), iron ore and concentrates (3.2%), raw cotton (2.8%), diamonds (2.7%), saw logs and veneer logs (1.8%), platinum (1.7%), ore and concentrates of other non-ferrous metals (1.3%), copper ore and concentrates (1.0%) and copper and copper alloys (0.8%). These ten products accounted for roughly 89% of total Chinese imports from that region in 2006. As exporters of these products, Brazil, Chile and Peru are major competitors of African countries. As suppliers of these products to China, Latin America and the Caribbean compete directly with Africa.

In services, Africa has become a key market for Chinese construction and engineering firms. According to official Chinese statistics, "contracted projects", "labour cooperation" and "design consultation" in Africa were estimated to total US$ 2 billion in 2001. In 2006, the turnover on contract labour stood at US$ 9.5 billion, accounting for 31% of China's offshore contracted projects. With the services sector, two-way traffic in tourism is growing rapidly. Latin America and the Caribbean has not been a major target for Chinese services companies.

Chinese investment (FDI and other financial flows), long awaited in Latin America and the Caribbean, is flowing increasingly to Africa. According to Chinese authorities, of Chinese non-financial overseas FDI stock, valued at US$ 75 billion in 2006, US$ 48 billion was directed towards Asia, while US$ 20 billion was channelled towards Latin America and the Caribbean. Meanwhile, the corresponding figure for Africa was US$ 2.6 billion accounting for 3.4 %, destined mainly for Sudan, Zambia, Algeria, Nigeria, South Africa, Egypt and Congo. Chinese FDI in Africa has increased sharply in recent years. In October 2007, for instance, the Industrial and Commercial Bank of China agreed to purchase 20% of Standard Bank Group of South Africa for US$ 5.6 billion. China is also reported to have: (i) expanded the list of African exports which enter free of duty; (ii) provided preferential trade credits; and (iii) established a large fund to support Chinese FDI in Africa. The last two components of trade and investment promotion measures are being implemented by China Exim Bank, through which the Chinese government disburses all its foreign aid, and the China Development Bank. In September of 2007, the Exim Bank signed an agreement to finance 6.5 billion United States dollars' worth of improvements on Congo's infrastructure, and 2 billion dollars' worth of construction and refurbishment of mines, using mineral reserves as collateral. The following month, a similar deal was signed with China Development Bank. In addition, China is reported to have provided debt relief on its own terms to African countries; in 2000-2002, it wrote off overdue obligations worth US$ 1.3 billion, and in 2006, it announced its intention of cancelling debt of close to US$ 1 billion.

Source: Economic Commission for Latin America and the Caribbean (ECLAC), on the basis of United Nations Commodity Trade Database (COMTRADE); Ministry of Commerce of China, 2006 Statistical Bulletin of China's Outward Foreign Direct Investment; Jian-Ye Wang and Abdoulaye Bio-Tchané, "Africa's burgeoning ties with China. Maximizing the benefits of China's increasing economic engagement with Africa", *Finance and Development*, Washington, D.C., International Monetary Fund (IMF), March 2008; *The Economist*, "A special report on China's quest for resources", 15 March 2008.

Figure VI.14
CHINA'S IMPORTS, BY REGION AND TECHNOLOGICAL INTENSITY, 2006
(Percentages)

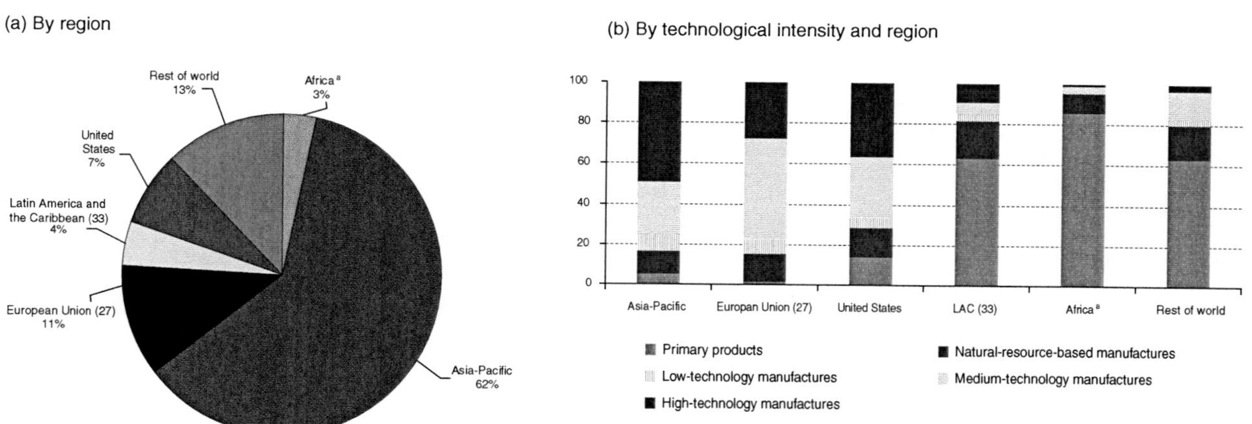

Source: Economic Commission for Latin America and the Caribbean (ECLAC), on the basis of official information from the database of the United Nations Conference on Trade and Development (UNCTAD).
[a] Africa comprises 54 countries in the African continent.

A major feature of intra-Asian trade and FDI dynamism has been China's dramatic emergence as a key player and one of the hubs of the world economy, around which a major trade reorganization is unfolding in Asia. For many neighbouring countries in Asia, China is becoming a staging post for exports to the United States and European markets (ECLAC, 2007b).

Remarkably, the network of regional trade centered in China developed outside the ambit of regional trade agreements. The "Asia Factory" grew out of the unilateral liberalization of trade in parts and components together with FDI flows and appropriate investment climates, which have been the key elements of Asia-Pacific's intraregional trade. This represented a major change in the Asian development model before China emerged as an economic power. An important element of the fragmentation of manufacturing processes in the region was Japan's loss of comparative advantages in manufacturing production, which led Japanese firms to slice their production processes and outsource more labour-intensive stages to the neighbouring countries of East Asia. This "hollowing out" of the Japanese economy was replicated in Taiwan Province of China, Republic of Korea, Singapore and Hong Kong SAR, thereby deepening the process of creating the "Asia Factory." Lastly, China's entry on to the international economic stage further eroded the industrial comparative advantages enjoyed by the higher-income East Asian countries, making offshore production more attractive. Rising wage levels in China are now enticing other Asian countries to invest elsewhere inside and outside Asia (see box VI.2).

Box VI.2
INDUSTRIAL DEVELOPMENT IN CHINA AND THE IMPACT OF RISING LABOUR COSTS

China's impressive and sustained economic growth in recent years has brought with it a series of consequences, which need to be taken into account when one looks at economic trends in the Asia-Pacific region and how they may impact Latin America and the Caribbean.

This sustained growth has improved the average income of the Chinese population, through higher incomes, allowing for more domestic consumption of goods and services. On the other hand, the comparative advantages enjoyed by China in world markets are increasingly being eroded by domestic factors such as increased labour costs, higher inflation, shortage of skilled labour, particularly in the medium- and high-technology manufacture and services sectors, and external pressures for higher prices of imported inputs, such as energy, mineral commodities and food, and the appreciation of the yuan.

In early 2008, the Chinese government implemented a new labour law, providing for increased social security, stronger unions and legal guarantees in contracts and dispute resolution, which will have an impact mainly on private SMEs whose activities are basically labour-intensive, and have low value added. At the same time, the government has decided to reduce export subsidies for commodity-exporting companies. The new labour law might reduce the low-cost labour advantage of China in the short term, in particular for private companies, but in the longer term should bring increased certainty in this area, promoting training within companies in order to retain personnel and reducing the current high turnover that exists within the different industries. All these factors are affecting China's manufacturing industry, including those firms operating in the special economic zones in coastal provinces such as Jiangsu, Zhejiang and Fujian. As a result, some changes in the current manufacturing industry in China are expected, in particular in relation to future capital investment and the global competitiveness of Chinese industry.

Box VI.2 (concluded)

There are significant differences between average wages and gross domestic product between Chinese provinces, particularly between the coastal and inner lands. For example, while Henan Province ranked fifth in GDP across China in 2006, its average wage ranked second to last among 31 provinces. A comparison of labour costs in selected Asian countries and Ecuador (see figure below), shows that wages are significantly lower in Viet Nam, the Philippines, and India, while Indonesia and Ecuador have similar labour cost levels to those in the cheapest provinces in China. Thailand, on the other hand, shows higher wages than all the other places selected.

In conclusion, Viet Nam and India, in particular, might become a challenge for China by attracting foreign capital and providing cheap labour. However, China continues to have some provinces with low labour costs and a large production scale, which would compete with Ecuador and Indonesia.

COMPARISON OF AVERAGE WAGES FOR SELECTED CHINESE PROVINCES AND OTHER COUNTRIES

(Dollars per month)

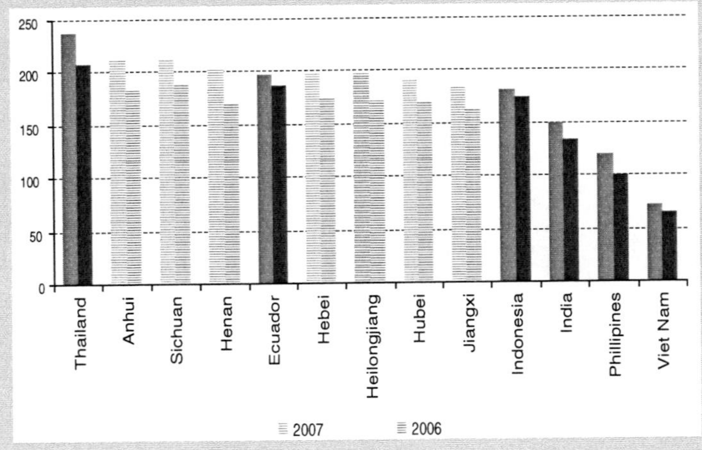

Source: Economic Commission for Latin America and the Caribbean (ECLAC), on the basis of National Bureau of Statistics of China for data for Chinese provinces and The Economist Intelligence Unit (EIU) for data for other countries.

4. Latin American and Caribbean FDI

The Latin American and Caribbean region was able to double its average annual FDI inflows from US$ 38.3 billion to US$ 74.3 billion between 1993-1997 and 1998-2002 before seeing them fall to US$ 72.3 billion during 2003-2007. During the last period, notwithstanding an absolute increase in the value of inward FDI, the region's share of FDI from global sources and developing countries has shrunk. It has also decreased as a percentage of GDP (down from 4% in 2004 to 3% in 2006) whereas in other developing regions, FDI/GDP ratios have been rising (ECLAC, 2007a). In addition, in stark contrast to the case of developing Asia, FDI flows to the region plummeted during the four years after the Asian crisis (1999-2003), with the sharpest falls occurring in MERCOSUR and the Andean Community. It took MERCOSUR more than four years to recover to the pre-crisis level, while inflows to the Andean Community's countries have still not caught up (see figure VI.15).

Of the FDI host countries, historically the United States has been the most important source of FDI in Latin America (see figure VI.16). In the 1990s, Spain came to play a leading role, being the most important FDI source for a number of Latin American countries. In the present decade, the country's weight in FDI inflows to the region declined from 23% in 1997-2001 to 10% in 2002-2006. Asia-Pacific as a region has been a very minor investor, accounting for only 2.8% in 1997-2001 and 3.5% in 2002-2006 of total inward FDI, estimated at US$ 8.9 billion for each period. On the other hand, the share of intraregional FDI in total FDI inflows in Latin America doubled (from 5% to 10%) during the same period. This was due to the emergence of a number of companies of Latin American origin, the so-called trans-Latins.

Figure VI.15
FDI INFLOWS INTO LATIN AMERICA AND THE CARIBBEAN, 1980-2007
(Millions of dollars)

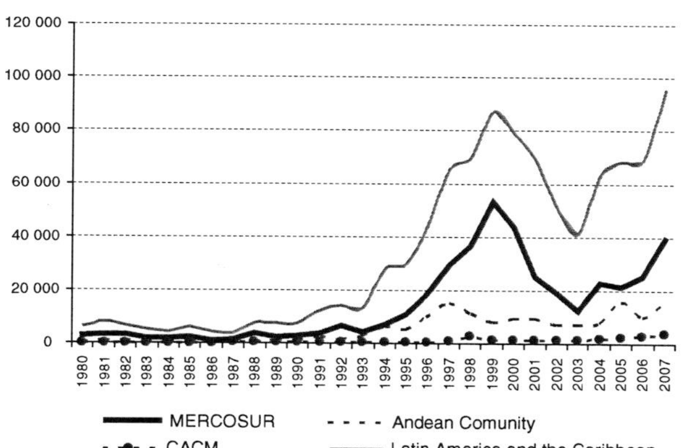

Source: Economic Commission for Latin America and the Caribbean (ECLAC), on the basis of official information.

Figure VI.16
LATIN AMERICA'S INWARD FDI, BY REGION, 1997-2006
(Percentages)

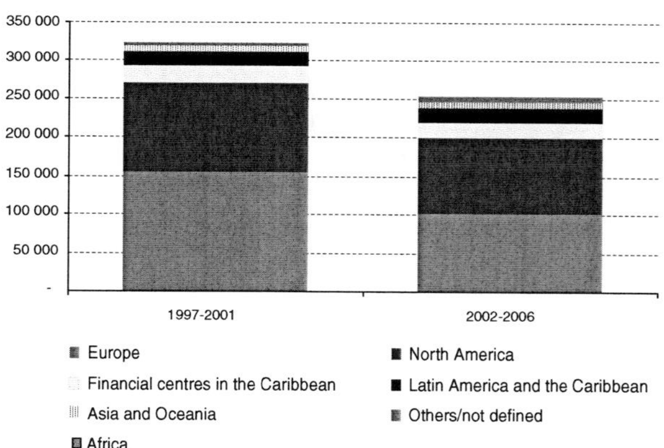

Source: Economic Commission for Latin America and the Caribbean (ECLAC), on the basis of official information.

The subregions of Latin America attract different kinds of FDI depending on the corporate strategies underlying the investment. Historically, natural-resource-seeking FDI, one of the predominant types, has been channelled into the Bolivarian Republic of Venezuela, Argentina, and the Andean countries in the case of petroleum and natural gas, and Chile, Argentina and Peru in the case of minerals.[11]

Another type, market-seeking inward FDI, has been attracted primarily to the larger markets in the region, such as Brazil and Mexico. Chile has also been a major recipient of this type of investment. In the goods sector, the automotive, food and beverage and chemical industries have stood out, while in services the focus has been on financial services, telecommunications, retail trade, electricity and natural gas distribution. This type of investment is considered to promote new local economic activities and increase local content by creating and deepening of production linkages, strengthening local entrepreneurial development and improving local services and national systemic competitiveness. The drawback of this type of FDI is that in many cases it does not promote internationally-competitive goods and services, and it tends to crowd out local companies.

Efficiency-seeking inward FDI, geared towards exports to third markets, (especially that of the United States) has been directed primarily to Mexico in the electronics, automotive and apparel industries and to Central American countries for apparel and some light electronics. Factors conducive to this type of investment include the continued restructuring of these industries in the United States and opportunities associated with free trade agreements with the United States, particularly NAFTA and the Dominican Republic- Central America - United States Free Trade Agreement (CAFTA-DR). Factors that may dissuade investors from boosting this type of investment include increasing competition from China and other Asian countries and the expected withdrawal of fiscal incentives or subsidies for export processing zones under the World Trade Organization (WTO) rules (ECLAC, 2007a).

In general terms, Mexico and Central American countries are typically recipients of a relatively large proportion of efficiency-seeking FDI, mainly from United States TNCs in the motor vehicle, electronics and apparel industries, while South America has received more market-seeking FDI, primarily from European TNCs in a few manufacturing industries (motor vehicles, food products, beverages and tobacco), a number of services (finance, telecommunications, retail commerce, electricity and gas distribution), and natural-resource-seeking FDI, mostly from Anglosaxon TNCs in petroleum, natural gas and mining. TNCs whose parent companies are based in developing Asia do not seem to have participated actively in any of the three categories mentioned above.

Efficiency-seeking inward FDI is usually considered to be conducive to exports of manufactures, to the conversion of an export platform into a manufacturing centre, improved international competitiveness, transfer and assimilation of foreign technology, training of human resources, creation and deepening of production linkages,

---

11 The performance of natural resource-based FDI in the region in recent years reflects the tension between two forces: the sustained rise in commodity prices and changes in the legal conditions for natural-resource exploration and exploitation in some countries. These combined forces have led some foreign investors to abandon the region, to restructure their investments or to hold off on new investments, while others have announced new projects. Some trans-Latin firms and foreign investors from other developing countries, especially China and India, have shown a growing interest in this type of FDI in Latin America.

and local entrepreneurial development. However, this type of FDI also has several shortcomings; the low-value-added trap; a major focus on static rather than dynamic local comparative advantages, a heavy dependence on imported components, and a lack of industrial agglomeration, the risk of crowding out local companies, a race to the bottom in salaries, problems in labour and environmental standards, and a race to the top in TNC incentives. Many FDI projects in Latin America, regardless of their origin, share these shortcomings.

As the recent experience of Latin America's automotive industry indicates, an increasing number of inward FDI projects combine both "market-seeking" and "efficiency-seeking" types (ECLAC, 2008). In general, the industry is becoming more "export-oriented" and the major players operating in Latin America are adopting a corporate strategy quite distinct from the previous one, which was based primarily on the exploitation of local markets. The companies are acting more as "regional" players, taking advantage of preferences that various regional trade agreements offer. This change of strategy has attracted a few motor vehicle makers from Asia to start producing in the FDI-recipient countries instead of importing finished vehicles. This transformation, however, has not yet resolved the persistent problems facing the Latin American automotive industry, namely high import contents and lack of backward and forward linkages, including deficient networks of local parts and components suppliers.

An important feature of Latin American FDI is the huge increase of outward FDI channelled primarily to enterprises within the region itself. Thanks to the competitive advantages of the natural resources in their markets of origin, several trans-Latins have progressed from being exporters to being global producers. Many of the trans-Latins' efficiency-seeking investments in the manufacturing sector have been directed outside their home region. In the area of motor vehicles and parts, the main investments were motivated by proximity to customers, the benefits to be derived from the development of products and solutions and the need to avoid trade barriers. An interesting case in Asia is the case of Nemak (part of the Alfa group) which announced the construction of a new production plant in China. This company also purchased the operations of the high-technology aluminium-component manufacturer, Tk Aluminum, in China. The Brazilian company, Marcopolo, launched a project with Tata Motors to supply the Indian market. As a rule, however, the geographic scope of trans-Latins' operations still does not go much beyond the region of Latin America and the Caribbean, with just a few cases extending to the United States or Europe. In Asia, these companies play a very insignificant role. (ECLAC, 2007a).[12]

5. Impediments to biregional FDI

The low level of Asian FDI channelled to Latin America over the last two decades is linked to intra-industry corporate activity in East Asia and to the fact that Latin American and Caribbean countries have not been part of the interaction between trade and FDI, which serves to relocate production across national boundaries, thus creating a two-way, or even a triangular trade flow among participating countries. Latin American industrialization of the 1980s and 1990s brought about a clearly different trade and investment relationship: companies in Latin America continue to pursue an international strategy based on advantages in their respective home countries, whether arising from an abundance of natural resources, expertise in developing and processing these resources, or their capabilities and competitiveness in selling the processed resources or industrial commodities internationally. In services, large companies in the region have expanded their businesses on an international scale into two or more countries, in such fields as energy, communications, transportation, and financial services. Asian investors have rarely participated in the privatization process of these sectors.

In addition, market-seeking FDI in Latin America and the Caribbean has been too "inward -looking" and has not contributed sufficiently to the building of local manufacturing capacities and international competitiveness. One of the major reasons for a low level of trade and investment flows between the two regions relates to the lack of the so-called "efficiency-seeking" FDI, which is the type most common in Asia-Pacific. Also, in those cases where they do exist in Latin

12 One exception is that in 2006 the food companies Bimbo and Gruma, which were already strong players in Latin America, the United States and Europe, began investing in Asia. Bimbo purchased the Chinese operations of the Spanish firm Pan Rico. Gumba bought Rositas Investments in Australia and invested in food production projects in China and Japan, investing an estimated US$ 100 million (ECLAC 2007a, p. 51).

America, they suffer from the typical shortcomings of this type of FDI, namely, their "enclave" nature, low value-added trap and the lack of industrial clusters. One way of fostering trade and investment relations with Asia-Pacific would therefore be to promote this type of FDI on the Latin American side, and to address the problems that it usually engenders for the national economy. In this regard, it is interesting to note that Japan's Economic Partnership Agreement (EPA) with Mexico contemplates, in several chapters of the agreement, numerous technical cooperation measures for improving Mexican industrial capacities and international competitiveness, points that are not common in typical free trade agreements with the United States (ECLAC, 2008).

The fact that FDI flows between the two regions have lagged far behind the dynamic trends of total FDI flows in both is due not only to the inter-industry nature of trade flows but also to other economic and social factors. Lack of knowledge of corporate strategies in the other region, due to cultural, geographic and historical factors, is one important consideration. The scarcity of information, especially about recent trends in trade and FDI, regional integration and existing business opportunities in the other region, is another important impediment to reciprocal trade and investment. The lack of a well-established network among companies, large companies and SMEs alike, is an obstacle to strategic alliances and corporate association. Despite profitable opportunities, the high sunk costs of ventures, and the risks involved for single investors may also continue to act as formidable barriers.

As the Asian experience attests, a country's comparative advantage is strongly influenced by that of neighbouring countries. What matters more in today's globalized international economy is the region's market size, natural resource endowments, production cost structures, patterns of specialization, availability of skilled and unskilled labour, R&D capabilities and infrastructure as well as the harmonization of the "behind-the-border" measures and domestic regulations. In this context, regional integration has a lot to offer. In pursuit of the so-called "dynamic effects" of integration, most new regional integration goes beyond conventional arrangements addressing trade in goods and involves attempts at comprehensive disciplines and rules. Such schemes envisage liberalization of trade in services, factor movements, harmonization of regulatory regimes, environmental and labour standards as well as many domestic policies perceived as affecting international competitiveness. Cooperation in harmonization of norms as well as strengthening of infrastructure, physical and human alike, by way of regional integration, is also of growing importance. Despite substantial progress in these areas, by way of various initiatives through subregional and regional integration and free trade agreements signed with the United States, the European Union and several Asian countries, Latin America still lags behind Asia-Pacific in this regard.

6. Proliferation of trade agreements in Asia-Pacific: consequences for Latin America and the Caribbean

As examined in the foregoing sections, until recently, Asian regional integration consisted of burgeoning intraregional trade, based on the increasingly complementary production and trade components of the different countries' manufacturing sectors. Intra-industry trade (IIT) expanded significantly as the specific advantages of production and marketing chains were exploited more effectively. This process of de facto (market-led) integration in Asia-Pacific is now being supported by de jure (government-led) integration; and strong production and trade relations are being complemented by free trade agreements of various types that aim to consolidate those links. A clear characteristic of the process in Asia and the Pacific is the fact that several large regional economies, such as Japan, China, India, Republic of Korea and Taiwan Province of China, are abandoning their traditional reluctance to sign preferential agreements and join trade blocs, and have decided to sign bilateral or plurilateral trade agreements with other economies both within and outside the Asia-Pacific region. Asia-Pacific is consolidating its production integration through agreements that currently cover over 60% of its total trade (for more details, see ECLAC, 2007a; Rosales and Kuwayama, 2007).

The two approaches to integration, de facto and de jure routes, should be ultimately complementary. Integration of markets through use of formal trade agreements leads to greater legal certainty, clearer and more enhanced transparency of " the rules of the game" among businesses and "lock-in" the results of de facto integration achieved so far. Meanwhile, integration by this route may be unsuccessful if the underlying economic factors are not favourable or if countries and sectors share only a few production and trade complementarities. Given, on the one hand, the divergent patterns of regional integration between the two regions and, on the other, the proliferation of trade agreements in each (a definite trend that will orient future biregional trade debates and discussions), the important point is not necessarily to sequence the two approaches as Aminian et. al. (2008) suggests, but rather to seek ways of establishing synergies between them.

As discussed elsewhere (ECLAC, 2008), the de jure approach is needed to address the existing tariff and non-tariff barriers that impede greater trade flows between the two regions. Biregional cooperation and strategic business alliances are also called for in order to improve marketing/distribution and transport systems and other physical infrastructures, whose deficiency tends to increase transaction costs and thereby jeopardize future biregional business opportunities. The two regions should also work together to enhance international competitiveness and innovation capabilities not only for individual countries but also for each region as a whole.

E. Conclusions and recommendations

With imminent risks bearing down on the world economy and the emergence of a new geography of the world economy increasingly centered around Asia-Pacific, Latin American and Caribbean authorities should redouble their efforts to identify and capitalize upon the potential complementarities between the region and Asia-Pacific. Latin America and the Caribbean should take advantage of its current favourable position to lay the foundations for sustained trade and investment relations by creating biregional business alliances, enhancing cooperation in innovation and human capital in order to diversify trade, add greater value and knowledge to exports, and help create more stable conditions for growth.

One of the reasons for the limited biregional trade and investment flows is the lack of intra-industry trade between the two regions. Although there exists substantial intra-industry trade in each region, trade of this type across the two regions is still scarce. The fact that current intra-industry trade flows account for a relatively small proportion of biregional trade points not only to vast possibilities that may lie ahead, but also to enormous challenges that confront future biregional cooperation in trade and investment.

Inter-industry trade still accounts for the bulk of trade flows: exports from Asia-Pacific are manufactures, while Latin American and Caribbean exports are mainly primary commodities. Whereas the region's exports as a whole contain a growing proportion of manufactures, the opposite is true for its exports to Asia-Pacific. Shipments of food items and minerals and metals represent an increased share of total exports to Asia-Pacific, reflecting the region's comparative advantages and the potential of those markets. In contrast, the experiences of Central America and particularly Mexico point to an investment and trade strategy different from the one adopted in the rest of the region. Given the divergent pattern of international specialization between the two regions, the continued expansion and deepening process of international production chains of Asia-Pacific, together with the present strong demand for commodities, would offer the countries of Latin America and the Caribbean new production possibilities and export opportunities.

The list of products exported by the region to Asia-Pacific is becoming more diversified: it now includes a number of new products such as fishery products and pig meat, along with high-technology manufactures that include electronic microcircuits and telecommunications equipment and data-processing machinery. The presence of these manufactures indicates that Latin America is beginning to integrate, albeit sporadically, into the extensive supply-chain networks that are prevalent in the Asia-Pacific region.

It is also possible to detect some biregional trade flows that are of an intra-industrial nature and are increasing, though still at an incipient stage. In general, Mexico's trade with Asia-Pacific shows higher Grubel Lloyd indices than those for other Latin American countries. Costa Rica and Brazil are beginning to show some degree of intra-industry trade with that region. On the side of Asia-Pacific, Singapore, Australia and New Zealand are moving into intra-industry trade with Latin America and the Caribbean. In short, there has been a breakthrough from a pure inter-industry trade type to a trade structure that is a little more intra-industry-oriented.

Both intraregional FDI flows in Asia-Pacific and FDI inflows into emerging Asia have been a genuine promoter of de facto regional integration in this region; the FDI originating not only from the major developed countries but also from within emerging East and South-East Asia have been major investors for each Asian country over the years. In this region, there exists a clear "trade and investment" relationship, which promotes intra-industry and intra-firm trade and a greater "slicing-up" process of complex cross-border international supply chain networks.

East and South-East Asia can be viewed as a highly integrated "factory", in which the previous national production processes have been dismantled and dispersed to the lowest-cost locations across the region. An important element of the fragmentation of manufacturing processes in the region was Japan's loss of comparative advantages in manufacturing production, which led Japanese firms to slice their productive processes and outsource more labour-intensive stages to the neighbouring countries of East Asia. This "hollowing out" of the Japanese economy was replicated in Taiwan Province of China, the Republic of Korea, Singapore and Hong Kong SAR, thereby deepening the process of creating the "Asian Factory." China's later entry onto the international economic stage further eroded the industrial comparative advantages enjoyed by the higher-income East-Asian countries, making offshore production more attractive. Notably, this entire regional trade creation occurred outside the ambit of regional trade agreements but together with investment attraction policies.

There is also growing concern at the assumption that the benefits of Asia's buoyancy may not be fully exploited by non-Asian countries, owing to the formation of an informal (de facto) trade bloc, now supported by formal (de jure) integration in Asia-Pacific. Those countries make up an increasingly broad, widening and complementary group in which development is disseminated in concentric circles, thanks to intra-industry regional trade and intraregional FDI. In view of these trends, countries of Latin America and the Caribbean need to strengthen their trade links to make their production more complementary with that of Asia-Pacific, and establish trade and investment partnerships, in addition to trade agreements, which would provide new access to these markets and help these countries to integrate into Asian production and export chains.

Apart from the natural-resource-based FDI, one predominant type of FDI in Latin America and the Caribbean, "market-seeking" FDI, has been too "inward-looking" and has not contributed sufficiently to the building of local manufacturing capacities and international competitiveness. One of the major reasons for the low level of trade and investment flows between the two regions is the lack of the so-called "efficiency-seeking" FDI, the type most common in Asia-Pacific. And when they exist in the region, they suffer from the typical shortcomings of this type of FDI, namely, their "enclave" nature and the low-value-added trap as well as a lack of industrial clusters. In seeking to deepen trade and investment relations with Asia-Pacific, the region could therefore consider adopting a two-fold approach: promoting this type of FDI on the Latin American side, and addressing the drawbacks that usually affect national economies in general and the export sector in particular.

Concerning the more efficient and coordinated exploitation of comparative advantages, a number of recent experiences show that value can be added to commodity exports and knowledge can also be incorporated. Although more difficult than in manufacturing sectors, it is also possible to integrate commodities into production and marketing chains in Asia and the Pacific; this calls for a systemic approach that covers the production process, trade logistics, sea and air transport, and marketing and distribution in the final consumption market. To the extent that this is based on alliances with Asia-Pacific's investors, the initial export of commodities will become a complex of activities involving goods, services, investments and financing. Strategic partnerships should be created to increase value added throughout the production and marketing chain, and mutually beneficial technological partnerships should be developed (to apply advances in biotechnology to agro-industry, mining, forestry and fisheries, for example).

The countries of the region also urgently need to make the most of the current dynamism in the Asia-Pacific region and develop new linkages to move forward in the area of innovation and competitiveness (a weak link in the Latin American regional experience), strengthen links between trade and investment, and consolidate production and technological linkages. The Asia-Pacific region offers investments that could provide complementary financing for major initiatives, especially in the areas of infrastructure and energy. An interesting challenge is to identify the infrastructure and energy projects where Asian investment might be most needed, to speed up the implementation of projects, which would make it possible not only to strengthen the trade facilitation and investments link with Asia-Pacific but also to generate externalities for Latin America's own regional integration process. It would thus be advisable to link the strategic partnership with that region with an update of regional integration, to achieve unified markets, support increasingly common standards and provide more legal guarantees.

A number of market-access problems still exist. In Asia-Pacific, high ad valorem equivalents (AVEs) are applied to agricultural products and a number of natural-resource-based manufactures —precisely the product lines in which the Latin American and Caribbean region has major export interests and strong comparative advantages. The challenge facing the region is therefore to engage more actively in the Asian production and distribution chains with exports that face the highest levels of protection. In this regard, the countries of the region are encouraged to pursue better market access to that region, either on a bilateral basis or jointly, in a more coordinated manner.

For a number of reasons (including the prospect of securing better market access) Japan, Republic of Korea, China, and Singapore have engaged in free trade agreements and strategic partnerships with Latin America. Such agreements include those signed by: (i) Japan with Mexico and with Chile, and the joint study carried out with Argentina (with a view to be expanded to MERCOSUR); (ii) China's FTA with Chile and the almost finalized negotiations with Peru; (iii) Korea's FTA with Chile, Korea's preliminary negotiations with Mexico, and the joint study which supports an FTA between Korea and MERCOSUR; (iv) Singapore's FTA with Panama and the strategic partnership with Chile (through the Trans-Pacific Strategic Economic Partnership Agreement or P4), and Singapore's attempts aimed at an FTA with Mexico (stand-by) and signing of an FTA with Peru in May 2008; (v) Thailand's finalized negotiations for an FTA with Peru, and the discussions initiated with MERCOSUR and with Chile, both subject to the assessment of preliminary joint studies; and (vi) Malaysia's negotiations (already at an advanced stage) with a view to a bilateral agreement with Chile. India, at the same time, has signed trade agreements with Chile and with MERCOSUR, and has, for some time, been engaged in preliminary talks with Colombia and Venezuela under a limited trade liberalization process aimed at securing the partial elimination of tariffs on a restricted number of goods.

On the plurilateral front, the divergent positions within the Andean Community make it improbable that this regional block will move forward with trade liberalization initiatives in the short term with economic blocs of Asia, despite the talks that have already taken place, especially with India. The most recent initiative and probably the one with most prospects so far is the upcoming meeting of trade ministers of ASEAN and MERCOSUR, which will be convened by Brazil for November. There are no concrete objectives in view at this point in terms of a process towards a free trade agreement, but this meeting is definitely aimed at forging closer economic ties between the two regions, given their respective comparative advantages and the mutual benefits to be derived.

Other options available to the region for achieving better market access to the Asia-Pacific market might include: (i) creation of a trade bloc with East Asia to promote further trade liberalization (whether within the framework of APEC (FTAAP) or otherwise), which might include more than the three Latin American members (Chile, Mexico and Peru); this would help to achieve greater uniformity and convergence of rules and disciplines between the FTAs signed by APEC member countries and those signed by Latin American and Caribbean countries; (ii) promotion of intra-APEC trade and investment, by way of simplification and harmonization of the rules of origin (ROO) present in the majority of FTAs signed by APEC members and much greater flexibility in accumulating ROO among the different integration schemes and the FTAs in the region; (iii) the possible enlargement of the Trans-Pacific Strategic Economic Partnership Agreement, or "P4" (EPA), extending its geographic coverage for future FTA negotiations, for example, to Peru, Mexico, Colombia and Thailand; (iv) coordinated support by the three current Latin American APEC member countries in seeking APEC membership for other countries of the region; and (v) the strengthening and more active participation of the countries of both regions in the Forum for East Asia-Latin America Cooperation (FEALAC), the only forum of its kind which goes beyond the concept of the Pacific Rim. Chile, Mexico and Peru should play a critical role in coordinating positions and working together on different fronts in order to promote integration not only in APEC-related forums but also within and between other intraregional schemes.

The countries of these two regions could consider future action in other areas, in particular in improvement of infrastructure and energy. The public and private sectors of Latin America and the Caribbean should work together with Asian counterparts engaged in investment promotion to coordinate regional portfolios of projects in these two areas. One particular challenge for improving efficiency is the lack of information on the maritime and air transport system serving the two regions. In this regard, there is a need to analyse the available and planned transport channels between the two regions by: (i) studying the composition of commodity trade flows; (ii) looking at the maritime and air transport system, particularly its structure and vessel capacity and the export potential and import demand of both regions; and (iii) strengthening SME industry and trade associations to achieve scale economies for SME exporters through clusters or other forms of association, assisted by information dissemination using information and communications technologies (ICTs).

Bibliography

ADB (Asian Development Bank) (2007), *Asian Development Outlook*, Manila.

Aminian, Nathalie, K.C. King and Francis Ng (2008), "Integration of markets vs. integration by agreements", *Policy Research Working Paper*, No. 4546, World Bank, March.

Ando, Mitsuyo (2005), "Fragmentation and vertical intra-industry trade in East Asia", document presented at the Claremont Asian Regional Integration Workshop, Claremont, California 25 February.

Ando, Mitsuyo and Fukunari Kimura (2005), "Global supply chains in machinery trade and the sophisticated nature of production/distribution network in East Asia", July, unpublished.

ASEAN Secretariat (n/d) [online] http://www.aseansec.org/

Durán, José, Nanno Mulder and Osamu Onodera (2008), "Trade liberalization and economic performance: East-Asia versus Latin America 1970-2006", *OECD Trade Policy Working Paper*, No. 70, Paris, February.

Durán, José and Mariano Alvarez (2007), "Shipping costs: a rising challenge to the region's competitive development", *FAL Bulletin*, No. 256, Santiago, Chile, Economic Commission for Latin America and the Caribbean (ECLAC), December.

Durking, J. and M. Kryegier (2000), "Differences in GDP per capita and the share of intra-industry trade: the role of vertically differentiated trade", *Review of International Trade-Economics*, vol. 8, No. 4.

ECLAC (Economic Commission for Latin America and the Caribbean) (2008), "Latin American strategy on trade and investment towards Asia-Pacific: 'Market-led' integration for greater participation in Asia-Pacific supply value chains", document prepared for the project "Study on Latin American strategy on trade and investment towards Asia-Pacific" (JPN/08/001), Government of Japan.

___ (2007a), *Foreign Investment in Latin America and the Caribbean, 2006* (LC/G.2336-P), Santiago, Chile. United Nations publication, Sales No. E.07.II.G.32.

___ (2007b), *Latin America and the Caribbean in the World Economy, 2006. Trends 2007* (LC/G.2341-P/E), Santiago, Chile. United Nations publication, Sales No. E.07.II.G.85.

___ (2006), *Foreign Investment in Latin America and the Caribbean, 2005* (LC/G.2309-P), Santiago, Chile. United Nations publication, Sales No. E.06.II.G.44.

EIU (Economist Intelligence Unit) (2008), "World Investment Service" [online] http://www.eiu.com/.

Export-Import Bank of Korea (n/d) [online] http://www.koreaexim.go.kr.

Fukao, Kyoji, Hikari Ishido and Keiko Ito (2003), "Vertical intra-industry trade and foreign direct investment in East Asia", *RIETI Discussion Paper Series*, No. 03-E-001.

Haddad, M. (2007), "Overview of rules of origin in East Asia: how are they working in Practice?", *Trade Issues in Asia: Preferential Rules of Origin—Policy Research Report*, Washington, D.C., World Bank.

Hiratsuka, Daisuke (2006), "Outward FDI from and intraregional FDI in ASEAN", *Discussion Paper*, No. 77, Tokyo, Institute of Developing Economies, November.

IMF (International Monetary Fund) (2007), *Regional Economic Outlook: Asia and Pacific. World Economic and Financial Surveys*, October.

JETRO (Japan External Trade Organization) (2007), *2007 JETRO White Paper on International Trade and Foreign Direct Investment (Summary). Increasing Utilization of Asian FTAs and Growth Strategies for Japanese Companies*, Tokyo.

___ (2006a), *2006 JETRO White Paper on International Trade and Foreign Direct Investment (Summary). Japanese Corporate Activity in New Growth Markets and the Emerging East Asian Free Trade Zone*, Tokyo.

___ (2006b), "Report examines effects of Japan-Mexico EPA one year after its entry into force", *Press release*, April.

Kawai, Masahiro and Ganeshan Wignaraja (2007), "ASEAN+3 or ASEAN+6: which way forward?", *ADB Institute Discussion Paper*, No. 77, Tokyo, Asian Development Bank Institute.

Kawasaki, Kenichi (2003), "The impact of free trade agreements in Asia", *RIETI Discussion Paper Series*, No. 03-E-18, Tokyo, Research Institute of Economy, Trade and Industry (RIETI).

Kimura, Fukanari and Mitsuyo Ando (2004), "The economic analysis of international production/distribution networks in East Asia and Latin America: the implication of regional trade agreements", document presented at the Conference of the Latin America/Caribbean and Asia/Pacific Economics and Business Association (LAEBA) and the Pacific Economic Cooperation Council Trade Forum, APEC Study Centers Consortium (ASCC), Viña del Mar, 26-29 May.

Kinoshita, Toshihiko (2004), "Economic Integration in East Asia and Japan's Role", Washington, D.C., Waseda University/Carnegie Endowment for International Peace.

Kuwayama, Mikio (2001), "Hacia una nueva alianza de comercio e inversión entre América Latina y Asia-Pacífico", *Documento de divulgación*, No. 12, Buenos Aires, Institute for the Integration of Latin America and the Caribbean (INTAL)/Integration, Trade and Hemispheric Issues Division (ITD)/Statistics and Quantitative Analysis Unit (STA), Inter-American Development Bank (IDB).

METI (Ministry of Economy, Trade and Industry of Japan) (2007), "kaigai jigyo katsudo kihon chosa" [Basic (trend) survey of overseas business activities] No. 36.

___ (2006), *Trends in Overseas Subsidiaries. Quarterly Survey of Overseas Subsidiaries.*

Ministry of Commerce of China (n/d), "Invest in China" [online] http://www.fdi.gov.

___ (2006), *2006 Statistical Bulletin of China's outward Foreign Direct Investment,* Beijing.

Morrison, Charles E. (2006), "An APEC trade agenda", *An APEC Trade Agenda? The Political Economy of a Free Trade Area of the Asia Pacific*, The Pacific Economic Cooperation Council/The APEC Business Advisory Council.

Rosales, Osvaldo and Mikio Kuwayama (2007), "América Latina y China e India: hacia una nueva alianza de comercio e inversión", *Comercio internacional series*, No. 81 (LC/L.2656-P), Santiago, Chile, Economic Commission for Latin America and the Caribbean (ECLAC). United Nations publication, Sales No. S.07.II.G.6.

Secretariat of Economic Affairs, Office of Mexico-Japan Economic Partnership Agreement (n/d) [online] <http://www.mexicotradeandinvestment.com>.

Tharakan, P.K.M. (1989), "Bilateral intra-industry trade between countries with different factor endowment patterns", *Intra-Industry Trade- Theory, Evidence and Extensions*, P.K.M. Tharakan and J. Kol (eds.), London, MacMillan.

The Economist (2008), "A special report on China's quest for resources", 15 March.

UNCTAD (United Nations Conference on Trade and Development) (2006a), *Trade and Development Report 2006* (UNCTAD/TRD/2006). United Nations publication, Sales No. E.06.II.D.6.

___ (2006b), *World Investment Report 2006: FDI from Developing and Transition Economies: Implications for Development* (UNCTAD/WIR/2006), New York, October. United Nations publication, Sales No. E.06.II.D.11.

Wakasugi, Ryuhei (2007), "Vertical intra-industry and economic integration in East Asia", *Asian Economic Papers*, vol. 6, No. 1.

Wang, Jian-Ye and Abdoulaye Bio-Tchané (2008), "Africa's burgeoning ties with China. Maximizing the benefits of China's increasing economic engagement with Africa", *Finance and Development*, Washington, D.C., International Monetary Fund (IMF), March.

World Bank (2007), *East Asia & Pacific Update - 10 Years after the Crisis*, Washington, D.C.

WTO (World Trade Organization) (2008), *International Trade Statistics 2007*, Geneva.

Yoon, Ryong, Deok (2007), "Korea's Outward FDI in Asia: characteristics and perspectives", document presented at the Indian Council of Research in International Economic Relations (ICRIER) Workshop on Intra-Asian FDI Flows, New Delhi, Habitat Centre, 25- 26 April.

Chapter VII

Prospective studies: a tool for enhancing international integration

Introduction

Just as matters relating to international conditions, multilateral negotiations, regional integration and trade relations among countries, regions or continents are important for the evolution of trade, competitiveness and innovation capacity are increasingly crucial for tackling the economic and social challenges that countries now face.

In an era of globalization, export development is an important source of growth. Statistics show year after year that growth in international trade far outstrips that of world output and is one of its main engines. Trade also has the ability to stimulate a culture of competition, obliging firms to increase productivity and seek new markets. Furthermore, it encourages investment and helps to diversify production and consumption. Above all, however, in today's globalized, dynamic and changing world, global trade promotes knowledge, innovation, best practices and the incorporation of new technologies. In effect, as a result of globalization, firms have to deal with the reconfiguration of production systems and the continual emergence of new technologies. Witness the leading role now being played by information technologies, biotechnologies and the possibilities offered by nanotechnology. Firms are finding that they must adopt these new paradigms in order to participate now and in the future in the continual contest for markets, in which competitiveness and innovation are the keys to success.

Some emerging economies (China, India and others) have locked into the advantages of globalization and the continual emergence of new technologies to excellent effect, displacing the industries of many Latin American and Caribbean countries. In some cases, firms from the region have found niches in which they are competitive, but others have been pushed out of markets, leading to higher unemployment and worsening poverty. Although these developments can be foreseen, there is rarely a long-term strategy in place to deal with them. With the competitiveness-innovation link growing ever closer, countries lacking this link are worse placed to scale up the value of exports, have less capacity to incorporate knowledge into the goods they produce, diversify their export structure or achieve dynamic export development, while their ability to defend local industry is weakened.

As noted in the ECLAC report *Structural Change and Productivity Growth - 20 Years Later. Old problems, new opportunities* (ECLAC, 2008), although major strides have been made in Latin America and the Caribbean, the region is losing ground in comparison with certain Asian and Eastern European countries. Two of the main obstacles to competitiveness are the limited diversification of export products and the slow incorporation of innovative know-how into products and processes.

Some societies are better prepared to take advantage of future opportunities and to strengthen their position in global trade. Previous editions of *Latin America and the Caribbean in the World Economy* have looked at a number of cases, including the innovation and export development strategy developed by countries such as Finland, Ireland, Malaysia, the Republic of Korea, Singapore and Sweden. They have also analysed the cases of Australia and New Zealand, whose export structures are still heavily based on natural resources, but which have developed strategies and to develop new industries to add value and knowledge to the products they export.[1]

A new study that includes Spain and the Czech Republic, as well as these countries, and which is summarized in chapter VI of the report mentioned above (ECLAC, 2008), underlines the fact that a feature shared by these countries —whose policies, culture and history are very different— is the concerted action of the State to promote export development and competitiveness based on a vision of the future. In these countries, such a vision is manifested in medium- and long-term export development strategies and their implementation through public-private partnerships that seek consensus or, at least, understanding with respect to basic strategic guidelines.

In the effort to move ahead with consensus-seeking, prospective or foresight exercises have become an instrument used not so much for projecting an increasingly uncertain future, but for socializing information to create networks of different stakeholders and form expert analyses, all of which contributes to strategy definition and policy decision-making.

Prospective exercises have no single definition, but they increasingly tend to draw on a broad range of stakeholders to help define probable future scenarios —building alternative futures— and seek effective ways to tackle them. Countries that have a shared vision of the future and are able to trace paths towards a stronger position at the international level may then use these scenarios to gain ground in terms of competitiveness and strategies for technological development and innovation. With a view to impacting on the future, foresight work includes participation, consensus-building and information stockpiling, thus contributing to decision-making and planning.

Prospective studies tie in with national efforts to strengthen innovation and competitiveness in several ways. First, these studies can help identify technologies that may be crucial in building up a country's future competitiveness. Prospective exercises help design science and technology projects that guide State budgets and private-sector activities. Second, these exercises facilitate linkages between technology and know-how and the market, meaning that they stimulate the practical application of scientific research findings. This is a matter of identifying innovation priorities as regards future scenarios in areas offering new medium- and long-term opportunities for firms. Prospective exercises can serve to identify such opportunities, anticipate obstacles and put forward policies for advancing along the path or paths that have been identified. Third, prospective exercises allow long-term partnerships to be strengthened among researchers, firms from different industrial sectors, the academic world, government and, in general, different areas of society.

The following section uses specific examples from different countries to describe how prospective exercises have been implemented and used to create strategies for export development and innovation. This process is not common in Latin America and the Caribbean, so the progress achieved in other countries and continents can help promote the use of such exercises in order to enhance the region's international integration.

A. Foresight analysis, export development strategies and international integration

Prospective or foresight analysis consists of a systematic and organized enquiry into long-term behaviour patterns regarding different issues. Numerous analytical approaches can be found in the literature on this area, which has aroused mounting interest at the international level.[2] Over the last few decades, however, and for different reasons, understanding

1 See New Zealand Ministry of Economic Development (2005) and Backing Australia's Ability (2004).

2 Masini (2006), Cuhls (2003), Cuhls and Jaspers (2004), Cariola and Rolfo (2004).

of the prospective process moved away from the simple exercise of projecting the future as an extrapolation of the past, giving way to a more complex vision that is oriented more towards decision-making in the present. The participation of a large number of stakeholders —including scientists, professionals, businesspeople and public authorities— helps pave the way for intelligent, systematic and participatory planning and creation of development strategies designed to improve a country's long-term competitive position at the international level.

The most systematic work carried out on the application of forward-looking analysis at the country level was undertaken during the 1990s in countries such as Austria, France, Germany, Japan, the Republic of Korea, Sweden and the United Kingdom, although today such work has extended to most European countries, Australia and New Zealand, while Japan and the Asia-Pacific Economic Cooperation (APEC) forum have promoted the practice in Asian countries. These exercises have been carried out mostly at the national level, but have also been implemented at regional and sectoral level. As will be seen further on, they have been developed as a policy tool and play an important role in the strategic vision used to strengthen international integration.

One example among many that illustrate the relationship between foresight analysis and export development can be found in Germany, whose economy depends heavily on exports with a high knowledge content. Germany has recognized that its technological efficiency is one of its main advantages when competing in the world markets, and is aware that German firms will be able to remain highly competitive in the long term only to the extent that they continue to invest in research and development (R&D), develop new technologies, and quickly transform innovations into marketable goods. The country has used prospective studies to identify technologies that can play a decisive role to increase future competitiveness. The specific goal of its latest prospective exercise, entitled Futur (2001-2005), was to investigate areas of research able to attract funding, and the way those studies were subsequently implemented and used was crucial. The knowledge obtained from the studies, later helped to establish priorities for technological research and technology policies applied to highly export-oriented sectors such as the automobile industry, nanotechnology, information and communications technologies (ICTs), and the health and energy sectors.

1. Strategic areas of export development and prospective exercises

Strategy analysis in countries studied outside the region (ECLAC, 2008) found four strategic pillars supporting programmes and policies to strengthen international integration: attracting foreign direct investment (FDI), coordination and internationalization of small and medium-sized enterprises (SMEs), export promotion, and innovation. These pillars are not equally important in all the countries (see table VII.1), but together form a system of policies and programmes that are sustained in the medium term, and which represent the architecture of an export development strategy.

Table VII.1
FOUR STRATEGIC PILLARS OF INTERNATIONAL INTEGRATION [a]

	Attracting foreign direct investment	Coordination and internationalization of SMEs	Export promotion	Innovation
Australia	√			√
Czech Republic	√		√	√
Finland				√
Ireland	√	√	√	√
Malaysia	√	√	√	√
New Zealand		√	√	√
Republic of Korea		√	√	√
Singapore	√	√	√	√
Spain [b]		√	√	√
Sweden				√

Source: Economic Commission for Latin America and the Caribbean (ECLAC), on the basis of official reports from the relevant countries.
[a] The √ sign indicates a strategy that has been formally established and implemented.
[b] Refers to the autonomous communities.

Attracting foreign investment, for example, has played a key role in the strategies of small countries trying to make swift progress in the area of industrialization and export of high-technology products with value added, such as Ireland, Malaysia, Singapore and, lately, the Czech Republic. As a result of intense external competition, the current strategy in these countries is to maintain or improve the domestic business climate and be more selective in implementing investment attraction programmes, placing emphasis on higher-technology production and services sectors.

The choice of policy to attract foreign investment is no small matter and foresight exercises provide the opportunity to form a consensus on which activities are to benefit from incentives. At present, priority is given to industries and services with a high knowledge and value content, and to investments in R&D. These exercises, which engage different private and public-sector stakeholders, have improved decision-making and increased policy efficiency. Ireland and Singapore and, to a certain extent, Malaysia offer interesting examples of such processes. In these countries, the search for strategies to deal with future challenges involves not only local stakeholders, but also international advisory panels. Every year, the Government of Singapore convenes a meeting at the highest political level, involving managing directors from large multinational firms and government representatives, to analyse global and Asian trends along with technological and strategic changes. As an instrument of future analysis, this meeting not only represents a forum to share information related to domestic strategies, but also fosters a network of contacts in the international market that helps identify opportunities for the country.

The strategic pillar consisting of the internationalization of firms has a number of dimensions: (i) integration of local firms into international value and export chains; (ii) integration of firms as suppliers of transnational corporations with a local presence; (iii) technological upgrading, particularly for SMEs; and (iv) training in exporting and foreign investment, also mainly for SMEs. Prospective exercises have proven useful in selecting the activities and sectors on which to target human and financial efforts. In the case of the Republic of Korea, the Ministry of Trade, Industry and Energy (MOTIE) has conducted foresight analyses to build consensus on policies and identify the country's strategic priorities up to 2030 (Choi, 2003; Seok-Ho and others, 2006).

Export promotion is another strategic pillar for improving information regarding possible foreign markets, helping to promote a country's image, linking suppliers with buyers, and improving the quality of goods and services, along with market access. In some countries, these programmes and policies are developed within the framework of internationalization and innovation programmes.

As shown in table VII.1, the innovation pillar represents the strategy most often used for export development, which shows how important it is in steadily increasing the productivity and competitiveness of goods and services. Countries' future international integration depends on the creation of new products and services, and the upgrading of productive processes. It is no surprise, therefore, that the number of foresight studies in Europe and Asia directly increases in relation to the innovation strategies they produce. In the case of Ireland, the main objective of the last prospective exercise was to ensure sustained competitive advantages and improve the country's standard of living. Hence, the government attached particular importance to promoting society's understanding of how science and technology could help the country tackle future needs. Specifically, it set about raising economic stakeholders' awareness of how investment in research, science and technology would help Ireland to transition towards a knowledge society. The exercise also helped to establish networks linking firms with basic sciences, applied sciences and government policies and, lastly, it fostered a culture of reflection on markets, technological opportunities and the ongoing challenges faced by the country.

Following the examples of Germany, Japan and the United Kingdom, the Republic of Korea has carried out three technology futures exercises, which have involved a growing number of stakeholders working together in panels of experts, businesspeople, academics and even consumers, to assess potential areas of technological development for the country. Together with establishing networks to spread information and knowledge, later strengthened by government policies, the results of these exercises provided inputs for five-year plans in the areas of science and technology that have guided State budgets and private-sector activities.

The process has developed since the start of these prospective analysis exercises in respect of their direction and the methodologies used. The exercises carried out in Europe and, later, Asia initially focused on technology foresight, with which competitiveness was believed to be closely linked. Prospective exercises were seen as the key to resolving the dilemma between the need to establish priorities (because of the cost of upgrading, limited resources or the complexities of scientific decision-making) and pressure to obtain value for money and socio-economic impact.

Given that methodologies are generic, however, and can be used with different goals, the process shifted towards a new approach to competitiveness-building, in which not only R&D were important, but also the articulation of technology and knowledge with the market. New scientific or technological know-how could not remain confined to laboratories or universities, but had to be used to add value to products and processes through marketing, thus giving rise to innovation strategies. It was thus a matter not only of identifying research priorities based on scientific opinions, but of analysing future outcomes for firms in areas that offered new opportunities in the long term. Foresight analysis was used to identify such opportunities, possible obstacles and policies for advancing along the paths identified. This involved the participation not only of scientists in the exercise, but also of industry, consumers and government authorities working in the areas of production, marketing and technological dissemination.

Box VII.1 describes an example of foresight analysis focused on competitiveness-building in one of Norway's main export areas: aquaculture. The example illustrates the way such analysis helped establish a public-private alliance to outline the industry's future, through a discussion involving industry, scientists, other professionals and government authorities. Interestingly enough, although the goal of the exercise was to identify the future of a particular industry, the agency that initiated the exercise was the Research Council of Norway, demonstrating that in a country that uses state-of-the-art technology, the future is closely linked with R&D and the search for strategic solutions.

Box VII.1

A PROSPECTIVE STUDY IN NORWAY: AQUACULTURE 2020

In 2003, the Research Council of Norway invited representatives from the aquaculture industry, research communities and public authorities to take part in a discussion on the future of Norwegian aquaculture, entitled Aquaculture 2020. The initiative aroused considerable interest on the part of institutions and private individuals. Some 150 basic and five more complex scenarios were drawn up, one of which was used as the basis for strategic recommendations and initiatives targeting stakeholders in the areas of research, government, trade and industry. The scenarios proposed within the framework of Aquaculture 2020 were used to present a series of different outlooks regarding the potential of Norwegian aquaculture up to 2020, and to explain what had taken place up to that time.

The exercise found that research alone can not resolve all the problems encountered and that, to produce results, research investment should be coordinated with business and trade development strategies established by commerce and industry and by the State. Second, given that research in different areas should be connected and enriched transversally, it was concluded that joint action in technological and professional fields such as ICTs, materials technologies, biotechnology, along with social and market research, is fundamental for the development of new and important areas of knowledge and to identify strategic solutions for the development of aquaculture.

As a result of this process, the Research Council of Norway has been using prospective analysis as a tool to develop large-scale research programmes involving skilled professionals from different firms, and representatives of State, research and educational institutions, working together to provide long-term foresight analysis. This work identifies the central issue in each case and fosters discussion regarding the future, creating a productive collaboration effort that would not have been possible if the stakeholders involved were not meeting on a daily basis.

The Aquaculture 2020 report that resulted from this exercise does not purport to provide a comprehensive or scientific analysis. What it deals with is the future or, more specifically, a range of possible or alternative future scenarios. The report was issued with the aim of improving the basis for the sector's development programme, as commended to the Research Council of Norway for the 2004-2005 period.

Source: Economic Commission for Latin America and the Caribbean (ECLAC), on the basis of Research Council of Norway "Aquaculture 2020: Transcending the barriers - As long as...", 2005 [online] http://www.forskningsradet.no /CSStorage/Flex_attachment/Aquaculture_2020_eng.pdf.

Today, foresight analysis is also applied to sectoral strategies and even to general development issues such as economic, social and sustainable development. In this context, the discipline has evolved through the convergence of trends in public policy analysis, strategic planning and future studies, and brings together the main agents of change in order to develop a strategic outlook based on advance intelligence. As shown by Masini (2002) the importance of foresight analysis lies not only in anticipating what the future holds, but also in deciding what path to follow.

The end results of prospective exercises —the outcome of the recommendations and policy decisions deriving from them— have yet to be measured. Some authors, however, have identified six functions that prospective analysis should fulfil; these represent intermediate results and feed into policy implementation. These functions are: (i) to provide the advance information or "intelligence" to which State authorities and other stakeholders have access during the exercise and which broadens the knowledge base used to take decisions; (ii) to facilitate policy implementation, by building a shared vision among all stakeholders regarding the present situation and future challenges, as well as establishing shared networks and viewpoints; (iii) to promote participation by different stakeholders —including civil society— in decision-making, so increasing the transparency and legitimacy of policies; (iv) to support policy definition, translating the results of the collective process into specific options for policy design and implementation; (v) to reshape the political system by introducing long-term challenges; and (vi) to demonstrate to the public that policies are based on rational information (see Da Costa and others, 2006).

Lastly, the body of experience in prospective analysis reveals certain keys to making the most of such exercises and ultimately producing policies that are truly effective for shaping long-term patterns. Based on the experience of a country such as Ireland, several recommendations may be made (Boyle, O'Donnell and O'Riordan). One of these is to link the long-term focus with current issues and policies in order to increase the stakeholders' interest in such exercises and the likelihood of their success. In addition, although in prospective exercises learning is obtained mainly from other experiences, it always has to be adapted to specific circumstances, which calls for training and planning.

It has also been noted that for such exercises to be well focused, it is necessary to form some kind of steering committee made up of different stakeholders, to be responsible for (among other things) coordinating and overseeing the foresight exercise and facilitating the search for consensus or understanding. Since the members of such a committee must obviously be well informed, they should include experts in the different issues that need to be addressed and consult their own and other specialists' research during the course of the exercise. Another recommendation is to use the process to establish networks of scientists, industry, consumers and experts, which should remain active in the long term. Multiple methodologies should be used for prospective analysis, including situation planning, workshops and Delphi or other methods in order to structure thinking over the long term. These methodologies can help identify strategies or implement policy recommendations related to the future. Lastly, Boyle, O'Donnell and O'Riordan found that the most successful exercises are those that translate into a plan of action as a mechanism for implementing the strategy. Given the current challenges for strengthening Latin American and Caribbean integration at international level, familiarity and use of these policy instruments may be extremely useful.

2. A broad array of methodologies and instruments

Between the late 1940s, when future studies were first undertaken, and today, when foresight analysis has become a public policy instrument, the methodology used for such exercises has broadened enormously. Although different countries carry out prospective exercises in a large variety of ways, generally reflecting their own individual traits as well as the characteristics of each exercise, the set of methodologies available is common to all of them. Those methodologies include those corresponding to the preliminary study phase, which are generally conducted by specialized researchers. Multiple techniques are used at this stage, including the preparation of models and simulation, extrapolation of trends, expert panels, Delphi techniques (structured collection of knowledge from experts, from which conclusions are distilled), review of literature, retrospective analysis, and so forth. Other techniques are incorporated during the process in the interaction with different stakeholders, such as analysis of strengths, weaknesses, opportunities and threats (SWOT analysis), cross-impact analysis, brain storming and citizen panels, which are used to analyse trends and create scenarios.

(a) Engaging stakeholders

In recent times, a key component of these exercises has been strong stakeholder engagement. Experience has shown that the more stakeholders are involved, the more effective the policy, and that this is just as important as the skills of those responsible for implementing the policy (see Havas, Schartinger and Weber, 2007). Exercises such as Futur 2001-2005 in Germany, Future 2020 in the United Kingdom, the latest Delphi study conducted in Japan and the exercise for the period 2003-2004 in Sweden mobilized stakeholders from many different spheres, forming highly representative groups of corporate executives, representatives of industrial organizations, scientists, consumers, labour associations and government authorities.

The way the stakeholders participate depends on the type of exercise and the methodology used. A number of phases have been identified, however, each with different degrees of engagement and participation (see figure VII.1). At the diagnostic or exploration phase of the exercise, the degree of participation can be limited by the specificity of the issues, but the number of stakeholders convened increases considerably at the decision-making phase, then narrows down again at the stages of implementation and coordination.

The first stage, then, consists of establishing or choosing the issues or projects on which the exercises are to be carried out, and the second is to apply the particular methodology of the prospective exercise. The method used at the first stage may be an intensive workshop, in which a select group of academics or experts chooses potential subjects for analysis. By the second stage, there should be a team qualified in foresight methodology behind each issue, supported by an expert advisory group This was the procedure employed in the last foresight exercise conducted in the United Kingdom.

Figure VII.1
PHASES OF STAKEHOLDER ENGAGEMENT IN A FORESIGHT ANALYSIS PROCESS

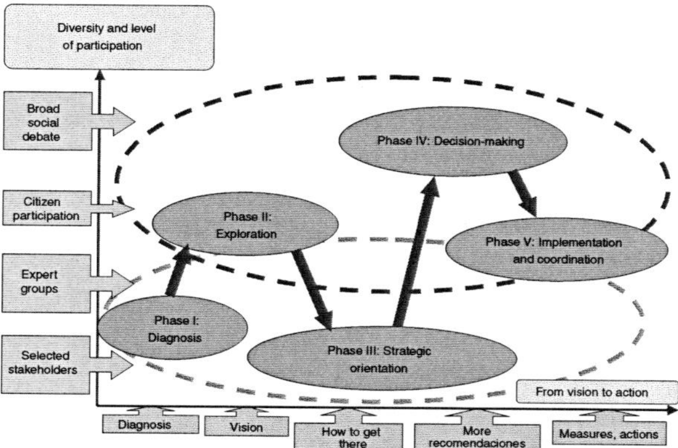

Source: Economic Commission for Latin America and the Caribbean (ECLAC), on the basis of O. Da Costa and others, "The impact of foresight on policy-making: Insights from the FORLEARN mutual learning process", 2006.

The strategy of the exercise is different in each case and requires intensive use of the available tools. The strategy design is the most flexible point as regards possible techniques. Yet all strategies have a common feature: they are typically participatory and inclusive, with either intensive workshops or joint work by the participants over a longer period of time. One of this methodology's peculiarities is that the exercise is coordinated by a team that is neutral, from outside the sector being discussed. This generates new combinations of stakeholders, leading to a more multi-disciplinary and cooperative vision of the issue, which would be difficult to achieve if the people directly involved were running the project.

Lastly, the greatest successes of these exercises cited by the authorities coordinating them include, first, their capacity to generate consensus or, at the very least, understanding about the options and roads to strengthening the respective country's international position and, second, their ability to create mechanisms to consolidate long-term partnerships between researchers, firms in different sectors of industry, academia and governments and, in general, different walks of society.

(b) Developing future scenarios

In recent times, foresight exercises have also drawn on future scenarios methodology (Berkhout and Hertin, 2002 and DTI, 2002). This approach can be very useful in countries that need to set up medium- and long-term strategies, precisely because it is used to delineate the basic conditions or context on which the different scenarios are based, which helps to develop more effective strategies. This methodology enables analysis of the different dimensions of each of the scenarios, including trends in the global market, economic and sectoral trends in the country and employment and social trends, among others. The key to the exercise is to look beyond the horizons that are normally visible, in international trade, for example, in order to identify the potential and the opportunities arising from both the markets and developments in science and technology.

The United Kingdom Department of Trade and Industry (DTI) uses this methodology. In the last exercise conducted in 2002, the scenarios were based on two dimensions: social values, from the most individualistic to the most community-oriented (DTI, 2002), and the measurement of governance systems, which ties in with government structure and decision-making.

The first dimension affects social priorities, policies and patterns of economic activity. In Latin America, the community side of the social dimension could be equated with organized civil society, which lobbies and works for policies orientated towards social integration.

With regard to the second dimension, one extreme corresponds to autonomy —power remaining at the national level— and the other to interdependence —power shifting to supranational institutions, such as the European Union. An equivalent exercise for Latin America would be the development of scenarios of greater or lesser regional integration, which would have a key impact on infrastructure and, especially, energy.

But scenarios can have multiple dimensions, which also depend on what direction countries are exploring. For example, scenarios could be developed around the Doha Round of trade talks, which would be particularly relevant for the MERCOSUR countries. Or around the future outcomes of negotiations on climate change, including the potential participation of Brazil, China and India in the Kyoto Protocol accords. But whatever dimensions are chosen for scenario-building, the key aspects of each must then be determined as a function of their possible impact on the domestic and international context in the future.

3. The leadership provided by governments

While there are academic bodies and research institutes devoted to futures analysis, the onus has been on governments to take the initiative as regards foresight exercises as such, that is, as a tool for decision-making and strategy-crafting. At the same time, since this discipline started up in the developed countries, where competitiveness has been closely linked to technological development, the greatest advances have occurred in science and technology. In the United States, foresight work has been spearheaded by the Department of Defense, while in Japan, the National Institute of Science and Technology Policy (NISTEP) conducts Delphi studies on a regular basis. In the Republic of Korea, the Science and Technology Policy Institute (STEPI) has a group working on futures analysis. In the United Kingdom, prospective exercises are part of the mandate of the Office of Science and Technology (OST), while the Australian Science and Technology Council was responsible for an exercise denominated "Matching science and technology to future needs". Similar bodies steer prospective processes in Canada, China, Hungary, New Zealand, South Africa and Thailand. In Austria various departments of the Austrian Academy of Sciences are still responsible for this area, and in Sweden foresight exercises are conducted by a consortium formed by the Royal Swedish Academy of Engineering Sciences with representatives of industry and the public sector.

The concept of competitiveness as being linked to innovation is generating concern about the market side, that is, how to market new process and products or business models. This has led to the inclusion of new actors and made it necessary to share the organization of exercises with other ministries. In the United States, for example, the Department of Commerce has been brought on board, as has the Ministry of Economic Affairs, Commerce and Industry in Japan. In Finland, what is now the Ministry of Employment and Economic Affairs (formerly the Ministry of Trade and Industry) and the Finnish Funding Agency for Technology and Innovation (TEKES) are the agencies responsible for foresight exercises (see box VII.2).

Box VII.2
TECHNOLOGY FORESIGHT IN FINLAND

Technological development and innovation have become key resources for growth and competitiveness in the Finnish economy and are expected to remain so in the future. In many organizations, prospective analysis in this area is now an essential part of strategy development in order to remain technologically competitive.

Unlike many other countries, Finland does not have a formal national-level foresight process that could be used as background for setting R&D priorities. Nevertheless, technology foresight exercises are used, applied and developed in many forms and at various organizational levels in the innovation system. The Ministry of Trade and Industry set up a project to coordinate technology prospective activities in Finland in 2001 and that task has been carried on thereafter.

This project's main purpose was to formulate scenarios and viewpoints for innovation policy, analyse different processes of evolution and develop new theoretical approaches, from long-term systematic research to public debate.

Several networks have been created under the project, including an expert network, a foresight network involving all the ministries and a high-level committee comprising representatives of the Ministry of Trade and Industry, the Finnish Funding Agency for Technology and Innovation (TEKES) and the Technical Research Centre of Finland (VTT), as the nucleus responsible for technology policy issues.

The main areas of technology foresight for the crafting of technology and innovation policy in Finland have been as follows:

(i) Essential changes and trends in the economic environment.
(ii) Key issues regarding globalization, internationalization, integration, regulation, information society development, development of the European Union and technological changes in society.
(iii) Sustained growth and development, ageing and other long-term changes in society.
(iv) Changes and trends in national innovation and production systems, such as the dynamics and long-term development of industrial clusters and the business environment.

TEKES is the main public agency financing applied and industrial R&D in Finland. Its technology strategy is based on close and intensive interaction, discussion and continuous learning with firms, research institutes, industrial organizations and other technology-policy peer groups. This work also takes international trends into account by using the agency's wide contact network.

Technology foresight studies are often associated with technology evaluation programmes in the same field. This type of foresight study may be denominated embedded studies, which incorporate evaluation, technology foresight and technology assessment. These projects also provide a platform for the creation of development tools and methods of technology foresight for programmes in this area.

A number of studies have analysed Finland's technology foresight activities and compared them with European practices, identifying a number of challenges for Finland. These include systematic and comprehensive analysis of the potential risks of technological development; balanced assessment of different R&D areas; sound, transparent and well-documented foresight processes; and all the aspects stakeholders must bear in mind in processes of foresight, estimation and evaluation.

Source: Economic Commission for Latin America and the Caribbean (ECLAC), on the basis of Eija Ahola, "Technology Foresight within the Finnish Innovation System", document presented at the Second International Conference on Technology Foresight, Tokyo, 27 and 28 February 2003.

B. Foresight in Latin America and the Caribbean and lessons from experiences in the rest of the world

Although foresight analysis has been carried out in Latin America and the Caribbean, it has not been a systematic government practice at the sectoral, subnational or national levels (except in a few countries). In most cases, foresight exercises have been used sporadically, with the region's countries lacking the capacity to adapt them creatively to their situations.[3]

The experiences of European and Asian countries that use foresight show that these exercises can be extremely useful, not only for looking at and modelling the future, but also for harmonizing the visions of different stakeholders and reconciling these with opposing interests. Multilateral institutions including the Organisation for Economic Co-operation and Development (OECD), the European Union and APEC support such exercises and help countries to identify and study phenomena that may affect their future, also creating the conditions for the development of a common vision. For instance, the aim of the OECD International Futures Programme is to help countries tackle the complexity and uncertainty of today's world, through the creation of a platform for policymakers and other stakeholders to compare visions and ideas, by taking account of the viewpoints of others and establishing a dialogue that leads to a greater understanding of the phenomena involved and guidelines for the future. The European Union has the Foresight for the European Research Area (FORERA), which aims to promote foresight activities in Europe as a basis for the open coordination of future visions, the facilitation of decision-making and the provision of assistance, long-term guidelines and guidance for stakeholder dialogue on research and innovation policies at the European level. APEC has the Center for Technology Foresight (CFT), which was set up in 1998 as part of the National Science and Technology Development Agency (NSTDA) in Bangkok. Its main aim is to develop and disseminate foresight capacity and planning tools to help APEC economies to face rapid changes and social challenges. With this in mind, APEC has adopted a fairly broad definition of foresight as a systematic attempt to glimpse the future of science, technology, society, the economy and their various interactions, for the purposes of social, economic and environmental benefits. To achieve this, APEC carries out: foresight projects (in the broadest sense of the term); regional, sectoral and organizational foresight studies; training in the latest generation of foresight studies; and regional and national strategic planning.[4]

As a region, Latin America and the Caribbean has no such agencies, despite the many challenges it faces and the ever-increasing demands of competitiveness. Given that the main competitors of the region's countries have a long-term vision and have agreed upon a common strategy to strengthen their position in the world economy (resulting in a clearly defined course of action), it is obviously important for Latin America and the Caribbean to follow a course based on long-term strategic guidelines that translate into specific actions in the present. This is vital in order to coordinate and link effective policies.

1. The search for national vision on the road to competitiveness

Foresight exercises help to identify a national vision for facing the future in a consensual way. One highly illustrative example was implemented by the Australian Labour Prime Minister in April 2008.[5] This involved convening 1,000 people grouped according to 10 issues, and their joint efforts served to define the country's priorities for the future. The issues analysed in Australia are not toofar removed from the challenges facing Latin American and the Caribbean countries: productivity, training and education, the future of the economy, future direction of rural industries, climate change and water (a key issue for Australia) and the long-term health strategy.

3 See Popper and Medina (2008).

4 For more information on the OECD International Futures Programme, the European Union's Foresight for the European Research Area (FORERA) and the APEC Center for Technology Foresight (CFT), see http://www.OECD.org, http://forera.jrc.ec.europa.eu/ and http://www.apecforesight.org/, respectively.

5 *Australia 2020 Summit, Initial Summit Report*, April 2008.

In the initial stage of the exercise, the assembly of actors with different interests generated some contention but also facilitated an understanding of the challenges involved, put various possible solutions on the table, enabled stakeholders to make contact and get to know each other and eventually led to understandings and even consensus on key issues for the country's development. Many Latin American and Caribbean countries could benefit from such an initiative. One positive aspect is that the dialogue leaves ideology and parties to one side, as participants look to the future to solve concrete problems and come up with viable options for strengthening national competitiveness in the long term.

Between 2003 and 2004, Sweden carried out a similar exercise, the conclusions of which are presented in "Inspiration for Innovation: Swedish Technology Foresight 2004".[6] In Sweden, the search to identify the course of the country's future development was carried out in a shorter form. The country's cutting-edge technology and the effects of the constant forces of globalization led the Swedish to the conclusion that the investment specialization should be deepened. Eleven sectors were selected, grouping 100 areas of knowledge and technological development, including interactive technology, functional materials, sustainable food production and health-care technology. As a means of strengthening collaboration among companies, academia and the government, these results were incorporated into Sweden's innovation strategy, which guides the programmes and incentives for its implementation.

2. Foresight in energy: a means of overcoming obstacles to competitiveness

Foresight exercises help to identify ways of breaking down obstacles to competitiveness or to achieve consensus and establish strategic guidelines as a result. One example is energy policy. Although foresight exercises are not commonplace in Latin America and the Caribbean, Brazil and the Bolivarian Republic of Venezuela have some experience in this area.

In 2005, the State petroleum company of the Bolivarian Republic of Venezuela, Petróleos de Venezuela S.A. (PDVSA), carried out the first technological foresight study on fuels and advanced vehicles, with a view to defining future scenarios for its products over the next 10 or 20 years (Paez, 2005). In terms of fuels, the exercise revealed a wide range of opportunities and threats, which in a global context could become major challenges and opportunities for the company. The policy recommendations that arose from the exercise included the creation of a corporate technology strategy to promote the search for new products and fossil fuels for future markets, timely investment in technology to produce high-quality fossil fuels and the need to explore new business opportunities in Asia and Latin America and the Caribbean, as well as socially and environmentally responsible energy diversification in all markets. The usefulness of the exercise clearly depends on its capacity to influence decision-making in enterprise and government.

In Brazil, a foresight exercise was carried out into the sustainability of the ethanol industry. Current oil prices, the higher cost of cereals and rapid technological change in the Brazilian ethanol industry made the product into the most competitive biofuel in the world. Added to this is the potential demand from the United States when the tariffs on ethanol are eliminated in 2009. Although the strong international position of ethanol bodes well for the industry, major challenges remain, as detailed by the foresight exercise.[7]

The study concluded that, although rising world demand for ethanol would be a driving force of development in the industry, the negative externalities will also be considerable unless appropriate strategic planning is carried out. Public policy should be used to solve problems relating to ownership rights and land-use planning, and to react to the opportunities of a new regional development based on the deconcentration of the bioenergy industry. The study also highlighted the need to increase State support for R&D and technological transfer, motivate the private sector with mechanisms to promote best practices in corporate governance and social responsibility, and strengthen the response to the markets' efficiency requirements and environmental pressures.[8]

---

6 Swedish Technology Foresight (2004) [online] www.tekniskframsyn.un.

7 The exercise was carried out by the Institute for Agricultural Economics, as part of a project on the direction of public policies for the ethanol industry in the state of São Paulo and the public-policy research programme of the Foundation to support research in the state.

8 In Brazil, the Center for Strategic Management and Studies (CGEE) carries out foresight studies in different areas.

There are several countries in the region whose energy matrix will not cover future requirements. Carrying out national foresight exercises would enable countries to formulate alternative scenarios and, above all, achieve consensus among the various actors on the subject of viable options that may have opposing effects. At the regional level, these exercises would optimize the use of energy, with direct effects on competitiveness. With this in mind, the Latin American Energy Organization (OLADE) carried out an energy foresight study of its 26 member countries in 2006 (OLADE, 2006). The exercise was organized by countries and subregions —Mexico, Central America, the Caribbean, Andean countries and the Southern Cone— and covers the period up to 2018. The study presents the ratio between supply and demand by country and subregion for the entire range of energy products, and compares this with what the ratios would be in scenarios of high and low levels of integration.

As with any study of this nature, some assumptions have been made about the world order, such as the strong surge in demand from China, the United States and India, which will particularly affect demand for petroleum in the transport sector. There has also been a mushrooming of searches for alternatives to conventional petroleum and its petroleum products. The study also uses regional assumptions. A scenario with low levels of integration (with only a few consolidated infrastructure projects, mainly in natural gas and electricity) would result in lower competitiveness and slower rates of growth and development. In a high-integration scenario, regional competitiveness, growth and development would all increase. An analysis of the results of the foresight study clearly shows the economic benefits of integration by subregion, given the energy-production capacity of some countries and the energy requirements of others.

The problem with this type of exercise is that, rather than producing consensus on political decisions, it tends to represent more of an analysis of the future, with conclusions that do not result in a strategy to be implemented by the countries involved. This is illustrated by the different approach to foresight used in other regions, including in some Nordic countries (Denmark, Finland, Iceland, Norway and Sweden).[9] These countries are making efforts to design and apply a strategic vision in the energy sector for the next 30 years. The exercise carried out involved 16 agencies from the spheres of academia, industry, energy companies and associations from the five countries, plus a wide range of European experts from the areas of research, industry and government. The aim of the foresight exercise was to help the companies, research institutes and governments of the five countries to define priorities for the energy industry, especially in terms of introducing hydrogen energy. The exercise enabled these countries to develop collaborative projects, set up networks of scientists and investment companies and create a critical mass to lend weight to their projects in the international arena. In addition to the specific research findings, the exercise has made it possible for a group of small countries to join forces and combine their material resources, knowledge and determination to tackle the energy challenges of the future.

3. Foresight studies at the sectoral level

In Latin America, sectoral foresight exercises have been promoted by the United Nations Industrial Development Organization (UNIDO). In 2005 a futures exercise was conducted for the South American fishing industry, covering Chile, Colombia, Ecuador and Peru. This exercise served to generate cooperation agreements to increase productivity and competitiveness in the export chain, define regional R&D programmes and propose technology upgrades in products and sectors related to the fishing industry. In addition, the project produced recommendations regarding follow-up to the exercise and the need to establish a regional fisheries policy; promoted investment in modernization and technological upgrading in the industry; proposed the creation of a regional training and technology alert centre and, lastly, established a quality of origin framework for products from the region (UNIDO, 2006).

If such exercises had been carried out in Chile's salmon farming industry several years ago, the main stakeholders (industry representatives, workers, scientists, international experts and public authorities) might have reached an understanding to develop a sustainable growth strategy based on innovation and environmental stewardship. This might well have avoided the diseases that are now hurting the output of one of the country's main export products. Conversely, the exercise carried out in the Norwegian fish-farming industry (see box VII.1) generated joint action by scientists and professionals in ICTs, materials technologies and biotechnology and social and market

9 Nordic H2 Energy Foresight, *Building the Nordic Research and Innovation Area in Hydrogen, Summary Report*, January 2005.

researchers, to contribute to the development of new and important know-how and strategic solutions to carry the industry forward in the long term.

Sectoral foresight exercises can be used to discover the potential existing in new sectors. In Ireland, for example, such exercises have been carried out to ascertain the social, economic and market trends that will prevail in the country up to 2015. The exercises encompassed the following sectors: chemicals and pharmaceuticals (the sector with the largest share in exports); ICTs (seeking to increase exports of high-tech services); manufacturing processes and materials (especially in computing and medical equipment); health and life sciences; natural resources (agro-industrial and marine foods and forestry products); energy, transport and logistics; and construction and infrastructure. In each of these areas the exercise built consensus among government representatives, experts, scientists and industry members on the scientific research and technological progress needed to ensure competitiveness and better living standards in the future.[10]

Foresight exercises have been carried out in Latin America too, one example being those conducted in Uruguay (Ramos, 2002), which had some interesting features compared with those carried out in other countries of the region. The first is that the process was headed by the Office of the President of the Republic, which meant that the exercise was not isolated from the sphere of decision-making. Second, it involved 170 specialists, including business representatives, academics and government authorities, which conferred legitimacy upon its resolutions. The report on the exercise also mentioned its limitations: the actors' difficulty in developing a vision of the future and in separating long-term scenarios from the analysis of current conditions and the pressure on the State to correct them. It was decided to concentrate scientific and technological effort and policies and investment on the following areas:

- Biotechnology in the agrifood system, with a panel steered by the National Institute of Agricultural Research (INIA)
- Energy, with a panel steered by the Faculty of Engineering of the University of the Republic
- Transport and logistics, with a panel steered by the Faculty of Engineering of the University of Montevideo

Prospective exercises are also useful in mapping out the future of an industry in crisis and looking for alternatives. One example is Dutch agriculture, which recently went through a crisis involving animal health, food safety and outbreaks of disease. The prospective exercise carried out by the National Council for Agricultural Research (NRLO) showed that new concepts would be needed to develop sustainable agriculture in the future. Prospective tools such as analysis of scenarios, in-depth interviews, specialist studies and trend analysis helped to set out the criteria for generating new concepts. One of the proposals, the idea of agroparks, consisted of grouping different farms in a single industrial estate, thus enabling the recycling of energy, minerals, water and carbon dioxide.

The eco-industrial concept of agroparks represents, in many ways, a paradigm shift, with agricultural activity no longer confined to the countryside, but carried out also in semi-urban settings. Contrasting with the paradigm of specialization, different branches of agriculture come together to recycle materials (carbon dioxide, energy, water and minerals). Although the pilot projects are still under way, the experience and learning gained from the prospective exercise were so significant that NRLO was turned into an Innovation Network Rural Areas and Agricultural Systems, as it was considered that foresight activities are more effective when they are integrated into systems of innovative processes. In relation to agroindustry, the example of Uruguay mentioned earlier suggests that certain countries of the region have many advantages, but these are not well enough known nor has any strategy been developed to unlock all of their potential. Adding value through innovation is one of the major challenges in this regard, and foresight exercises offer a way to map out the future of those sectors in the region.

C. Conclusions

Latin America and the Caribbean is lagging behind in certain areas of export development and competitiveness. Moving ahead in this regard involves a dual challenge: catching up with other countries, while avoiding the lag generated by continual technological development, which is even faster in the era of globalization. In the world of today, the effort to increase countries' competitiveness and strengthen their international integration cannot be left to the invisible hand of the market, but calls for a

10 See ICSTI Ireland (1999).

medium- and long-term strategy based on collaboration between the public and private sectors. This is borne out by the experience of economies that have leapfrogged in terms of export development and growth, closing the gap with higher-income countries.

As discussed in this chapter, foresight exercises nourish this process. Experience shows that such tools are useful for developing consensus on how to build a desirable future that is also "achievable" in the long term, by compiling the information available from different stakeholders, analysing and evaluating it and jointly identifying priorities and strategic lines to be taken into consideration in the present. Generally speaking, foresight exercises help to build understanding and accords among the relevant stakeholders around strategic pillars of development. This might be in relation to a future vision of the country, to sustainable growth, or to more specific objectives such as innovation strategy.

Foresight exercises make use of multiple methodologies to achieve consensuses or agreements and translate them into policy proposals, and this feeds into decision-making on the part of the authorities. Experience suggests that the wider the engagement of the stakeholders and the more democratic the process, the more sustainable the long-term strategies deriving from it. But turning the exercise into a strategy and a plan of action also requires leadership and a coordinating body, resources, parameters and a system that promotes collaboration between the public and private sectors and in which policies and programmes can be put into practice.

Although these exercises are quite new, historically speaking, their use is growing very rapidly at the international level. As noted earlier, however, foresight is an incipient discipline in Latin America and the Caribbean and there is still a great deal of room to make more comprehensive use of these tools to help create either national innovation programmes to build up technological capacities or, more broadly, export development strategies to compete in the world of tomorrow. The exercises carried out in the region have not yet reached the stage of impacting on policy. Government cycles also deprive the recommended actions of continuity. Nevertheless, the participants and stakeholders view prospective exercises as positive experiences. Building consensus about how to tackle obstacles to competitiveness or future challenges greatly strengthens support for policies and, especially, their sustainability over government cycles. Such exercises are thus useful for moving ahead with the development of long-term strategies.

The process of prospective analysis is a goal in itself, because it leads to broad participation, consensus-building and the creation of networks. It is also important to achieve effective or practical results, however, given the great potential of foresight work as a policy tool, whether in the area of FDI attraction, international expansion of SMEs or science and technology policies that can help make a country more competitive internationally. While foresight exercises obviously do not eliminate the incertitude of the future, they can help to lessen it by reducing the uncertainty that the lack of a national innovation and competitiveness strategy can add to the business climate.

Bibliography

Amanatidou, E. and K. Guy (2006), "Interpreting foresight process impacts: steps towards the development of a framework conceptualising the dynamics of 'foresight systems'", document presented at the second international seminar "Future-Oriented Technology Analysis: Impact of FTA Approaches on Policy and Decision-Making", Sevilla (Spain), 28 and 29 September.

APEC CFT (APEC Center for Technology Foresight) (2005), "Introducing foresight and the APEC Center for Technology Foresight" [online] http://www.tmc.nstda.or.th/apec/.

Australia 2020 Summit. Initial Summit Report (2008), April.

"Backing Australia's Ability. Building our Future through Science and Innovation" [online] http://backingaus.innovation.gov.au/.

Banthien, H., Kerstin Cuhls and N. Ludewig (2004), "About the Futur Process", *Participatory Priority Setting for Research and Innovation Policy: Concepts, Tools and Implementation in Foresight Processes. Proceedings of an International Expert Workshop in Berlin*, K. Culhs and M. Jaspers (eds.), Fraunhofer IRB Verlag.

Berkhout, F. and J. Hertin (2002), "Foresight Futures Scenarios: Developing and Applying a Participative Strategic Planning Tool", *Greener Management International*, No. 37 [online] http://www.greenleaf-publishing.com/productdetail.kmod?productid=92.

Boyle, Richard, Orla O'Donnell and Johanna O'Riordan (2002), "Promoting longer-term policy thinking", *CPMR Policy Paper*, No. 22, Committee for Public Management Research [online] www.cpmr.gov.ie/publications/discussion-papers/promoting-longer-term-policy-thinking.pdf.

Cariola, Mónica and Secondo Rolfo (2004), "Evolution in the rationales of foresight in Europe", *Futures 36*, vol. 10.

Choi, Youngrak (2003), "Technology Roadmap in Korea, Stepi, Session 5: Foresight Activities in Asian Countries" [online] Http://Www.Nistep.Go.Jp/Ic/Ic030227/Pdf/P5-1.Pdf.

Cuhls, Kerstin (2003), "Government Foresight Activities in Germany: The Futur Process" document presented at the Second International Conference on Technology Foresight, Tokyo, 27-28 February [online] http://www.nistep.go.jp/IC/ic030227/pdf/s3-2.pdf.

Cuhls, Kerstin and Michael Jaspers (eds.) (2004), *Participatory Priority Setting for Research and Innovation Policy: Concepts, Tools and Implementation in Foresight Processes. Proceedings of an International Expert Workshop in Berlin*, Fraunhofer IRB Verlag.

Cuhls, Kerstin and Hariolf Grupp (2001), "Status and prospects of technology foresight in Germany after ten years" [online] http://www.nistep.go.jp/achiev/ftx/eng/mat077e/html/mat077ae.html.

Da Costa, Olivier and others (2006), "The impact of foresight on policy-making: insights from the forlearn mutual learning process", *Technology Analysis and Strategic Management*, vol. 20, No. 3.

DTI (Department of Trade and Industry of the United Kingdom) (2002), "Foresight Futures 2020: Revised Scenarios and Guidance" [online] http://www.foresight.gov.uk/publications/current_round_general_publications/foresight_futures_2020_revised_scenarios_and_guidance/dti_ff_web.pdf.

ECLAC (Economic Commission for Latin America and the Caribbean) (2008), *Structural Change and Productivity Growth - 20 Years Later. Old problems, new opportunities* (LC/G.2367(SES.32/3)), Santiago, Chile.

Eija Ahola (2003), "Technology Foresight within the Finnish Innovation System", document presented at the third session of the Second International Conference on Technology Foresight, Tokyo, 27-28 February.

Georghiou, L. (2001), "Third generation foresight: Integrating the socio-economic dimension", Proceedings of International Conference on Technology Foresight, Science and Technology Foresight Center of NISTEP, Japan [online] http://www.nistep.go.jp/achiev/ftx/eng/mat077e/ html/mat077oe.html.

Georghiou, L. and others (2004), "Evaluation of the Hungarian Technology Foresight Programme (TEP). Report of an International Panel", Manchester University [online] http://www.nkth.gov.hu/english/technology-foresight/evaluation-of-the, May.

Havas, Attila, Doris Schartinger and Mathias Weber (2007), "Experiences and practices of technology foresight in the European region", *Second Technology Foresight Summit. Conference Proceedings*, Budapest, 27-29 September, Vienna, United Nations Industrial Development Organization (UNIDO).

ICSTI (Irish Council for Science, Technology and Innovation) (1999), "Technology Foresight Ireland" [online] http://www.forfas.ie/icsti/statements/tforesight/overview/tforeire.htm.

Martin, Ben (2001), "Technology Foresight in a Rapidly Globalising Economy", document prepared for the Regional Conference "Technology Foresight for Central and Eastern Europe and the Newly Independent States", United Nations Industrial Development Organization (UNIDO), Vienna, 4-5 April [online] http://www.unido.org/fileadmin/import/12614_ReportRegConfedited.pdf.

Martin, Ben and John Irvine (1989), "Research Foresight: Priority-Setting in Science", London, Pinter Publishers [online] http://www.sciencedirect.com/science/article/B6V77-45GSH7P-10/2/28330b1ea6bc03fa485e0125068e363e.

Martin, Ben and Ron Johnston (1999), "Technology Foresight for 'Wiring Up' the National Innovation System-Experiences in Britain, Australia and New Zealand", *Technological Forecasting and Social Change*, vol. 60.

Masini, Eleonora (2002), "A vision of futures studies" *Futures 34*, vol. 3-4, April.

___ (2006), "Rethinking futures studies", *Futures 38*, vol. 10, December.

Miles, Ian and Mike Keenan (2003), "Ten Years of Foresight in the UK", document presented at the the Second International Conference on Technology Foresight, Tokyo, 27-28 February, [online] http://www.nistep.go.jp/IC/ic030227/pdf/p3-1.pdf.

Ministry of Economic Development of New Zealand (2005), "Economic Transformation" [online] http://www.med.govt.nz/templates/StandardSummary.

NISTEP (National Institute of Science and Technology Policy of Japan) (2005), "The 8th Science and Technology Foresight Survey - Delphi Analysis" [online] http://www.nistep.go.jp/index-e.html, May.

Nordic H2 Energy Foresight (2005), "Building the Nordic Research and Innovation Area in Hydrogen. Summary Report" [online] http://www.risoe.dk/rispubl/SYS/syspdf/Nordic_H2_05004-29.pdf.

OLADE (Latin American Energy Organization) (2006), "Prospectiva energética de la región" [online] http://

www.olade.org.ec/documentos2/articulos/2006-09-17-articulo%20ARR.pdf.

Paez, D. (2005), "Primer ejercicio de prospectiva tecnológica de PDVSA en combustibles futuros y vehículos avanzados", Caracas.

Popper, Rafael and Javier Medina (2008), "Foresight in Latin America. Cases studies: Brazil, Colombia and Venezuela", document presented at the International Panel "Evaluación en prospectiva", Bogotá, 3-4 June.

PREST (2006), "Evaluation of the United Kingdom Foresight Programme", Manchester Business School [online]_http://www.mbs.ac.uk/research/engineering-policy/researchprojects/documents/Foresight_Evaluation_Final_Report_June_2006.pdf, March.

Ramos, A. (2002), "Programa de prospectiva tecnológica Uruguay 2015: principales recomendaciones", Montevideo, Presidency of Uruguay and United Nations Industrial Development Organization (UNIDO).

Seidl da Fonseca, Ricardo (2006), "UNIDO Regional Initiative on Technology Foresight. The Second Policy Conference: Ways to European Future - A Dialogue between Policy Makers and Foresight Practitioners", Chzech Republic, 11-12 May [online] http://www.eranet-forsociety.net/policyconference/files/16-Seidl%20da%20Fonseca%202006.PPT.

Seok-Ho, Son and others (2006), "Priority setting of future technology area based on Korean technology foresight exercise", *Technology Management for the Global Future*, vol. 3, No. 8-13, July.

Swedish Technology Foresight (2004), "Inspiration for Innovation: Swedish Technology Foresight 2004" [online] www.tekniskframsyn.nu.

The Research Council of Norway (2005), "Aquaculture 2020, Trascending the Barriers - As Long as ..." [online] http://www.forskningsradet.no/CSStorage/Flex_attachment/Aquaculture_2020_eng.pdf.

UKCIP (UK Climate Impacts Programme) (2001), "Socio-economic scenarios for climate change impact assessment: a guide to their use in the UK Climate Impacts Programme" [online] http://www.ukcip.org.uk.

UNIDO (United Nations Industrial Development Organization) (2006), "Technology Foresight Programme", Investment and Technology Promotion Branch [online] http://www.eranet-forsociety.net/policyconference/files/16-Seidl%20da%20Fonseca%202006.PPT.

Zackiewicz, M., G. Jannuzzi and I. Macedo (2004), "Technology futures analysis as a decision problem: the case of Brazilian Energy Technology Foresight", document presented at the seminar "New Technology Foresight, Forecasting and Assessment Methods", Sevilla (Spain), 13-14 May.

Publicaciones de la CEPAL / *ECLAC publications*

Comisión Económica para América Latina y el Caribe / *Economic Commission for Latin America and the Caribbean*
Casilla 179-D, Santiago de Chile. E-mail: publications@cepal.org
Véalas en: www.cepal.org/publicaciones
Publications may be accessed at: www.eclac.org

Revista de la CEPAL / *CEPAL Review*

La *Revista* se inició en 1976 como parte del Programa de Publicaciones de la Comisión Económica para América Latina y el Caribe, con el propósito de contribuir al examen de los problemas del desarrollo socioeconómico de la región. Las opiniones expresadas en los artículos firmados, incluidas las colaboraciones de los funcionarios de la Secretaría, son las de los autores y, por lo tanto, no reflejan necesariamente los puntos de vista de la Organización.

La *Revista de la CEPAL* se publica en español e inglés tres veces por año.

Los precios de suscripción anual vigentes para 2008 son de US$ 30 para la versión en español y de US$ 35 para la versión en inglés. El precio por ejemplar suelto es de US$ 15 para ambas versiones. Los precios de suscripción por dos años (2008-2009) son de US$ 50 para la versión en español y de US$ 60 para la versión en inglés.

CEPAL Review first appeared in 1976 as part of the Publications Programme of the Economic Commission for Latin America and the Caribbean, its aim being to make a contribution to the study of the economic and social development problems of the region. The views expressed in signed articles, including those by Secretariat staff members, are those of the authors and therefore do not necessarily reflect the point of view of the Organization.

CEPAL Review is published in Spanish and English versions three times a year.

Annual subscription costs for 2008 are US$ 30 for the Spanish version and US$ 35 for the English version. The price of single issues is US$ 15 in both cases. The cost of a two-year subscription (2008-2009) is US$ 50 for Spanish-language version and US$ 60 for English.

Informes periódicos institucionales / *Annual reports*

Todos disponibles para años anteriores / *Issues for previous years also available*

- *Balance preliminar de las economías de América Latina y el Caribe, 2007, 180 p.*
  ***Preliminary Overview of the Economies of Latin America and the Caribbean, 2007**, 180 p.*
- *Estudio económico de América Latina y el Caribe 2007-2008, 152 p.*
  ***Economic Survey of Latin America and the Caribbean 2007-2008**, 146 p.*
- *Panorama de la inserción internacional de América Latina y el Caribe, 2007. Tendencias 2008, 160 p.*
  ***Latin America and the Caribbean in the World Economy, 2007. 2008 Trends,** 148 p.*
- *Panorama social de América Latina, 2007*, 294 p.
  ***Social Panorama of Latin America**, **2007**, 290 p.*
- *La inversión extranjera en América Latina y el Caribe*, 2007, 228 p.
  ***Foreign Investment of Latin America and the Caribbean, 2007**, 206 p.*
- *Anuario estadístico de América Latina y el Caribe* / ***Statistical Yearbook for Latin America and the Caribbean*** (bilingüe/*bilingual*), 2007, 434 p.

Libros de la CEPAL

96 *Familias y políticas públicas en América Latina: una historia de desencuentros*, Irma Arriagada (coord.), 2007, 424 p.
95 *Centroamérica y México: políticas de competencia a principios del siglo XXI*, Eugenio Rivera y Claudia Schatan (coords.), 2008, 304 p.
94 *América Latina y el Caribe: La propiedad intelectual después de los tratados de libre comercio*, Álvaro Díaz, 2008, 248 p.
93 *Tributación en América Latina. En busca de una nueva agenda de reformas*, Oscar Cetrángolo y Juan Carlos Gómez-Sabaini (comps.), 2007, 166 p.
92 *Fernando Fajnzylber. Una visión renovadora del desarrollo en América Latina*, Miguel Torres Olivos (comp.), 2006, 422 p.
91 *Cooperación financiera regional*, José Antonio Ocampo (comp.), 2006, 274 p.

90 *Financiamiento para el desarrollo. América Latina desde una perspectiva comparada*, Barbara Stallings con la colaboración de Rogério Studart, 2006, 396 p.
89 *Políticas municipales de microcrédito. Un instrumento para la dinamización de los sistemas productivos locales. Estudios de caso en América Latina*, Paola Foschiatto y Giovanni Stumpo (comps.), 2006, 244 p.
88 *Aglomeraciones en torno a los recursos naturales en América Latina y el Caribe: Políticas de articulación y articulación de políticas*, 2006, 266 p.
87 *Pobreza, desertificación y degradación de los recursos naturales*, César Morales y Soledad Parada (eds.), 2006, 274 p.
86 *Aprender de la experiencia. El capital social en la superación de la pobreza*, Irma Arriagada (ed.), 2005, 250 p.
85 *Política fiscal y medio ambiente. Bases para una agenda común*, Jean Acquatella y Alicia Bárcena (eds.), 2005, 272 p.
84 *Globalización y desarrollo: desafíos de Puerto Rico frente al siglo XXI*, Jorge Mario Martínez, Jorge Máttar y Pedro Rivera (coords.), 2005, 342 p.
83 *El medio ambiente y la maquila en México: un problema ineludible*, Jorge Carrillo y Claudia Schatan (comps.), 2005, 304 p.
82 *Fomentar la coordinación de las políticas económicas en América Latina. El método REDIMA para salir del dilema del prisionero*, Christian Ghymers, 2005, 190 p.
82 ***Fostering economic policy coordination in Latin America. The REDIMA approach to escaping the prisoner's dilemma***, Christian Ghymers, 2005, 170 p.

Copublicaciones recientes / *Recent co-publications*

Fortalecer los sistemas de pensiones latinoamericanos. Cuentas individuales por reparto, Robert Holzmann, Edward Palmer y Andras Uthoff (eds.), CEPAL/Mayol, Colombia, 2008.

Competition Policies in Emerging Economies. Lessons and Challenges from Central America and Mexico, Claudia Schatan and Eugenio Rivera Urrutia (eds.), ECLAC/Springer, USA, 2008.

Estratificación y movilidad social en América Latina. Transformaciones estructurales en un cuarto de siglo, Rolando Franco, Arturo León y Raúl Atria (coords.), CEPAL/Lom, Chile, 2007.

Economic growth with equity. Challenges for Latin America, Ricardo Ffrench-Davis and José Luis Machinea (eds.), ECLAC/Palgrave Macmillan, United Kingdom, 2007.

Mujer y empleo. La reforma de la salud y la salud de la reforma en Argentina, María Nieves Rico y Flavia Marco (coords.), CEPAL/Siglo XXI, Argentina, 2006.

El estructuralismo latinoamericano, Octavio Rodríguez, CEPAL/Siglo XXI, México, 2006.

Gobernabilidad corporativa, responsabilidad social y estrategias empresariales en América Latina, Germano M. de Paula, João Carlos Ferraz y Georgina Núñez (comps.), CEPAL/Mayol, Colombia, 2006.

Desempeño económico y política social en América Latina y el Caribe. Los retos de la equidad, el desarrollo y la ciudadanía, Ana Sojo y Andras Uthoff (comps.), CEPAL/Flacso-México/ Fontamara, México, 2006.

Política y políticas públicas en los procesos de reforma de América Latina, Rolando Franco y Jorge Lanzaro (coords.), CEPAL/Flacso-México/Miño y Dávila, México, 2006.

Finance for Development. Latin America in Comparative Perspective, Barbara Stallings with Rogério Studart, ECLAC/Brookings Institution Press, USA, 2006.

Los jóvenes y el empleo en América Latina. Desafíos y perspectivas ante el nuevo escenario laboral, Jürgen Weller (ed.), CEPAL/Mayol Ediciones, Colombia, 2006.

Condiciones y políticas de competencia en economías pequeñas de Centroamérica y el Caribe, Claudia Schatan y Marcos Ávalos (coords.), CEPAL/Fondo de Cultura Económica, México, 2006.

Aglomeraciones pesqueras en América Latina. Ventajas asociadas al enfoque de cluster, Massiel Guerra (comp.) CEPAL/Alfaomega, Colombia, 2006.

Reformas para América Latina después del fundamentalismo neoliberal, Ricardo Ffrench-Davis, CEPAL/Siglo XXI, Argentina, 2006.

Seeking growth under financial volatility, Ricardo Ffrench-Davis (ed.), ECLAC/Palgrave Macmillan, United Kingdom, 2005.

Macroeconomía, comercio y finanzas para reformar las reformas en América Latina, Ricardo Ffrench-Davis (ed.), CEPAL/Mayol Ediciones, Colombia, 2005.

Beyond Reforms. Structural Dynamics and Macroeconomic Theory. José Antonio Ocampo (ed.), ECLAC/Inter-American Development Bank/The World Bank/Stanford University Press, USA, 2003.

Más allá de las reformas. Dinámica estructural y vulnerabilidad macroeconómica, José Antonio Ocampo (ed.), CEPAL/Alfaomega, Colombia, 2005.

Gestión social. Cómo lograr eficiencia e impacto en las políticas sociales, Ernesto Cohen y Rolando Franco, CEPAL/Siglo XXI, México, 2005.

Crecimiento esquivo y volatilidad financiera, Ricardo Ffrench-Davis (ed.), Mayol Ediciones, Colombia, 2005.

Pequeñas y medianas empresas y eficiencia colectiva. Estudios de caso en América Latina, Marco Dini y Giovanni Stumpo (coords.), CEPAL/Siglo XXI, México, 2005.

Coediciones recientes / *Recent co-editions*

Espacio iberoamericanos: la economía del conocimiento, CEPAL/SEGIB, Chile, 2008.

Hacia la revisión de los paradigmas del desarrollo en América Latina, Oscar Altimir, Enrique V. Iglesias, José Luis Machinea (eds.), CEPAL/SEGIB, Chile, 2008.

Por uma revisão dos paradigmas do desenvolvimento na América Latina, Oscar Altimir, Enrique V. Iglesias, José Luis Machinea (eds.), CEPAL/SEGIB, Chile, 2008.

Hacia un nuevo pacto social. Políticas económicas para un desarrollo integral en América Latina, José Luis Machinea y Narcís Serra (eds.) CEPAL/CIDOB, España, 2008.
Espacios iberoamericanos: comercio e inversión, CEPAL/SEGIB, Chile, 2007.
Espaços Ibero-Americanos: comércio e investimento, CEPAL/SEGIB, Chile, 2007.
Visiones del desarrollo en América Latina, José Luis Machinea y Narcís Serra (eds.), CEPAL/CIDOB, España, 2007.
Cohesión social: inclusión y sentido de pertenencia en América Latina y el Caribe, CEPAL/SEGIB, Chile, 2007.
Social Cohesion. Inclusion and a sense of belonging in Latin America and the Caribbean, ECLAC/SEGIB, Chile, 2007.
Espacios Iberoamericanos, CEPAL/SEGIB, Chile, 2006.
Espaços Ibero-Americanos, CEPAL/SEGIB, Chile, 2006.

Cuadernos de la CEPAL

92 *Estadísticas para la equidad de género: magnitudes y tendencias en América Latina*, Vivian Milosavljevic, 2007, 186 pp.
91 *Elementos conceptuales para la prevención y reducción de daños originados por amenazas naturales*, Eduardo Chaparro y Matías Renard (eds.), 2005, 144 p.
90 *Los sistemas de pensiones en América Latina: un análisis de género*, Flavia Marco (coord.), 2004, 270 p.
89 *Energía y desarrollo sustentable en América Latina y el Caribe*. Guía para la formulación de políticas energéticas, 2003, 240 p.
88 *La ciudad inclusiva*, Marcello Balbo, Ricardo Jordán y Daniela Simioni (comps.), CEPAL/Cooperazione Italiana, 2003, 322 p.

Cuadernos estadísticos de la CEPAL

35 Resultados del Programa de Comparación Internacional para América del Sur. Solo disponible en CD, 2007.
34 *Indicadores económicos del turismo*. Solo disponible en CD, 2006.
33 *América Latina y el Caribe. Balanza de pagos 1980-2005*. Solo disponible en CD, 2006.
32 *América Latina y el Caribe. Series regionales y oficiales de cuentas nacionales, 1950-2002*. Solo disponible en CD, 2005.
31 *Comercio exterior. Exportaciones e importaciones según destino y origen por principales zonas económicas. 1980, 1985, 1990, 1995-2002*. Solo disponible en CD, 2005.
30 *Clasificaciones estadísticas internacionales incorporadas en el banco de datos del comercio exterior de América Latina y el Caribe de la CEPAL*, 2004, 308 p.

Observatorio demográfico *ex Boletín demográfico* / *Demographic Observatory formerly Demographic Bulletin* (bilingüe/*bilingual*)

Edición bilingüe (español e inglés) que proporciona información estadística actualizada, referente a estimaciones y proyecciones de población de los países de América Latina y el Caribe. Incluye también indicadores demográficos de interés, tales como tasas de natalidad, mortalidad, esperanza de vida al nacer, distribución de la población, etc.

El Observatorio aparece dos veces al año, en los meses de enero y julio. Suscripción anual: US$ 20.00. Valor por cada ejemplar: US$ 15.00.

Bilingual publication (Spanish and English) proving up-to-date estimates and projections of the populations of the Latin American and Caribbean countries. Also includes various demographic indicators of interest such as fertility and mortality rates, life expectancy, measures of population distribution, etc.

The Observatory appears twice a year in January and July. Annual subscription: US$ 20.00. Per issue: US$ 15.00.

Notas de población

Revista especializada que publica artículos e informes acerca de las investigaciones más recientes sobre la dinámica demográfica en la región, en español, con resúmenes en español e inglés. También incluye información sobre actividades científicas y profesionales en el campo de población.

La revista se publica desde 1973 y aparece dos veces al año, en junio y diciembre.

Suscripción anual: US$ 20.00. Valor por cada ejemplar: US$ 12.00.

Specialized journal which publishes articles and reports on recent studies of demographic dynamics in the region, in Spanish with abstracts in Spanish and English. Also includes information on scientific and professional activities in the field of population.

Published since 1973, the journal appears twice a year in June and December.

Annual subscription: US$ 20.00. Per issue: US$ 12.00.

Series de la CEPAL

Comercio internacional / Desarrollo productivo / Desarrollo territorial / Estudios estadísticos y prospectivos / Estudios y perspectivas (Bogotá, Brasilia, Buenos Aires, México, Montevideo) / ***Studies and Perspectives*** (The Caribbean, Washington) / *Financiamiento del desarrollo / Gestión pública / Informes y estudios especiales / Macroeconomía del desarrollo / Manuales / Medio ambiente y desarrollo / Mujer y desarrollo / Población y desarrollo / Políticas sociales / Recursos naturales e infraestructura / Seminarios y conferencias.*
Véase el listado completo en: www.cepal.org/publicaciones / *A complete listing is available at*: www.cepal.org/publicaciones

كيفية الحصول على منشورات الأمم المتحدة

يمكن الحصول على منشورات الأمم المتحدة من المكتبات ودور التوزيع في جميع أنحاء العالم . استعلم عنها من المكتبة التي تتعامل معها أو اكتب إلى : الأمم المتحدة ، قسم البيع في نيويورك أو في جنيف .

如何购取联合国出版物

联合国出版物在全世界各地的书店和经售处均有发售。请向书店询问或写信到纽约或日内瓦的联合国销售组。

HOW TO OBTAIN UNITED NATIONS PUBLICATIONS

United Nations publications may be obtained from bookstores and distributors throughout the world. Consult your bookstore or write to: United Nations, Sales Section, New York or Geneva.

COMMENT SE PROCURER LES PUBLICATIONS DES NATIONS UNIES

Les publications des Nations Unies sont en vente dans les librairies et les agences dépositaires du monde entier. Informez-vous auprès de votre libraire ou adressez-vous à : Nations Unies, Section des ventes, New York ou Genève.

КАК ПОЛУЧИТЬ ИЗДАНИЯ ОРГАНИЗАЦИИ ОБЪЕДИНЕННЫХ НАЦИЙ

Издания Организации Объединенных Наций можно купить в книжных магазинах и агентствах во всех районах мира. Наводите справки об изданиях в вашем книжном магазине или пишите по адресу: Организация Объединенных Наций, Секция по продаже изданий, Нью-Йорк или Женева.

COMO CONSEGUIR PUBLICACIONES DE LAS NACIONES UNIDAS

Las publicaciones de las Naciones Unidas están en venta en librerías y casas distribuidoras en todas partes del mundo. Consulte a su librero o diríjase a: Naciones Unidas, Sección de Ventas, Nueva York o Ginebra.

Las publicaciones de la Comisión Económica para América Latina y el Caribe (CEPAL) y las del Instituto Latinoamericano y del Caribe de Planificación Económica y Social (ILPES) se pueden adquirir a los distribuidores locales o directamente a través de:

Publicaciones de las Naciones Unidas
2 United Nations Plaza, Room DC2-853
Nueva York, NY, 10017
Estados Unidos
Tel. (1 800)253-9646 Fax (1 212)963-3489
E-mail: publications@un.org

Publicaciones de las Naciones Unidas
Sección de Ventas
Palais des Nations
1211 Ginebra 10
Suiza
Tel. (41 22)917-2613 Fax (41 22)917-0027

Unidad de Distribución
Comisión Económica para América Latina y el Caribe (CEPAL)
Av. Dag Hammarskjöld 3477, Vitacura
7630412 Santiago
Chile
Tel. (56 2)210-2056 Fax (56 2)210-2069
E-mail: publications@cepal.org

Publications of the Economic Commission for Latin America and the Caribbean (ECLAC) and those of the Latin American and the Caribbean Institute for Economic and Social Planning (ILPES) can be ordered from your local distributor or directly through:

United Nations Publications
2 United Nations Plaza, Room DC2-853
New York, NY, 10017
USA
Tel. (1 800)253-9646 Fax (1 212)963-3489
E-mail: publications@un.org

United Nations Publications
Sales Sections
Palais des Nations
1211 Geneva 10
Switzerland
Tel. (41 22)917-2613 Fax (41 22)917-0027

Distribution Unit
Economic Commission for Latin America and the Caribbean (ECLAC)
Av. Dag Hammarskjöld 3477, Vitacura
7630412 Santiago
Chile
Tel. (56 2)210-2056 Fax (56 2)210-2069
E-mail: publications@eclac.org